Bas Princen (November 2004)
Photographs of the Palestinian Arab village of Sur Bahir, the Jewish Israeli settlement
of Har Homa and the surrounding urban landscape of East Jerusalem.

CITY OF COLLISION

Jerusalem and the Principles of Conflict Urbanism

Edited by Philipp Misselwitz and Tim Rieniets

Editorial Team: Zvi Efrat, Rassem Khamaisi, Rami Nasrallah

Birkhäuser – Publishers for Architecture

Basel · Boston · Berlin

Partners

Berlin University of the Arts

Universität der Künste Berlin

International Peace and Cooperation Center (IPCC)

Bezalel Academy of Arts and Design, Jerusalem

Bezalel Academy
of Arts and Design
Jerusalem

ETH Swiss Federal Institute of Technology Zurich,
Institute for Urban Design

ETH
Eidgenössische Technische Hochschule Zürich
Swiss Federal Institute of Technology Zurich

Made possible by

Robert Bosch Stiftung

ROBERT BOSCH STIFTUNG

Allianz Cultural Foundation

Allianz
Kulturstiftung

Berlin University of the Arts

Universität der Künste Berlin

ETH Swiss Federal Institute of Technology Zurich,
Institute for Urban Design

ETH
Eidgenössische Technische Hochschule Zürich
Swiss Federal Institute of Technology Zurich

Arthur Goldreich Trust

ayt
קרן ארתור גולדרייך
Arthur Goldreich Trust

Goethe-Institut Jerusalem

GOETHE-INSTITUT

Bibliographic information published by Die Deutsche Bibliothek

Die Deutsche Bibliothek lists this publication in the Deutsche Nationalbibliographie;
detailed bibliographic data is available on the internet at http://dnb.ddb.de.

© 2006 Birkhäuser – Publishers for Architecture, P.O. Box 133, CH-4010 Basel, Switzerland
Part of Springer Science+Business Media

Printed on acid-free paper produced from chlorine-free pulp. TCF ∞
Layout and cover: Tom Unverzagt, Leipzig
Printed in Germany

ISBN-10: 3-7643-7482-9
ISBN-13: 978-3-7643-7482-2
www.birkhauser.ch

9 8 7 6 5 4 3 2 1

ESSAYS

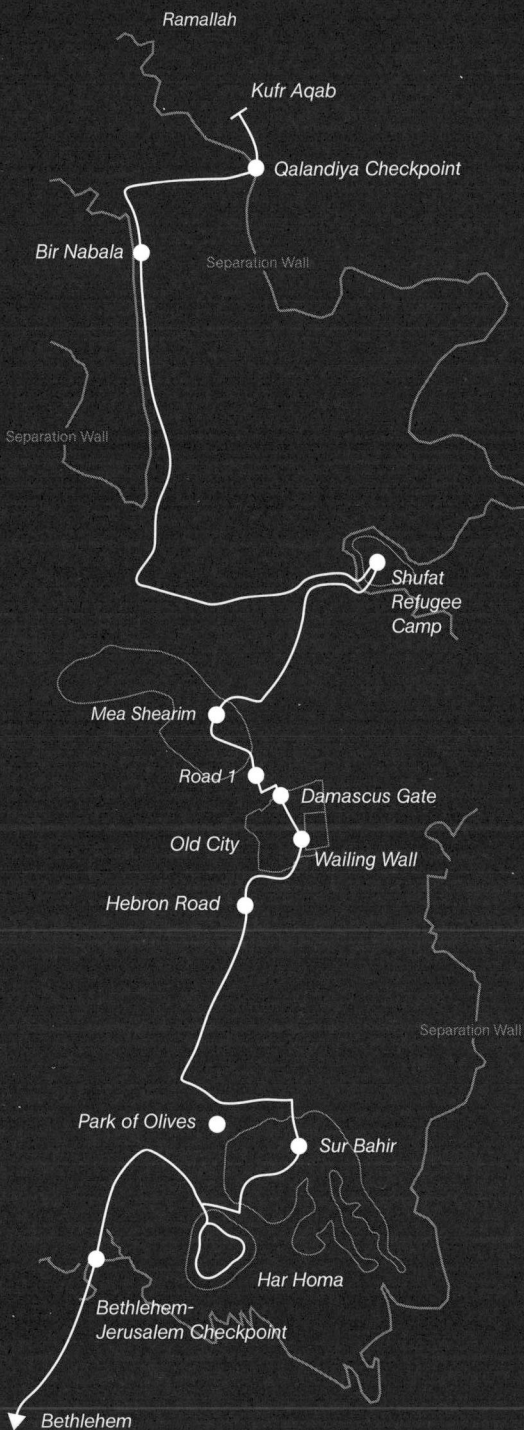

Ramallah

Kufr Aqab

Qalandiya Checkpoint

Bir Nabala

Separation Wall

Separation Wall

Shufat
Refugee
Camp

Mea Shearim

Road 1

Damascus Gate

Old City

Wailing Wall

Hebron Road

Separation Wall

Park of Olives

Sur Bahir

Har Homa

Bethlehem-
Jerusalem Checkpoint

Bethlehem

PREFACE

LEARNING FROM/FOR JERUSALEM

In 2003, we launched an open research process incorporating Palestinian, Israeli, and European participants. Our endeavor set out to understand the production of space in Jerusalem, in light of the Israeli-Palestinian conflict, and the city inhabitants' parallel strategies of resistance, adaptation, and survival. These initial goals, however, were soon caught up in dramatic developments around the city. At the time of this publication, the construction of the Israeli Separation Wall in the Jerusalem area is in its final stages, with grave consequences for Palestinians inside and outside the city, and despite an admonitory ruling by the International Court of Justice in The Hague. Israeli occupation of the rest of the West Bank continues through settlement expansions, permanent restrictions on movement, and checkpoint regimes. In response, Jewish Jerusalemites have been exposed to a sustained series of deadly suicide attacks. Prospects for a renewed peace process seem more distant than ever.

Simultaneously, recent years have witnessed an increase in violent conflicts unfolding in urban environments. Political, religious, ethnic, or cultural conflicts have affected Baghdad, New York, London, Paris, and Istanbul and influence our perceptions about, and use of, space. Despite its peculiarities, Jerusalem must be considered against this global horizon. Cities are being transformed through government measures against the backdrop of a pervading fear of terror threats—be they real or imagined. In the end, urban diversity itself is perceived as a potential threat: attacks from within are anticipated in the form of disguised fundamentalists, extremists, assassins, and suicide bombers, fuelling suspicion of the unfamiliar. Security, control, and panic are all influencing contemporary urban spatial production; empty spaces, wastelands, parks, or roads can become new frontiers. Suburbs can be transformed into gated enclaves, and suburban shopping centers into fortresses. Jerusalem—once perceived as an isolated case, taken hostage as it were by the Israeli-Palestinian conflict—seems to have become now to be an antecedent for other cities' transformation. We believe that a study of an urbanism so extreme, as that of Jerusalem, will benefit our common understanding of the relationship between political violence and the production of urban space. In Jerusalem, these aspects have intensified over decades and in extreme ways only latent or less pronounced in other urban contexts.

When 30 Palestinian, Israeli, and European students of architecture met in Jerusalem for the very first time, the conditions surrounding their study appeared most unfavorable. At the height of the Second Intifada against the Israeli occupation of the Gaza Strip, West Bank, and East Jerusalem, most Palestinian-Israeli contacts were frozen. The cycles of successive retaliation, targeted killings, and suicide attacks fueled a downward spiral towards greater polarization. Technically, meetings became nearly impossible: Israel had imposed "closure" policies on the occupied West Bank that made Palestinian access to Jerusalem almost impossible. Israeli travel to the West Bank was made illegal through military order, and even Israeli trips to the eastern part of Jerusalem were commonly undertaken under armed guard. Despite all odds, participants resolved to escape momentarily from the bounds of collective identity and suffering, risking accusations of "normalization" in their dealings with the "enemy," in order to engage as individuals in a process of joint research.

This assemblage was made possible by the project "Grenzgeografien – geographies of conflict," a joint initiative of the International Peace and Cooperation Center in East Jerusalem, The Bezalel Academy of Arts and Design in West Jerusalem and the University of the Arts in Berlin, later joined by the Federal Technical University of Zurich. Our trilateral project investigated the production and use of urban space in the prototypical microcosm of the Palestinian Arab village of Sur Bahir and the Jewish settlement of Har Homa, which are situated as neighbors in Jerusalem's eastern periphery, next to the newly-built Separation Wall. Here competing interests and claims collide in full force, leaving deep imprints on the physical landscape and fabric of everyday life.

The unique trilateral composition of the teams allowed them to break everyday rules of urban segregation, moving transversally through ethnic barriers, buffer zones, and invisible walls. Momentarily, participants were able to bend stereotypical ethnic roles, thus gaining a new qualitative access to the city—access that has long been lost to Jerusalem's residents, including its professional and academic communities. Israelis and Palestinians entered spaces and were introduced to individuals, that were previously entirely inaccessible: Israeli students entered Palestinian neighborhoods (many for the first time), while many of the Palestinian students received for the first time Israeli access permits to the city and entered Jewish settlements. During the workshops that followed between 2003 and 2005, participants gathered unique material extracted from surveys, conversations with locals, and observations of everyday situations. Students negotiated and concluded their in-depth analysis by creating joint mapping projects, envisioning urban change under conditions of conflict, and assembling a unique atlas, which has now become part of this publication.

The results of these workshops encouraged us to open the project to a wider community of researchers and practitioners in a city where the conflict in all its manifestations has stymied bilateral engagement in professional discourse. Recognizing the limitations, not least of which was a lack of mandate, we were convinced of the productive possibilities for confronting difference and engaging in dialogue as professionals (rather than as politicians), including exposing and recognizing each side's biases, as well as the power imbalance at work. Forty local and international experts in the fields of architecture, urban and cultural studies participated in the conference, "Cities of Collision," held at the Van Leer Institute Jerusalem in November 2004, creating a new platform from which to consider Jerusalem in the context of recent global processes of urban transformation and new patterns of conflict. Their contributions and discussions resulted in the essays published in this volume.

READING JERUSALEM

Through this anthology of essays, maps, and photographic documentary, we offer readers a spatial and cultural insight into the dynamism, ambivalence, and complexity of life in Jerusalem. The complex and rapidly changing condition of Jerusalem does not allow for a comprehensive overview—nor can this publication offer proposals for solving the deep-rooted conflict that has kept the city and its inhabitants hostage for almost eight decades. Instead, contributions to this publication will open up different perspectives and provide qualitative insights into the political, cultural, and socioeconomic forces operating in the city. It also reveals the inhabitants' strategies of everyday survival, which can only be understood from a multilateral perspective. Still other essays will consider Jerusalem in relation to global processes of urban change, thereby offering new perspectives on a city that is usually viewed in isolation from its history or against the selective backdrop of the Middle East conflict.

Division and segregation has become an increasingly dominant paradigm, not just in the Middle East. This book is a plea for crossing boundaries and for preserving and treasuring eroding areas of fluidity—and not only in Jerusalem. It is hoped that this book will equip us with new insights and analytical tools for reading contested urban spaces in Jerusalem and elsewhere.

We would like to thank the partners and participants whose unyielding support has made this project possible.

The Editorial Team
Zvi Efrat (Bezalel Academy of Arts and Design, Jerusalem)
Rassem Khamaisi (IPCC Jerusalem)
Rami Nasrallah (IPCC Jerusalem)
Philipp Misselwitz (Berlin University of the Arts)
Tim Rieniets (ETH Zurich)

Philipp Misselwitz and Tim Rieniets

Jerusalem is an ancient cradle of human culture and one of the most important loci of three world religions. But as long as the city has existed, it has been the cause and breeding ground of conflicts, as well as the target and site of dispute and war. It is both victim and weapon. During this eventful history, the city has been destroyed several times, and its urban fabric exposed to ever-shifting ownership. Different cultures and ethnicities raise claims to the city as a symbolic cultural center. In more recent history, the city has been the staging ground for 80 years of violent conflict between Jews and Palestinian Arabs, each nurturing a long-established emotional and cultural attachment to the city, each claiming the city to be its legitimate capital.

During this period, Jerusalem has become a laboratory for the production of extreme spatial configurations. The process of urban transformation from a land-locked provincial town to a modern sprawling metropolis is intertwined with the Israeli-Palestinian conflict. Nowhere else has conflict over territorial and demographic control been so deeply inscribed into an urban fabric. The architecture of the urban landscape of Jerusalem, as well as the social and cultural behavior of its citizens, allow deep insight into the complexity of this conflict and the contradictory forces that impact the production of ordinary urban space.

Following a trilateral initiative to research the relation between conflict and the city, which begun in August 2003 with a series of student workshops, over 40 Palestinian, Israeli, and international authors contributed essays and photographs to this volume. In addition, local research compiled by the editors and students over the last three years was gathered into a series of cartographic maps and has been inserted into each chapter of the book. The contributions deliberately fuse internal and external perspectives, analyzing Jerusalem as a microcosm which—despite Israeli-Palestinian specificities—is also deeply linked to global processes of urban transformation and has become a burning-glass for events that take place elsewhere. In this introductory text, we will acquaint the reader with the themes that tie together this diverse set of contributions. The five main chapters of the book have been devised to emphasize our search for types and genres in spatial production, behavior patterns, and everyday practices, and to consider Jerusalem as an extreme model of everyday life under conditions of conflict.

ENCLAVES/EXCLAVES

Almost 40 years after the 1967 Six Day War and Jerusalem's military unification, the notion of the city as the "unified city" remains fragile rhetorical
acrobatics. In reality, residents of the city do not experience the urban territory as a continuum, but conduct their everyday lives within almost completely
separate socioeconomic cultural and spatial systems. Every aspect of the city
is invested with ethnicity, and a complex system of codes (wrought in architecture, signage, dress, etc.) helps residents to navigate through perceived safe
passages and protected environments. This extreme level of segregation has
produced a spatial landscape akin to an "archipelago" of isolated "islands" (Eyal
Weizman, page 86). As soon as military victory was achieved, fighting over permanent control of the city continued by other means. A war of *cement* and stone
radically changed the urban fabric. In this process, the border contours changed
from a continuous line (dividing Palestinian East Jerusalem from Jewish West
Jerusalem between 1948 and 1967) to a complex matrix of exclaves (settlements
for Jewish Israelis built in annexed East Jerusalem) and Palestinian enclaves,
served by segregated road systems and surrounded by buffer zones. While all
municipal resources were mobilized so that a redivision of the city would be
impossible, East Jerusalem's Palestinians refused to assimilate into the Israeli
system, nurturing their own parallel visions of Jerusalem as the religious
center and political capital of an independent Palestinian state.

The spatial logic of exclaves and enclaves did not begin with 1967, but date
back to the very beginnings of the Israeli-Palestinian conflict. Sharon Rotbard
finds a comparable simultaneous logic of spatial containment and territorial
control in the planning of early 20th-century kibbutzim, often referred to as
"homa umigdal" ("wall and tower"), alluding to their perimeter wall and watchtower which protected them against often hostile surroundings.

In the post-1967 era, the idealistic settlements of the early Zionist era have
been replaced by large-scale, state-controlled investment projects. Motivated
pioneers, eager to construct a Jewish homeland in Palestine, have been replaced
by suburban dwellers seeking convenient, American-style suburban living. Most
of the current 400,000 Jewish settlers have been lured across the Green Line by
state-subsidized financial incentives rather than a Greater Israel ideology. Successive Israeli governments have "succeeded in transforming much of the settlement enterprise into a socioeconomic and geographical process of metropolitan
suburbanization" (David Newman, page 119).

As a result of intense settlement construction in East Jerusalem, Palestinian
communities are forced within the spatial containment that characterizes the settlements: they lost their agricultural land reserves and became enclaves within a
space of Israeli hegemony—remaining largely excluded from Israeli political, social,
and cultural life. Analyzing the impact of Israeli settlement policies on Palestinians, Sari Hanafi argues, "in the Palestinian-Israeli conflict, the Israeli target is the
place" (Sari Hanafi, page 93). Hanafi characterizes the systematic Israeli settlement
project as "spacio-cide." "The weapons are not so much tanks, but bulldozers that
have destroyed streets, houses, cars, and dunum after dunum (one dunum equals
1,000 square meters) of olive groves. It is a war in an age of literal agoraphobia."

Polly Braden (October 2005): Photographic journey through the Jerusalem area during the festivals of Yom Kippur and Ramadan.

0 km: Kufr Aqab

0.1 km: Qalandiya Checkpoint

But despite the declared aim of maintaining a 70 percent Jewish majority, which is written into Jerusalem's master plan, Israel has been unable to stem Palestinian population growth, which far exceeds that of Israelis.

Endurance and resilience have been effective tactics for Palestinians. Prohibited from expanding beyond established built-up areas, villages and neighborhoods have become densely knit, crowded, and uncontrollable. Families invest cash in cement and mortar, upgrades and small extensions, improving daily life gradually by adding modern conveniences. The conflict between modernization and military occupation, between stubbornly preserved traditions and new lifestyles, between growing communities and lack of public institutions forces Palestinian neighborhoods into "urbanization without urbanity" (Rassem Khamaisi, page 121).

BARRIERS/LINKS

In Jerusalem, "[t]he quality, size, and nature of each road, one might say, is a fair indicator of whether Palestinians or Israelis move along it" (Shmuel Groag, page 176). A short drive along one of the convenient fast highways, with breathtaking desert views, links the settlements of East Jerusalem to western Jerusalem—cutting right through hostile territory, bypassing Palestinian neighborhoods without distracting their Israeli drivers.

In contrast, roads in Palestinian neighborhoods and villages suffer from chronic underinvestment. Residents rely on old, evolved "capillary road systems" (Shmuel Groag, page 177) whose non-hierarchical nature require familiarity. The result is the parallel and superimposed existence of two almost completely separate systems. With such inequality in spending of municipal resources, urban space becomes treacherous and unreliable, fuelling biases and distrust. Indeed, "the mundane is a strategic weapon" (Sharon Rotbard, page 110): a highway directly connecting settlements with Israeli territory is at the same time an invincible barrier for Palestinians who live next door, but have no access to it, and therefore is a symptom of Israeli "ethnocracy" (Oren Yiftachel and Haim Yacobi, page 172).

The most obvious and ruthless example of the dual presence of barriers and links within the same infrastructural system is the construction of more than 60 kilometers of Separation Wall in the Jerusalem area, which has radically altered physical and socioeconomic realities. Its absurdly meandering contours, combined with new roads and tunnels, fulfils the two (at times contradictory) principles of securing a "unified city" for a Jewish Israeli population while at the same time excluding many thousands of Palestinian Jerusalemites (Rassem Khamaisi and Rami Nasrallah).

MONUMENTS/NO-MAN'S-LANDS

The Separation Wall has become a photogenic asset for a global media persistently in search of new iconic images to represent the Israeli-Palestinian conflict. But Issam Nassar's research situates the Separation Wall within a larger historical continuum that denies Arab Palestinian cultural presence in the region, detectable in the works of European Christian photographers in the mid-19th century. Then Palestinian natives were "reduced to a backdrop upon which the biblical story could be substantiated, rather than recognized as a real place in the real world—attesting to real histories other than the Judeo-Christian narrative" (Issam Nassar, page 222). From this perspective, Nassar reconsiders the spatial impact of the Separation Wall and "the effect it has on one's imagination of the Other. The issue of seeing, or, in our case, not seeing, the Other may not be of enormous consequence in the short run, but...will have serious long term effects."

Fear and denial of the Other is equally present wherever Israeli and Palestinian urban fragments collide and produce a host of frontier spaces: territories of fear and anxiety, a hostile wilderness, excess space where garbage is dumped or fragments of ancient agricultural landscapes disintegrate.

Contradictory elements of decay are juxtaposed with areas orchestrated by Israeli designers, producing pockets of a highly-engineered and aesthetic (yet often equally deserted) landscape. The rural has been replaced by the suburban, the agricultural by the decorative, all symptomatic of a fight over identity, ownership, and aesthetic domination of the urban landscape.

Design is also strategically used to create a decorative veneer on spatial planning that effectively limits the expansion of Palestinian urban space. Vast tracks of Palestinian private land in East Jerusalem have been legally expropriated and designated as public green zones blocked from Palestinian construction, often later to be rezoned for the construction of Jewish settlements (see Amir Paz-Fuchs and Efrat Cohen-Bar). A naive trust in professional (versus political) planning ethics (see Naama Meishar and Yehotal Shapira) or financial incentives lures Israeli planners to accept these commissions for settlements, blurring agendas of good design and political planning.

CONFRONTATION/EXCHANGE

In Jerusalem, xenophobia is heightened and space is divided into that of "us" and "them," resulting in islands of cultural containment and social exclusion. Wherever possible, the crossing of ethnic boundaries is avoided. But a complete physical disengagement is equally impossible.

One of the most notorious sites of involuntary interaction is Qalandiya checkpoint, which separates the Palestinian suburbs of Jerusalem and Ramallah. Tamar Berger deconstructs the relationship between Israeli soldiers and Palestinians. Drawing on Michel de Certeau's distinction between "strategy, which is the domain of the powerful who possess a place and perspective of their own (e.g. a watchtower) and tactics, which is the "art of the weak," those who are limited by the givens of place and time." Berger discovers "a degree of Palestinian power and Israeli weakness, a place of resilience, even defiance. The Palestinians defy the brutality of the checkpoint with their very presence: passive in appearance, pacifist in practice, self-controlled and civil, as they transverse a threatening, humiliating obstacle" (Tamar Berger, page 253).

Such patterns yield to a muddling of roles, unveiling the schizophrenic conditions of a city that is politically "unified" but ethnically divided. "Tell me, did you occupy East Jerusalem or did we occupy you?" a Palestinian cab driver from East Jerusalem asks his Israeli colleague from West Jerusalem, cynically alluding to his own Israeli identity card, which allows him to pragmatically exploit some advantages of access to the other side. "I go wherever I want. I eat in your

restaurants, sleep with your women, and take your work. I think it was we who
occupied you in 1967" (Yaakov Garb, page 294). Palestinians often employ tactics
that undermine and erode the otherwise clear-cut roles and patterns of occupier
and occupied. In light of the recent housing crunch, Israeli newspapers report
an increase in Palestinians considering buying apartments even in Jewish settlements, that are generally a no-go zone for them. This trend could undermine
Jewish ethnic hegemony in the settlements, as involuntary Palestinian pioneers
employ techniques of camouflage and assimilation: a potential "Trojan horse."[1]

Thus social and economic innovation is born from need, as Rema Hammami
explores at Surda checkpoint. While suffering from humiliation, endless delays
and obstacles in arriving at school, work, and home, Palestinians "establish the
collectively understood, but individually achieved, daily resistance of simply getting there." Nevertheless, "the unlikely symbols of the new steadfastness are
not 'national institutions', but rather the subproletariat Ford van drivers, whose
semicriminal bravado is summed up by ubiquitous Nike 'No Fear' stickers emblazoned on their rear windshields" (Rema Hammami, page 257). These entrepreneurs are
ambiguous figures, easing everyday oppression but also benefiting from it.

Opportunism also fuels a fragile web of economic relationships between
Jews and Arabs in Jerusalem. The proximity of contrasting social cultures and
resources, the asynchronism of Arab and Jewish religious holidays, as well as the
salary gap between the two groups, has created economic possibilities for both.
Despite the persistence of two parallel economic centers, transport, and education systems, approximately half of East Jerusalem's workforce migrates into
West Jerusalem as day laborers, while cheaper goods and services in Palestinian
communities lure Jewish Jerusalemites. Although asymmetric power relations
dominate these economic exchanges, they effectively undermine the notion of
closed borders and strict segregation (see Michael Romann).

Service economies in West Jerusalem accessible to Palestinian employees—
health, transportation, or construction—are the only places where regular personal exchange takes place between Jews and Arabs. Despite a backdrop of fear
and hatred, these casual and inconspicuous work encounters in West Jerusalem
offer the opportunity to escape "the posturing and political declarations about
a united/occupied Jerusalem...[E]veryday passions, kindnesses, mischief, and
creativity weave us together" (Yaakov Garb, page 286).

INNOVATION/DESTRUCTION
"Kulanu yehudim!" ("We're all Jews!"), Yaakov Garb quotes a Palestinian cab
driver jokingly using the phrase Jews, sometimes use to express brotherly largesse to allude to the absurdity of his situation "ruling," as a Palestinian, Jerusalem's roads with a fleet of yellow cabs. The turn of phrase is symptomatic for the
contradictory dynamics emerging between the two opposing groups, each seeking
for, and protecting, its identity, but always in relation to the other.

These encounters are registered in language, fashion, lifestyle, or built environment, and reflect the struggle for identity and spatial belonging. Representations of identity in architecture embody the persistent tension and contradiction
between assimilation and rejection. Zionist architects seeking to create an inde-

pendent and recognizable Israeli architecture initially embraced an international style—which was eventually replaced by a fascination with the forms of Palestinian Arab villages: "the ultimate expression of locality" (Alona Nitzan-Shiftan, page 341).

The aesthetic appropriation of the Palestinian vernacular into a new style of Israeli architecture was paralleled by the physical and programmatic appropriation of a vast stock of buildings expropriated from Palestinian refugees. A particularly poignant example of is the home of the Baramki family. Between 1948 and 1967, the building lay along the Jordan-Israel no-man's-land dividing Jerusalem. After being confiscated, then serving as an Israeli military border post, it was later reopened as the "Museum on the Seam," with the municipality refusing to acknowledge the Baramki family's ownership of the home. Today the Baramki house serves "as a component of a different architecture of knowledge production" (Thomas Abowd, page 336).

Israeli cultural references are also found on the Palestinian side. Israeli settlements for example are often viewed with ambivalence: symbols of the occupation, yet a window on modernity and Western life-style at the same time, admired for their formidable organization and high-quality construction. These cross-cultural influences do not necessarily travel a direct route from Israel to Palestine or visa versa, however. Diaspora links in both communities play a role in these cultural importations. In fact, this backdoor route leads to the unintended approximation of both groups in the references of international capitalism. Cultural and political elites returning to Palestine during the Oslo period (1994-2000) introduced economic power and entrepreneurship, as well as new urban and architectonic models (see Sylvaine Bulle). Palestinian "gated communities" for new elites resemble their Israeli counterparts, and even apply settlement security strategies.

As such, beyond the visible processes of negation, a thin and unconscious cultural exchange is underway. The result is an unintentional urban productivity— a common culture located between the extremes of total rejection, on one hand, and subtle, unconscious hybridity, on the other.

However, these quiet tones rendered in architecture, lifestyle, or language are mostly drowned out by the ongoing noise of the intense conflict that has produced a city, which alters its physical form in an accelerated fashion. Urban change (Israeli road planning, spatial closures, construction of walls, fences, but also private Palestinian homes) that would normally require lengthy planning processes are implemented virtually over night—an uneasy, sometimes panicked dynamism. It is "a policy of scorched earth, rather than planning..." (Meron Benvenisti, page 38). Nationalist interest determines the city's development: political planning by the Israeli municipality but also the tactical responses of the city's Palestinian inhabitants.

EPILOGUE

From a Central European perspective, Jerusalem is frequently considered an uncanny reminder of an age long past: a conflict of colonial and terrorist violence that blurs distinctions between military and civilian, public welfare, and ethnic discrimination. Western European capitalist democracy is still seen as a universal concept dismissing both social revolutions and military conflict to the periphery of the developing world. It seems only natural then, to export this apparent success story to the Middle East, Asia, Africa, etc., in the role of morally superior arbiter engaged in political and moral mediation. From this skewed perspective, the roots of aggression such as New York's September 11th attacks, or the subsequent attacks in Madrid or London, could only be found in the jealousy, religious fanaticism, and barbarism that characterizes an "uncivilized" periphery. The apparently unexpected return of such violence to the "First World" city was shocking, and only seemed to reaffirm fears that "out there" barbarism still prevailed—now in the form of militant Islamic terrorism. In this light, Jerusalem's violent urban context appears as a dangerous disease to guard and protect oneself against.

Thus, the drastic measures adopted in the "War on Terror" have been justified as a means of protecting Europe and North America against outside threats. But in reality, such threats have been fused with the fears derived from internal conflicts resulting from long-term structural problems of the European and North American city: the same preventative security measures and rhetoric are readily used to "deal" with failed integration of migrant communities or increasing social polarizations. Lines between external and internal pressures are blurred.

What is changing European and American cities is not destruction by means of suicide bombings, but the growing fear of "the other" and the manner in which these suspicions are manifested in urban space. Government and private measures against the pervading fear of terror threats (be they real or imagined) have challenge the very freedom of the individual that was once heralded a triumph of the Western system. Urban diversity itself is perceived as a potential threat. "The worry here," writes Stephen Graham, "is that attempts will be made by governments (and the security-military-industrial complexes which have burgeoned since the advent of the 'war on terror'") to reengineer cities so that their porous, open, and intrinsically fluid spaces and systems become little more than an endless series of securitized passage points" (Stephen Graham, page 158).

As Western cities become cultural, socioeconomic and political microcosms of a globalized and diversified world, our mental map of the city should be redrawn, and the position of cities like Jerusalem vis-à-vis the European city revised. Geographic distance is no longer relevant. What seemed at the periphery of Central Europe is now in fact closer than ever. A change of perspective not only allows us to better understand the city and the dynamics through which conflict alters urban fabric, but also allows us to better understand the development—current and predicted—of the relation of conflict and the Western metropolis. Jerusalem is a laboratory for a conflict urbanism whose symptoms are already all too familiar.

While we suggest learning from Jerusalem's conflict urbanism today, it remains our hope for the future that perhaps a city, which has produced such an urbanism, can also serve as a laboratory for practices that undermine, erode, and transgress this condition.

1   Tom Segev, "Conceding Har Homa," February 1, 2006, www.haaretz.com

JERUSALEM, BETWEEN URBAN AREA AND APPARITION

FROM A MULTIETHNIC CITY TO NATIONALISM?
JERUSALEM IN THE EARLY TWENTIETH CENTURY

A conversation on Jerusalem with Meron Benvenisti and Salim Tamari
moderated by Michael Fischer and Philipp Misselwitz

Fischer and Misselwitz: Salim, in your recent research you have used diaries
written by Arab Jerusalemites in order to piece together a sense of what it was
like to live in Jerusalem during the early period of the British Mandate (1918-1921).
You have discovered that the authors identified themselves first and foremost as
citizens of Jerusalem, and only in a second instance, as belonging to a particular
ethnicity: as Arab Muslims, Arab Christians, or Jews. You have found a period
where modernity was viewed with excitement, through new kinds of public
institutions like street cafes, restaurants, and so on. Can we extrapolate your
findings to describe an essential quality of the Middle Eastern city at the beginning
of modernity: an urban environment accommodating a multitude of different,
more or less unstable identities, a city based on the paradigm of coexistence that
has since been lost?

Tamari: What can be constructed from these diaries is a transition between
two kinds of modernities: the Ottoman kind, which is usually seen as continuation
of a communitarian system, and British Mandate colonial modernity, which is
seen as ushering in a new era. It is often forgotten that the late Ottomans were
in fact the promulgators of notions of modern citizenship, which had immense
implications for the modernity of the city as a whole. In the period covering the
last third of the 19th century to the end of World War I, a new urban identity was
formed in Jerusalem, Beirut, Damascus, and in Anatolia, which was based on
class transformation, constitutional reform, and urban planning, and was often
expressed through citizens' departure from the confines of their dwellings in the
walled city or traditional family neighborhoods.

All these cities were composed of minorities and it is important to state that
I do not refer to ethnic minorities, which is a retrospective concept of Ottoman
minorities. Rather, we should speak of communities belonging to different religions or linguistic groups. The major change that affected coexistence between
these groups after the collapse of the Ottoman Empire and the beginning Mandate period was the emergent notion of nationality, which meant separating
from the notion of multiethnic, multicommunal Ottoman citizenship. The most
important of these was, of course, a sense of greater Arabness within Greater
Syria (that is, the area referred to as Bilad ash-Sham, or the Eastern Mediterranean Arab provinces)—some would call it Palestinian or Syrian nationalism.
Later, or probably in parallel, Palestinian regional identity was also affected by
the emergence of a separatist Jewish nationalism.

In fact, the Ottomans had introduced many features of these urban modernities, which the British and the French then claimed retrospectively. Already the first governor of Jerusalem, Ronald Storrs, defined Palestine and certainly Jerusalem not as a country with one potential citizenship, or even two nationalities, but as a country and city of three religions. To emphasize this, he combined the star of David, the crescent, and the cross in his emblem. This principle determined the way the British divided the Old City, issued national identity cards and passports, and so on. One could say that they actually created a regression in a certain budding notion of Ottoman modernity. We see these separate developments already in the period after World War I in the writings of Khalil Sakakini (on the Arab side) and Eliahu Elyashar (on the Jewish side).

Benvenisti: I'm reminded of my father who was born in Salonica in Greece. When he came to Palestine in 1913 to study amongst other Sephardic Jews, also Ottoman subjects, he did not consider this making *aliya* [immigrating, or literally, "going up"], as did other Ashkenazi Jews at the time. He simply moved to another place in the country. There was a very touching moment in my father's diaries where he said he came to Jaffa and he felt he had arrived home. One might think that he meant that he was coming home to the Holy Land, but no—he felt at home because he spoke the language and wore the same *tarbush* [fez] as Turkish officials. This moment was totally unlike the culture shock felt by Ashkenazi Jews on their arrival in a dusty Mediterranean city.

But I can agree with you only up to a point. What you are saying about Ottoman modernity seems to me somewhat anachronistic and nostalgic. In fact, the emergence of nationalism was fostered by the Ottomans, when it suited them. For instance, under the Ottomans, a split between the Christian community into Greeks and Bulgarians was created by the creation of a rival Bulgarian patriarch. Some Christians who defined themselves as "orthodox" became Greek nationalists, especially from Anatolia but also in Salonioca. Christians in Macedonia now became Bulgarians. Fighting broke out between the two factions, despite that 20 years prior they had all identified themselves as simply orthodox Christians.

Once World War I broke out, the paradigm of multiethnic citizenship was only supported by the Jews of Turkey and the Balkans. The Jews in Salonica, the majority of the city's inhabitants, remained the last believers in the Ottoman model of citizenship. With the emergence of nationalism, Jewish Salonica was finished, because it found itself between nationalities. Even in Palestine, there was initially a sense of solidarity with Turkey, which then dissipated because of the regime's cruelty and venality.

Tamari: Of course, the arrival of the British was preceded by the war, which had already destroyed the system out of which Ottoman reform was producing a nation of citizens, rather than subjects. This led to the recession of communal or city consciousness in favor of a wider regional consciousness, whether Shami [Syrian], or Palestinian. The war also led to a dramatic change in the way people conceived the Ottomans. As a result of the war, the Ottoman idea—of a multiethnic, multinational citizenship—died. One could say that this was a step backwards because of the great possibilities inherent in this broader frame of identification. Cities such as Jerusalem, and even more so Beirut, Damascus, and Istanbul, transformed from centers of cosmopolitan multinational citizenship to centers for ethnic enclaves, be they Turkish, Armenian, Greek, or certainly Arab.

Benvenisti: I do not think that World War I gave such an impetus to nationalism, which was already flourishing. To speculate that without this war we could have continued to live in an island of multiculture, in which definitions or entities are molded around community and religion, is wishful thinking. It is perhaps important to consider the special position of Arabs within the Ottoman Empire, as they had much more power than the Jews. Arabs of the Middle East, despite the fact that later on they sought to disassociate themselves from the Ottoman Empire, did not need nationalism. I believe that in Iraq today we see the very end of this Sunni Ottoman dominance that we saw vanishing in many other parts of the Middle East during the mid 1950s to late 1980s of the last century, and which remained only in the regime of Jordan. If we try to appropriate the lost paradigm of Jerusalem as a "city of communities" for the present we would return to something that, unfortunately has vanished, and will return only when we see the end of nationalism.

Fischer and Misselwitz: How did the shift towards nationalism and ethnic belonging affect the city of Jerusalem?

Tamari: We could say that the modern colonial impact and the creation of the Jewish state transformed a limited urban consciousness to one of belonging to the country as a whole. During the Ottoman period, there was a core geographic area inside which people identified themselves as coming from the city. I am editing a diary of an Ottoman soldier from Jerusalem during the Great War. For him, marrying outside the city of Jerusalem was unimaginable. He could imagine marrying a Christian or a Jewish woman from the city but not a non-Jerusalemite, because belonging to Jerusalem bounded the parameters of his experience and his consciousness. We can see that this identification works across religious boundaries; a fellow Jerusalemite was a Jew, or a Christian was primarily seen as a compatriot of a specific community. Then all of a sudden, a Jew in Arab Palestinian eyes became the European, the intruder from a different ethnic community which was contesting [ownership of] the land. The Jews of the city were no longer part of the national community, but joined with their European co-religionists who contested the Arab Palestinian's claim to the land. So the country as a whole, not the city, was the main arena of the conflict. For Jerusalem, one might say that this shift happened in the 1920s as a gradual and cumulative process that all of a sudden dawned on public consciousness. This process started immediately after the end of the British military government in 1922, and the beginning of the Mandate.

SPATIAL SEGREGATION: CHANGING URBAN PATTERNS DURING THE BRITISH MANDATE PERIOD

Fischer and Misselwitz: How did the shift from an inclusive city to a city of competing ethnicities affect the spatial and physical fabric of Jerusalem? If one looks at Jerusalem's late 19th century expansion beyond the Old City walls, one already finds a surprisingly clear division into ethnically homogeneous areas: Arabs in the north, Jews in the northwest, etc. If Salim's theory of Ottoman modernity is right, where are the urban typologies that manifested this?

Tamari: This happened as the middle classes and professionals moved beyond the city walls into areas where those families possessed or purchased land. In some of those areas, like Sheikh Jarrah, where the Muslim elites (Nashashibis, Jarallahs, and Husseinis) moved, we witness class and religious identity combine. The Jews had their planned communities in the western areas, near Mea Sharim, Yamin Moshe, or Montifiore. Similarly the Greek Orthodox middle classes and some of the Latin Arab Catholics built Talbiya and Katamon. Baqaa, by contrast, was mixed by religion but homogeneous in class character. It is one of the great paradoxes of the modernity of Ottoman Jerusalem that the developing new city consisted of religiously and spatially delineated communities of Jews, Christians, and Muslims, which were much more segregated than communities of the Old City, even though they were modern and secular.

Benvenisti: In order to understand the degree of encroaching separation, one has to differentiate between residential neighborhoods and the business district. Outer residential areas were always segregated due to land ownership, which Salim described. But in more central areas like Sheikh Jarrah or Romema, mixing was important at least until the late 1920s. But if we look at Jerusalem's main business district around Julian's Way and Jaffa Road, we find that it was completely mixed until 1948. The way to measure the degree of separation here would be to research the archives of the Arab-owned Rex Cinema on Princess Mary Street (today's Shlomzion HaMalka) and find out how many Jews went there. You would find that vast numbers attended. Even I remember going there as a child in 1946 on Saturday evening or Friday evening when cinemas were closed in Jewish areas.

Fischer and Misselwitz: What impact did the administrative reforms and planning efforts of the British authorities have? Salim mentioned earlier that the British introduced strict divisions between three religious groups. How did this sectarian thinking manifest itself in the sweeping reforms that were supposed to modernize the city?

Tamari: One of the most dramatic reforms was the division of the Old City. The British Mandate authorities retroactively divided the area into four communities: Muslim, Armenian, Christian, (Arab) and Jewish. While Armenians, Muslims, Christians, and Jews always existed as distinct communities, the British tried to delineate them as administratively separate quarters. If one reads the demographic map of the late Ottoman period, there was a great deal of mixture in the Muslim quarter—which was substantially inhabited by Jews and Christians. Religious labeling of these communities was noted by foreign visitors, but was not recognized by the Ottoman administration, nor by the natives of the city. Equally, there were many Muslim families living in the so-called Jewish quarter, and a few Muslims in the Christian quarter. The only quarter which was actually "ethnically pure" was the Armenian quarter, because it was delineated by the Armenian convent and its administration.

Fischer and Misselwitz: What about urban planning? The British authorities expended great efforts not only in surveying the existing fabric, but also in planning the future expansion of the city.

Tamari: Planning is a very interesting notion here. Early plans by Sir William McLean and Charles Ashbee, drawn at the invitation of Colonel Storrs after World War I and later expanded by the Sir Patrick Geddes and Henry Kendall plans, showed that the British envisioned what you might call a "garden city" (based on romantic English notions of urban use). Those were particularly influenced by city planner Ashbee—an accomplished follower of William Morris in England. Here we see a dichotomous vision of Jerusalem dividing the Old City and New City. The British envisaged the Old City behind the walls as a "pickled" city— a preserved living archeological museum comprised of historic buildings and pathways. This concept of museum-city involved renovation schemes whose objective was to protect and insulate history from modernist intrusions. The New City beyond the walls was designated as an area of modernist planning and habitat. Both Old and New cities were supposed to be linked by gardening and landscaping projects within which the iconic Old City could be appropriately staged. All the buildings that had linked these parts were to be erased, and in fact this process was begun by removing all the commercial establishments and landmarks erected in the immediate vicinity of the walls near Jaffa Gate, Damascus Gate, and the New Gate. Part of this overall scheme of preservation was the enforcement of a municipal law, already on paper from the late Ottoman period, which dictated that all new buildings must be constructed from local stone— ensuring a degree of uniformity and aesthetic control over height and material.

But we have to remember that British planning had little chance of actually being implemented for fiscal reasons and due to the chief planners' short tenure. The British budget for the civil administration of Palestine had to be raised locally (from taxes) and most of it was consumed for defense operations during the Arab Revolt (1936-1939), whose aim was to oppose British sponsorship of Jewish home rule in Palestine (the Balfour Proclamation).

Benvenisti: British planning was much more reactive than proactive. The Kendall plan in particular is a totally overrated and unimportant document. It was published only four months after the end of the British Mandate in 1948. Kendall did not really plan much but simply accepted and aestheticized what was happening any- way. He could not have planned it because you cannot plan a mixed Jewish-Arab neighborhood when Jews and Arabs wanted to built their own areas. To me the garden city plan was largely determined by the ability and success of the Jews in buying land. When the Jews succeeded in purchasing the neighborhood of Rehavia from the Greek Orthodox Church, they built the Jewish neighborhood of Rehavia. When they could buy the land of Talpiot, they built Talpiot.

But apart from its planning regulations, British planning hardly affected the expanding city, which resulted instead from competition between Jews and Arabs over land. This story continues until the present day. Until this moment, urban planning in a traditional sense is totally unimportant. After the 1948 War, it was not the western city government but the Jewish National Fund or the state that grabbed as many abandoned Arab properties as they could. Each time the Israeli Ministry of Housing hastily built an ugly neighborhood on a hilltop, and ruined the place with bad planning and bad construction, they moved on to another one. It was and still is a policy of scorched earth, rather than planning. You build a section

0.2 km: Qalandiya Checkpoint

0.6 km: Qalandiya Checkpoint

as if you are at war and have one objective: to conquer a strategic spot. Whatever could be touched and claimed was claimed. The real planners are politicians and bureaucrats. Architects and urban planners become mere technicians, who never raise value questions and are without ethical considerations.

Architectural plans do not explain what is happening now in Jerusalem either. Israeli planners have always opportunistically smelled what the government or municipal authority wants and then jumped on the opportunity. The same story is now repeating itself in the case of the E-1 planning project which is supposed to link Maale Adumim and municipal Jerusalem. Planners and architects are fighting one another to have a chance to plan that monstrosity without thinking about politics, quality, sustainability, and so on. Planning is certainly not what formed the current fabric of Jerusalem. It's only the politicians and the violence that determined the planning of Jerusalem.

Tamari: I agree that private interests changed the Mandate city much more effectively than public planning. But after 1948, the relationship between civil consciousness and land ownership changed dramatically. The notion of private versus public ownership of land was subsumed under a different rubric, with the emergence of the Jewish state as a key agency of power. Suddenly, virtually all Arab property was expropriated by the Jewish state under the Absentee Law regulations (which made use of the expulsion of Palestinian refugees from their localities) and then nationalized in order to create new Jewish communities (in Israel, freely-held private land amounted to a miniscule percentage of the total land area) which was then leased to new Jewish immigrants who arrived after 1948.

After 1967, the State of Israel also claimed land in East Jerusalem and the West Bank which had belonged privately to Jewish citizens before 1948—even though those Jewish owners themselves were unable to claim it. Those appropriations included properties primarily in the Jewish quarters of Jerusalem's Old City and in Hebron, the villages of Silwan or Sheikh Jarrah, or the area of Neve Yaacov, Atarot, etc. To my knowledge there is only one original family who actually "went back" to the Jewish Quarter of Jerusalem. Of course, Arabs were not permitted to reclaim land in West Jerusalem or Israel that had belonged to them before 1948. These are areas that are hundreds of dunams larger than those claimed by Israel on behalf of antebellum Jewish communities. After 1967, Israel also claimed public properties in East Jerusalem, by making itself the successor of the Jordanian state. In addition, vast tracks of land in Jerusalem (as well as in the rest of the West Bank) were expropriated in the public's name. Later, these holdings were used almost exclusively to build neighborhoods for Jews. Israel created a legal fiction in which the "public" was defined as the "Jewish public," which allowed many settlers—with government backing—to claim Palestinian property as their own. In very few cases have Israeli courts accepted challenges to this massive scheme of land theft.

Benvenisti: During the Mandate period, the city administration barely functioned. To say that under the Mandate existed a kind of civic fraternity, with both sides participating in public life is totally wrong. It's part of the nostalgia that people feel about the British Mandate with memories of Jews and Arabs having tea at the King David Hotel. Ever since the beginning of the national era, city hall was contested. Everything was based on ethnicity. In the early days of the Mandate, the Jews still agreed to continue the tradition of giving the mayor's office to the Muslims while Christians and Jews would determine the deputy mayors. But tensions soon became worse, and eventually the British totally dismissed the municipal council and appointed a British commissioner.

Tamari: I think you are also recreating a segregationist vision which was the product of the 1936 Rebellion. It is true that there was substantial residential segregation. But as you have pointed out yourself, there was an integrated city. People mixed not only commercially with joint businesses, but also in the social domain, with common ritual celebrations of a quasi-religious nature. These included the festivals of Nabi Rubeen, al-Khader (St. George), and Nabi Musa. Above all, social interaction between communities was very common and was not at all a ritual cohabitation, but one based on neighborhood coexistence. The fact that these exchanges were limited, and the fact that there was also communal conflict later on, does not correspond to the segregationist model of the city that appeared only in the 1930s. In this regard, collective memory is short lived and tends to paint a picture of conflict that goes back to "time immemorial."

Benvenisti: This is not my understanding of history. I must be the pessimist and you the optimist. I remember vividly how I was raised in the last house on Gaza Road, on the border of the Rosh HaIr quarter in Katamon. Our house was the last house between Jerusalem and the Arab village of al-Malha. I remember how we fought with the Arab children all the time.

Tamari: I was saying that segregation happened after the rebellion, not before. I am not only including the British Mandate years but also the late Ottoman period that preceded it.

Benvenisti: To me, the Ottoman period is a different era all together. I'm not saying that those who lived under the British did not have good friends across the sectarian divide. But one cannot draw any conclusions from that. Then you would also have to call the period between 1967 and 1973 a "golden era" when there was frequent exchange between middle class Jews and intellectual Palestinians.

Tamari: The point is not that Jews and Arabs lived together well and then there was a rupture and then they went back again. I think what happened is that people did not think of themselves as Jews and Arabs but they gradually became Jews and Arabs. Before that there were communities in Jerusalem and many of the Jews identified with neighborhoods with Muslims and Christians, which took the form of business partnerships, social visitations, and neighborly bonds. I should mention here that in Eliahu Elyashar's memoirs, relations between Sephardic Jews and Muslims were described as much better than between Jews and Christians, who vied occupationally for contested clerical positions within the imperial domain.

POLITICAL PLANNING

Fischer and Misselwitz: You have described a powerless municipality during the British Mandate, which was left to react to and sanctify an increasingly segregationist city. The post-1967 Israeli municipal structure, which sees itself as an authority for a "reunified" city, is completely boycotted by Palestinians in East

Jerusalem and services in the eastern part are poor. The municipality remains
the exclusive agent for Jewish citizens, yet planning schemes are developed all
the time. What are the aims and objectives of this process of planning? Can we
speak about planning?

Benvenisti: First of all, we have to remember that the municipal borders of
post-1967 are an invention by the Israelis. They were determined by politics,
not by planning. So we should not talk about East Jerusalem, but of a politically-
motivated Israeli intrusion into areas that did not belong to them. If Arabs could
equally acquire land and build in the entire city, we could begin talking about
planning. All the investment poured into this area served the political agenda
to cement the imposed unification through facts on the ground: the shifting of
a huge Jewish population into the area beyond the Green Line (UN-administered
armistice line between Israel and Jordan, 1948-1967) with the intention of
encircling the Arab population and acquiring vast stretches of land.

Fischer and Misselwitz: But that does not mean that planning does not exist.
Planning is always political, serving political goals, and planners are agents of
political programs. Perhaps the extent to which politicians determine spatial and
demographic issues is unique in this conflict. Would it be right to say here that
politicians are not just commissioning planners, but act as planners themselves?

Benvenisti: If we talk about planning in Jerusalem, we cannot talk about benign,
positive planning. Major planning decisions for the long-run are made by cabinet
ministers and the army, with almost no urban consideration or consistent thinking.
Planners and public objections are arrogantly ignored. Sectarian and partisan
Israeli interests are always predominant and legitimate Palestinian needs are
rejected as an expression of hostility.

Fischer and Misselwitz: You are describing a very asymmetrical relationship
between institutions serving the interest of Jewish Israelis, and Palestinians who
do not have a representative body to press for their rights. But is this relationship really simply a relationship between the powerful and the weak? Despite
tight planning restrictions, Palestinians continue to build and expand like never
before. Can we speak here also of facts on the ground established by the disen-
franchised and discriminated part of the population—a strategy in which informal
planning is played out against formal planning?

Tamari: I think we have to be wary of conventional academic wisdoms here. It
has become very fashionable among anthropologists to talk about the oppressed
resisting by creating facts on the ground through illegal building and so on. This
seems to me a rather unconvincing way of describing this situation, particularly
on the part of social scientists who use this paradigm. (I am referring to fashionable James Scott-style explanations that seek forms of resistance in the manner
that ordinary citizens adapt to situations of oppression by "bending" the law—for
example, by creating unauthorized housing schemes.) The individual solutions of
building a house here or adding a room there will never accumulate to real qualitative improvements. The problem definitely has to do with the helplessness of
ordinary people against a colonial system that creates a regime of discrimination—
denying them building permits, and limiting their freedom of movement through
checkpoints and barriers, all on the basis of their ethnic identity.

At the Madrid Peace Conference in 1991—and in all subsequent peace negotiations—Palestinians were forced to confine themselves to the future of "East Jerusalem" as the basis of negotiations. This was a mistake. We accepted "West Jerusalem" as Israeli domain, even though the Partition Plan of 1947 established the whole city as a corpus separatum. That was the period (in 1991) when Palestinians should have said, "You claim Arab Jewish-owned property in Atarot, and in the Jewish quarter of the Old City, and we claim pre-1948 Palestinian property from Katamon, Malha, and so on." Of course that did not happen and the PLO (Palestine Liberation Organization) accepted the weakness of their position as a part of the negotiating paradigm. This led logically to the conclusions that US President Bill Clinton and Israeli Prime Minister Ehud Barak tried to impose in the Camp David negotiations in 2000 and in Taba in 2001, when the proposed division of the city was to divide East Jerusalem between Palestinians and Israelis.

PLANNING A JOINT FUTURE?

Fischer and Misselwitz: Is it possible to develop a joint, mutually acceptable vision for the city? What agencies could undertake such a project? How should it be done?

Tamari: There are so many think tanks supported by the Europeans today where the assumptions I suggested above limit the nature of the solution. This is wishful thinking by social scientists, as none of them actually embody in their paradigms a radical questioning of the current power relationship between Israel and the Palestinians in discussing the future of the city. Utopian visions can be useful as a way of transcending reality and reminding ourselves of other futures. But with the power relations so overwhelming stacked against the Palestinian side, all these futurist schemes become abstract and self-congratulatory.

Benvenisti: I totally agree with Salim on this issue. Thank God, I can afford not to be part of this peace industry, but others need to live. The first step should be to question the spatial limits of Jerusalem. We should forget about the notions of "East Jerusalem" and "West Jerusalem," or the vast and monstrous area that the Israelis call "Greater Jerusalem." We can think of this inflation of territory we call "Jerusalem" as a balloon; one thing I would want is to pierce that balloon and to compact Jerusalem, to de-Jerusalemize Jerusalem: to return to the Old City and forget the rest for the next 50 years.

Let's think about Jerusalem as a museum: the Old City. The rest, we just invented. I see this as a way of overcoming fatigue from the obsession about Jerusalem. One example of this fatigue was the Israeli elections for the Jerusalem mayor in 2003. No Israeli politician or legislator was ready to stand for election. Why? People couldn't have cared less about Jerusalem. Those who cared about Jerusalem were bigots! Right wing orthodox, ultra-orthodox, and maybe some of the Arabs, too. I am saying that maybe we have to wait for Jerusalem to be drawn into a stupor of boredom. The less you discuss Jerusalem, the better the chances that there will be a solution.

Tamari: Another way is to push these parameters of discussing the future of the city so as to propose them for the whole country, and not to limit them to the city itself.

Benvenisti: Exactly. That is also a possibility. Either you expand the whole thing endlessly, or contract it. You say, "Listen, what is Jerusalem?" Jerusalem is the Old City. Maybe if you want, Mandatory Jerusalem. Let's take Kendall's Plan and say that is Jerusalem. Here we can identify things that are really contested. But outer settlements like Har Homa are not Jerusalem; they are really part of Beit Sahur. Why do we have to add to Jerusalem's misery also Har Homa, which was build on confiscated (in other words, stolen) land.

I can detect some glimmer of hope on the Israeli side. People are getting sick and tired of using the name of Jerusalem in vain. You heard that from the Israeli delegation to the Geneva process who said, "We did not pray 2000 years for Shufat." And there is willingness even among Likud people (as you can see from the fence that Israel is constructing) to give up the notion of the sanctity of former Jerusalem mayor Teddy Kollek's 1967 borders of Jerusalem. Maybe in that lies a future.

BORDERS, WALLS, PARTITIONS

Fischer and Misselwitz: Can we turn back to the question of power? It could also be a dangerous fiction to forget the agencies of power. What are the possibilities and leverages for subverting the current asymmetrical power relationship? Is the two-state, two-capital solution still the only position? What would be the implications for Jerusalem if we follow the bi-national state or the two-state paradigm?

Tamari: I do not want to play that game because I do not believe that we have a choice today between having one state or two states. I think both ideas are problematic. The abandonment of the territorial solution is very problematic politically because it means that you cannot, as a matter of priority, struggle against land confiscation, against settlements, and against territorial expansion. Why? Because you would instead be in the mindset of fighting for equal citizenship. To abandon the territorial claims is a politically shortsighted position, because it transforms the issue of Palestine primarily into an issue of civic rights. On the other hand, to behave as if we are in the first Intifada and are on the road to independence—i.e. the creation of two sovereign states—is also blind because it means ignoring the last 20 years of eroding possibilities for a viable state on our side. There is one political economy in the entire country now; the idea that there is an independent Palestinian Authority is deceptive. It may make many Palestinians feel good that they have their own passports and flag, but these are not at all real. So, obviously we have to think of the paradigm that can transcend this dichotomy of two states versus one state.

Benvenisti: Both propositions are already part of one continuum, although many people use one state versus two states religiously or as if they are dichotomous. In certain aspects, we already have two states with rigid borders, but those borders apply to Palestinians only. At the same time, we also have a unitary state without any regard for borders, where the Israelis are dominant.

One might refer to the model of Bosnia or the unimplemented model of Cyprus. What is most important [in these models] for our purposes, is the fact that the international community has understood the advantages of preserving territorial integrity, preferring "soft" internal boundaries to rigid dividing lines which would have made it difficult to travel freely and hinder economic recovery.

Alterations in international borders disturb the existing geopolitical balance and gives rise to tensions in nearby countries. For example, resolution of the Kurdish problem via the partition of Iraq (or even by creating a federation) would send dangerous political shockwaves throughout the three neighboring states which have large Kurdish minorities (Iran, Turkey, and Syria). It is therefore preferable to retain the recognized international borders—which are like a mosaic, in that every little change distorts the picture and causes problems—and to aim, if possible, for "soft" internal boundaries.

Fischer and Misselwitz: Can you explain a bit more?

Benvenisti: Rigid borders lie between two states with a border separating them. There is no question that we need a clear identity of ethnicity and territory, which this model provides. But we face the problem of how to define identity, ethnicity, and territory. One should discuss the one-state concept using either the Western model of a unitary state such as France, or face the idea of multiracial South Africa. That is why Israelis always discuss demography, because they are trying to relate demography and voting patterns. But this is not always the case. One could create a federated Palestine-Israel with internal soft borders that will keep ethnic identity attached to territory. And therefore—to return to Jerusalem—Jerusalem definitely needs soft boundaries between ethnically-defined areas. I think we can work on that without using the dichotomy of one versus two states, but rather think about one state and two states as a continuum. We should select and choose from both concepts. A unitary state by itself is not going to work because the problem here is with collective, rather than individual, rights. But the concept of surgical partition will also not work because the current power relationships guarantee that Israeli interests will prevail. What we have to find is ideally something in between.

For the first time in Zionist history, Israelis have now acknowledged the fact that there are Palestinians. There are Palestinians, and therefore you cannot ignore them by building settlements in their midst. Suddenly, they understand that there are Palestinians that they cannot absorb. And the price for that is the withdrawal from Gaza, but also eventually from areas beyond the Green Line.

Fischer and Misselwitz: Do you mean that if the dispute shifts to a dispute about borders, leftists and Palestinians will try to push the wall westwards a little bit here, a little bit there, in order to improve situation for Palestinians?

Benvenisti: You cannot tell the Palestinians that they have to live with what is going to be 8% of historic Palestine. They will not accept it, and it is not sustainable.

Tamari: We should remember that the nature of the Jewish city is also changing, including the notion of citizenship within Israel. Also, the country's relationship to the Diaspora is changing in a very intriguing way. The idea of dual nationality, for example, creates great possibilities, not only for the Jews but also for the Arabs. It is conceivable that the effect of the 1.2 million Russian immigrants in Israel (many of them not Jews) will inject into the Israeli nationality prospects that transcend the Mizrahi-Ashkenazi dichotomy. If we then add the dual nationality that many Israelis share with European countries or the US, it could become increasingly possible for Israelis to accept that Israel is part of the world and not part of "Fortress Judaica."

If Israel redefines itself as part of the global community, the wall on its eastern frontier, already seen as illegal by the international community, will be rejected by many Israelis as defining their borders. These are countervailing tendencies. Israel itself is redefining itself as a corporate entity. The terms of trade, the relationship with the United States, the relationship with the European Commission, and ultimately new ways of looking at Palestinians will make the wall itself an anathema.

Benvenisti: If you consider the immediate implications of the wall on Jerusalem, it is creating great urban problems and long term upheavals. I still hope that Israelis will not be successful, because eventually the sheer power of the incision created by the wall will leave the West Bank divided into two, maybe three, separate cantons, with roadblocks designed as international crossings in Bethlehem, Betuniya, Qalandiya. Perhaps Palestinians have no choice but to accept this in the short term. But then it will simmer and accumulate. Most sociologists, and planners think that there is always a positive future. But there is never a future, there is always only the present. If Israel succeeds in implementing the same principles in the northern and southern West Bank that were implemented in Gaza, including the partition of the West Bank by Maale Adumim, and Palestinians placidly accept this, this is the final victory of Zionism. But it will be a pyrrhic victory.

Tamari: There will always be people who accept and people who resist. And I think there are too many factors that mitigate against a long-term solution. If what you are saying is true, then the wall will become a border, an ethnic border. But it will become an embarrassment, just as the Berlin Wall was for Germany. Israel wants to be part of Europe, not only economically and politically, but culturally. I think it will be very difficult to maintain its status vis-à-vis the international community while maintaining ethnic segregation within its own boundaries. Turkey is another good example of this trend. As Turkey inches closer towards the European Union, conditions will be forced on it which will make ethnic segregation and linguistic restrictions increasingly difficult. In the foreseeable future, the Israeli wall, currently justified by security and defensive rationalizations, will become such a monstrosity that it will change the attitude of the Europeans and the Americans towards the State of Israel.

Benvenisti: You know, I would say something even stronger: that the whole notion that we are discussing of a geographical entity called "Jerusalem" is false. Jerusalem is a fiction. As a historian, I could never understand the notion that boundaries create communities. Usually we say that nationalism emerged in an area, and then borders were defined around that definition of nationalism. We all know that the colonial experience is just the opposite.

Here I see how an administrative political definition creates a geographical concept, and then people accept it. I would suggest to you that what we are discussing is not Jerusalem but the problems that we would like to attach to Jerusalem because we need to define for ourselves an agenda. There is no longer an objective entity such as Jerusalem, because when we ask now, "What is Jerusalem?" we get answers that speak more of the political, economic or cultural point of view of the definer. According to the Israeli municipal definition, Jerusalem now covers an area of 124 square kilometers. This is monstrous and totally fictitious.

Fischer and Misselwitz: Is it more fictitious than, for instance, the boundary of any other metropolis?

Benvenisti: We cannot compare a contested city like Jerusalem, where boundaries and demography are considered political issues, to the problems of London or other metropolises. Here, everything is a political statement more than an urban statement.

Conflict and
Urban Transformation

1553

Census by Ottomans shows Jerusalem population as comprised of 1,650 Jews, 10,000 Muslims and 1,650 Christians.

1860

First Jewish settlement outside Jerusalem's walls, Mishkenot Shaananim, completed at the behest of British Jewish philanthropist Sir Moses Montefiore.

British Rule

November 2, 1917

The British Foreign Office writes to Lord Rothschild (in the Balfour Declaration) to express Britain's commitment to the establishment of a Jewish national home in Palestine, without prejudice to the civil and religious right of the non-Jewish population.

December 11, 1917

British General Allenby defeats Ottoman forces and enters Jerusalem, Palestine is placed under British military administration.

1919

Third wave of Jewish immigration begins, comprised of 40,000 eastern Europeans, many steeped in the socialist ideology that formed the backbone of the kibbutz movement (1919-1923). From 1924 to 1929, another 82,000 Jews arrive, and between 1929 and 1939, Nazism spurs a new wave of 250,000 Jewish immigrants.

April 1920

Palestinian riots break out in Jerusalem, five Jews are killed and several hundred wounded.

Timeline

British Mandate Begins

June 1922

Palestine Mandate given to Britain by League of Nations. Haj Amin al-Husseini is appointed Grand Mufti of Jerusalem.

August 23-29, 1929

Tensions break into open violence. Palestinians clash with British forces in Jerusalem; residents of Hebron and Safed turn on their Jewish neighbors, killing 113. British authorities dispatch the Shaw Commission to investigate.

February 2, 1933

Palestinians declare general strike to protest Jewish immigration.

November 12, 1936

Peel Commission recommends the partition of Palestine between Arabs and Jews, a recommendation accepted by Britain; Palestinians establish the Arab Higher Committee.

May 17, 1939

MacDonald ["Third"] White Paper rejects former partition and envisages a creation of one state with an Arab majority and Jewish participation in the government. Jewish immigration limited to 75,000 over five years, and thereafter limited by Arab consent.

1944

British census shows that Jerusalem population as comprised of 92,143 Jews, 32,039 Muslims, and 27,849 Christians.

June 22, 1946

The underground Irgun ["Etzel"] bombs Jerusalem's King David Hotel, where British government headquarters were located. The group also hangs two British sergeants in revenge for death sentences placed on Etzel members.

"From time to time, we absorb aliyah [immigration]. The crowding in the tents gets worse…We are living three to a tent: I, my chaver [lover], and her–my neighbor–number three' in the family. Only a thin cloth separates us from her. We have lived like this for two years already…And sometimes, I think: can someone living under different circumstances understand what price the absorption of aliyah demands of a chaver kibbutz?" *Poet Rachel (1934), writing from Kibbutz Daganya*

"We shall fight the war against Hitler as if there were no White Paper, and the White Paper as if there were no war." *David Ben Gurion (1939)*

"We have clashing interests with the [Palestinian] Arabs everywhere, and these interests will continue and the clashes will increase… and once again I hear the answer rise from within me: only a [Palestinian Arab] population transfer and evacuation from this country, so it becomes exclusively for us [Jews] is the solution. This idea remains with me, especially today, and I find comfort in it, in the face of the enormous difficulties involved in land purchase and settlement." *A March 18, 1941 diary entry by Yosef Weitz, director of the Jewish National Fund's Land Settlement Department*

"I used to sit in [Jerusalem's Postal Café] every afternoon, where we used to encounter its cosmopolitan clientele… The discussion was always on the same themes: Jewish migration, Arab resistance, Jabotinsky's insurrection, the battle of Tel Hai in northern Palestine, the rebellion in Jaffa [1921], and the clashes between Arabs and Jews. These discussions included ideological debates, which were translated to us in the vernacular. From them we became familiar with the basic tenants of socialism, anarchism and bolshevist doctrines." *Najati Sidqi, communist author writing his memoirs just after World War I, in Mudhakkarat Najati Sidqi, edited by Hanna Abu Hanna*

"I remember one time there was a big feast and King Abdallah was attending…someone told the king that Sheikh Hussam teaches his daughters how to play the piano and sends his daughters to foreign schools. My father stood in front of the king and cited some of the Prophet's sayings about education and culture in front of everybody [and] told him that the Prophet said, 'you should pursue your education even if it takes you to China,' and that education was a requirement for every Muslim man and woman…" *Saida Jarallah, the first Muslim Palestinian woman to study abroad in 1938, cited in Ellen Fleischman's "Mandate Memoirs," Jerusalem Quarterly File 2*

July 18, 1947

British return the illegal immigrant boat "Exodus 1947" back to Europe, where the passengers are sent to an internment camp.

November 29, 1947

United Nations General Assembly votes for the partition of Palestine and the creation of a Jewish state (Res. 181), 33 in favor, 13 opposed and 11 abstaining.

State of Israel Created

May 14, 1948

Israel declares its independence; 12 hours later Arab forces and Jewish irregulars engage in a battle that ends on June 11, with Jewish forces in control of 76.9% of mandate Palestine, and 85% of Jerusalem. Hundreds of thousands of Palestinians flee the fighting, fearing the fate of villages like Jerusalem's Deir Yassin, where Jewish forces killed civilians and then advertized their fate. As many as 80,000 refugees leave western Jerusalem.

December 9, 1949

The United Nations votes to internationalize Jerusalem and its surroundings, establishing the city as a "corpus separatum" between Jordan and Israel.

Israel Consolidates Its Control

1950

Absentee Property Law passed March 14, whereby any person who on November 29, 1947 was a citizen or resident of Arab states, or who was a Palestinian citizen who had left his or her place of residence was classified as an "absentee." Absentee property is vested in the custodian of absentee property, which then "sells" it to the Development Authority authorised by the Israeli parliament. The "Law of Return" is passed in July, whereby any Jew is entitled to full Israeli citizenship.

May 28, 1964

The Palestine Liberation Organization (PLO) is established, based on the 1936 structures of the Arab Higher Committee. Fateh, the faction founded in the late 1960s and headed by Yasser Arafat, carries out its first military attack against Israel in 1965, and comes to dominate the PLO in 1969.

June 5-11, 1967

The Six Day War between Israel and Egypt, and Jordan and Syria, places new territory under Israeli control: all of Jerusalem, the Sinai, Golan Heights, Gaza Strip, and the West Bank. Six thousand Palestinians are evicted from the Mugrabi Quarter in Jerusalem and their homes demolished to open space around the Western Wall.

Israel's Settlement Program

June 27-28, 1967

The Knesset writes into law the annexation of East Jerusalem, comprised of 6.4 km² of Jordanian Jerusalem and 64 km² of the nearby West Bank, including several villages and lands from neighboring villages.

September 27, 1967

Settlers move into Kibbutz Kfar Etzion in Hebron. Israeli settlements are planned this year in a pattern embodied in the Allon plan, strategically placed in Jerusalem and its immediate suburbs, the Jordan Valley, the Jericho desert area, the southern Gaza Strip, and the Golan Heights.

March 21, 1968

Palestinian fighters repel an Israeli attack at the Jordanian village of Karameh along the Jordan-Israel border. While Fateh's losses are far greater than Israel's, the event galvanizes Palestinians, more firmly entrenches the course of guerilla warfare, and places the Palestinian cause on the international agenda.

October 6–24, 1973

In a surprise Yom Kippur attack, Egypt and Syria invade Israel. The military move, while quickly a failure, generates great concern within Israel about military readiness.

July 30, 1980

Israel declares Jerusalem its "eternal undivided capital," and the seat of government. The UN condemns the move in Resolution 478.

Palestinian Uprising

December 9, 1987

A civilian uprising is sparked in the Occupied Territories, known in Arabic as the "Intifada" or "shaking off." It is run by local committees in the Occupied Territories and characterized by strikes, boycotts, and public demonstrations. The Israeli response is first surprise, and then a violent crackdown.

April 1993

Israel first publicizes its "Greater Jerusalem" concept comprised of 440 km², and incorporating the settlements of Maale Adumin and Givat Zeev. Underlying the plan were attempts to maintain a Jewish majority in the city, despite Palestinian population growth.

Oslo Accords Signed

September 13, 1993

Signing of the Declaration of Principles between Israel and the PLO. The plan calls for several stages of Israeli troop redeployment before final status talks over borders, major security issues, refugees, settlements, and Jerusalem.

March 31, 1993

Israel begins a policy of "closing" Israel and Jerusalem to Gaza and West Bank residents; security permits instituted for travel and checkpoints established to enforce the policy.

"A fraction of the Palestinian people…is promised a fraction of its rights (not including the national right to self-determination and statehood) in a fraction of its homeland (less than one-fifth of the area of the whole); and this promise is to be fulfilled several years from now, through a step-by-step process in which Israel is to exercise a decisive veto power over any agreement." *Fayez Sayigh (1974), responding to autonomy formulas proposed at multi-lateral talks*

"Those who call us terrorists wish to prevent world public opinion from discovering the truth about us and from seeing the justice on our faces. They seek to hide the terrorism and tyranny of their acts, and our own posture of self-defense." *Yasser Arafat (November 13, 1974), speech to the United Nations in New York*

"The conclusion to be drawn from this uprising is that the present state of affairs in the Palestinian occupied territories is unnatural and that Israeli occupation cannot continue forever. Real peace cannot be achieved except through the recognition of Palestinian national rights, including the right of self-determination and the establishment of an independent Palestinian state on Palestinian national soil." *January 14, 1988 statement by "Palestinian nationalist institutions and personalities from the West Bank and Gaza"*

"Every time the negotiations advanced, [PLO Chairman Yasser Arafat] would say, 'Without Jerusalem? Without Jerusalem?' But, of course, he went without Jerusalem." *A Palestinian close to Arafat on Israeli-Palestinian negotiations, in the New Yorker 1996*

"Settlement throughout the entire Land of Israel is for security and by right… The disposition of the settlements must be carried out not only around the settlements of the minorities [Palestinians] but also in between them. This is in accordance with the settlement program adopted in Galilee [inside Israel] and in other parts of the country, with the objective of reducing to the minimum the possibility for the development of another Arab state in these regions." *1979 guidelines of a settlement committee of the Israeli government and World Zionist Organization, as quoted in Howard Sachar's A History of Israel*

"For Jewish Jerusalem I did something in the past 25 years. For East Jerusalem? Nothing! What did I do? Nothing! Sidewalks? Nothing! Cultural institutions? Not one! Yes, we installed a sewerage system for them and improved the water supply. Do you know why? Do you think it was for their good, for their welfare? Forget it! There were some cases of cholera there and the Jews were afraid they would catch it." *Teddy Kollek (1990) mayor of Jerusalem from 1965–93*

"We have come from Jerusalem, the ancient and eternal capital of the Jewish people… We have come to try and put an end to the hostilities, so that our children, our children's children, will no longer experience the painful cost of war, violence and terror." *Israeli PM Yitzhak Rabin (1993) at the Washington, DC signing of the Oslo agreements*

October 26, 1994

Israel and Jordan sign a bilateral peace accord. Jordan thus relinquishes any possible claims to the West Bank, but maintains a presence over Muslim institutions in Jerusalem.

Palestinian Authority Established

December, 1995

The Israeli Ministry of Internal Affairs applies a policy stating that Palestinian Jerusalemites (not full Israeli citizens) will lose their residency rights in the city if they have lived outside its borders for more than seven years.

January 20, 1996

Palestinians, including Jerusalem residents, hold first general presidential and legislative elections: Yasser Arafat wins the vast majority of the presidential vote and Fateh dominates the parliamentary elections. While a parliament building is constructed in Abu Dis (outside Jerusalem's municipal borders but integrated with the city), Palestinian political life is conducted largely in Ramallah. The parliament building is never used after a subsequent Israeli crackdown on Jerusalem Palestinian political institutions.

1999

Palestinian census shows that despite Israeli figures which put the number of Jerusalem identity card holders at 200,000, only 85,805 Palestinians are living within the Jerusalem municipal boundaries (the remainder were therefore at risk of losing their residency status).

July 11-25, 2000

Final status talks break down at Camp David, despite personal intervention by US President Bill Clinton. The status of Jerusalem is the deal breaker.

"Israel is not to carry out unilateral measures that might affect the results of the negotiations. There is a big difference between the peace mentality and the war mentality. Peace needs two sides while war can be decided by one party… Based upon all this, we view the Israeli plans to build new settlements and open up new settlement roads as a 'declaration of war.'" *PLO Executive Committee Member and unofficial Jerusalem minister Faisal Husseini (1995) to the Palestine Report*

"Those in the traditional opposition [to the peace process] did not participate in the election. So what you have are different degrees of agreement and different perspectives and approaches. We still don't have a crystallized political life…" *Hanan Ashrawi (1996), Independent Jerusalem member of the Palestinian parliament*

"Jabal Abu Ghneim is the door to Bethlehem and is adjacent to the Islamic holy places of al-Aqsa Mosque and the Dome of the Rock. With this settlement [Har Homa], they want to isolate the holy places so as to have free rein in them… The objective is not only to build 38,000 housing units 120 meters from the al-Aqsa Mosque, but to destroy the Islamic and Christian holy places." *Palestinian Authority President Yasser Arafat, in the al-Watd newspaper, March 3, 1997*

"Jerusalem will not be on the negotiating table with the Palestinians at any time in the future… Israel's agreement to the Oslo Accords was intended to remove Jerusalem from any negotiations. Other compromises are necessary in order to avoid the need for compromises over Jerusalem." *Shimon Peres in The Jerusalem Post, February 13, 1996*

"I don't sign orders to destroy the houses of Jews, only of Arabs." *Haim Miller, deputy mayor of Jerusalem (Yediot Aharonot, February 7, 1998)*

"Everyone there [in the West Bank] should move, should run, should grab more hills, expand the territory. Everything that's grabbed, will be in our hands, everything that we don't grab, will be in their hands." *Then-Israeli opposition leader Ariel Sharon to the right-wing Tsomet party (1998)*

"The Arabs must be made to feel afraid, since the IDF [Israeli army] isn't doing it. They aren't afraid of the IDF, so we have to make them fear us. When the settlers put up a roadblock, the Arabs stay two kilometers away. When the IDF does it, they aren't afraid." *Lenny Goldberg of the Beit El settlement north of Ramallah in Haaretz*

Al-Aqsa Intifada Begins

September 29, 2000

The second Palestinian uprising explodes with civil unrest that is met by unprecedented Israeli military force. It is sparked by the visit of opposition leader Ariel Sharon to Jerusalem's Aqsa Mosque, and is dubbed the "Al-Aqsa Intifada," reflecting a turn towards religious symbols in Palestinian nationalism. Soon the stonethrowing turns to military-style attacks on Israelis both in the Occupied Territories and Israel.

January 28, 2001

Talks at Taba where discussions center around Jerusalem settlement blocs as Palestinians and Israelis try without success to pick up from where the Camp David talks left off.

March-April, 2002

Israel commences Operation Defensive Shield, reinvading every West Bank town (save Jericho) turned over to Palestinian Authority security control through the Oslo accords. Thousands are arrested and massive property damage incurred. Suicide bombings are carried out in Israel at an unprecedented pace; in the month of March, 135 Israelis are killed.

Unilateralism

June 2002

Israel begins constructing a series of electronic fences, concrete walls, patrol roads, and guard towers surrounding West Bank population centers.

June 24, 2003

With US leadership, the "Quartet" comprised of the United States, the European Union, the United Nations and Russia, drafts the "Road Map," a staged plan intended to get Palestinians and Israelis back to final status negotiations.

"What happened, and is still happening in Al Aqsa [mosque] and in the rest of the Palestinian territories, where victims are falling in the dozens and the wounded in the hundreds, is a defense of Islamic and national holy rights. It will have dangerous ramifications on the Arab and Islamic worlds, which will threaten the peace process and warn of the start of consecutive waves of violence, bringing the area back to the time before the peace process—full of destruction and hate and bloodshed on both sides." Al Quds editorial, October 1, 2000, translated by the Palestine Report

"In a very short time we will see the West Bank divided into three major cantons and ten other enclaves, and all the Palestinian people will be surrounded and besieged. Because of past experience, we won't now believe someone who only talks about this issue, because it seems that in this 'peace' we are always paying the price. People have now learned that 'peace' is meant only to satisfy Israel's needs, while no one seems to care about the occupation." Activist Jamal Jumaa (bitterlemons.org, August 11, 2003)

"The terrible pictures we see here are stronger than every word," Mr Sharon said. "It's interesting to speculate what kind of Palestinian state they want... What are they talking about? This terrible thing that we are seeing is the continuation of the Palestinian terror and we must fight and struggle against this terror." Ariel Sharon at the site of a Jerusalem bus bombing that killed 19 people, including the bomber, and injured over 50 (Guardian, June 18, 2000)

"As the wall is being built, we are discovering that it is virtually impossible to create full physical separation between Israelis and Palestinians, and to do so in a humanitarian way. There is no such thing as a 'good' wall in Jerusalem because you cannot simply ignore the cumulative effects of policies of a generation that created this delicate weave of arteries and veins that made us inseparable." Lawyer Danny Seideman (2004)

November 11, 2004

PLO Chairman and Palestinian Authority President, Yasser Arafat, dies after months of confinement in his Ramallah headquarters. His advisors request that he be buried in Jerusalem, but Israel denies the request.

August 12-15, 2005

Israel undertakes "disengagement" from the Gaza Strip and four settlements in the northern West Bank. The move is advocated by Prime Minister Sharon as a further push for separation, and an attempt to stem demographic concerns of a Jewish minority controlling a Palestinian majority.

January 25, 2006

The Islamist movement, Hamas, wins a sweeping victory in the Palestinian parliamentary elections, including four out of six seats in Jerusalem, where Palestinians came out to vote in unexpectedly high numbers. The elections mark the denouement of the Fateh movement and the weaknesses of the Oslo accords, which Hamas has typically rallied against.

"There is American acknowledgment that in any final status agreement there will be no Israeli withdrawal to the 1967 lines…. This acknowledgment appears in two ways: understanding the facts determined by the large Israeli settlement blocs such as making it impossible to return to the 1967 lines, and implementation of the concept of 'defensible borders.'" *Prime Minister Ariel Sharon to the Knesset, concerning an April 14, 2004 US letter of assurances*

"If they want peace, they must know that what is happening in the Gaza Strip must happen in the West Bank and East Jerusalem." *Palestinian negotiator Saeb Erekat (August 2005).*

"This is an option that we will take into consideration when we feel that the Israelis accept our rights and admit that we have rights in Jerusalem, we have rights over the area where the Israel is built settlements and built the Israeli annexation and confiscation wall." *Member of Hamas parliament Aziz Dweik (2006), when asked if the new Palestinian government will recognize Israel.*

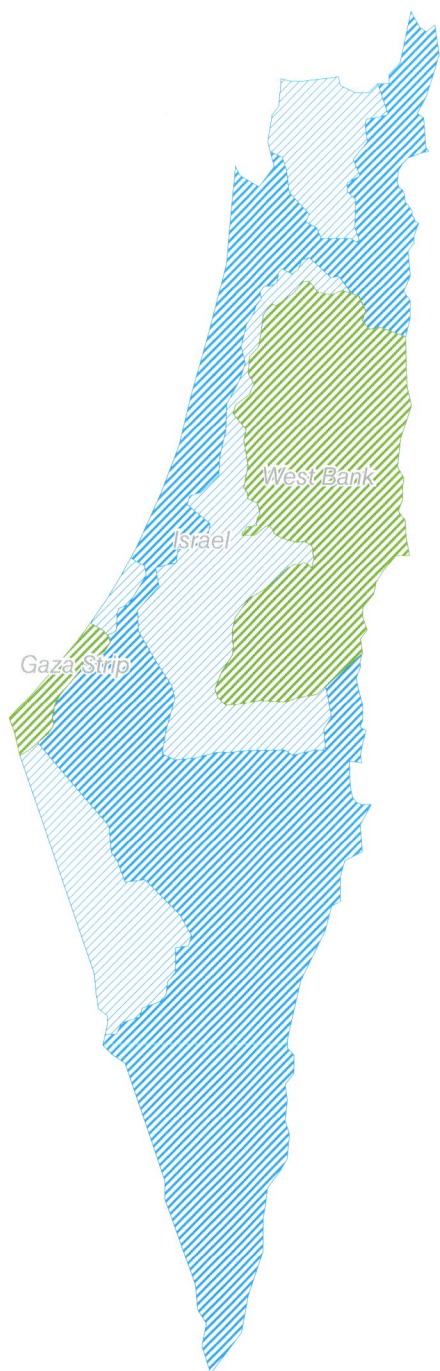

Palestine
(British Mandate)

West Bank

Israel

Gaza Strip

2001

Golan-Height

West Bank

Israel

Gaza Strip

From British Mandate to Oslo
Israel (1917-2001)

Great Britain received the League of Nation's
Mandate in 1922 to facilitate the founding of
an independent state of Palestine. But tensions
between the Zionist movement and Arab resistance proved irresolvable. The UN Partition Plan
of 1947 was rejected by the Arab states, and
the subsequent 1948 War resulted in the founding of the State of Israel. More than 700,000
Arab Palestinians fled and where forced out. In
the Six Day War of 1967, Israel gained control
over Egypt's Sinai Peninsula, the Syrian Golan
Heights, Jordanian West Bank and Egyptian
Gaza Strip. Palestinians themselves have revolted
in two intifadas. The Oslo Accords (1993) and
the Road Map (2004) held out the possibility
of an independent Palestinian state, but core
issues remained unsolved.

1917-1948

Under British mandate

1948-1967

Under British mandate

The State of Israel

Temporary Occupied by Israeli forces
(1948-1949)

2001

Oslo area A/B
(full/partial control of the Palestinian Authority)

Oslo Area C
(full Israeli control)

Israel

0   20   40   60   80   100 kilometers

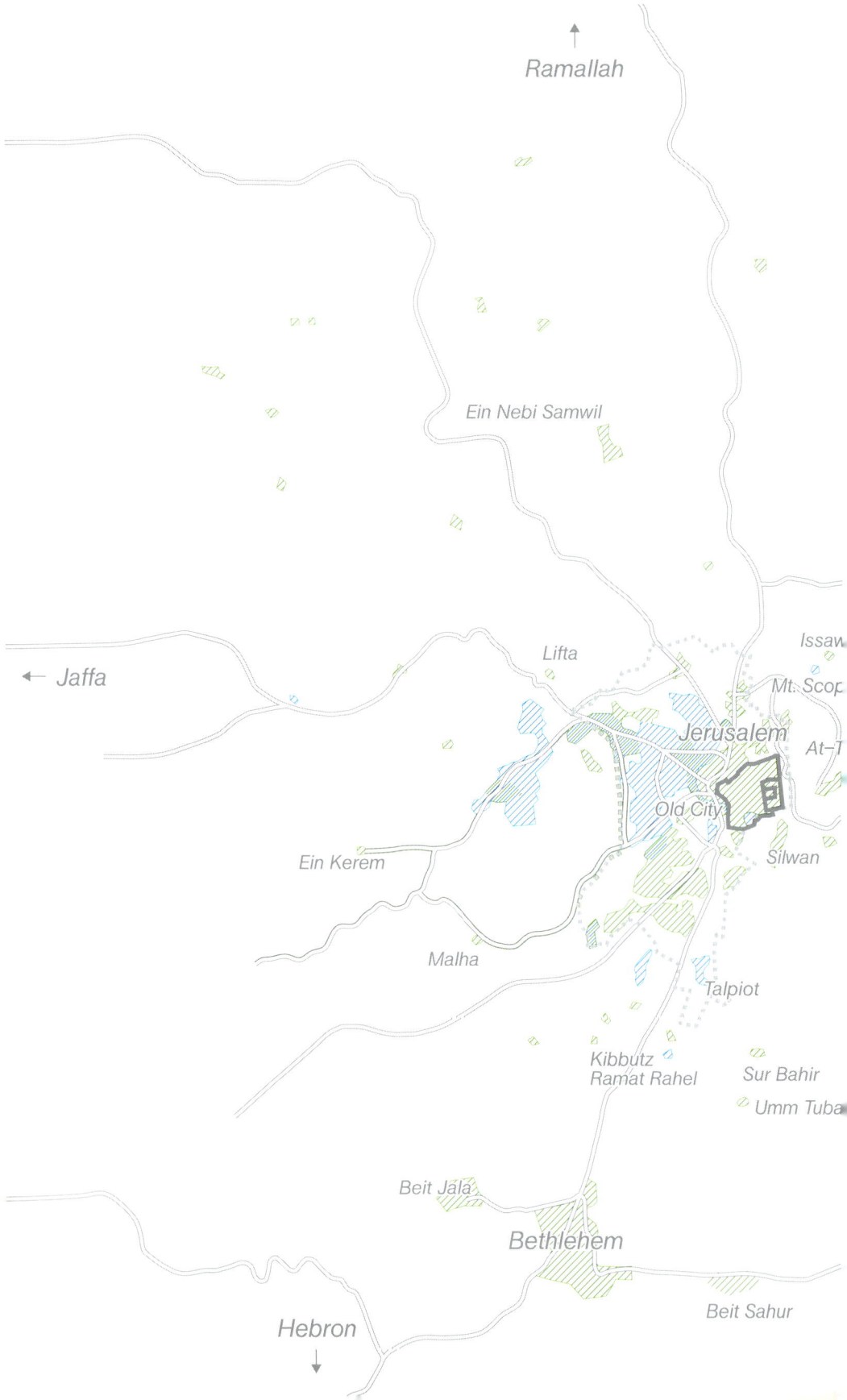

Ramallah

Ein Nebi Samwil

Jaffa

Lifta

Issaw

Mt. Scop

Jerusalem

At-T

Old City

Silwan

Ein Kerem

Malha

Talpiot

Kibbutz
Ramat Rahel

Sur Bahir

Umm Tuba

Beit Jala

Bethlehem

Beit Sahur

Hebron

British Mandate
Jerusalem (1917-1948)

With the collapse of the Ottoman Empire in
1917, the larger political and cultural framework
for a multicultural city had evaporated. Citizenship now became increasingly defined in terms
of ethnicity. Fuelled by the British Mandate's
(1920-1948) ambiguous promise of a European-style nation-state, Jews and Arabs were
drawn into a struggle for hegemony. Tensions
and eventually near civil war overshadowed the
hopes and potentials connected to the city's
enormous growth from 60,000 to 200,000
inhabitants in only 30 years. The effects on
Jerusalem's social, economic and cultural fabric were disastrous: Modernization, economic
growth and expansion were increasingly driven
by ethnic interests. While some mixed areas
remained, new neighborhoods were strictly
segregated.

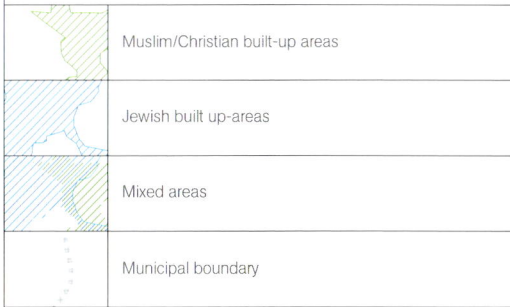

Jericho →

Abu Dis

Muslim/Christian built-up areas

Jewish built up-areas

Mixed areas

Municipal boundary

0   1   2   3   4   5 kilometers

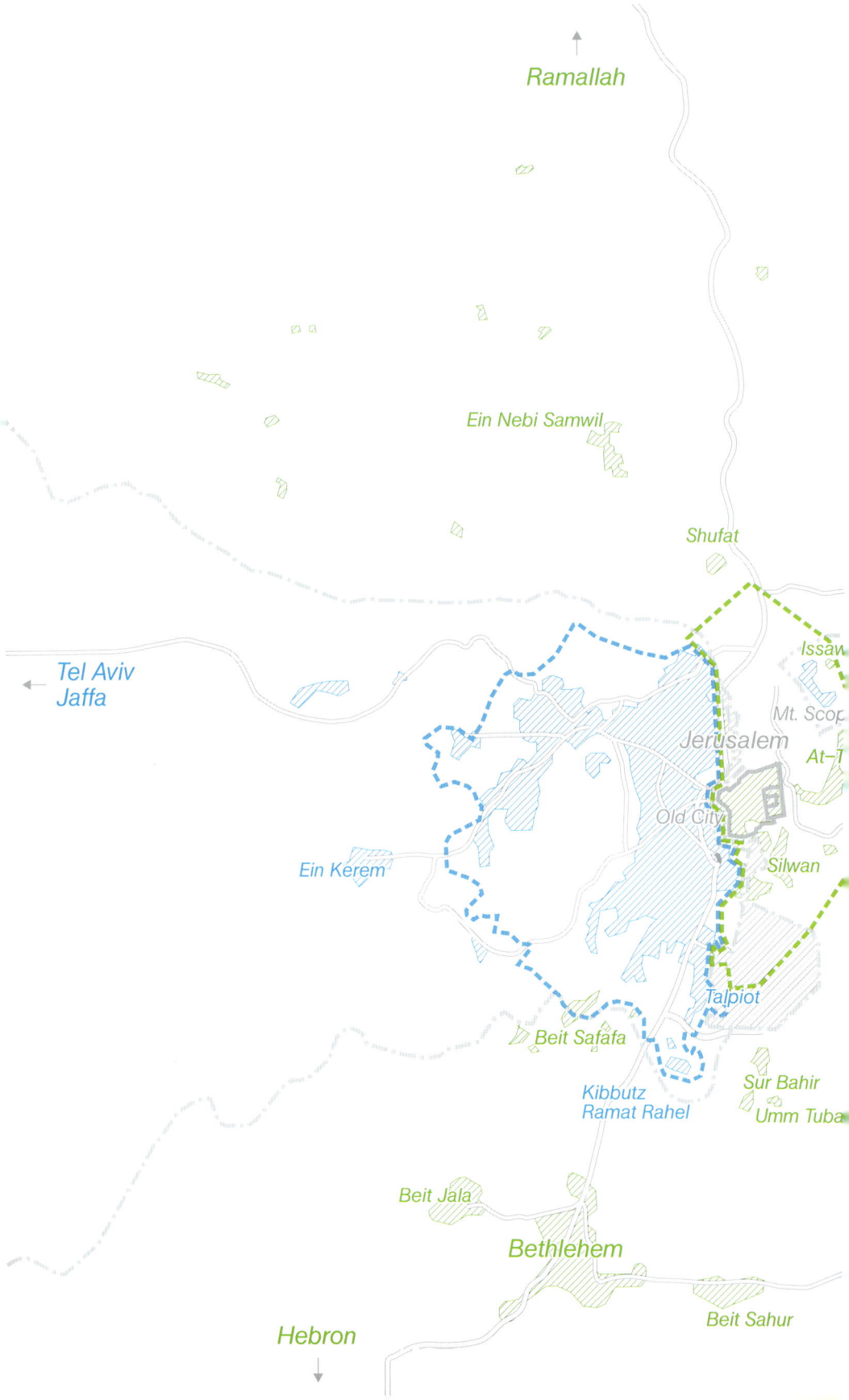

Ramallah

Ein Nebi Samwil

Shufat

Issaw

Tel Aviv
Jaffa

Mt. Scop

Jerusalem

At–T

Old City

Ein Kerem

Silwan

Talpiot

Beit Safafa

Sur Bahir

Kibbutz
Ramat Rahel

Umm Tuba

Beit Jala

Bethlehem

Hebron

Beit Sahur

Divided City
Jerusalem (1948-1967)

Unable to provide a solution to the ethnic conflict in Palestine, the British deferred to the newly established United Nations. On 29 November, 1947, the United Nations Partition Plan for Palestine was adopted (Resolution 181), which resolved that Palestine would become a confederation between Jewish- and Arab-controlled areas and an internationalized Jerusalem-Bethlehem area as a corpus separatum. The plan failed. Violence evolved into a full-scale war after the British withdrawal in May 1948, resulting in the largest population displacement in the city's history: 45,000 Arab Jerusalemites and almost 30,000 villagers residing within the Jerusalem district lost their properties and livelihoods and became refugees from areas which were annexed into the newly-founded Israeli state. More than 30 Jerusalem villages either vanished from the map or were expropriated and transferred to Jewish ownership, reflecting similar processes at work in the rest of Palestine. Jews fled the now Jordanian-controlled Old City and other neighborhoods. A UN administered armistice line (the Green Line), split the city into a Jordanian half and an Israeli half.

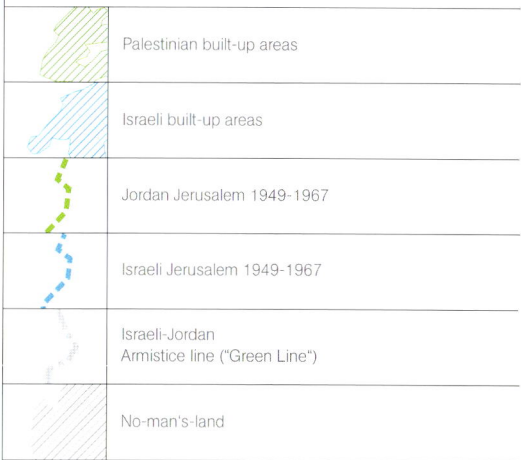

Jericho →

Abu Dis

	Palestinian built-up areas
	Israeli built-up areas
	Jordan Jerusalem 1949-1967
	Israeli Jerusalem 1949-1967
	Israeli-Jordan Armistice line ("Green Line")
	No-man's-land

0   1   2   3   4   5 kilometers

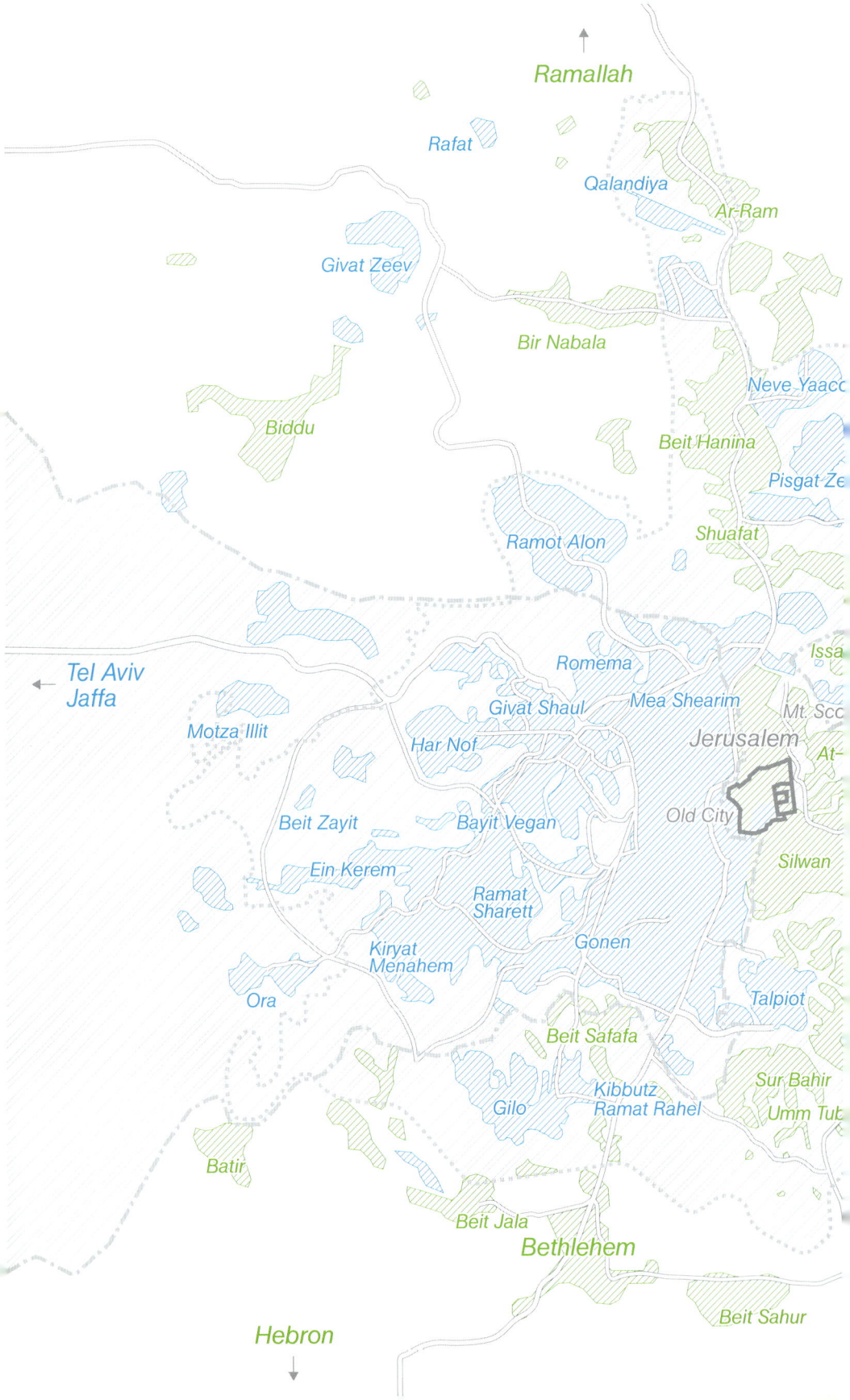

Ramallah

Rafat

Qalandiya

Ar-Ram

Givat Zeev

Bir Nabala

Neve Yaaco

Beit Hanina

Pisgat Ze

Biddu

Shuafat

Ramot Alon

Issa

Tel Aviv
Jaffa

Romema

Mea Shearim

Mt. Sco

Jerusalem

Givat Shaul

At–

Motza Illit

Har Nof

Old City

Silwan

Beit Zayit

Bayit Vegan

Ein Kerem

Ramat
Sharett

Kiryat
Menahem

Gonen

Ora

Talpiot

Beit Safafa

Sur Bahir

Kibbutz
Ramat Rahel

Umm Tub

Gilo

Batir

Beit Jala

Bethlehem

Beit Sahur

Hebron

Forced Unification
Jerusalem (1967-1987)

After the Six Day War, Israel annexed Jordanian
East Jerusalem, including some of the territory
of the now-occupied West Bank, and included
it within enlarged municipal boundaries. This
annexation has yet to be legally recognized
by the international community. While a relative fragile calm prevailed, war by other means
continued over spatial and demographic control
over the city. Based on the expropriation of
Palestinian lands, Israel created room for vast
building programs designed to cement the city's
unification. Despite these overwhelming new
facts on the ground, Jerusalem continued to be
divided along ethnic seam lines—lines no longer
constituted through physical barriers, but a complex system of invisible walls surrounding interconnected communal archipelagos. Palestinians
were able to continue to live with some degree
of autonomy and even economic progress,
maintaining separate school and public transport
systems, usually retaining their Jordanian citizenship, and boycotting to vote for the Israeli municipal authority. A privately-funded "building boom"
exploded on the city's periphery, as Palestinians
were mostly unable to obtain building permits
inside the Israeli municipal boundaries.

Jericho →

Maale Adumim

Abu Dis

	Palestinian built-up areas
	Israeli built-up areas
	Jerusalem and annexed East Jerusalem areas
	Israeli-Jordan Armistice line ("Green Line")
	Municipal boundary

0   1   2   3   4   5 kilometers

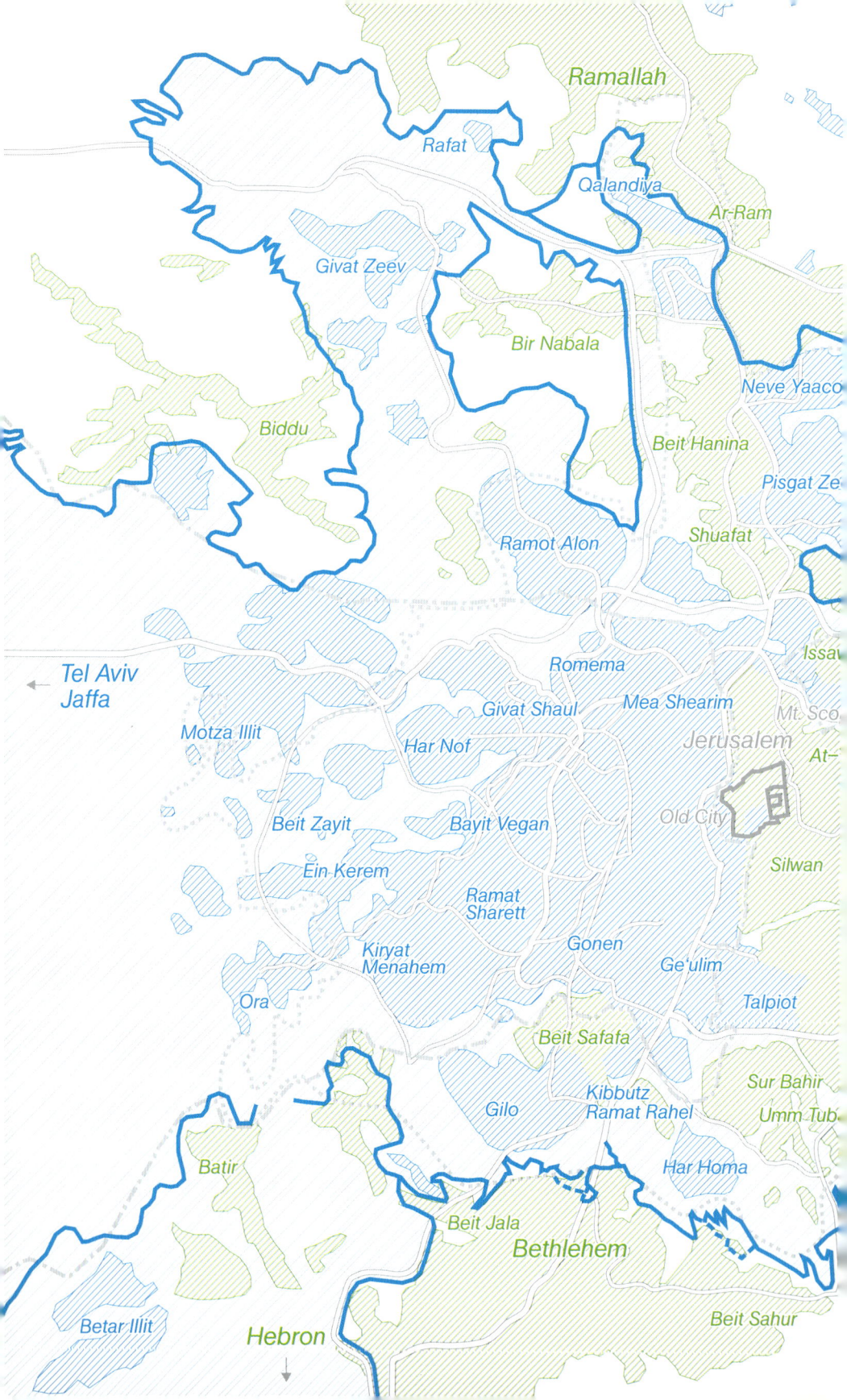

Ramallah

Rafat

Qalandiya

Ar-Ram

Givat Zeev

Bir Nabala

Neve Yaaco

Beit Hanina

Pisgat Ze

Biddu

Ramot Alon

Shuafat

Tel Aviv
Jaffa

Romema

Mea Shearim

Issa

Givat Shaul

Mt. Sco

Motza Illit

Har Nof

Jerusalem

At–

Old City

Beit Zayit

Bayit Vegan

Silwan

Ein Kerem

Ramat
Sharett

Kiryat
Menahem

Gonen

Ge'ulim

Ora

Talpiot

Beit Safafa

Sur Bahir

Gilo

Kibbutz
Ramat Rahel

Umm Tub

Batir

Har Homa

Beit Jala

Bethlehem

Beit Sahur

Betar Illit

Hebron

Walled City
Jerusalem (1987-2005)

Conflict ignited again during the first Intifada
(1987-1993) against the persisting Israeli occupation. International pressure forced both parties
to end violence and formally recognize a two
state principle. Negotiations led to the signing of
the 1993 Oslo Accords. But limited self-rule for
the Palestinians was combined with a new set
of restrictive policies. Israeli checkpoints were
set up limiting travel to and from Jerusalem,
thus severing the eastern city from its West
Bank hinterlands. Settlement construction was
stepped up and Palestinian suicide attacks on
Israeli civilians continued. The failure of Oslo to
solve the Jerusalem crisis in part led to the
collapse of the peace process in 2000, and then
the al-Aqsa Intifada: an interminable cycle of
military incursions, suicide attacks, and collective
punishment. In this atmosphere, Israel was able
to impose far-reaching physical changes justified as temporary anti-terrorist measures. An 8
to12-meter-high wall and fence complex follows
a contorted path seeking Israeli demographic
and spatial hegemony, while maintaining the
pretence of a united city.

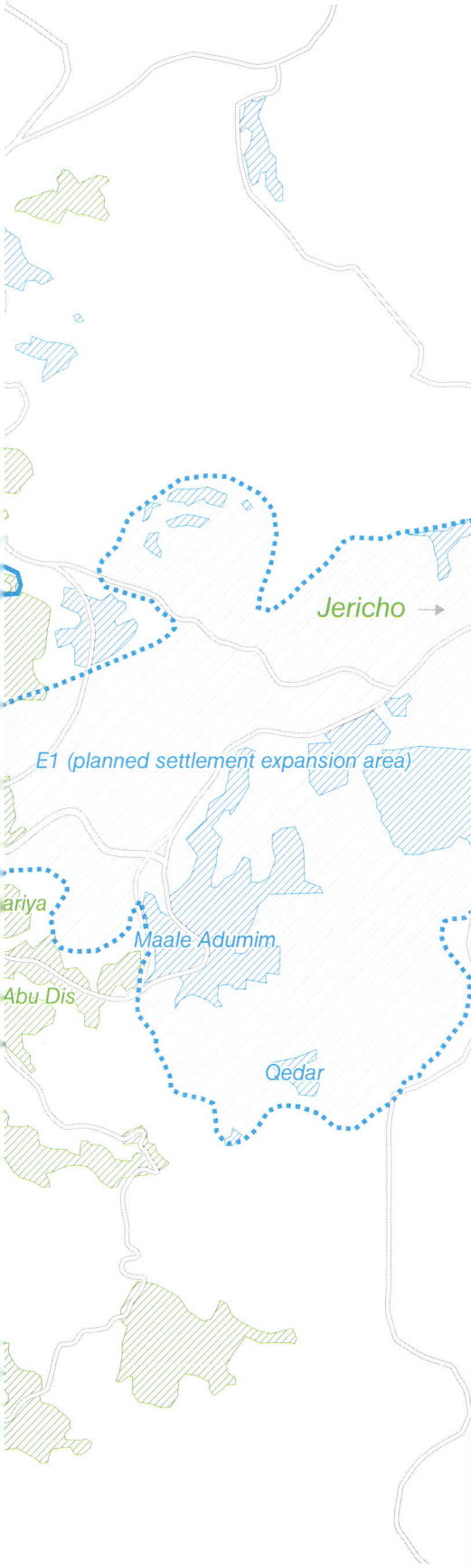

Map labels: Jericho, E1 (planned settlement expansion area), ...ariya, Maale Adumim, Abu Dis, Qedar

	Palestinian built-up areas
	Israeli built-up areas
	Area enclosed by Seperation Wall/Fence
	Israeli-Jordan Armistice line ("Green Line")
	Municipal boundary
	Separation Fence/Wall
	Separation Fence/Wall route subjected to further completition

0   1   2   3   4   5 kilometers

Jerusalem

Sur Bahir

Jabal Abu Ghneim

Bethlehem

Arab Village
Sur Bahir (1841)

Sur Bahir was founded on the upper slopes
of a rocky hill, overlooking four valleys (wadis)
that slope in a south-eastern direction towards
the Jordan valley rift. The village consisted of
several tight building clusters around courtyards
(*hosh*). Each cluster belonged to different patri-
lineal extended families (*hamula*). The dwellings
themselves were domed, constructed entirely
from local limestone, and often located above
rock caves. They were situated in such a way
that they allowed residents to easily guard crops
and olive groves in the fertile cultivated valleys.
Agriculture determined the rhythms of village life
and, during harvest periods families often stayed
overnight in field storage houses (*qusur*). Village
lands were defined through the accumulation
of individual and extended family land holdings,
as well as common land (*moshaa*). In the tightly
knit, self-contained community, no formal property lines were required; territorial boundaries
were remembered over generations through oral
descriptions of trees, rocks, or retaining walls as
markings.

Built-up areas

0 | 100 | 200 | 300 | 400 | 500 meters

Jerusalem

Kibbutz
Ramat Rahel

Sur Bahir

Umm Tuba

Jabal Abu Ghneim

Bethlehem

New Neighbors
Sur Bahir (1925)

Sur Bahir remained unaffected by the early years of British rule, which concentrated on regional reorganization and town planning schemes. Villages continued to develop in an organic way according to traditional rules (based on Islamic shariah law, which allots and develops property according to relative plot size, property lines, building height, and construction density) and without the interference of an external planning regime which imports and copies planning strategies in a top-down process (see Khamaisi in this volume). Slowly, the village begun to spread along the mountain ridges between the agricultural valleys. Later, the British initiated extensive land surveys which, for the first time, defined a village boundary around the family land holdings and common lands, thus facilitating a gradual shift from communal to private land that had begun during Ottoman land reforms. Life in Sur Bahir begun to change with the foundation of Kibbutz Ramat Rachel in 1926. Three years later, the kibbutz was attacked and burned down in one of the first major outbursts of tensions. The kibbutz was rebuilt a year later; between 1936 and 1939 it again was the site of violence from Palestinians protesting Zionist immigration.

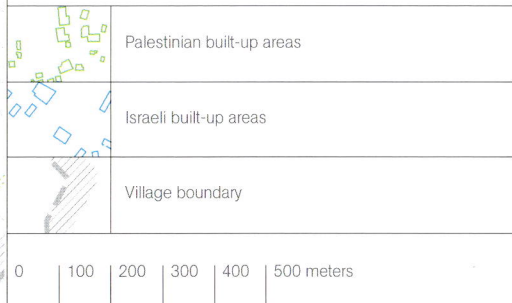

	Palestinian built-up areas
	Israeli built-up areas
	Village boundary

| 0 | 100 | 200 | 300 | 400 | 500 meters |

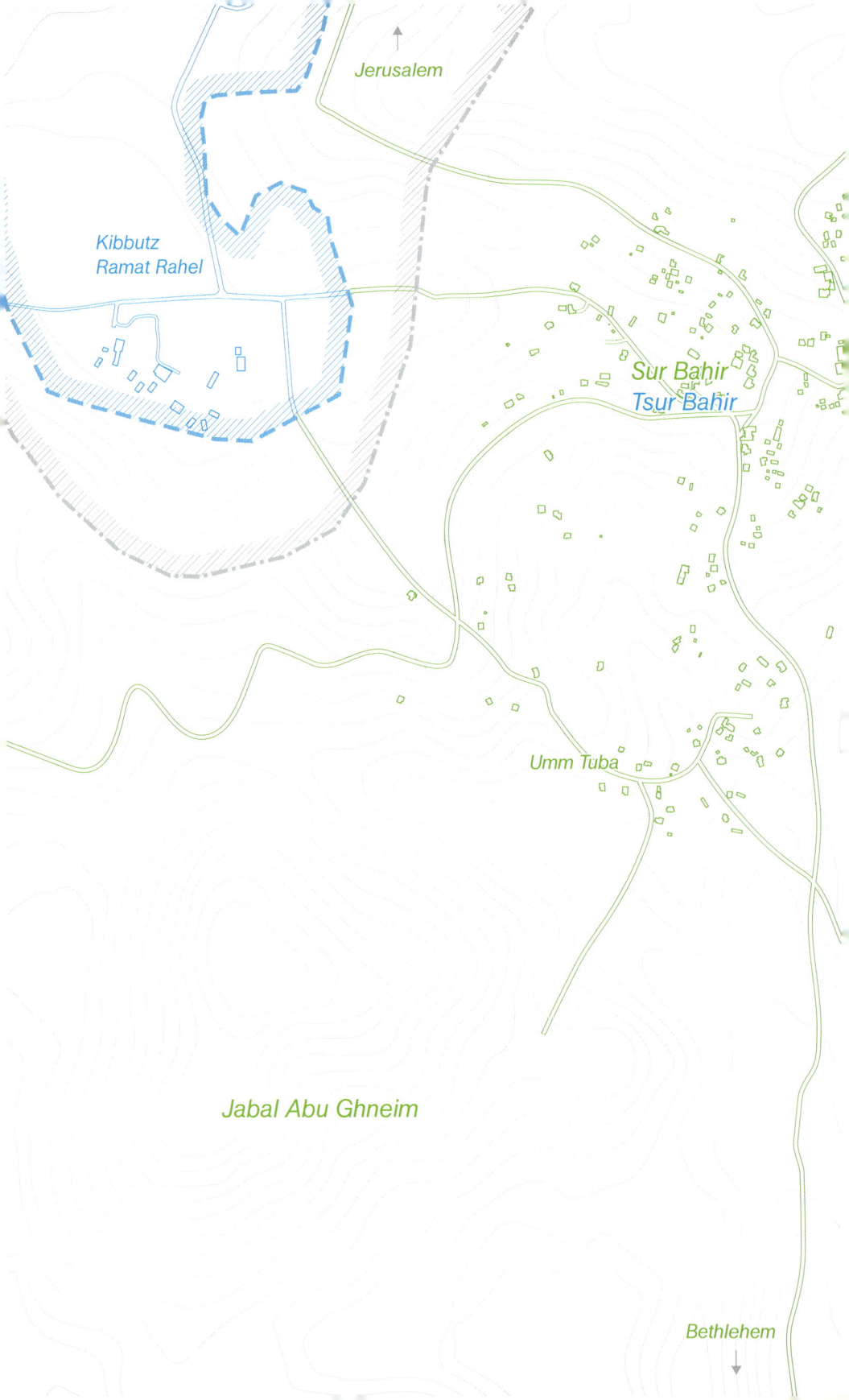

Jerusalem

Kibbutz
Ramat Rahel

Sur Bahir
Tsur Bahir

Umm Tuba

Jabal Abu Ghneim

Bethlehem

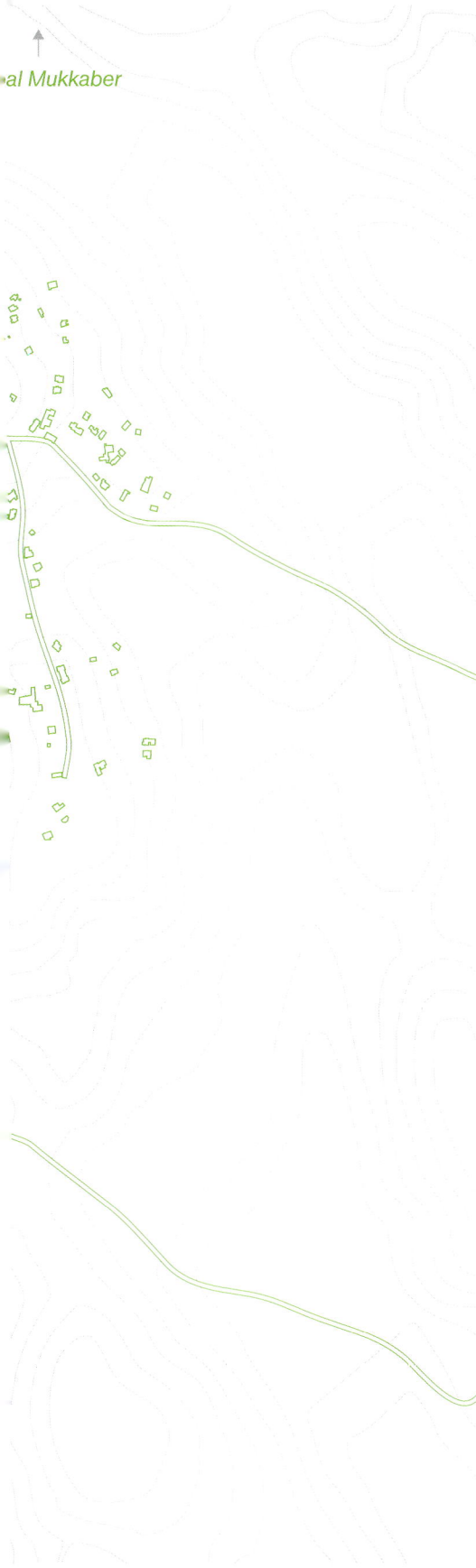

al Mukkaber

Frontier Zones
Sur Bahir (1949)

The dramatic events that engulfed Jerusalem
in the late 1930s and 1940s (culminating in
the division of the city, expulsion of population,
and demolition of most of Jerusalem's western
villages) led to an equally dramatic change
for Sur Bahir and the neighboring kibbutz. The
new UN-administered armistice line was drawn
immediately to the northwest of the village,
around Ramat Rahel, which was completely
destroyed for the second time in the war. Suddenly, village and kibbutz were positioned on the
geopolitical frontier between Israel and Jordan,
separated by a broad strip of no-man's-land. The
destroyed kibbutz was quickly rebuilt as a strategic outpost overseeing the most south-eastern
frontier of West Jerusalem. With the historic road
under Israeli control, Sur Bahir now became an
important north-south passage point connecting
Bethlehem and East Jerusalem, reinforced by
an outpost of the Jordanian Army. But general
economic stagnation and Jordanian underinvestment in Jerusalem slowed village growth and
many of its younger generation emigrated.

Palestinian built-up areas

Israeli built-up areas

Israeli municipal boundary

Israeli-Jordan
Armistice line ("Green Line")

0 | 100 | 200 | 300 | 400 | 500 meters

Jerusalem

Kibbutz
Ramat Rahel

Sur Bahir
Tsur Bahir

Umm Tuba

Jabal Abu Ghneim

Bethlehem

Inclusion and Exclusion
Sur Bahir (1987)

After the 1967 War, Sur Bahir became part of annexed territory absorbed into Israeli municipal Jerusalem. The border fortifications between the village and the kibbutz (which was destroyed and rebuilt for a third time) were dismantled. Redrawing of boundaries meant that some 1,000 dunums (1 dunum equals 1000 m²) of village lands and houses to the east were separated from the village, together with Sur Bahir's cultural resources, remaining in the West Bank. Vast village plots to the north were expropriated and declared public "green areas." Refusing to accept its annexation into Jerusalem or adopt Israeli citizenship, Sur Bahir's inhabitants continued to identify themselves as Palestinian villagers. But the young generation quickly recognized the advantages of accessing Israel's job market and social security system. Agricultural traditions were soon abandoned and new cash earned mainly in Israel's low-skilled labour market became available for home construction. Eager to limit Palestinian development and demographic growth, the Israeli municipality and its planning authority prohibited construction beyond the existing built-up area and delayed the creation of a master plan for decades.

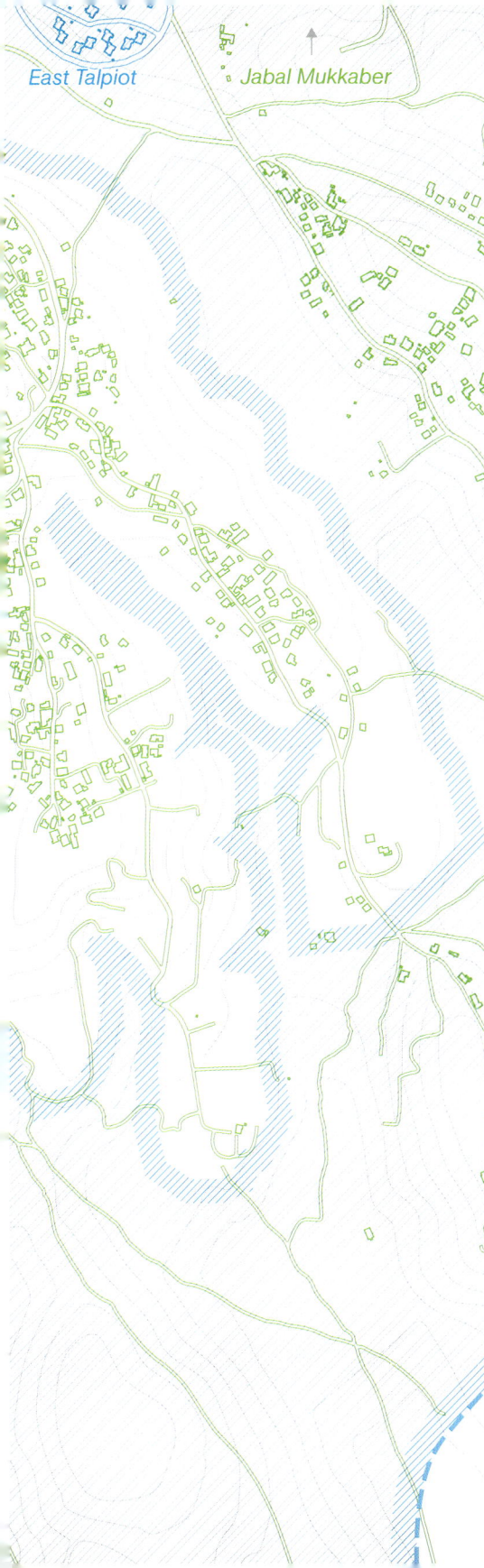

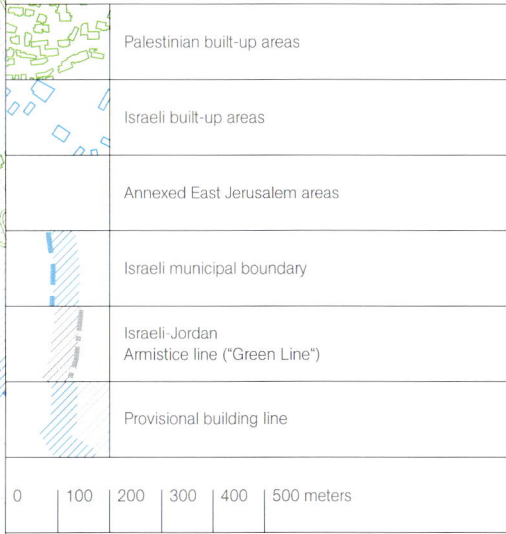

	Palestinian built-up areas
	Israeli built-up areas
	Annexed East Jerusalem areas
	Israeli municipal boundary
	Israeli-Jordan Armistice line ("Green Line")
	Provisional building line

0   100   200   300   400   500 meters

Jerusalem

Kibbutz
Ramat Rahel

Sur Bahir
Tsur Bahir

Umm Tuba

Jabal Abu Ghneim
Har Homa

expansion area
for Har Homa

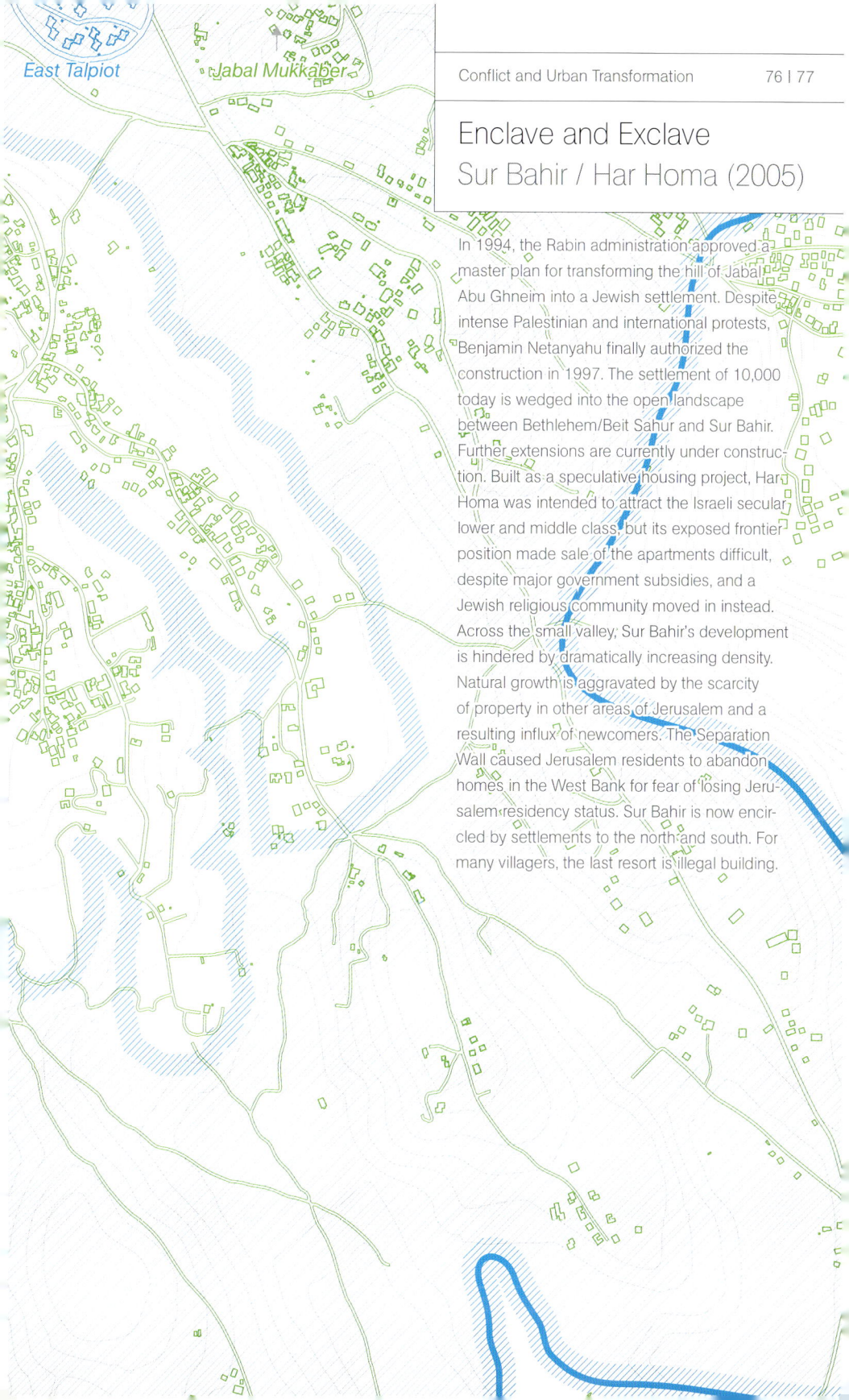

Enclave and Exclave
Sur Bahir / Har Homa (2005)

In 1994, the Rabin administration approved a master plan for transforming the hill of Jabal Abu Ghneim into a Jewish settlement. Despite intense Palestinian and international protests, Benjamin Netanyahu finally authorized the construction in 1997. The settlement of 10,000 today is wedged into the open landscape between Bethlehem/Beit Sahur and Sur Bahir. Further extensions are currently under construction. Built as a speculative housing project, Har Homa was intended to attract the Israeli secular lower and middle class, but its exposed frontier position made sale of the apartments difficult, despite major government subsidies, and a Jewish religious community moved in instead. Across the small valley, Sur Bahir's development is hindered by dramatically increasing density. Natural growth is aggravated by the scarcity of property in other areas of Jerusalem and a resulting influx of newcomers. The Separation Wall caused Jerusalem residents to abandon homes in the West Bank for fear of losing Jerusalem residency status. Sur Bahir is now encircled by settlements to the north and south. For many villagers, the last resort is illegal building.

Settlements

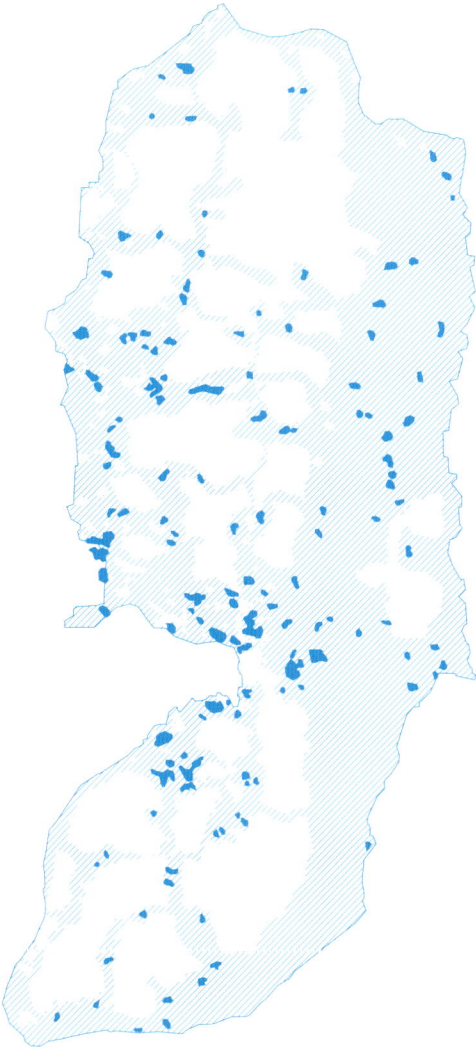

Palestinian urban areas

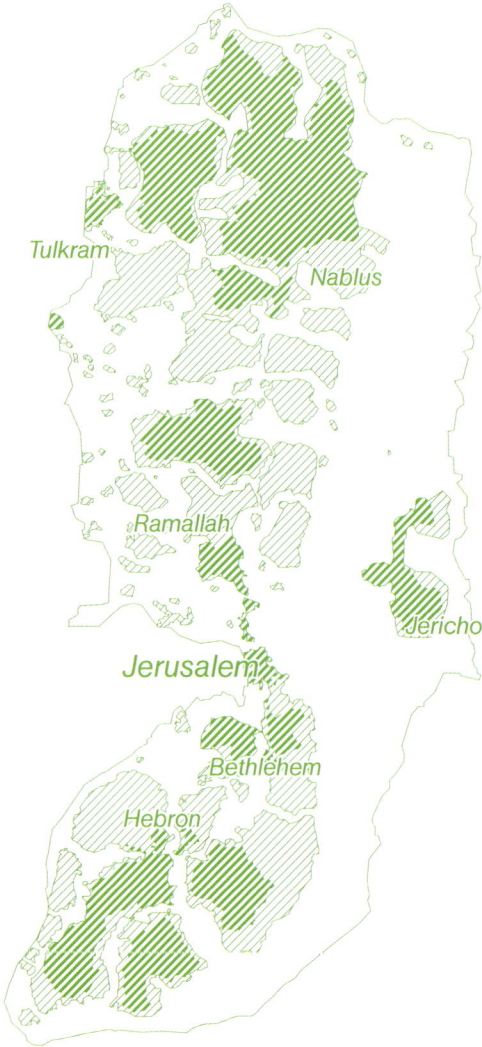

Tulkram

Nablus

Ramallah

Jericho

Jerusalem

Bethlehem

Hebron

Archipelago
West Bank / Jerusalem

The establishment of Jewish settlement in the
West Bank since 1967, the political partition of
territories according to the Oslo agreements
(2001) and the construction of the Separation
Fence/Wall have produced a spatial landscape
of enclaves and exclaves. Settlements have
fragmented and encircled Palestinian neighborhoods, dismembering their spatial, social,
and economic fabric and destroying their land
reserves for agricultural use and urban developments. As a result, Palestinian villages and
neighborhoods are forced within the same kind
of spatial containment that characterizes the
settlements. They have become enclaves within
a space of Israeli hegemony.

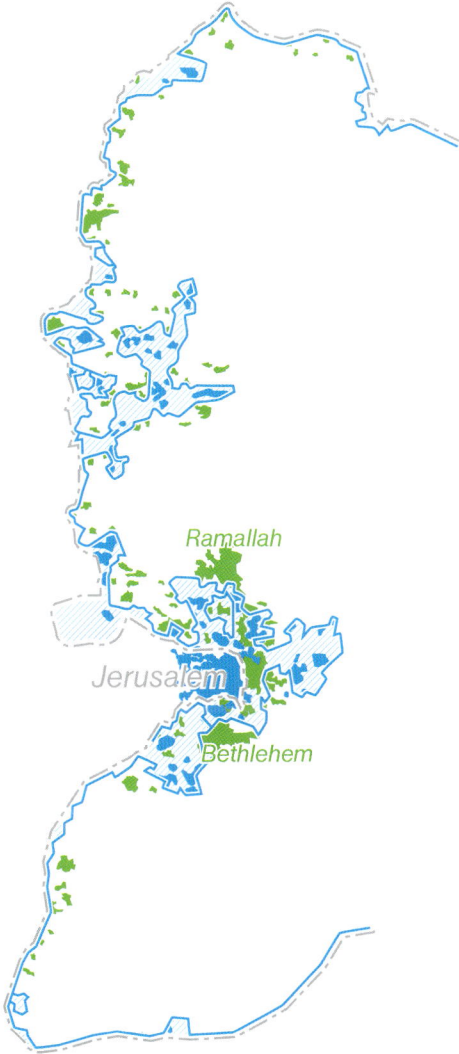

Ramallah

Jerusalem

Bethlehem

	Settlements
	Oslo Area C (full Israeli control)
	Settlements
	Palestinian urban areas
	Oslo Area A (full control of the Palestinian Authority)
	Oslo Area B (Palestinian civil control, Israeli military control)
	Walled cities
	Israel-Jordan Armistice Line (1948-1967)
	Separation Fence/Wall
	Urban areas
	Westbank annexed to Israel

0 | 10 | 20 | 30 | 40 kilometers

Concept and copyright

Tim Rieniets, Philipp Misselwitz

Sources

Timeline: Charmaine Seitz with Karen Lee Brachah, Mona Dajani and Yehuda Greenfield-Gilat.

B'tselem - The Israeli Information Center for Human Rights in the Occupied Territories, *The West Bank - Jewish Settlements and the Separation Barrier*, (Jerusalem, 2004).

International Peace and Cooperation Center IPCC, Rami Nasrallah, Rassem Khamaisi, Michael Younan, *Jerusalem on the Map* (Jerusalem, 2005).

Le Monde Diplomatique (edit.), *Atlas der Globalisierung*, taz Verlags- und Vertriebs GmbH, (Berlin, 2003).

Project Grenzgeografien (International Peace and Cooperation Center IPCC Jerusalem, Bezalel Academy of Art and Design Jerusalem, University of the Arts Berlin, ETH Swiss Federal Institute of Technology Zurich), *Trilateral Student Workshops* (Jerusalem, 2003-2005).

Survey of Palestine, *Jerusalem Area (scale 1:1,250)*, (1946).

Survey of Palestine, *Jerusalem Area (scale 1:20,000)*, (1943).

The Applied Research Institute - Jerusalem (ARIJ), *A Geopolitical Atlas of Palestine - The West Bank and Gaza* (Jerusalem, 2004).

United Nations, Office for the Coordination of Humanitarian Affairs (OCHA), *Closure Maps* (2005).

United Nations, Office for the Coordination of Humanitarian Affairs (OCHA), *West Bank Barrier Route Projections: Preliminary Overview* (2005).

ENCLAVES EXCLAVES

Extensive ethnic segregation in Jerusalem has produced a fragmented spatial landscape consisting of isolated "exclaves" and "enclaves." The Green Line that once divided the city into two halves has been transformed into a complex, three-dimensional matrix. Israeli settlement construction in East Jerusalem and the West Bank is guided by the spatial principle of isolation, which protects inhabitants against a perceived hostile landscape. In the process, settlements dismember the spatial, social, and economic fabric of the surrounding Palestinian neighborhoods and villages, and destroy their land reserves for agricultural use and urban developments. As a result, Palestinian villages and neighborhoods are forced into a spatial containment similar to that of the settlements. They become enclaves within an area of Israeli hegemony, yet are excluded from Israeli political, social, and cultural life.

PRINCIPLES OF
FRONTIER GEOGRAPHY

Eyal Weizman

If borders are abstract lines which designate the edges of jurisdictions, barriers make those limits physical. Since the mechanization of warfare in the 19th and 20th centuries, and the relatively symmetrical power maintained across borders between more or less equally armed national armies and allied coalitions, defense is no longer conceptualized on a local or urban scale, but at the level of immense linear constructions along the edges of national space. Borders were fortified to control the movement of armies, as well as to regulate the movement of goods, labor, information, wealth, and disease into the body of the state. The demarcation and fortification of borders had a complementary project: the issuing of travel documents and passports, which was significant in creating and sustaining the political model of a sovereign national entity. Fixed borders came to embody a state of "peace" wherein the consolidation of citizenship and the homogenization of languages and cultures could take place.

War is an extreme boundary-framing condition. The trenches of World War I— barriers on a continental scale—are a case in point. They proved that shovels and barbed wires could become strategic weapons capable of paralyzing the movements of two opposing coalition armies. Stephen Kern described them thus:

"Trenches zigzagged through the land, outlining the ever-changing facets of the front and linking areas of military operations behind. Nearest the enemy was the front line, from which shallow 'saps' ran into no-man's-land and led to the most forward observation posts, grenade throwing posts, and machine-gun emplacements. About two hundred yards behind that was the support line in which the men spent most of the time living in dugouts cut into the dirt walls in deeper chambers tunneled down as far as thirty feet... Several hundred yards behind that was the reserve line, and communication trenches ran perpendicular to, and connected all three... From an aerial perspective the trench system gave the terrain a Cubist-like composition of irregular geometricized forms." (Kern, 2003:305)

Post-World War I strategic doctrine relied on the principles of linear defense as manifested in three major fortification systems, two of them built along the volatile French-German border: the German West Wall was designed to hold off the French Army while the *Wehrmacht* was defeating its enemies to the east. Facing it was the French Maginot Line, designed to delay the *Wehrmacht's* westward *Blitzkrieg* until French reserves could be drafted. The German Atlantic Wall was designed to prevent an Allied invasion of the German-occupied continent along the Atlantic coast. However, the increased capacity for rapid maneuver and the integration of air and ground forces made it easy to bypass or pierce these lines, eventually rendering them obsolete.

Poisonous gas, so decisive in breaking the territorial integrity of the trench lines in World War I, is also allegorical: it expresses another kind of flexible territoriality, quite opposite to the linearity and solidity of stable space. The shifting territoriality of gas was realized in the drifting milieu of a deadly microclimate without front or back. "With gas warfare, the trigonometry which had governed military theory in an unbroken continuity since the days of Roman siege-catapults, gave way to a fiendishly complex multiparameter calculus, in which the simple variants of propulsive force, air resistance, gravity and distance were complicated by the addition of wind-direction and speed, air-pressure, humidity and temperature" (Connor, 2003). The territoriality inaugurated by gas warfare was one of process rather than form. The ability of gas to diffuse and infiltrate, and its effectiveness against a static enemy, undoubtedly helped to dissolve the front line and the territoriality of clear edges.

The collapse, during World War II, of the static linear model of warfare turned long fortified lines into giant monuments to the absurdity of standing still in battle and believing in eternal territorial control. The last fortified line to have entertained the fantasy of solid defense was the Israeli Bar-Lev Line, built on the eastern bank of the Suez Canal, only to collapse in the 1973 Arab-Israeli War— itself, the last symmetrical battle to be fought between state armies of relatively equal force. In a victory of flow over stasis, the giant sand dykes of the Bar-Lev Line were eroded by high-pressure water jets. After the collapse of the Iron Curtain, and the end of the period of military balance, a different political space and type of military engagement—low-intensity, nonsymmetrical conflict between regular armies and paramilitary organizations—gradually staged a return.

The frontier is antithetical to fortified lines. Against the geography of stable, static places, and balance across sovereign borders, the frontier is a space of "flow." It is a military and political pattern of elastic and shifting geography, a zone of contact that cannot be represented by lines. The frontier can be associated with a variety of political forms, past and present, such as city-states, empires, and colonizing states. If sovereign borders are linear and fixed, frontiers are deep, fragmented, and elastic.

FLEXIBLE GEOGRAPHY

Despite a common perception, the frontier did not originate with the expansion of Europe into America, Australia, or Africa. It was part of the territoriality of premodern empires. The margins of the Roman and Chinese Empires, as well as those of the Aztecs and the Inca, were deep, shifting, and scantily defined domains of cultural exchange and warfare where battles took place with people defined since ancient Greece as "barbarians." These empires were based upon a flexible relationship between center and periphery, defined by power, commerce, and affiliation rather than territorial proximity. In this respect, the geographic form of ancient empires could be seen as a strong center with a flexible circumference. "Barbarians" were not only an amalgamation of primitive warrior-tribes; they were often highly organized and cultured settled or semi-nomadic peoples.

Zones of imperial control were extended not only through the conquest, occupation, and annihilation of "barbarians," but also through their "acculturation" with a single language or religion; the flattening of differences and the melting of "foreignness" into the social and economic pots of the empire.

The pattern of any frontier's geographical expansion is irregular. It shifts with changing climate, geology, and technological possibilities. It pours across pastoral steppe grasslands in an attempt to grab and fence off sizeable fields; it follows the narrow and splintering arteries of geological strata; it traces the ridges of metal and mineral deposits above ground in work camps, towns, and cities, or occupies geographical "islands" over isolated energy fields. The pattern of habitation across a frontier draws a diagram not only of the balance of power between colonizers and "barbarians," but of the economic and technological level and social organization of the colonizers themselves. Pockets of control continuously expand or contract. Temporary lines of engagement and confrontation, marked by makeshift boundaries, are not limited to the edges of the occupier's space, but exist throughout the depth of its territory.

ENCLAVES

Contemporary geopolitical space has several frontier characteristics. Instead of being demarcated by continuous lines, it has come to resemble a territorial patchwork of introvert enclaves. Anselm Franke, Ines Weizman, and I have described these enclaves as "islands," and their organization as "archipelago" (though what surrounds them is not the sea). Isolated from their external conditions, these homogenized extraterritorial enclaves lay outside the jurisdiction that physically surrounds them. They can be found in the form of zones of humanitarian intervention, military camps, or international transport, trade, and manufacturing hubs. The international-law principles of "suspended sovereignty" and "extraterritorial jurisdiction," upon which "islands" rely, violate the traditional juridical territoriality of the sovereign state and call the Westphalian border-based statesystem into question.

The noncontiguous nature of borderlines and the fragmentation of space are mirrored by temporal nonsequentiality. Actions do not unfold in a consistent, linear manner. At no point across the American Frontier was there a clear line between colonized territories and yet-to-be-colonized territories. The area had been broken into settlement pockets surrounded by uncultivated land—itself cut up by forts, roads, and railway lines. Often this splintered geography folds in from the edge of the territory to its interior. Frontier conditions can be found to varying degrees wherever one looks at a geographically expanding power. The "barbarians" are never organized behind fixed lines, they are always already inside. The border is in fact everywhere: around every public and private property and infrastructure, taking the form of local or regional fortifications and security apparatuses epitomized by today's roadblocks, checkpoints, fences, walls, CCTV systems, and sterile perimeters.

Popular fears have recently provoked the reconceptualization of the border. The US is attempting to reborder its own national space using a set of new technologies, laws, and practices that extend its jurisdiction. The project of creating

2.6 km: Begin Road near Bir Nabala

13.1 km: Shufat Refugee Camp

a "virtual border" aims to extend American surveillance networks, so as to compile and share vast amounts of biometric and other data that would make it possible to identify and intercept "terrorists" while still "abroad." This extension of US borders reflects, according to Michael Sorkin, the American ideology of the frontier. It creates a frontier zone between the territory of the US and its extended virtual border where an archipelago of extra-territorial detention and investigation centers mete out "frontier justice" beyond any legal jurisdiction.

POINTS AND LINES

The military geometry of the historical frontier was based on a relation between points and lines. Relatively autonomous forts scattered across the periphery provided an intricate matrix of control over the terrain. Strongholds have often been military colonies inhabited by civilized veterans/soldiers who were given land rights in return for fulfilling the task of frontier management and defense. Across the American West, native nations, cattle barons, and bandits shared at least one threat: the creeping domestication of the territory by farmers who, fencing themselves in and parceling out the great plains, brought with them a rigid code of law enforcement and private property. Law itself was territorialized, ultimately through the production of boundaries and hierarchies, zones and enclaves, mapping, and land registry. Land registry projects rarely recognized the rights of "natives" over lands in their possession the way they recognized the ownership rights of colonizers. Across Australia, New Zealand, and North America, land rights were based on the 18th century territorial fantasy of a *terra nullius*—an empty land where natives were no different from nature, having therefore no established rights to the environment. If rights were granted, such as in the case of reservations, they often did not extend vertically to include natural resources just below the surface.

Roads are crucial for frontier geographies. Without them, there could be no military deployment, expansion, or supply, no commerce, and thus, no culture. Colonial routes, like France's *routes nationals*, designed in, or inspired by the Schools of Highway and Bridges, were laid in straight lines across mountains and valleys, and stood for the rational, Cartesian power of the state. Lines of communication and transportation can function as wedges that open up "alien terrain" for further colonization, enabling larger populations to migrate and inhabit settlement-points. Paths of communication may also create effective barriers that honeycomb local populations into isolated enclaves of limited habitat. In this respect, the role of rivers is an index of the difference between frontier and border geographies. For states, rivers are often "natural" borders that mark the edge of territories.[1] They serve as physical icon for an imagination that naturalizes the state as a complete, indivisible territory of an a-temporal patrimony.

Points and lines are interdependent instruments that merge military and civilian architecture. The distribution of settlement-points[2] across the frontier requires a complex set of lines to connect them.[3] However, the reliability of movement and transport along these lines depends on the strong-points placed to protect them. As such, the frontier resembles a dynamic battlefield played out in slow motion. It regularly shifts from offensive expansion—seeking the temporary occupation of new strategic points and securing their lines of supply—to defensive organization designed to protect territorial gains from counter-offensives.

Frantz Fanon described colonial occupation as a complex compartmentalized system, which at every point is divided into two. Colonial occupation, when securely settled, can be understood as a geometry of state power, but at the expansion stages it may exhibit dynamic topological characteristics similar to the network-based geography of the colonized.

The initial relation and encounter between colonists and natives can sometimes appear "reciprocal" with feedback mechanisms of mimicry and counter-mimicry. Recurring frontier myths tell of the fragile "immigrant" hardened into a "native," transgressing the limit between civilization and wilderness, combating barbaric forces, gaining a right to settlement by the destruction of local "evil," and finally assuming something of the character of the "natives" just destroyed.

In his 1893 lecture, "The Significance of the Frontier in American History," Frederick J. Turner announced the closure of the American frontier, contending that American democracy would not have developed as it did without incorporating some of the rough and rugged characteristics of frontier individuality and the values of "personal freedom" into the national repertoire. He described the frontier as liberation from a stifling European culture and urbanized East Coast. "What the Mediterranean Sea was to the Greeks, breaking the bonds of custom, offering new experiences, calling out new institutions and activities, that, and more, the ever retreating frontier has been to the United States" (Turner, 1893:). The qualities of liberty and autonomy, as well as those of intolerance to law, order, and all things metropolitan, were typical of attitudes that developed in isolated frontier forts and settlements, to the extent that the open space of the frontier could be declared no less than "the conceptual terrain of republican democracy." (Negri and Hardt, 2000:168). But Turner's lecture not only described, it manufactured the cultural imaginaries and coherent narrative that helped to sustain, justify, and even celebrate expansion at the expense of native nations. Beyond the American myth of do-it-yourself frontier individuality, frontier colonization largely depended "on organized expansion of large capitalist enterprises and on urban financial speculation that funded them," (Hirst, 2005:78, 84) as well as on organized military defense and new institutional forms.

FRONTIER VIOLENCE

Of the 70 recognized political conflicts in the world today, only six manifest themselves as war between two or more sovereign states, while at least half are carried on outside the juridical framework of any sovereign power. In frontier lands, no rules of conduct bind the conflicting parties. All boundaries are provisional and permeable. Affiliations, enmities, and loyalties are temporary. The violence used to pacify frontiers cannot be accommodated within the legal framework of the modern state. Murder and other crimes go unrecorded and no truces are permanent. Since the gradient of state-power diminishes towards the periphery, political initiatives shift from the institutions of the center to those of the edge. Inhabitants of the frontier thus exercise strong political leverage over "mainland" politics, an influence often misused by the state itself. Criticized for their brutality, colonial powers have often claimed they lacked effective means to enforce their own laws on the periphery of their territories, or claim that the criminal actions carried out by their agents are exceptions that do not reflect the rule. Often, however, these powers profit in psychological effect and/or territorial control from the brutal and illegal "local initiatives" of armed settlers or rough soldiers, without having to take responsibility for the latter's actions. Colonizing states may excuse what is effectively the rule as an exception, and exceptions as the rule. Governments sometimes create the atmosphere that allows certain crimes to take place.[4] When the frontier seems to degenerate into complete lawlessness, it is because its "organized chaos" is often generated from the center.

The perpetuation of violence is deemed a necessary condition for the pacification of the frontier. Provocation produces resistance or counter-violence and thus the very justification for further suspending due process or military restraint. A legal paradox is thus created: states may suspend both national and international laws, act in breach of international conventions without any international mandate, effectively creating a lawless domain, yet criminalize all acts of resistance against it as illegal. Frontiers offer a variety of zones of legal exception where crime and murder are possible. Accordingly, Achilles Mbembe describes colonies as "zones in which war and disorder, internal and external figures of the political, stand side by side or alternate with each other. As such, the colonies are the location par excellence where the controls and guarantees of judicial order can be suspended—the zone where the violence of the state of exception is deemed to operate in the service of 'civilization'"(Mbembe, 2003:19).

The fragmented frontier creates a shifting legal geography of exception positioned outside the conditions of modernity and progress, or, using Giorgio Agamben's words, creates "zones of indistinction" the edges of which are elastic, shifting, and incoherent. For Agamben, temporariness is integral to the function of the "state of emergency" and the rules of exception. A "temporary" state of emergency and/or application of martial law allow the frontier to maintain a level of lawlessness that would not be tolerated were they considered permanent. The situation will remain "temporary" as long as needed for victory to be achieved, and for the frontier to be domesticated. Only then, can the "closed off" frontier be endowed with the "normal" laws of the state. From 19th and early 20th century "pacification" to late 20th century and early of 21st century "peace keeping," frontiers embody the temporary instability of the "stability" to come.

Frontier violence is never confined to the actions of regular armies or paramilitary organizations. Struggle over land and habitat redefine every act of living, settling, extracting, harvesting, or trading as violence itself. In the frontier zone, the settler is a militarized and armed civilian and military actions and resistance are carried out in the midst of, or against, civilian populations. In a frontier environment a distinction is maintained between two kinds of lives: modern and primitive. Natives have so often been associated with the landscape, as noted before, that "when European men massacred [natives] they somehow were not aware that they had committed murder." (Mbembe, 2003:23)

The territorial architecture of the "war on terror" has placed the imaginary space of the frontier at the forefront of global consciousness, and extended its legal, social, and military characteristics across a new geopolitical construction site. The militarization of global and legal infrastructures have turned economic enclaves into outposts and trade channels into temporary alliances and militarized trajectories. A new global geography of fragments, micro-conflicts, newly erected barriers, and fortifications can be found across this borderless state of territorial ambivalence.

1   The Oder/Neisse between Germany and Poland, the Amur/Heilong Jiang between Russia and China, the Jordan between Israel, the occupied West Bank, and the Kingdom of Jordan.

2   Roman fortresses, the Chinese steppe-forts, Crusaders' castles, the fortified settlements of the Conquistadors, the British Raj's hill stations in Northern India, French blockhouses across the Vietnamese and Algerian frontiers, American air bases on Pacific or Atlantic islands, the suburban settlers' outposts on the West Bank.

3   The paved roads of the Roman Empire, the mountain passes of the Crusaders, the railway and the telegraph lines of the American West, the bypass highways of the West Bank, the effective routes of strategic bombers for the US Air-force.

4   According to Israeli historian Benny Morris, it only took David Ben Gurion making his wishes for the expulsion of the Palestinian population known to IDF (Israelie Defense Forces) top brass in 1947-1948 for them to launch into action.

Selected Biblography

Ariella Azoulay and Adi Ophir, *Bad Days* (Tel Aviv: Resling Press, 2002).

Zygmunt Bauman, "Living (Occasionally Dying) Together in an Urban World," in *Cities, War and Terrorism*, ed. Steven Graham (Oxford: Blackwell Press, 2004).

Gideon Biger, *Land of Many Borders* (Be'er Sheva: Ben Gurion University Press, 2001).

Steven Connor, "An Air That Kills: A Familiar History of Poison Gas." Paper delivered at the "Death By Technology" conference, Birkbeck College, May 30, 2003.

Gilles Deleuze and Félix Guattari, *A Thousand Plateaus, Capitalism and Schizophrenia* (New York and London: Continuum Books, 2004).

Hastings Donnan and Thomas M Wilson, *Borders: Frontiers of Identity, Nation and State* (Oxford: Berg Publishers, 1999).

Frantz Fanon, *The Wretched of the Earth* (London: Penguin books, 2003).

Derek Gregory, "Defiled Cities," *Singapore Journal of Tropical Geography* 24, (3) (2003).

Derek Gregory, *The Colonial Present, Afghanistan, Palestine, Iraq* (Oxford: Blackwell Publishing, 2004).

Paul Hirst, *Space and Power, Politics, War and Architecture* (London: Polity Press, 2005).

Richard Howitt, "A Nation in Dialogue: Recognition, Reconciliation and Indigenous Rights in Australia," *Hagar* 2 (2001).

Stephen Kern, *The Culture of Time and Space, 1880-1918* (Cambridge: Harvard University Press: 2003).

Eric Lichtblau and John Markoff, *Accenture Is Awarded U.S. Contract For Borders*, New York Times, June 2, 2004, http://www.nytimes.com.

Achille Mbembe, "Necropolitics," *Public Culture*: 15 (1), 2003.

Benny Morris, *The Birth of the Palestinian Refugee Problem, 1947-1949*, (Cambridge: Cambridge University Press, 1987).

Antonio Negri and Michael Hardt, *Empire* (Cambridge: Harvard University Press, 2000).

Michael Sorkin, "Bush in Space," in *World Architects* (series), ed. Eyal Weizman: *Domus Magazine*, December 2004.

Frederick J Turner, "The Significance of the Frontier in American History," originally read at the meeting of the American Historical Association in Chicago, July 12,1893 and first published in the *Proceedings of the State Historical Society of Wisconsin*, December 1893.

Martin Warnke, *Political Landscape, The Art History of Nature* (London: Reaktion Books, 1994).

Eyal Weizman, Ines Weizman, and Anselm Franke, "Islands, the Geography of Extra-Territoriality," *Archis* Magazine, December 2003.

Sari Hanafi

THE SPACIOCIDE OF PALESTINE

Compared to other colonial and ethnic conflicts such as Rwanda-Burundi, Serbia-Bosnia, ect, the 1948 war did not, relatively speaking, produce many casualties. The notion of *al-Nakba* (the Catastrophe) is based on refugeehood and the loss of land, rather than the loss of life. Even after five years of Intifada, the number of victims is relatively low,[1] certainly if compared to the six week killing rampage in Rwanda which saw some 800,000 people massacred. The Israeli colonial project is not a genocidal project but a "spacio-cidal" one. In every conflict, belligerents define their enemy and shape their mode of action accordingly. In the Palestinian-Israeli conflict, the Israeli target is the place. The Jerusalem Emergency Committee, a working group set up by Jerusalem-based NGOs (non-governmental organizations) after the April 2002 Israeli invasion of the West Bank, reported on the systematic destruction of public places: all but two Palestinian ministries and 65 NGOs were partially or totally destroyed. What was striking about this wanton destruction was the vandalism. To seize documents and computer hard drives from the Ministry of Education can be "understood" within the framework of a military quest for information that would "prove" that the Palestinian educational system "produced incitement and engendered suicide bombers," but why did soldiers also have to smash the computer screens and tear apart the furniture?

During the war years in the former Yugoslavia, architect Bogdan Bogdanovich was one of the first to coin the term "urbicide" to describe the destruction of Balkan cities. Serbian nationalism romanticized rural villages, where a single community spirit predominated. The city, in this context, was a symbol of communal and cultural multiplicity, the antithesis of the Serbian ideal. In the Palestinian occupied territories, the entire landscape has been targeted. The weapons are not so much tanks, but bulldozers that have destroyed streets, houses, cars, and dunum after dunum (1 dunum equals 1,000 square meters) of olive groves. It is a war in an age of literal agoraphobia, the fear of space as articulated by Christian Salmon in 2002, seeking not the division of territory but its abolition. A trail of devastation stretches as far as the eye can see: a jumble of demolished buildings, leveled hillsides, and flattened vegetation, both wild and cultivated. This barrage of damage has been wrought not only by the bombs of traditional warfare, but by industrious, vigorous destruction, which has toppled properties like a vicious tax assessor. It is "spaciocide," not urbicide. It is more holistic, incorporating "sociocide" (targeting Palestinian society as whole)[2], "economocide" (hindering the movement of people and goods) and "politicide" (destroying Palestinian National Authority (PNA) institutions, and other physical embodiments of national aspirations)[3]. The climax of these policies so far, has been the destruction of a third of the Jenin Refugee Camp.[4]

The Israeli agenda in this Intifada (2000–2005) has been to induce what one Israeli minister called "voluntary transfer," i.e. get rid of the Palestinian population by transforming the Palestinian topos to atopia, by turning territory into mere land. It is through spaciocide that Israel is preparing such an exodus, and since the Intifada began in 2000, some 100,000 Palestinians have left the country (3.3 % of the Palestinian population of the West Bank and Gaza).

Palestinians have been forced to migrate internally as well. In Hebron, for instance, some 5,000 people (850 families) have left the Old City to neighboring villages because of Jewish settler vigilantism and Israeli army imposed curfews.

House demolitions are another tactic used to provoke transfer. From September 2000 to September 2005, 73,567 housing units in the West Bank and Gaza were damaged and 7,633 were completely destroyed.[5] And the numbers just keep climbing. Transfer is also realized with the "denaturalization" of some 200,000 Palestinians trapped between Israel's West Bank fence/wall and the Green Line (UN-administered armistice line between Israel and Jordan, 1948-1967), who now find themselves neither in Palestinian territory nor in Israeli territory, but rather stateless and space-less.

This "spaciocide" has been made possible by the division of the Palestinian occupied territories into A, B, B-, B+, C, H1, and H2 zones, which was a consequence of the Oslo Accords. In these "twilight" zones, Palestinian infrastructural development has been almost impossible, due to spatial fragmentation, but also to the fragmentation of the Palestinian political system. The Palestinian National Authority (PNA), for example, cannot implement water reservoir projects for villages in zones A or B if the pipeline passes through zone C. The paving of a new road between Bethlehem and Hebron was halted in 1999 because Israel did not authorize it to pass through zone C. There has been significant urban development in zones A and B, but these are always surrounded by Israeli zones of control, curtailing the possibilities for commercial, industrial, or residential expansion—including those projects financed by international agencies.

THE CHARACTERISTICS OF SPACIOCIDE

Spaciocide is a strategic colonial ideology applied in Israel/Palestine regardless of the "peace process." Even after the signing of the Oslo Accords, the area of the settlements doubled and the number of settlers living in them tripled (from 120,000 to 430,000—including East Jerusalem).

Spaciocide ignores and denies the development needs of the Palestinian community. No reliable Israeli demographic studies have been conducted on the Palestinian population of the occupied territories. The only "solid" studies have been those of Israeli anthropologists working on the *hamula* (clan) system for surveillance and regulation purposes.

Spaciocide is of a three-dimensional nature, as Eyal Weizman has elaborated in "The Politics of Verticality." Countless unsettled issues regarding underground sewage, aquifers, water reservoirs, tunnels and bridges, archaeology, etc. piled up on the Israeli-Palestinian negotiating table have made it clear to the parties negotiating the "peace process" that a two-dimensional solution to the conflict is untenable. The Israeli approach has been to offer Palestinians limited sovereignty on the ground, while retaining control of the subsoil and the airspace. In other words, creating a kind of sovereignty sandwich: Israel-Palestine-Israel, across the vertical dimension. Peace technicians (the people who are always drawing new maps for new solutions) have arrived at some far-fetched proposals for solving the three dimensional problems of international borders.

Spaciocide shapes not only the place, but also its boundaries. Israeli colonial practices entail the constant redrawing of borders, creating a new type of frontier: portable, porous, and hazy—a border in motion if you will. The border designates two spaces that are completely different: Palestinian space and settlement space. The Israeli occupation determines what will be illuminated and what will remain in the dark; what will be rendered visible or invisible, accessible or inaccessible.

Spaciocide aims to transform the Palestinian occupied territories into Bantustans, or noncontiguous enclaves or, in the words of Adi Ophir and Ariella Azoulay, camps.[6] It is interesting to note that in August 2004, the IDF (Israeli Defense Forces) presented the World Bank with a plan for new roads, bridges, and tunnels to be built and utilized by Palestinians and financed by the international organization. The implication being that Israel is no longer committed to a future Palestinian state with territorial contiguity so much as transportational contiguity.

This is spaciocide at the macro level. Certainly future research should examine how this kind of planning functions at the micro levels, i.e. the interaction between colonizer and colonized, or: how social actors resist this planning and transgress these power structures.

COLONIAL BIO-POWER, BARE LIFE, AND THE STATE OF EXCEPTION

How did spaciocide become possible in the Palestinian occupied territories? The sovereign power, according to Giorgio Agamben, routinely distinguishes between those who are to be admitted into "political life" and those who are to be excluded from it as the mute bearers of "bare life." The process he describes is one in which people and bodies are categorized in order to manage, control, and monitor them, reducing them to a life which is bare, i.e. to mere "vegetative" beings, apart from the social, political, and historical attributes that constitute them as individual subjects. And the task at hand is the identification of mechanisms through which the state is able to insert itself into citizen/colonized bodies as a measure of sovereign power, enacting specific forms of violence by the rule of the exception—through which sovereign power is defined—and turning all life and all political struggles into battles, once again, over bare life. Such forms of sovereignty can be found in the way colonial powers manage bodies according to colonial and humanitarian categories.

Developing Michel Foucault's exploration of biopower, Giorgio Agamben demonstrates how sovereignty carries with it a "power over life" by rule of exception, i.e. being above the law—as its constituting force—but also safeguarding its application. Agamben sees two models of power, a juridical one—focused on the problem of the legitimacy of Western power (the problem of sovereignty), and a nonjuridical one—centered around the problem of the effectiveness of Western power. These two models meet in the dimension of exception. The sovereign, according to Carl Schmitt, is the one who may proclaim the state of exception; this person is not characterized by the order that she or he institutes, but by the suspension of this order. This temporary suspension becomes a new and stable spatial arrangement inhabited by the naked life (of people without political rights) that cannot be inscribed into the order. The sovereign has the right to suspend the validity of law, a right that is, of course, not inscribed in the constitution.

Foucault contested traditional approaches to the problem of power, which had been based exclusively on juridical models ("what legitimizes power?") or institutional models ("what is the state?"). He stressed the passage from a "territorial state" to a "state of its population" and the increased prominence of a nation's health and biological life as a problem of sovereign power. This growing inclusion of man's natural life into the mechanisms and calculations of power, translated, for the first time in history, into the possibility that power both protects life and authorizes its destruction. In this view of sovereignty, populations are objective matter to be administered, rather than potential subjects of historical or social action. This does not mean that subjects cannot emerge and resist this sovereignty, but that sovereignty attempts to reduce the subjective trajectories of individuals to bodies. Thus, indistinct, displaced, localized, and colonized bodies come to be classified and defined as refugees, stateless people, residents of zones A, B, B-, B+, C, H1, H2 (Oslo categories), inhabitants of areas in front of Israel's West Bank fence/wall, or behind it, potential terrorists (post-9/11 categories), etc. Populations are assigned different statuses as legal subjects; individual lives are suspended in an ontological no-man's-land. The objective of this classification is primarily to exclude[7] and make possible the spacio-cidal project.

The political project of the Palestinian people (or the "political people" to borrow Gérard Bras' terminology) is transformed into a collection of distinct subgroups who become antagonists in the pursuit of their own interests vis-à-vis the conflict and its possible solutions: it is in the interest of the Palestinian residents of Jerusalem to stay outside the Palestinian national project, as Israel transforms the occupied territories into Bantustans; the geographical fragmentation of the West Bank and Gaza create two (or more) distinct entities with different populations animated by their own stereotypes and power struggles; to say nothing of the Palestinian citizens of Israel or Palestinian refugees in the diaspora. This process became possible as the exercise of sovereign power (as actuality but also as potentiality) created not only zones of indistinction between the inside and outside (of the nation, town, or home), but penetrated the entire political/social field, transforming it into a dislocated bio-political space in which modern political categories (e.g. Islamist/nationalist, right/left, private/public, dictatorial/democratic) are entering a post-political realm of dissolution.

13.2 km: Shufat Refugee Camp.

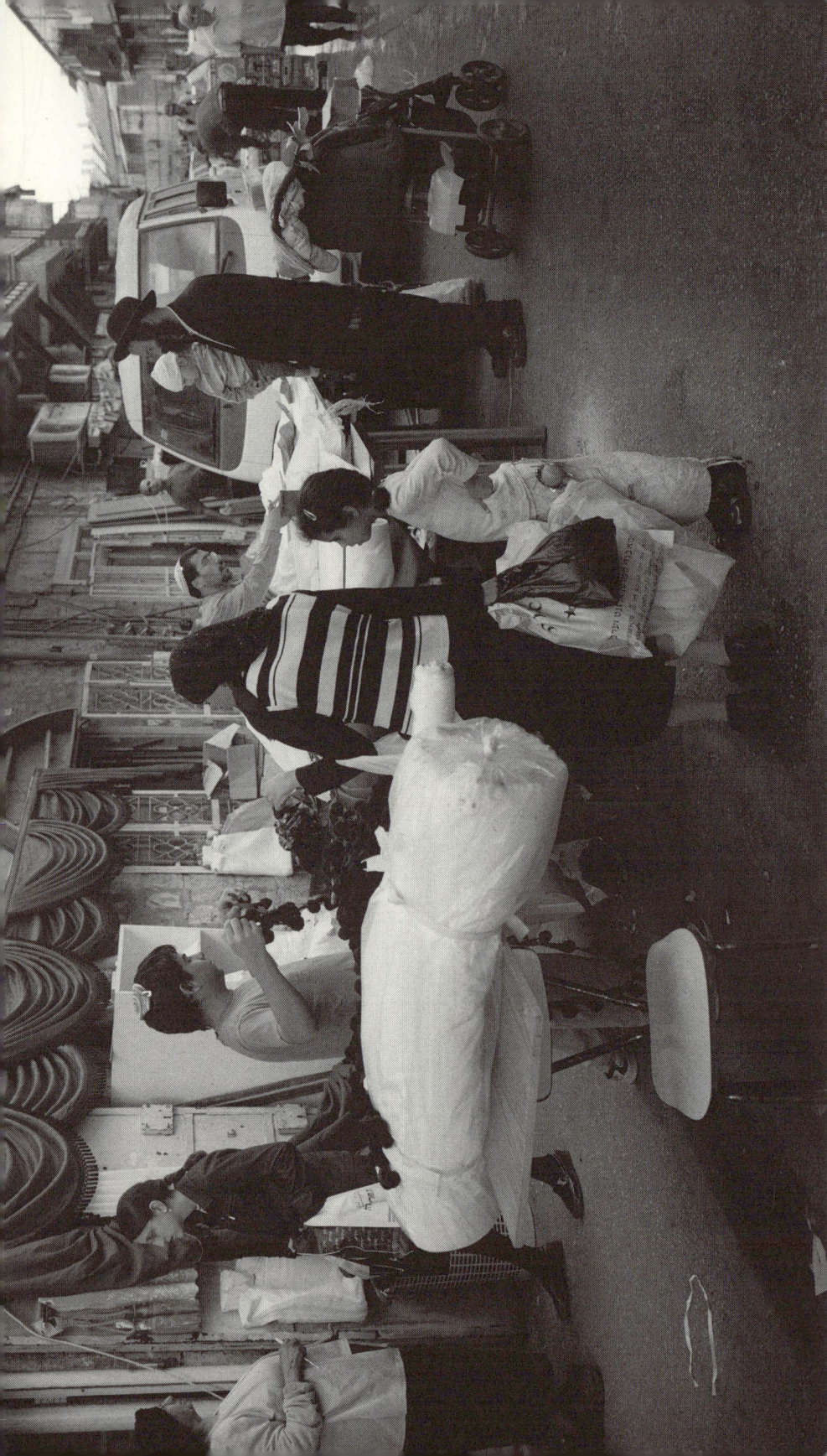

But sovereignty does not work according to one-way exclusion. Palestinians are excluded from the recourse of the law, but remain subject to it. Their lives are regulated and restricted by Israeli statutes and military orders which apply even to the private spheres of marriage and children. Palestinian citizens of Israel can no longer marry their West Bank and Gaza kinfolk and compatriots since a recent Israeli High Court ruling legitimated a 2003 law, barring "family reunification" from "mixed" couples. The case of Palestinian Jerusalemites is the epitome of exclusion/inclusion: included by virtue of the unilateral Israeli annexation of their city and excluded from municipal services, master plans, and civil liberties big and small; they live in a segregated city in which they are residents, but not citizens.

The international community's inability to see Israel as a colonial state stems from the fact that its democratic practices for Jewish citizens living in the State of Israel overshadow its dictatorial practices for the Palestinians living in the state of exception: Palestinian citizens of Israel; Palestinian Jerusalemites; Palestinian residents of the different zones of the occupied territories; Palestinian refugees inside and outside the camps, inside and outside the country.

With this state of exception, Israel is able to restrict Palestinian residential construction in East Jerusalem and then "legally" destroy houses built without a permit. With the same state of exception, Palestinian residential construction in the various zones of the occupied territories is also constrained. Military order 418, called "Order for the Planning of Towns, Villages and Buildings (Judea and Samaria)," outlines the requirements for obtaining building permits. Article 7, called "Special Powers," grants the High Planning Council the power to "amend, cancel or suspend for a specified period the validity of any plan or permit; to assume the powers allocated to any of the committees mentioned in article 2 and 5; to grant any permit which any of the committees mentioned in article 2 and 5 are empowered to grant [...]; to dispense with the need for any permit which the Law may require." (Coon, 1991:280) In other words, the sovereign power can use these exceptions to annul its own regulations.

This is a regime of exception that renders conceivable the idea that in certain "legal" circumstances, it is possible to kill without judicial intervention. It can be said that the Palestinian is a *homo sacer*—one who, according to Agamben, may be killed without due process and without the killer being punished. Israel's frequent extra-judicial killings are made possible because Israel exercises its sovereignty in a manner that permits it to kill without committing homicide or celebrating a sacrifice; it is, rather, the actualization of a "capacity to be killed" inherent in the condition of the colonized: the Palestinians. The international community, with its silence and/or timid protestations, encourages Israel to continue in this vein.[8] During any number of invasions of Palestinian towns, the Israeli army has declared the town a closed military zone, barring foreigners and journalists from accessing it. In the regime of exception, it is important to keep the exception invisible. Israel and the United States have insisted, since the second year of the current Intifada, on a ceasefire rather than an end to occupation making negotiations security-related rather than political.

Israel's "spaciocide" is enabled through biopolitics, the sovereign's capacity to proclaim the state of exception and enforce a state of suspension. However, the colonized do not take these mechanisms lying down. They use violent and non-violent modes of resistance, constructing home and society, making themselves visible, mobilizing global movements. And Palestinian "voluntary transfer" has its Israeli counterpart: indicators show Israel being "quit" too, as the year 2003 saw the least immigrants since 1975.

RESISTING THE COLONIAL ORDER: THE SUBJECTIVITY OF THE COLONIZED

Biopolitics make spaciocide possible, and spaciocide creates deterritorialized bodies; Palestinians without a place in territory, refugees without land. Spaciocide leaves body without space. Such bodies, then, attempt to regain their subjectivity by blowing him/herself up together with an enemy. Spacio-cidal politics then become suicidal politics, where uprooted bodies become bodies ready to explode. The uprooted body is a body without relationship to territory; it is a body in orbit, a satellite, an uncontrollable and unsupervised object bound to take revenge. In the unipolar and Imperialist era under the hegemony of the United States, revenge does not adhere to geographical and political boundaries but is played out on a global stage. But violence is not the only form of resistance. To counter the Israeli spacio-cidal project, Palestinians transgress the regime of exception by constructing their habitat without permits, even at the risk of demolition. A study on Palestinian diaspora investment in the occupied territories showed heavy invest-ment in construction. To gain a foothold in Palestine, some of Palestinians living abroad buy or build a "vacation" apartment or house. Others build for their family members in Palestine. The Palestinian Central Bureau of Statistics conducted an "Existing Building Survey" and a study of "Expenditure and Consumption Levels," estimating individual investments from the diaspora in private construction in Palestine at some $170 million in 1996 and some $200 million in 1997.

PERSPECTIVE

Biopolitics and the regime of exception are reinforced, in the case of Israeli and Palestinian actors, by the chain of victimization. In a mirror of distorted perspec-tives and projections, Israelis see themselves as The Victims, an exceptionality stemming from the exceptionality of the Holocaust. Palestinians also see them-selves as the ultimate victims (the *last* colonized people with the *largest* refugee group in the *longest* unresolved political conflict) and construct this excep-tionality beginning with al-Nakba. In the same sense that Israeli "spaciocide" is informed by the Zionist myth of "a land without people for a people without land," Palestinian refugees nurture a dream of a land without refugees for refu-gees without a land. The Palestinian refugees of the West Bank and Gaza, but also of the diaspora, have greater attachment to the land of Palestine than to the people of Palestine. In interviews, they often insist on talking about property, land, the Mediterranean Sea, al-Aqsa Mosque, Birim Church, but avoid the question of how they might live, and with whom.

I am not suggesting that cooperation between Palestinian returnees and their Jewish neighbors is impossible, but that it is necessary to think of return not only in terms of geography but also in terms of society.

1   As of October 2005, the figures are 3,891 Palestinian dead and 29,222 Palestinian injured; 1,074 Israeli dead and 7,520 injured. For Palestinian numbers see Palestinian Central Bureau of Statistics in www.pcbs.org/martyrs/list.aspx; for Israeli numbers see www.idf.il/SIP_STORAGE/ DOVER/files/7/21827.doc.

2   Sociocide, a concept developed by Palestinian political scientist Saleh Abdel Jawad, denotes policies used by one political entity for the total destruction of another, not only as a political entity, but also as a society in all its dimensions. The final objective of sociocide is the complete replacement of one society by another.

3   For instance, the destruction of Gaza Port as a symbol of commercial autonomy, or the cancellation of the Palestinian international phone code (970).

4   The invasion of this camp in April 2002 resulted in the damaging of 1,846 homes, of which 680 were completely destroyed and 1,166 partially destroyed.

5   Palestinian Bureau Central of Statistics, www.pcbs.org/martyrs/dest_a.aspx.

6   Communication at the conference "The Politics of Humanitarianism," Van Leer Institute, March 2004.

7   As Agamben noted, biopolitics is the original exclusionary function of Western politics.

8   Communication by Adi Ophir at the Mada conference in Nazereth, 2003

Selected Bibliography

Giorgio Agamben, *Moyens sans fins. Notes sur la politique* (Paris, Éditions Payot et Rivages, 1997).

Giorgio Agamben, *Homo Sacer. Sovereign Power and Bare Life* (Standford: Standford University Press, 1998).

Meron Benvenisti, "The West Bank Data Project—A Survey of Israel's Policies," (Washington: American Enterprise Institute for Public Policy Research, 1984)

Anthony Coon, *Town Planning Under Military Occupation: An Examination of the Law and Practice of Town Planning in the Occupied West Bank*, (Dartmouth Publishing Group, 1992

Michel Foucault, *Dits et écrits* (Paris: Gallimard, 1994).

Rema Hammami, Sari Hanafi, and Elizabeth Taylor, "Destruction of Palestinian Institutions. Preliminary Report," April 13,2002, commissioned by Jerusalem NGOs Network, Jerusalem.

Sari Hanafi, "Contribution de la diaspora palestinienne à l'économie des Territoires: investissement et philanthropie" in *Maghreb-Machrek* 161 (November, 1998).

Sari Hanafi, "Report on the Destruction to Palestinian Institutions in Nablus and Other Cities (Except Ramallah), Caused by IDF Forces Between March 29 and April 21," 2002, http://www.jmcc.org/new/02/apr/destruction.htm.

Sari Hanafi, "The Impact of Social Capital on the Eventual Repatriation Process of Refugees. Study of Economic and Social Transnational Kinship Networks in Palestine/Israel," in *Exile & Return. Predicaments of Palestinians and Jews*, eds. Ann Lesch and Ian Lustick (Philadelphia: University of Pennsylvania Press, 2005).

Sari Hanafi and Linda Taber, *Donors, International organizations, local NGOs. The Emergence of the Palestinian Globalized Elite* (Ramallah: Muwatin and Institute for Jerusalem Studies, 2005).

Sina Najafiand and Jeffrey Kastner, "The Wall and the Eye," *Cabinet Magazine* online, (9), (Winter, 2002/03).

Mariella Pandolfi, "Moral Entrepreneur, Souveraineté mouvementé et Barbelés. Le bio-politique dans les Balkans postcommunistes," in *Anthropologie et Sociétés*, numéro spécial, eds. M. Pandolfi, and M. Abélès, *Politiques jeux d'espaces*, 26 (1), (2002).

Christian Salmon, "The Bulldozer War," *Le Monde Diplomatique* (May, 2002).

Anita Vitullo, "People Tied to Place: Strengthening Cultural Identity in Hebron's Old City," *Journal of Palestine Studies*, 33 (129), Fall, 2003.

Eyal Weizman, "The Politics of Verticality," *www.opendemocracy.net*.

WALL AND TOWER

THE MOLD OF ISRAELI ADRIKHALUT

Sharon Rotbard

ARCHITECTURE AND *ADRIKHALUT*

The Jewish settlement project over the past century has given birth to two architectural traditions: Eretz Israeli *architecture* and Israeli *adrikhalut*. Eretz Israeli
architecture refers to architecture made by Jews in Eretz Israel ("The Land of Israel,"
aka "Palestine") before the declaration of the State of Israel. Israeli *adrikhalut* is
an architectural tradition of Hebrew-speaking Jews in the State of Israel and the
Palestinian Occupied Territories after the declaration of the State of Israel.

The distinction between these traditions is chronological and political, but
also linguistic: the evolution from one to another required a sharp move from a
European architectural culture to an invented Hebrew one.

While the architect, as Adolph Loos suggested, is "a builder who learned
Latin," the *adrikhal* is one who has forgotten his foreign mother tongue, but also,
does not always speak Hebrew properly, either. And besides, Hebrew was still a
language in the making.

Apparently, architecture and *adrikhalut* are synonymous, and thus used inter-
changeably and sometimes simultaneously. Maybe that's why the Technion (Israel
Institute of Technology) in Haifa fashions "architects" and Tel Aviv University
produces "*adrikhals*," and in addition to the historical Union of Israeli Architects
(UIA), there is today a new association of *adrikhals* (the infamous IAUA). Despite
their foreign origins, i.e. Greek and Acadian, and the fact that both can be found
in the Hebrew dictionary, *adrikhalut* is used more commonly nowadays and is
perceived as somehow more "Hebrew" than its counterpart. Interestingly, the
meanings of architect and *adrikhal* are quite different, revealing two opposing
conceptions of the role of the architect and his/her relationship to physical reality:
while the Greek *archi-tect* refers to the proud "master of tectonics," the Acadian
ard-heikhal denotes a humbler role as the "slave of the palace."

MASTERS AND SLAVES

The uniqueness of the Israeli condition is revealed through the dialectic between
master and slave, between architecture and *adrikhlut*. If any planned physical
reality is produced in three dimensions: the political, the urban, and the architectural—architecture is no less political than it is urban. Nevertheless, architecture's relationship to politics depends on its ability to define itself as an autono-

mous discipline, to impose its own agenda and to realize it physically. While acts of modern architecture were formulated throughout the Western world under the illusion of autonomy and structured in a complex relationship between theory and practice, in Israel they were governed primarily by political circumstance and significance. Compared to the Western architecture that had the luxury of covering its political tracks under books and manifestos, in Israel it is impossible to ignore architecture's simple, concrete truths.

The most significant aspect of both Israeli traditions: architecture and *adrikhalut*, overt and covert, are their political dimensions. In Israel, architecture, just like war, is a continuation of politics by other means. Every architectural act executed by Jews in Israel is a Zionist act, be it calculated or not. The political program of "building the Land of Israel" is a fundamental component of every building in Israel, and the political facts they create are more dominant and conclusive than any stylistic, aesthetic, experiential, or sensual impact they may have.

Renewal, settlement, and construction of the Jewish State have been the declared objectives of the Zionist movement, including its architectural traditions. The new architecture, new house, and new town have been both site and means for realizing Jewish settlement. Building Eretz Israel is the central value and key metaphor of the new national ethos: "We came to this land to build and be built!"—sang the pioneers of the 1920s. In Israel, building is an educational tool, an official language, an ideology.

This has dictated to the Eretz Israel architect, and even more so to the Israeli *adrikhal*, a paradoxical list of priorities, according to which, political ideology and architectural theory merge, depend on each other, confront one another, hide and are hidden from the other. Every practicing architect in Israel is confronted with a situation wherein distinctive "architectural" dilemmas are infused with critical political implications.

From its inception, the Zionist movement used modern architecture to create its places. It was a marriage of convenience, as both sought a new place: the former needed one, and the latter strove to create one. As an extension of the European modern architectural debate, Eretz Israeli architecture managed to maintain the appearance of a normal, Western, modern architectural tradition. One must remember that normality, Westernness and modernity have always been the Zionist movement's most powerful strategic weapons.

Since the declaration of the State of Israel, architecture has been openly mobilized. The new Hebrew speaking "native" tradition, Israeli *adrikhalut*, had to meet the political needs of the times (conquer frontiers, occupy territories, distribute populations, house immigrants) and, if possible, proclaim itself as doing so. Israeli *adrikhals* at their best have been true servants of the palace, serving the Zionist project to varying degrees of integrity, humility, dedication, and responsibility, as they tried to enable political ideology to infiltrate through architectural forms, and simultaneously enable architectural doctrines to express themselves through programs inspired or dictated by politics. The architectural dimension of architecture—that cultural or spiritual aura of the built object and the surplus value of the building act—served at its best as a mere accessory, and at its worst as pure camouflage.

Having forsaken the would-be universal viewpoint held by Western architects (and Eretz Israeli architects) rooted in the dialectics of theory and practice, Israeli *adrikhalut* is rooted in the dialectics of politics and architecture; this is where its dilemmas, blind spots, and paradoxes are to be found. Israeli *adrikhalut* produces impressive architectural objects but lacks a critical, comprehensive view of itself; mobilized by political ideologies, it sets facts in concrete that are inherently political, but lack political awareness.

THE SETTLEMENT OFFENSIVE

Although dated from the period of the Eretz Israeli architectural tradition, the *Homa Umigdal* ("Wall and Tower") settlements of the 1930s were a first expression of a Jewish native architectural tradition, i.e. *adrikhalut*. As an architectural phenomenon initiated and executed almost entirely "without architects" in the service of political objectives, Wall and Tower was a true realization of the concept of *adrikhalut*, and certainly a direct response to the demands of the palace.

Volunteers on their way to establish the Ein Gev kibbutz at the Sea of Galilee (photo: Zoltan Kluger, 1937)

Building the first hut at the Ein Gev kibbutz
(photo by Zoltan Kluger, 1937)

Wall and Tower responded to the "Great Arab Revolt" that erupted in Palestine/Eretz Israel in April 1936. The revolt began with riots in Jaffa (nine Jews were killed and dozens more wounded[1]), followed by a general strike. It included economic measures such as a commercial boycott and a ban on land sales to Jews, as well as organized armed struggle. The "Great Arab Revolt" was the first mass-based reaction on the part of the Palestinian population to the Zionist settlement project, and certainly the first broad-based organized political expression of a new Palestinian identity. For the Jewish population, and especially the Zionist organization the revolt offered a golden opportunity to devastate the Palestinian economy and accelerate the establishment of a Jewish State. Facing Palestinian resistance to Jewish settlement in rural areas, and growing difficulties in the purchase of lands, the Zionist organizations elaborated a coordinated strategy of "settlement offensive" throughout the country. The idea was to establish, in the shortest time possible, a chain of new settlements that would create a Jewish continuum and define the future borders of the state. This continuum took the shape of the letter "N" from the Jordan Valley in the north, to the Beit Shaan Valley, to the Jezreel Valley, through the coastal plane, to the Negev desert in the south.[2] In this settlement offensive the main tactical tool was Homa uMigdal—Wall and Tower.

WALL AND TOWER

Wall and Tower is a seemingly defensive, but in fact offensive, system of settlement invented in 1936 by members of kibbutz Tel Amal (today kibbutz Nir David—a kibbutz [plural kibbutzim] is an agricultural collective found in Israel) in the

Beit Shaan valley. The invention, attributed to Shlomo Gur,[3] was developed by architect Yohanan Ratner.[4] From the start, the objective of this fortified communal settlement was to seize control of land that had been purchased by the Jewish National Fund (JNF)[5] but could not be settled.

The system was based on the hasty construction of a wall made of prefabricated wooden molds filled with gravel and surrounded by barbed wire. All in all, the enclosed space formed a 35 × 35 meter yard. Within this enclosure, a prefabricated wooden tower was erected from which it was possible to view the surrounding area. Four shacks housed a "conquering troop" of 40 people. Between the years 1936 and 1939, some 57 such outposts were established throughout the country and rapidly developed into permanent collective settlements of the kibbutz and moshav type.

The Wall and Tower settlement had to meet several tactical conditions: it had to be planned so it could be constructed in one day, and later, in one night; it could protect itself long enough for backup support to arrive; it could be visible to other settlements and accessible by motor vehicle.

TEL AMAL

The first Wall and Tower outpost was established at the site that later became kibbutz Tel Amal in the Jezreel Valley. The kibbutz members, who first formed a collective in Tel Aviv, were searching for land upon which to settle. When several of them arrived at kibbutz Beit Alfa, they understood that the members of that kibbutz wanted to establish another settlement east of their own, where there was a large Bedouin encampment, so it would not be the most remote settlement in the area. Although the land surrounding kibbutz Beit Alfa had been bought by the JNF, from Arab owners in Beirut, it was used by Bedouins as pastures in winter. The members of kibbutz Tel Amal set up camp near Beit Alfa and began to cultivate the land. With the outbreak of the Arab Revolt in 1936, their settlement attempts were thwarted when the Bedouins set fire to

Putting up the tower at the joint Wall and Tower Settlement of kibbutz Massada and kibbutz HaGolan Shaar in the Jordan Valley (photo: Zoltan Kluger, 1937)

Tel Amalk kibbutz in the Beit Shaan Valley
(photo by Zoltan Kluger, 1937)

their camp. This attack led the Tel Amal group to initiate, together with the residents of Beit Alfa and other nearby settlements, new means of defense against the Bedouins, who were said to be armed with British rifles. A formula was devised for the construction of four shacks surrounded by sandbags. This soon developed into double walls filled with gravel up to the windows and observation posts.

This design raised two objections: that it would not provide sufficient defense between the huts, and that the walls would not withstand the pressure of the gravel. After further calculations, it became clear that with little additional cost it might be possible to surround the huts with a yard, and around the yard build a wall with an observation tower and a light projector. Shlomo Gur consulted Yohanan Ratner, and returned with a drafted plan for a rectangular wall with four defensive positions at its corners. The proposal was submitted to the Regional Committee, which accepted it, declaring a new era of fortified walls.

Following the success of the Tel Amal experiment, Wall and Tower operations were executed throughout the country, "sometimes seven outposts in a single night," recounted Gur (Azoulay, 2000:27-35), who participated in the organization of some 50 such operations. These nocturnal missions were always reinforced by nearby settlements, and coordinated by the Zionist leadership.

SUSTAINABLE OCCUPATION

The historical importance of the settlement offensive and Wall and Tower was immense: there is no doubt that without those 57 Wall and Tower outposts spread strategically throughout the Galilee, the Jordan Valley, the Jezreel Valley, and the Negev, the fate of the State of Israel in 1948 would have been entirely different. The Wall and Tower outposts set along the "N" scheme configured the borders of the State of Israel until 1967, and shaped its only consensual outline.

The success of the settlement offensive defined state strategy in the years to come. Settlement has became one of the Israeli Defense Forces' (IDF's) main missions, and soon after its formation in 1948, Ben Gurion created a special military unit, the NAHAL (acronym for "Pioneering Fighting Youth"), which combines combat and settlement activities. As he explained the NAHAL's purpose to its soldiers in the unit's inaugural parade: "not with silent stone fortifications but with labor and the creation of a living human wall—the only wall that is able to resist the enemy's weaponry. The only sustainable occupation resides in building." (Ben Gurion, 1986:104).

HISTORY

Wall and Tower holds a mythical place in Israeli history. Nonetheless, despite its potent symbolism of sacrifice, dedication and heroism so central to the civic education of every Israeli Jew, and its current and tragic reincarnation in the separation fence/wall, Wall and Tower is conspicuously absent from the Israeli architectural canon, which has busied itself in the last decade with fabricating a dubious narrative about the "White City" of Tel Aviv's so-called "Bauhaus" style. While making every possible effort to canonize the Israeli version of the International Style, Israeli adrikhalut has ignored not only one of the most architectonically unique phenomena of the 1930s—and the only one relevant to the politico-spatial situation today—but also the sole local architectural phenomenon that received international recognition in the 1930s themselves.

It is therefore not surprising that in 1937, one year after the establishment of kibbutz Tel Amal, a model of Wall and Tower was chosen for the Palestine-Eretz Israel Pavilion at the World Exposition in Paris—the expo remembered in architectural history as the one that garnered the gold medal for Albert Speer's German Pavilion.

Wall and Tower expresses the characteristics and dilemmas of the Israeli built environment, revealing the tensions between its impulses and internal contra-dictions. It is the site of all Israeli oxymorons: "offense through defense," "intrusive siege," "the camp as home," "introverted expansion," "permanent temporality," "house-arrest." The figure of the oxymoron is stamped in the genetic code of the Zionist project and has accompanied it since Theodor Herzl wrote the novel Alt-neuland ("The Old-New Land"), translated into Hebrew (the living dead language) simply as "Tel Aviv."[6] Perhaps the greatest oxymoron of all is the notion of Israel as a "Democratic Jewish State."

Enclaves
Exclaves

PROGRAM

As metaphor for the Israeli practice of *fait accompli*, Wall and Tower is paradig-matic of all Jewish architecture in Israel, germinating the program and mold of Israeli *adrikhalut*, i.e. its future characteristics across the board: hasty translation of political agendas into acts of construction; occupation of territory (surfaces) through settlement (points) and infrastructure (lines); prioritizing the security functions and military capabilities (both defensive and offensive) of buildings; and the informed use of modernity—organization, administration, prefabrication, logistics, and communication.

As time went by and new settlements were established using more sophis-ticated means, the two essential functions of Wall and Tower—fortification and observation—held fast and replicated themselves on every scale. They dictated the location of new settlements on mountain and hill tops and the technological efforts of the Israeli space program (satellites, etc.). They contoured the land-scape as a network of points, as an autonomous layer spread over an existing landscape, transforming the country by dividing it not according to natural, territorial, and cadastral divisions, but according to dromological divisions, such as transportation speed and infrastructure lines. Thus, in the occupied territories today we find two superimposed countries: "Judea and Samaria" above—the land of settlements and military outposts, four-lane bypass roads, bridges, and tunnels; and "Palestine" beneath—the land of villages and towns, pot-holed roads, and dirt paths. Ultimately, Wall and Tower had a decisive effect on the way Israelis perceive the space in which they live, which in turn maps out their values: observers vs. observed, Cartesian ghetto vs. chaotic periphery, threatened culture vs. "desert makers" (in the words of Ben Gurion), city vs. frontier, past and future vs. present, Jews vs. Arabs.

The combination between hasty settlement through military or paramilitary means in civilian camouflage, the seclusion of an ideologically homogenous community behind fortified walls, and the panoptical observation of the sur-rounding area has replicated itself countless times and in countless forms since the first days of Wall and Tower. The "settlement point" system has been integrated into national master plans throughout Israel's history, such as the plan drawn up in the 1970s for the Judaization of the Galilee, and in the current "spontaneous" expansion of Israeli settlements in the occupied territories. Throughout, ideological and social homogeneity has been largely maintained—

be it through an existing core of founders or through mechanisms that filter new residents according to ideological, social, and economic criteria. Whatever the reasons for homogeneity, the repetition of this settlement pattern, in which there is congruence between geographic location and social status, ideology and ethnic identity, it has been one of the most prominent characteristics of the Israeli built landscape.

THE WALL

Although the state of Israel has never had fixed recognized borders, it has continuously toyed with them in its attempts to define itself geographically and socially. The history of Israel is replete with plans detailing possible borderline scenarios. The map of the State of Israel is like a palimpsest bearing different traces of this quest: the 1947 UN partition line, the 1949 armistice green line (UN-administered armistice line between Israel and Jordan, 1948-1967), the 1967 cease fire purple line, the 1974 forces' separation blue line, the various Oslo "peace" boundaries. The physical expression of these borderlines vary from the barbed wire of Jerusalem's demarcation line, to the "Fatima Gate" of the "Good Fence",[7] from the bunkers of the "Bar Lev Line"[8] to the electronic separation fence/wall under construction today in the West Bank. A similarly desperate quest for borders, limits, and partitions can be seen on any number of scales throughout of the Israeli landscape and built environment. If the phenomena of gated communities is relatively new to most Western societies, in Israel it is quite normal to find kibbutzim, moshavim (a moshav [plural moshavim] is a cooperative agricultural settlement), suburbs, towns, and cities surrounded with a physical borderline: walls, chain-link fences, barbed wire, not to mention the Eruv borderline defining the limits of the Sabbath zone.[9]

Much has been said and written about the link between external threats on the State of Israel, real or imagined, and the formation of social cohesion and national unity. In Wall and Tower, we see exactly how this link is established: the priorities of Wall and Tower outposts stipulated that first the wall was to be built, then the observation point, and later the houses. In contravention of its expansionist ambitions, the Wall served to perpetuate the residents' ghetto mentality and impulse for enclosure. Seclusion within the wall separates the settlement from its environment and defines the new community not only as those who choose to live "inside," but also as those who are under threat from "outside." Shlomo Gur himself admitted that one of the reasons Tel Amal searched for land upon which to settle, was in order to keep the collective from dismantling.

THE POINT

As a strategy, Wall and Tower realized the drive for territorial expansion and conquest by establishing new "settlement points," suggesting that the "point" on the map was more important than the "settlement" it denoted; that is, the location of the settlement had more importance than its actual existence. In Wall and Tower, the settlement point on the map was a point within a strategic network of points, and its placement was determined by an optimal vantage point. The network was spread in such a way, so that every outpost had

eye contact with another, enabling the Towers to transmit messages through
Morse code using flashlights by night and mirrors by day. The settlement point
was first and foremost an observation point: erecting the Tower was the point
in whole.

THE TOWER

The Tower was the spearhead of industrialization and modernity not only due
to its logistical and technological characteristics, but because it transformed the
environment into the object of industrial and instrumental scrutiny. The vantage
point had its own accompanying technologies, such as binoculars and light projectors, and was organized as a systematic project to be managed and manned.
Beyond the military implications of the vantage point, or to borrow from Paul
Virilio, I see therefore I kill, the panoptic observation of the "tower"[10] determined the power relations between the Wall and Tower settlements and their
surroundings even before the land was cultivated and its agricultural economic
exploitation commenced.

As an initiative intended to organize the logistics of the gaze, Wall and Tower
transformed, literally from one day to the next, the territory it occupied. Henri
Lefebvre characterized agrarian time and space as a heterogeneous combination
of variables such as climate, fauna and flora, while claiming that industrialized
time and space tends towards homogeneity and unity. Despite the fact that the
Wall and Tower outposts were erected in established agrarian regions, the organized observation points were sufficient for transforming these territories into
industrialized spaces. A few such panoptic observation posts had the power to
unify an entire agrarian region and eradicate, through one strategic threat, the
complex economic and cultural differences that distinguished Arab nomads from
farmers from urbanites in 1930s Palestine. The very instrumentalization of the
territory with a gaze, invested the landscape with scenarios and schemes, threats
and dangers, infusing places and objects with tactical possibilities, situating them
within a strategy, and unifying them into one "political" space—to use Lefebvre's
terms.[11] Wall and Tower transformed the landscape into a battlefield, a scene of
conflicts, a frontier—in other words, into a city.

THE CAMP AND THE DOMAIN

As an almost dimensionless point in space, Wall and Tower is more of an optical
instrument than a place—an all-seeing eye that cannot see itself. Nevertheless,
with its wall, its tower, and its four shacks, Wall and Tower is a rough draft of
a place. Despite its resemblance to European medieval urban imagery, Wall and
Tower paints in a most vivid manner the concrete scheme of the Israeli place:
the camp and the domain.

The camp and the domain divides the territory into two main functions—
lands to be settled and lands to be exploited. This division has shaped the
Israeli attitude toward territory; the military logic at the basis of the territorial
relationship between the camp and the domain can be likened to the economic
logic that distinguishes the urban from the rural elsewhere. The concrete translation of the camp and the domain on the ground, be it in the form of a kibbutz

or a moshav, imposed architectural solutions where the camp is perceived as a unified, coherent entity surrounded by a vast unbuilt domain, cultivated collectively (in the kibbutz), or separately (in the moshav). Above all, this division, characteristic of rural settlements, underlies one of Israel's greatest social injustices: unlike Western countries, where the socioeconomic structure is based on social tradition (Europe) or economic practice (USA), the Israeli class system has been based on the distribution of the country's most precious resource—land. In this sense, the settler may find him or herself at the height of the social ladder. If in the first years of the State his or her prestige was merely political and symbolic, it was soon enough translated in material terms. Even today, the question of the domain—who owns it, and what to do with it—seems no less complex and problematic than the question of Israeli borders, and is cause for much public debate.

CAMP

"The camp is your home—guard it well." This slogan, posted on countless Israeli army bases, can be seen as the essence of the settlement program. If the camp is home, and if it must be guarded, the fate of the camp's residents is to become prisoners of their own gaze.

The settlement effort involved a series of tasks, some of which were military and tactical, while others were civilian and strategic. This duality found expression in slogans such as "one hand on the plough, the other hand on the sword." Despite the frequent use of military means, a civilian appearance has always been maintained, and is still one of the Zionist enterprise's main objectives. This is why Wall and Tower, and later other forms of settlement, left the status of the place and its residents in doubt. In every type of politically motivated settlement enterprise, be it institutionally sanctioned or not, there is a mixture of a civilian and a military operation; a military operation in civilian clothing; enlisted civilians under army patronage.

"Civilianization" is the transformation of the soldier into the pioneer—who is able, if need be, to change clothes and transform back into a soldier at any time. The transformation of the camp into a home is the transformation of the paramilitary outpost into a permanent settlement. This is why would-be normalcy, a routine of civilian life, has always depended on a military presence, which in the long run, taxes collective resources far more than the act of settlement itself. In Israel, the mundane is a strategic weapon.

TROJAN HORSES

Wall and Tower spawned an original tradition of local Trojan horses, instruments of infiltration and other types of ambulatory, temporary, political, and hyperactive objects: the tent in the outpost and the mobile home in the settlements. These banal objects are ostentatious not because of how they look, but because of their potential for mobility, expansion, and transformation; because they threaten to change the temporary into the daily, the daily into the permanent and the permanent into the eternal; because of how they can turn the landscape into an arena of struggle.

There is no doubt that the appearance of new settlements was a spectacular event, an act of creating something from nothing, a spectacle of light[12] —tracing the trajectories of bullets and the echoes of explosions, both night and day. Shlomo Gur saw in Wall and Tower a prosaic answer to the problems of settlement. In an interview with Ariella Azoulay, he claimed to be indifferent to their visual effect. The reading offered here would be alien not only to the axiomatic perception he had of his system, but also to his sense of self as a "man of action." On the other hand, it is difficult to ignore the simple fact that in many Wall and Tower settlement operations, Gur was accompanied by photographer Zoltan Kluger and his team from the Oriental Photography Company, and Kluger's wages were paid for by The United Israel Appeal.

The Wall and Tower settlements of Ein-Gev and Massada/Shaar HaGolan, for example, were the subject and location of the first Hebrew Technicolor film shot in Palestine/Eretz-Israel: "Spring in Galilee" directed by Efraim Lisch (13 minutes, 1939) and produced by the JNF. Similarly, the JNF supported and promoted the first Hebrew Opera "Dan the Guard," which celebrated the Wall and Tower settlement of Hanita. The opera, based on S. Shalom's play "Shootings at the Kibbutz" (1936), was adapted in 1939 by composer Marc Lavry and writer Max Brod.

THE MOLD

As is usually the case in Israeli *adrikhalut*, the actual object is much more powerful than any image or metaphor. The real spectacle of Wall and Tower did not stem from the way it looked but from what it was, and what it did. It was, first and foremost, a wall. The wall was a program destined to become an "ideology," but it was also a plain wooden mold, 20 centimeters wide filled with gravel. The wall was a premonition of things to come, because whoever fills the mold with gravel, will not hesitate to fill it with other materials. Beyond the fact that it was a barrier, whose job it was to prevent unwanted infiltration and offer protection from bullets, the wall was a technological presentation and logistical *tour de force*: it was the promise, or the threat, of concrete.

1   My Grandfather, Benjamin Plascow, was always proud to remind me that he was the first man wounded in the "Events" of April 1936. He was stabbed in his chest on Jaffa Road on his way back from work at the Jaffa port. A tin cigarette box (today one of my family's dearest possessions) saved him from more serious injury.

2   Rafi Segal and Eyal Weizman describe the Zionist and Israeli settlement projects as a continual move from the valley to the mountain.

3   Shlomo Gur-Gerzovsky (1913-2000) was a founding member of kibbutz Tel Amal who became a national project manager following his success with Wall and Tower. Before the establishment of the state, he was responsible for planning the defense constructions of many settlements. After the establishment of the State, he was charged with Israel's first *grands projets*: the Hebrew University, the National Library and the Knesset in Jerusalem.

4   Yohanan Ratner (1891-1965), a trained architect and a former Red Army officer, was the chief architect and strategic planner of the Hagana, the pre-state predecessor of the Israel Defense Forces (IDF.) As a member of the Central Command during the 1948 war, Ratner was the only general to receive permission from Ben Gurion to keep his non-Hebrew family name. Later, he served as Dean of the Faculty of Architecture at the Technion in Haifa, where he was considered a reactionary and staunch opponent of modernist architecture.

5   The Jewish National Fund (JNF) was established in 1901 during the 5th Zionist Congress in Basel, Switzerland, in order to promote the purchase of land in Palestine for the Jewish people. To this day, the JNF is the most important player in the country's land regime. More than 90% of the

land in the State of Israel is designated as "state land" and managed by the Israel Lands Authority (ILA), which is controlled by a board of directors composed of a majority of JNF representatives. Since the JNF is an organ of the Zionist movement, these lands belong to the "Jewish People" rather than to the State of Israel or the citizenry of the state, which includes a sizable non-Jewish population.

6   *Altneuland* was published in 1902. In this futuristic novel, inspired by the tales of Jules Verne, Herzl relays the adventures of a young Jewish intellectual from Vienna, Dr. Friedrich Lowenberg, who meets a mysterious character named Kingscourt. The doctor and his companion decide to dissociate themselves from the decadence of Europe, and settle on a deserted island in the Pacific Ocean. On their way, they pass through the Land of Israel and find it in a state similar to that in which Herzl found Palestine during his historic 1898 visit. After 10 years on the island, Lowenberg and Kingscourt decide to resume their travels. They return to the Land of Israel and discover *Altneuland* (old-new land) settled and built according to Herzl's own program in his book *The Jewish State*. The first Hebrew translation of *Altneuland* was published in 1904 under the biblical title *Tel Aviv*, borrowed from the Book of Ezekiel. Tel Aviv, officially established five years later in 1909, appears to be the only city in the world named after a book.

7   The "Good Fence" is the Israeli name for the borderline that ran between the State of Israel and the "Security Belt" of Israeli-occupied Southern Lebanon from the 1978 Litany Operation to the IDF withdrawal in 2000.

8   The name of the defensive fortification along the Suez Canal, conceived in the late 1960s by then IDF Chief of Staff Haim Barlev.

9   The *Eruv* is a symbolic religious wire that surrounds every Jewish community in Israel, demarcating an area within which one can carry personal objects on the Sabbath, without it being considered "work" to do so.

10 Ariella Azoulay links this birds-eye view to another of Shlomo Gur's projects. In 1937, Gur photographed the rooftops of Jerusalem's Old City in order to plan the defense of the Jewish Quarter. Azoulay describes these photographs in detail in the introduction to her published conversations with Gur, interpreting them as a precursor to "the official eye of the State of Israel." (Azoulay, 2000:28); the mythical phrase ostensibly coined by a tired IDF soldier upon conquering Mount Hermon in 1973, calling it "the eyes of the state," should also be noted in this context.

11 This is a concrete example of Lefebvre's claim: "[A] landscape that has undergone instrumentalization becomes a political landscape." (Lefebvre, 1968:277-278).

12 See Paul Virilio's linkage between the light projectors of World War II anti-aircraft defense mechanisms and the emblem of 20th Century Fox, as well as other expressions of the spectacular, such as Albert Speer's Cathedral of Light in Nurnberg.

Selected Bibliography

Ariella Azoulay, *How Does it Look to You?* (Tel Aviv: Babel, 2000).

David Ben Gurion, "An Army for Defense and Building," speech recorded in the anthology *On Settlement, 1915-1956* (Tel Aviv: Hakibbutz Hameuhad, 1986).

Paul Virilio, *War and Cinema*, trans. Patrick Camillier (London and New York: Verso, 1989) [*Guerre et Cinema* (Paris: Cahiers du Cinema Editions de l'Etoile,1984)].

Henri Lefebvre, "Espace et Politique," in Henri Lefebvre, *Le Droit a la Ville* (Paris: Editions Anthropos, 1968).

Oded Yedaya, "Towards a Social Function: on Zoltan Kluger's Photography in the Period of Homa Umigdal," *Kav* 10 (July, 1990).

Rafi Segal and Eyal Weizman, "The Mountain," in *A Civilian Occupation*, eds. Rafi Segal and Eyal Weizman (London: Verso and Tel Aviv: Babel, 2003).

Theodore Herzl, *Altneuland* (Tel Aviv: Babel, 1997).

Yehezkel Frenkel, *10 Years*, a Tel Amal booklet, 1946.

Yehezkel Frenkel, "How We Arrived at Homa uMigdal," in *40 Years to Homa Umigdal*, a Tel Amal booklet, 1976.

Zeev Aner, "Shlomo Gur, The Man Behind Homa uMigdal," a monologue recorded in *The Days of Homa uMigdal*, ed. Mordechai Naor (Jerusalem: Yad Ben Zvi Press, 1986).

COLONIZATION AS SUBURBANIZATION

THE POLITICS OF THE LAND MARKET
AT THE FRONTIER

David Newman

Colonization in the traditional sense of implanting a civilian population and establishing settlements in an occupied territory has, with few historical exceptions, taken place in distant lands. The "mother" country encourages its citizens to settle these lands as a means of ensuring long-term territorial control. Colonizing populations gradually take over local rule, supporting the mother country by transforming direct military domination into a quasi-civilian form of administration, albeit backed by a strong military presence. Traditional colonization of this kind also results in the creation of first and second class societies, with the settlers enjoying full legal and economic rights, while the local, indigenous populations (if they have not been subject to genocide) are bound to subsistence economies and barred from major positions of power.

It is against this well documented "model" of colonization that I discuss the settlement of the West Bank and Gaza by Israel in the past thirty years (1975-2005), following Israel's occupation of these territories in 1967. Many have argued that the Zionist, and later Israeli, settlement and land colonization project before 1967 differs from that which has taken place in the West Bank and Gaza in the past 30 years, because of the legal status of the territories in question, the nature of the military/civilian administration, and the perceived morality and/or justice of the cause. Though it could also be argued otherwise—that one process of settlement and land colonization follows the other—this paper limits its discussion to the West Bank and Gaza alone.

GEOGRAPHIC AND ECONOMIC CHARACTERISTICS OF SETTLEMENT COLONIZATION IN THE WEST BANK AND GAZA

The process and objectives of Israeli colonization in the West Bank and Gaza were not vastly different from those of European countries in Africa, Asia, and the Americas, namely to ensure long term territorial control through the implantation of a civilian population that would build homes, farms and factories, and breed new generations of settlers who would see these lands as their homeland. But in many other respects, the mechanisms of Israeli colonization have been vastly different.

First, Israeli settlers were spurred on by an ideology in which they saw themselves as "liberating" (rather than "occupying") the colonized territory and returning it to its "rightful" owners—the Jewish people. Second, the territory in question was physically adjacent to the mother country, requiring families to move no more than a few kilometers from their previous homes. Third, while settlers changed their place of residence, most kept their places of employment inside Israel, easing the dislocation of relocation and, in effect, transforming the colonization process into little more than a suburban commute. Fourth, the settler movement has been largely middle class and educated, with many settlers being part and parcel of the Israeli administrative elite.

RELIGIOPOLITICS

Religion as colonization ideology plays a major role in explaining how some 250,000 settlers (not counting those in East Jerusalem) came to live in the West Bank in a relatively short period of time. Although by no means is the entire settler population "religious," the majority fall into this category, and their lead-

ers are active in the Gush Emunim ("Believers Bloc") movement and the National Religious Party (NRP). Since most settlers believe that the occupied territories belong to them by right of a Divine Promise, and that they were "redeemed" in a miraculous war of Divine Intervention, they are not prepared to relinquish them (at least not without a fight), for the sake of territorial compromise in the framework of a future peace agreement with the Palestinians.

Road advertisements for new settlement construction projects in the West Bank (photo: editorial team, 2006)

The decision-making process of many settlers is determined by the rulings of charismatic religious leaders, whom adherents regard as more legitimate than elected officials. This is of particular significance when it comes to religious rulings "forbidding" the relinquishing of territories once they have come under Israeli-Jewish control. Some religious-nationalist leaders have called upon their followers in the army to refuse orders to evacuate settlements, as this is interpreted (perhaps solely by them) as a direct contravention of the religious precept of preserving the integrity of the "cities of our God." This clash between religiopolitics and the rule of law manifested during the recent Gaza disengagement.

GEOGRAPHICAL PROXIMITY AND THE LAND MARKET

The West Bank and Gaza are territories adjoining the State of Israel. As such, Israeli colonization takes place in its own "backyard." For most settlers, colonization in the West Bank and Gaza has been no more than "residential relocation" for political motives (the vision of "Greater Israel"), economic motives (better quality of life), or both.

Like most land markets in metropolitan areas, the price per dunum falls in accordance with its distance from the urban center, in our case Tel Aviv—Israel's economic and cultural capitol. Families seeking larger, detached houses with a yard are forced into suburban and exurban areas where land costs are low. During the 1980s, at the height of West Bank colonization activities, land prices took a sharp downturn the moment one crossed the Green Line (UN-administered armistice line between Israel and Jordan, 1948-1967). So as to encourage potential settlers to settle, especially those not motivated by ideology, religion or politics, the state offered occupied West Bank lands at extremely cheap rates, in some cases *gratis*. All the homeowner really had to pay for was the house. This was a considerable incentive for people who were not opposed to relocating beyond the Green Line in order to exchange cramped apartments for spacious villas. The slogan "five minutes from Kfar Saba" (read: five minutes further from your place of employment, but much better housing conditions) appealed to many settlers in this period. With the paving of highways linking Jerusalem and Tel Aviv to their exurban hinterlands, one came to feel that they were living not in "Greater Israel" but in a greater metropolitan area.

SUBURBANIZATION AND COMMUTING

The Gush Dan metropolitan area, at the center of which stands Tel Aviv, was limited to north/south growth, as the west was cut off by the Mediterranean Sea and the east by the Green Line. The conquest of the West Bank in 1967 effectively opened up the urban hinterlands of Jerusalem and Tel Aviv in directions previously considered "ex-territoria." But suburban colonization was limited in the first decade of occupation due to the Labor government's preference for agricultural settlements, especially in the Jordan valley, in the framework of what became

known as the Allon Plan. This plan privileged settlement in peripheral and frontier regions, leaving most of the hilly areas of the West Bank unsettled (among other reasons, due to high Palestinian population density). However, this changed with the Likud government in 1977, and the subsequent development of a suburban com- muter belt along the Green Line in the 1980s. The dominant Zionist/Israeli tenets of location, territorial control, and settlement planning shift-

Showroom with models for new apartments in the settle- ment of Har Homa (photo: Jörg Gläscher, 2004)

ed from rigid, centralized rural agricultural cooperative communities (kibbutzim and moshavim[1]) to the looser, more *laissez faire* private residential communities typical of Western postindustrial societies.

The suburbanization of colonization opened up the settlement option to groups that had previously been excluded from such activity, not least because they had no interest in becoming part of an agricultural or cooperative commu- nity. The proximity between their new and old homes meant that they could keep their jobs but also their vocational preferences, and that the government did not have to expend resources to create new places of work. Employment in the settlements is usually limited to public sector jobs (e.g. education) or manage- rial positions in specially created and highly subsidized private sector industrial zones. And just as land for housing is cheap, so too is land for business (and often tax free).

Throughout Israel's history, successive governments have promoted a settle- ment policy of population dispersal to the periphery by offering lower taxation rates and a range of economic benefits aimed at encouraging residents to stay in places that suffer from a "double peripherality": peripheral location and economic hardships. But these policies have enjoyed only limited "success," and could not keep the children of poor immigrants from migrating to the urban centers in search of social mobility. The construction of settlements in the occupied territories, however, changed this policy altogether. In order to encourage people to relocate beyond the Green Line, the government provided settlers with incentives previously offered only to communities in the Negev or the Galilee—but this time it was for settling the geographic center of the country, just "five minutes from Kfar Saba." In effect, they were offered a "double centrality": central location with the economic benefits of the periphery).

Much of the Israeli public bought into this arrangement, despite the fact that the geographic, demographic, political, and economic realities of the settlements are vastly different from those of the country's real frontier communities. Why, given these preferable conditions, would anyone not opposed to settling in the West Bank or Gaza have chosen a peripheral "development town" when he or she could receive the same financial support in a middle class residential community?

SOCIOECONOMIC COMPOSITION OF THE SETTLER POPULATION

Suburbanization is a middle class activity. The suburban myth is built around the notion of professional families with children improving their standard of living by fleeing crowded city centers for "open space" and "fresh air"—where they will find less noise and pollution, better public education, and more community solidarity. Suburban communities in the Western world normally exhibit higher levels of education and employment in the tertiary and professional sectors. This is also true of the settlements of the West Bank and Gaza, thanks to the public and private funds poured into these communities.

One might think that the working class residents of "development towns" would have spearheaded the campaign against the settlements, if only because of the "unjust" allocation of resources. But this has not happened. Most "development town" residents have remained faithful to right wing political parties, especially the governing Likud party, as it has been perceived as the only political outlet for social protest against the hegemony of the Labor party—which founded the state, and with it, its innumerable inequities.[2]

METROPOLITAN COLONIZATION IN THE JERUSALEM *HINTERLAND*

Before 1967, Jerusalem's suburbs grew west of the city—the only direction not obstructed by the Green Line. After the annexation of East Jerusalem in 1967, suburban development extended in other directions, creating wedges between the Palestinian neighborhoods and suburbs of the city. Several West Bank settlements, such as Maale Adumim to the east, Beit El to the north, and the Gush Etzion settlement bloc to the south, function as Jewish suburbs of Jerusalem. Like the suburban settlements along the Green Line, residents of these settlements commute to work in Jerusalem, but go home to larger, detached houses with yards. Jewish Jerusalem has become intertwined with its West Bank environment, making the eventual evacuation of these settlements that much more difficult, and that much less likely. Following the Gaza disengagement, the focus of territorial struggle shifted to Maale Adumim, the largest most populous settlement in the West Bank, as right wing politicians are demanding its expansion

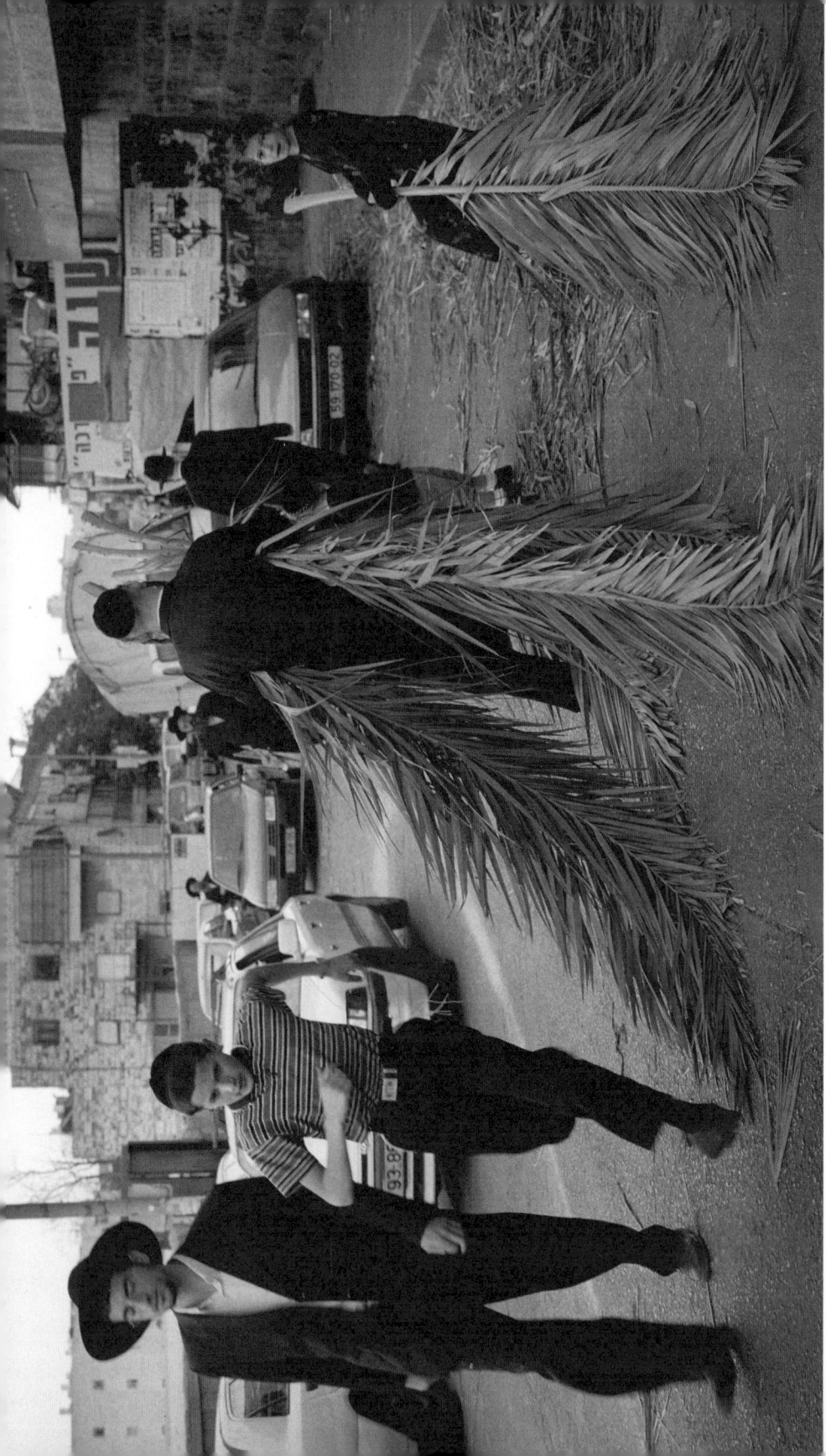

17.2 km: Mea Shearim

and municipal linkage to Jerusalem. Within this metropolitan region known as "Greater Jerusalem," functional space is dual—with Israeli and Palestinian communities living side by side, but experiencing their daily lives of working, shopping, studying, commuting, etc. like different universes.

THE IMPACT OF THE SEPARATION FENCE/WALL ON THE SETTLEMENT INFRASTRUCTURE

The route of the newly constructed separation fence/wall (ostensibly for "security purposes," i.e. to prevent Palestinian suicide bombers from entering Israel) has been determined by, and will in turn determine, the process of settlement expansion. While the major settlement blocs are included on the "Israeli side" of the barrier, many isolated and remote settlements now find themselves on the "outside" (the Palestinian "inside") or the "wrong" side. For them, this is a clear indication that even a right wing Israeli government will not insist on keeping them in the framework of a future territorial agreement, certainly in light of the recent Gaza disengagement.

IMPLICATIONS OF THE GAZA DISENGAGEMENT

Heated opposition to the Gaza disengagement notwithstanding, its actual implementation took place without any major problems and the specter of violence was, in retrospect, exaggerated. While many non-settler Israelis empathized with the settlers who were forced out of their homes, it did not shift public opinion from overwhelming support for the disengagement itself. Had the settlers crossed the line between perceived "legitimate" and "illegitimate" civil disobedience, support for their cause, or at least their civil rights, would have rapidly deteriorated. Mainstream settler leaders were acutely aware of this, knowing they had to contain the ferocity of their constituents' opposition. Since the disengagement, they have been harshly criticized by West Bank settlers for backing down from more aggressive modes of resistance. What the Gaza disengagement showed the Israeli public was that wholesale settlement evacuation is possible. At the same time, future evacuations in the West Bank—the settlement heartland—will probably be met with stronger opposition than it was in Gaza, not least because consensus for withdrawal from these areas is not as widespread as it was for Gaza.

"SUBURBAN" COLONIZATION

While the primary objectives of colonization are political and territorial—in the West Bank and Gaza as elsewhere—Israeli settlers and the successive governments that implanted them have succeeded in transforming much of the settlement enterprise into a socioeconomic and geographical process of metropolitan suburbanization.

As in most suburban and exurban communities in Western industrialized and postindustrialized societies, people move to the suburbs because of what they perceive as better living conditions, while maintaining their places of employment in metropolitan areas. With significant improvements in Israel's transportation system, an increasing number of "development town" residents are commuting on a daily basis to their places of work in urban centers. While the longitudinal distances between the Galilee in the north and the Negev in the south and the center of the country are grater than the latitudinal distances between Tel Aviv and, say, the settlement of Ariel nestled in the heart of the West Bank, these gaps are narrowing.

If suburbanization, i.e. socioeconomic advancement, played a major part in making the settlement process possible despite its explicit political objectives, perhaps the converse is also possible: changes in patterns of Israeli suburbanization could bring about a decline in settlement, political processes notwithstanding.

1   Editors note: A kibbutz (plural kibbutzim) is a type of agricultural collective found in Israel. Its typical features include the collective ownership of property, communal living. A moshav (plural moshavim) is a type of cooperative agricultural settlement, generally based on the principle of private ownership of land and communal marketing.

2   For its part, the Likud has consistently promoted middle class settlement programs at the expense of the working class, coupled with laissez-faire, anti-welfare economic policies, especially under the tutelage of former Finance Minister Benjamin Netanyahu. However, the Likud has not been the only party to promote settlement. The colonization of the occupied territories began under Labor rule, and the greatest periods of settlement growth took place, perhaps ironically, during the Rabin and Barak governments of the 1990's. The recent election of Amir Peretz, a former "development town" mayor and trade union leader, as chairman of the Labor Party has the potential to turn this "traditional" voting pattern around. His emphasis on social welfare, coupled with support for the peace process—, which could necessitate the evacuation of most West Bank settlements, might herald a structural change in Israeli voting, but also in Israeli settlement—as it becomes less and less attractive in the post-Gaza disengagement era.

Selected Bibliography

Abu Ayyash Abdul-Ilah, "Israeli Planning Policy in the Occupied Territories," *Journal of Palestine Studies* 11 (1) (1981).

Michael Dumper, *The Politics of Jerusalem since 1967* (New York: Columbia University Press, 1997).

Tamar Hermann and David Newman, "Extra-Parliamentarism in Israel: A Comparative Study of Peace Now and Gush Emunim," *Middle Eastern Studies* 28 (3) (1992).

Aharon Keller, *Society and Settlement in the Land of Israel* (Albany: SUNY Press, 1992).

Baruch Kimmerling, *Zionism and Territory: The Socio-territorial Dimension of Zionist Politics* (Berkeley: University of California, Institute of International Studies, 1983).

David Newman, "The Territorial Politics of Exurbanization: Reflections on Thirty Years of Jewish Settlement in the West Bank," *Israel Affairs* 3 (1) (1996).

David Newman, "From 'Hitnachhalut" to "Hitnatkut': The Impact of Gush Emunim on Israeli Society and Politics," *Israel Studies* (2005).

David Newman and Leviah Applebaum, "Defining the Urban Settlement: Planning Models and Functional Realities in Israel," *Urban Geography* 10 (3) (1989).

Yuval Portugali, "Jewish Settlement in the Occupied Territories: Israel's Settlement Structure and the Palestinians," *Political Geography Quarterly* 10 (1991).

Shalom Reichman, "Policy Reduces the World to Essentials: a Reflection on the Jewish Settlement Process in the West Bank Since 1967," in *Planning in turbulence*, eds. D. Morley and A. Shachar (Jerusalem: Magnes Press, 1986).

VILLAGES UNDER SIEGE

ADAPTATION, RESISTANCE, IMPOSED MODERNIZATION AND URBANIZATION IN JERUSALEM'S EASTERN VILLAGES

Rassem Khamaisi

This essay will analyze the nature of ruralism, suburbanization, and urbanization in relation to the Palestinian "villages" located within the municipal boundaries of Israeli-annexed East Jerusalem. As a result of the planning regime of the Israeli-controlled Jerusalem municipality, Palestinians suffer from imposed urbanization. This experience of physical and sociocultural siege manifests a particular spatial fabric. Its elements include the physical restrictions and limitations imposed by external and politically-motivated planning, land and property expropriations; its outcomes comprise changing sociocultural systems, normative behavioral patterns, and value systems inside the communities themselves.

RURALISM VERSUS URBANISM

Traditionally, the term "ruralism" has referred to the way of life in small localities and villages with low population growth and physical density, where traditional customs and behavioral patterns evolve around an agricultural economy. In contrast, the notion of "urbanism" has included large localities, towns, and cities based on nonagricultural economies and characterized by high population growth resulting from immigration, density, social diversity and individualism. In the modern era, however, this dichotomy began to gray. Although the two might still be differentiated physically, functionally, and structurally, the complex processes of urbanization, modernization, and globalization force us to reconsider both terms (Huntington, 1997). On the one hand, Palestinian East Jerusalem could be said to exemplify the generic typologies of urbanized localities and communities: suburbanization and semiurbanization (Gonen, 1995), sustainable urbanization (Allen and You, 2002), newly urbanized systems (Eben Saleh, 2002) and urbanization without urbanity (Khamaisi, 2004). On the other hand, such terminology not only decodes the space, but then serves a crucial tool in implementing spatial policies within a larger urban system. This "recoding" is an instrument for regulating and restricting future development. Thus, we see that "ruralism," "urbanization," and "suburbanization" are not neutral terms, but language that wields territorial and geopolitical power in determining demographic development and the allocation of resources.

Until the middle of the 19th century, Jerusalem was defined by the Old City's defensive wall—an area of approximately 900 dunams (1 dunum = 1000 square meters) square (Ben Ariah, 1990)—and a number of surrounding small villages and their agricultural holdings. From the late 19th century and beginning of the 20th century, the population of Jerusalem began to grow, particularly due to the new geopolitical and administrative status of Jerusalem as a provincial administrative center under the Ottomans and then, from 1917, as the site of the British Mandate governorship. Growth was fuelled by Jewish immigration, as well as the natural growth of the Arab population. The new Jerusalem developed and expanded to the west and northwest, beyond Jaffa and Damascus Gate and along the road to Jaffa, to Baqaa in the south and Sheikh Jarrah in the north (Tamari, 1999). But in contrast to the rapid urban growth, the villages of the Jerusalem area were growing slowly and distinctly divided from the expanding city by open and agricultural areas.

While the British Mandate authorities concentrated on regional reorganization and town planning schemes, villages continued to develop in an organic way according to traditional rules (based on Islamic *shariah* law, which allots and develops property according to relative plot size, property lines, building height, and construction density) and without the interference of an external planning regime that imports and copies planning strategies in a top-down process. Village lands were defined through the accumulation of individual and extended family land holdings, as well as common land (*moshaa*). Territorial boundaries were generally defined by an oral tradition until the beginning of the 20th century, when British Mandate authorities implemented the Ottoman Land Law (1858) and Land Registration Law (1861).

The expulsion of all rural populations from western Jerusalem in 1948 radically changed the nature of the urban-rural relationship. As western Jerusalem was reinvented as the vastly expanded capital of the newly founded State of Israel, what physically remained of the villages was quickly replaced by new urban neighborhoods inhabited by an urbanized Jewish population. In East Jerusalem (which is the focus of this essay), the relationship between city and villages remained nearly intact: independent local councils governed villages surrounding a moderately-important Jordanian city.

SPATIAL POLITICS OF SIEGE

Only weeks after the end of the war, on June 27, 1967, the Israeli government decided to expand the municipal boundaries of West Jerusalem to the east. While the new boundaries were to deliver a "United Jerusalem" as eternal capital of Israel and the Jewish people, they were additionally carefully engineered to exclude as many Palestinians as possible, thus ensuring a 74.2% Jewish majority and limiting the Palestinian population in the city to a mere 68,600 (compared to 197,700 Jews). In acquiring the greatest area of land but the fewest number of Palestinians, the agricultural lands surrounding Jerusalem's eastern villages provided an ideal spatial reservoir. Seventy thousand dunams, comprised of the Jordanian Jerusalem municipality and the surrounding villages, were annexed by the Israeli Jerusalem municipality. The more populous village centers of Abu Dis, Ezariya, Ar-Ram, and Bir Nabala remained outside of the municipal boundary. The result was a reduction of the space used by Palestinians to less than 25,000 dunams or about 34% of the total area of annexed East Jerusalem. Approximately 10,000 dunams, or 15% of East Jerusalem remained open for new development.

The spatial impact of the new boundary regime and the land expropriations was dramatic. Palestinian villages like Sur Bahir, Beit Safafa, and Shufat lost most of their agricultural holdings and hinterlands. The spatial continuity between the villages was severed, and they were robbed of their natural spatial resources. In an unprecedented manipulation of good planning rhetoric, the expropriated areas were redesignated as "green areas" for public use, but "public" was now defined exclusively as Jewish and the "green areas" became sites of vast Jewish settlement projects. Through economic incentives and subsidies, more than 200,000 Jewish residents were moved into a series of bedroom communities linked to the western city by efficient road systems. Green buffer zones defined by invisible walls and boundaries were transformed into inhabited buffer zones secured by perimeter roads and walls. The sum effect was to block any possible expansion of the Palestinian villages.

POLITICAL PLANNING

Political planning extended beyond the redrawing of territorial boundaries and land expropriations. Urban planning regulations proved to be an equally effective instrument to control and limit Palestinian building activity. The absence of formal land parcellation in the Palestinian areas served as an excuse for declaring a moratorium on any one expansion project. Building lines were drawn around the already built-up fabric, freezing the boundaries of the villages and restricting construction opportunities to private land inside the villages. At the same time, official planning schemes were never developed or delayed (in the case of Sur Bahir, plans were commissioned 35 years after Israeli control). Palestinian applicants for building permits to this day endure a biased and discriminatory regime that holds little promise within the framework of the regulated plans. Without reason, permits are delayed or simply not given; Palestinians must therefore often choose between not building at all, or building only to have the home demolished. From 1967 to 2001, approximately 3,100 building *permits* were granted to Palestinians in East Jerusalem, while some 19,900 housing units were constructed.

Further, new plans for existing villages are consistently developed ignoring the spatial reality inside the villages, or available data on actual and future housing needs. Public housing schemes for Palestinians do not exist (other than the Nusseibeh project constructed in northern Beit Hanina in the 1970s). The current physical state of the villages—density without urbanity—is a direct result of this planning regime. In effect, the planning regime forced upon the villages prescribes ruralism through social-cultural diminution; an urban service infrastructure is denied, while communities are forced to urbanize territorially and economically. As spatial encircling prevented horizontal expansion of the built-up fabric of villages, villagers were left to fill in, renovate, add to, or extend already existing buildings, generating an ever-increasing physical density inside the villages. In the absence of an urban infrastructure and appropriate services, villages relied on the rural infrastructures of narrow roads and the organic principles of sprawl in building individual houses, family compounds, or commercial businesses and workshops. In the last decade, particularly the last Intifada, frequent closures have spurred the opening of some shops in communities like Sur Bahir.

Using the aesthetic argument of wanting to preserve the village's rural character, the Jerusalem municipality has *not* embraced and steered densification, rather it is fighting it by imposing a limit on building height and enforcing a building-to-plot ratio. The Old City and its surrounding villages were even declared a national preservation zone, which places tight limitations on any construction activity and provides excuses for legally demolishing structures that "spoil" the area's ruralism, regardless of whether or not those structures existed prior to 1967.

The hypocritical nature of this policy is exposed when one compares the rules that apply to villages like Sur Bahir with surrounding settlements, such as Har Homa. While Sur Bahir is forced to preserve its rural character through low buildings and restrictive plot-to-building ratios, the neighboring settlement is a mega-structure of interconnected multistory, prefabricated apartment blocks. The building rights given in Talpiot Mizrah (Jewish settlement) are 150%-170% per building plot, while in Palestinian Jabal al-Mukaber, building rights are a tifling 25% per building plot (Marom, 2004:69).

INFORMALIZATION

Economic recovery and population growth after 1967 spurred investment in the improvement, renovation, and extension of village homes, but denial of construction permits, the costs involved in obtaining a permit, or delays in the process caused many families to build illegally or semi-legally. These "illegal" building activities are not a new phenomenon, in fact, but actually began in the British Mandate period, as soon as planning regulations were instituted. But after 1967, illegal construction has been folded into the wider geopolitical and ethno-demographic conflict rather than being viewed as a civic problem, as under the British and Jordanians. Israeli authorities combat illegal housing with the ferocity of a security problem, while persistently ignoring regional overcrowding, lack of resources, and the impossibility of obtaining legal permits. Between 1992 and 2004, some 5,318 building offences were recorded by the Israeli-controlled municipality. Approximately 3,830 cases were taken to court, 574 stop work orders delivered, and 614 demolition orders issued. Two hundred and thirty-eight buildings were in fact demolished, none of them owned by Jewish Israelis (Marom, 2004:44).

CLOSURES

When Palestinians from the Jerusalem area participated in violent activities and demonstrations during the first Intifada (1987-1993), the Israeli authorities dramatically stepped up security measures. After the signing of the 1993 Oslo Accords with Palestinians, Israel installed temporary military checkpoints at the entrance points to most Palestinian neighborhoods and villages in East Jerusalem. This new policy of "closure," as it came to be called, was a long-term strategy aimed at shoring up Israeli domination. At the same time, permanent checkpoints limited migration into Jerusalem and reinforced the city's municipal boundary. Further, the new "center of life" policy retroactively applied in 1995, created a legal framework for confiscating the Israeli identity cards from thou-

17.8 km: Road 1

sands of East Jerusalemites, who had chosen to live in more affordable housing outside the municipal boundaries. (Any contact with the authorities, could entail residents being asked for myriad forms of proof confirming that the city of Jerusalem remained their "center of life"; loss of the identity card meant the loss of the right to live, work, and move in the city.) This new policy reversed the stream of out-migration and has since dramatically increased the pressure on the already-saturated Palestinian housing market inside the municipal boundaries.

The beginning of the al-Aqsa Intifada (since 2000) led to further intensification of these policies. The limits on access and movement are currently being transformed into a physical separation through the building of a series of walls and fences running through East Jerusalem, severing Palestinian populated areas from the city's heart. The concurrent gradual amplification of the separation of Palestinians in East Jerusalem from Palestinians living in the eastern surrounding territory has created a situation of concentrated siege, a siege perceived by Palestinians as a new stage of heightened occupation.

INTERNAL PRESSURES

This external geopolitical siege has had a profound impact on the internal spatial, socioeconomic, and cultural structure of villages; its effects are felt by the individual village dweller as well as the wider Arab community.

Cultural Fragmentation

At the time of East Jerusalem's annexation, 40% of the city's Palestinians (27,000 people) lived in an urban setting, while the remainder lived in 12 villages. The new 1967 municipal boundaries made Palestinian villagers and urban Jerusalemites, two very different social, ethnic, and cultural groups, into like-residents of the city of Jerusalem. But the new Israeli government had a political interest in sustaining and deepening existing ethno-religious or sociocultural divides (Muslim versus Christian, urbanite versus villager versus Bedouin, or even Jerusalemite versus Hebronite, native versus immigrant versus refugee and so forth). Since Palestinians rejected the new municipality as a representative body, the Israeli authorities instead began to make deals with individuals and sub-groups, thereby deepening sociocultural fragmentation and preventing organized resistance from a united Palestinian body. The empowerment of traditional *hamula* (extended family) networks and the fostering of local patriotism in the villages and neighborhoods proved an effective tool for stopping or slowing the growth of a powerful civil society that could demand rights and equal access to the city's resources. It must also be said that the Arab communities often readily accepted such policies, particularly after the traumatic events of the war and in light of new economic opportunities offered by Israeli markets.

Although the Israeli labor market was opened to all occupied Palestinians, the mobility of West Bank and Gaza Strip residents was severely restricted by direct military rule. By comparison, East Jerusalemites received Israeli identity cards designating them as "permanent residents" (not quite citizens) of Israel. The resulting privileges—access to the Israeli social security system and freedom of movement—led to more economic opportunities. Between 1967 and 1987, East

Jerusalem's population grew from 68,000 inhabitants to 139,000, a growth of 103% and disproportionately high if compared with an overall population growth of 68% for the entire municipal area. This growth was largely fuelled by natural increase (about 3.3% per year) and immigration from the rest of the West Bank, and Gaza, and many Jerusalem residents who had left the city before 1967 returned to seek employment opportunities. Other factors in the increase included the absorption by Jerusalem villages of residents from the Hebron region and West Bank periphery, and applications for Israeli residency papers for non-Jerusalem ID-carrying spouses and children.

Family Role and Power

In Palestinian rural tradition, land ownership determines economic resources and the social status of the family. Sale of land was generally frowned upon, including sales to neighboring families or newcomers. The continual fear of land expropriation and loss of Jerusalem identity status, as well as the futility of finding alternative housing inside the city, has heightened this impulse to secure and preserve family land for future generations. This tendency has significant consequences, as it further slows processes of urbanization by reducing development to private housing projects and limiting the land available for commercial or industrial endeavors. The family-based system of ownership equally suppresses regular market buying and selling and inflates land prices. As long as *hamulas* preserve their territory in the villages, no civic and national Arab Palestinian institutions have the power and authority to independently initiate and organize construction activities. Local traditional leaders, including the *muktars* connected to each village's major families, do not command all of the tools required to see the community out of ruralism and into selective urbanization. The absence of a civic society or an integrative municipal or a national planning regime adds to the growing tensions within the traditional structure of belonging. The power of the extended family preserves private interests and leads to a "voluntary" withdrawal from the interests of the public. Most village conflicts erupt over land boundaries; these are settled through mediation between families with the help of trusted outsiders.[1] In lieu of this, there is no independent and democratically selected body that villagers identify with and that can provide a suitable alternative to the Israeli court system.

Class Polarization

Jerusalem-area villages, like all rural societies, have been deeply affected by the outward migration of the educated middle classes. In communities where tribal values form the basis of social relations, and class advancement and employment opportunities are limited, new generations often seek refuge in more urban environments that have a higher degree of tolerance and are open to absorbing new migration. The recent economic recession and decline in job opportunities in Israel have increased the village unemployment rate and additionally impacted class inequalities. The current trend is a growing poor underclass. This transformation in class structure will cause increasing social disparities within Palestinian society and further widen the gap between cities and villages (Khamaisi and Nasrallah, 2003). Limited social mobility between classes adds to the latent, truncated and false urbanization of rural communities and further strengthens social localization and tribalism, as well as the stratification of Palestinian social groups in East Jerusalem.

CONCLUSION

The wider geopolitical, territorial and demographic conflict has engendered a process of latent and false urbanization in eastern Jerusalem villages. Urbanization in rural environments within the eastern Jerusalem area is characterized by a dichotomy between urban living standards and consumer behaviors on one hand and sociocultural behavior based on traditional norms and principles on the other (Huntington, 1997). The main indicator of this selective urbanization is population growth. Between 1967 and 2002, the Palestinian population in East Jerusalem's villages grew by 223% (as compared with a Jewish population growth of about 132%, and growth in the entire city of 156%) (Choshen, 2004) with an average natural increase of about 3% per year. These demographic characteristics fit traditional rural communities, despite that East Jerusalem villages are largely dependent on the urban space of Jerusalem. The traditional spatial model of Jerusalem's organic villages has radically changed physically into a model more similar to that of suburban communities, even as their social and cultural characteristics remain traditional.

---

1   This mediation practice is called the *sulha*, it incorporates agreed-upon community-monitored payments and punishments, and is widely used to solve all kinds of internal and external family disputes.

Selected Bibliography

Adriana Allen, et al., *Sustainable Urbanization: Bridging the Green and Brown Agendas* (London: UN-Habitat, Developmental Planning Unit, University College London, 2002).

Arieh Yehoshua Ben, "The Old and New City in the 19th Century," in *Studies in History of Jerusalem*, ed. Amnon Cohen (Jerusalem: Yad Yitzhaq Ben Tsvi, 1990, in Arabic).

Robert Brooks, et al., *The Wall of Annexation and Expansion: Its Impact on the Jerusalem Area* (Jerusalem: IPCC, 2005).

Maya Choshen, ed., *Statistical Yearbook of Jerusalem, 20, 2002/2003* (Jerusalem: The Jerusalem Institute for Israeli Studies, 2004).

Mohammed Abdullah Eben Saleh, "The Transformation of Residential Neighborhoods: the Emergence of New Urbanism in Saudi Arabian Culture," *Building and Environment* 37 (May, 2002).

Amiram Gonen, *Between City and Suburban: Urban Residential Patterns and Processes in Israel* (Avebury: Aldershot, 1995).

Samuel P Huntington, *The Clash of Civilization* (New York: Touchstone, 1997).

Rassem Khamaisi and Rami Nasrallah, eds., *The Jerusalem Urban Fabric* (Jerusalem: IPCC, 2003).

Rassem Khamaisi, "Urbanization Without Cities: The Urban Phenomena Among the Arabs In Israel," *Horizon in Geography* (2004).

Nathan Marom, *The Planning Deadlock: Planning Policies, Land Regularization, Building Permits and House Demolitions in East Jerusalem* (Jerusalem: Bimkom and Eer Shalem, 2004).

Salim Tamari, ed., *Jerusalem 1948: The Arab Neighborhoods and their Fate in the War* (Jerusalem: The Institute of Jerusalem Studies and Badil Resource Center, 1999).

REFLECTIONS OF SPATIAL PRESENTATION IN SUR BAHIR

A STUDY IN USE

Yehotal Shapira

Sur Bahir, located in southeast Jerusalem, was born in the sixteenth century as a small Palestinian agrarian community, and gradually developed into today's neighborhood of 12,000 inside the Israeli Jerusalem metropolis. This essay will trace the landscaping traditions and building heritages that characterized this transformation and its influence upon contemporary East Jerusalem planning confrontations. This tack differs from the predominant manner in Israel of examining the planning of Palestinian surroundings; usually these analyses use a critique with a specific trajectory: one moving forward, towards "progress" (Jabarin & Law-Yone, 1998:68-76). In many cases, Palestinian communities' traditional structural qualities are seen as objects for change or conservation via the professional architectural discipline, despite that these qualities are key to understanding the contemporary evolution of places and their actual possibilities.

Construction of house extension in Sur Bahir (photo: Khaled Dabash)

Traditional Ottoman dwelling in Sur Bahir (photo: Khaled Dabash)

This essay will tie architecture and landscaping to Hall's (1997:13-75) arguments that representations are part of broader cultural processes which organize, normalize, and give structure to the world, as crucial components in the creation of common values. As such, this essay will give precedence to the faith and customs of the community and its individuals in describing their relationship between building and culture. The memories and the planning problems described were informed by discussions with planner and Village Development Committee head Hassan Abu Aslah and Village Development Committee member Khaled Dabash.[1]

Ayal (1993) argues that Israeli academic writing on "The Arab Village" tends to construct Palestinians as the distinct Other. Certainly, new Israeli writing—no less this essay—is in danger of reproducing existing power relations within the scholarly realm, repeating discrimination against Palestinians by creating new versus old perspectives and hierarchies. All too often, analyses reenforce Euro-American notions and "utilize" the presence of discrimination as a platform for integration into the international professional discourse. In light of these dangers, I argue that the meaning of such writing lies in the greater mutual understanding gained by examining Palestinian and Israeli cultural differences.

MEMORY, HISTORY, AND TRADITION IN SUR BAHIR

Sur Bahir has been inhabited since the 16th century (Hutteroth and Abdulfattah, 1977:117). The village developed alongside the Bethlehem-Jerusalem intercourse, and the majority of its houses were located in caves away from agricultural lands (Hirschfeld, 1987:84; Kark and Oren-Nordheim, 1995:324-329). The land surrounding the caves was originally used for pasture land; over time it was cultivated and adjacent houses were built of locally-found stone.[2] Each nuclear family inhabited a one-room house encircling an inner open-air courtyard used by the entire extended family. The house had very small windows and was also used as a place for agricultural production and shelter for animals. Domestic areas were separated from those used for animal shelter by graduated inner platforms connected with staircases.

The religious-cultural need to shield women from public access, and the requirements of defending the community from marauders (until the end of the 19th century, the desert frontier near Jerusalem was the site of frequent clashes between villages and Bedouin raids) dictated introverted construction (Canaan, 1933:57-63; Fuchs, 1998:87-91; Hirschfeld, 1987:54-78). The internal courtyard had many uses: storing grain, cooking in a wood oven, playing, washing, offering hospitality, and sheltering animals. Its floor was made of stone and trodden earth, and along its length were ditches that led water run-off to cisterns, which were Sur Bahir's only source of water. When construction was initiated around the internal courtyard, the entire extended family and the rest of the village joined in the social event (Canaan, 1933:57-63).[3]

This intimacy with the earth inspired echoes of natural forms in the building culture. Structures contained rigorous repetitions of the rectangular room placed in height according to the topography. These rectangular rooms, slightly displaced from each other, created rich, multidimension forms reflecting the surrounding area, while the roof of the home was a stone cross chamber reminiscent of a vaulted sky. The hillside terraces continued into the house, divided vertically on different plateaus, adapted and varied according to the changing topography, each with its own use. There was a natural progression outward and no consideration given to the final frontal view of the site (Shapira, 2004).[4]

From the late 19th century onwards, Sur Bahir's buildings, spatial organization, and attitude towards the landscape began to change.[5] In parallel, Jerusalem-area villages' population size increased markedly by the end of the 19th century (Ben Arie, 1989:79-84). This process of modernization was both internally and eternally motivated. Building patterns and the location and status of open spaces were altered: stretching from a tightly-knit village, Sur Bahir began to extend along the nearby ridges. The animals were either removed from the house altogether, or left on the first floor while the living area was elevated to a second floor built from chiseled stones with larger windows in pairs with a supporting arch above them. Later, this second floor adopted a "triple" entranceway, characterized by two windows next to a door leading out upon a balcony. At times, even a third floor was constructed (Oren-Nordheim, 1985). The house was thus visually separated from its surroundings.

Now the home and the courtyard had changed places: the courtyard located at the center of the house had moved to surround the domicile. Buildings were newly planned in the center of the land plot. Structures once built in rigorous functionalism, where each was equal to the others, began to represent the individual in the public sphere through the use of varied chiseled stones and decorations. The façade's appearance was not only a sign of new technique, but of altered social perceptions; the individual was increasingly visible and represented, rather than being subsumed within the wider clan. This transformation additionally signaled altered perceptions concerning the expression of status and property ownership (Shapira, 2004).

Hassan Abu Aslah remembers that there were several functioning public open spaces in Sur Bahir, each one intended for a separate extended family. These were the new sites of social events and communal agricultural activity. Wheat was processed in a dry, fenced-in area marked by the British survey as the "threshing floor." Parties were also held here where guests danced the *debka*.[6] Wedding processions began at the groom's house, coursing along the road to the first crossroads above the Sur Bahir cemetery, where the *Fatiha*[7] was read near the burial structures of Sheikh Dawary's family (Canaan, 1927:4, 23). An additional common public area was the *saha*, a building used for the meeting of the men of the extended family.[8] This practice was upheld until the 1950s. All of the village's families used the cemetery at the center of the village; Sheikh Dawary's family graves (a saint's *maqam*) were one important place of prayer.[9] These structures were destroyed at the behest of the Muslim authorities, during a later period of delegitimation of Palestinian saint worship.

Agriculture was both a source of work and the foundation of leisure, with no separation between them (Canaan, 1928:139-140). Hassan Abu Aslah describes his experience: "In the olive-picking season, all the people gathered outside the house to harvest the olives. For me as a child it was a unique experience, climbing [the olive trees]. We grew squash on the plain [as] summer fruit. We would make a tent and sleep there for three months [or in a cave or a shed], taking the cat and the utensils and having a picnic. We would work—getting up in the morning and picking olives—and we would also go to the market to sell the produce and bring home some money. Feeling the morning dew wetting the feet was a real pleasure."[10]

The occupation of East Jerusalem in 1967 and the annexation of Sur Bahir accelerated the village's urbanization. This process was accompanied by decreasing agricultural activity.[11] Two forms of agriculture still take place in the village. First, olive groves are cultivated in the wadis, in place of previously varied crops. Olive groves do not require a great deal of labor or a large financial investment, and their cultivation does not restrict an urban existence. The olive groves are also used for maintaining ownership over land which is threatened by Israeli Jewish settlement expansion. Second, contemporary agriculture persists through domestic husbandry, comprised of caring for pigeons and chickens, and the tending of fruit trees alongside ornamental growth (Israeli and Western attributes are visible in the blooming plants and grass watered by irrigation hoses).

Building forms from various eras exist side by side in Sur Bahir, and are now interwoven—relics of caves sit beside houses with an inner courtyard, which in turn neighbor structure-saturated, modern building sites. Important traditional attributes persist with modern variations: today, the wider village participates in construction, and units are added on to a main structure ("building from the inside") according to need. These elements are integrated into contemporary technologies (take, for example, the home that rises five stories high, in order to house the growing extended family, each nuclear family on a different floor). Local motifs such as vaults appear frequently next to modern patterns, and all types of stones and cuttings creates affluence in style and form. Inner divisions are now horizontal, each room with its own purpose. The traditional room for entertaining guests remains in nearly every house.

The neighborhood is characterized by lack of official planning and invested resources, as well as an abundance of privately-driven buildings. The result is ad hoc, with residents turning private structures into educational buildings, arranging their own access routes, developing roads with shared private funding, and so on. Gaps arise in irrigation, potable water, electricity, and sewers. Furthermore, the community suffers from construction that lacks the usual official inspections related to safety, fire prevention, earthquake preparedness, and parking requirements. Conversely, urbanization processes in Sur Bahir are deeply affected by regulations issued by the Israeli planning authorities. The central problem in the community today is the lack of legally-built housing, since Israeli zoning permits construction only in the center of the village. In that area, upwards building is replacing the traditional horizontal structure, swallowing the urban fabric and leaving no room for nostalgia or reliance on local building heritage. Despite official restrictions that crowd built-up areas, the neighborhood does not have a single open public space built or maintained by the municipality, to compensate for the resulting squeeze (it has as yet built only a few public structures). "The municipality has the ability to requisite lands for this purpose, and plans were prepared for that matter," says Abu Aslah. "But this municipality does not want to invest in us and to develop the village."

In the village center, the crowded construction has infiltrated private courtyards. Resident Fuad Jadalah explains that, lacking any other alternatives for children to play, "we hang a swing inside the house. Ten years ago, people had open courtyards; now there's no room." The pressure to build houses close together has overridden the desire for protected outdoor areas for women and children. Nor has the crowding been stayed by the economic benefits of courtyard agriculture. Discriminatory planning pushes Sur Bahir residents to build homes without permits, and as a result, illegally-built homes are regularly demolished by the municipality. Heaps of rubble from demolished homes scar the neighborhood, a visible reminder of the choked space.

THE CLASH OF ISRAELI PLANNING AND PALESTINIAN BUILDING

The municipality orders that these homes be demolished because of a specific Israeli planning perspective. This perspective cannot allow a blind eye to be turned to the subversive act of extensive, illegal Palestinian building. Nevertheless, only a small portion of these orders are implemented. I suggest that this partial implementation of official Israeli policy, seen alongside insufficient planning and investment in Palestinian neighborhoods, is evidence of Israeli confusion and embarrassment about the ethics of this policy. The authorities' fears and dreams restrict their ability to acknowledge different community and national needs (see the related essay in this volume by Naama Meishar and Yehotal Shapira). Moreover, the contradiction between Israeli policy and implementation is a sign of the Israeli authorities' conflicted policies concerning Palestinians' basic human rights, and the failures of the Israeli representation of the self versus the Other in East Jerusalem.

Put simply, the authorities fail to sufficiently and fairly provide for the needs of these residents, and construct instead a picture of them as law-breakers. The lack of official responsibility leaves these residents helpless, forcing them to bypass legal obligations and positioning them as a public for which these legal obligations do not apply. This undermines the basic moral foundation of Israel's democracy with all its implications. But the vast uncontrolled construction also exposes the failure and lack of logic of Israeli planning policies. Designed to control building activities, the strict rules have the opposite effect. Israeli hegemony over planning and architectural representation is undermined by the sheer energy with which the urban fabric is transformed by the people themselves.

A central quality of Sur Bahir's building culture is its foundation in the consent of extended families. This quality runs headlong into Israeli planning policy, which is conducted by a central sovereign authority managing ownership over most of the state's land. The planning authority decides on a "professional" basis the fastest way to settle large areas of land with the maximum amount of construction and the greatest (Jewish) population. Here, the planning process occurs from an aerial perspective and with a tautological view of the result. Israeli authorities then accuse the Palestinian public of possessing a "primitive" culture, which is responsible for not filling the gaps left by public planning—i.e. the residents' "failure" to turn private land into public schools, gardens, and so on. But planning in areas privately owned by clans who transfer property by inheritance and who rarely sell land outside the family can only be based on consent between the private owners. In Sur Bahir, the residents did not want to share knowledge about the subdivision of ownership with the planners working for the authorities.[12] Therefore, despite their existence and use in the pre-modern and modern era, public spaces are rarely available. A decline in the traditional social power of the extended family in favor of the needs of nuclear families and individuals creates problems for the greater population. A community's everyday basic necessities should direct planning. I would argue that, alongside discrimination and distress, the occupation has introduced a particular mechanism of planning, and a specific version and tempo of modernization. Among the horizons denied by the occupation is the possibility of creating a self-determined mechanism of planning and a self-inspired tempo of modernization. The diverse cultural fabric of Jerusalem sets challenges to contemporary planning unlike few cities in the world. In this context, the acknowledgement of specific representation and presentation of cultural differences and communities needs is an essential prerequisite to planning and design.

1   Abu Aslah is the head of the village's development committee. He worked as a planner in the Jerusalem municipality during both Jordanian and Israeli control. Dabash has initiated many welfare projects in the village since the 1960s and has documented over years Sur Bahir's building heritage. I would like to thank Naama Meishar for her important comments on this essay and for her partnership in the process of recording some of these memories.

2   These stones were not chiseled. They were minimally cut in a style called *khamy*.

3   According to Reilly (1981:91), the collective organization of the village or extended family was manifested in common use of various structures (such as ovens, a barn or a boardinghouse) (also see Robinson, 1907:101).

4   This analysis was inspired by the analysis of an African village by T. T. Minh-Ha and J. P. Bourdier (1996) and by T. T. Minh-Ha using these apprehensions of cultural criticism (Minh-Ha, 1992, 1999).

5   The village's developmental processes and its gradual urbanization are evident in a comparison of aerial photographs and maps of the neighborhood: in a Palestine Exploration Fund map from 1878, the village is marked schematically on the Bethlehem-Jerusalem road. The village is marked in this map in a way that does not allow estimation of its size. Other Palestinian villages in the Jerusalem area were marked in the same manner. In a map from 1933 (scale 1:10,000), clusters of houses can be seen alongside the Bethlehem-Jerusalem road. In a map from 1943 (scale 1:1250), it is possible to see how the building in clusters began to disperse towards the tilled agricultural lands. Marks of caves appear in the area, as well as many waterholes between the houses and several places that served both for cultivating wheat and as a place of gathering for families from the same clan. Many buildings are marked on agricultural lands. The mosque grew immensely, and several other common buildings can be seen. An aerial photograph from 2002 shows the continued urbanization process, particularly along the main roads. An urban succession is evident in extensive areas, and there is almost no space (courtyard) between buildings. The buildings themselves grow both in width and in height over time.

6   *Debka* is a dance customary during Palestinian weddings.

7   The most prominent verse of the Quran, which is recited at most ceremonies. Today, village wedding processions follow the village streets, without visiting the local shrine.

8   In Sur Bahir there were at first three main families, each with its own *saha*. Over time, ten different *sahas* developed; today, one family has revived the custom and uses only one *saha* for special occasions.

9   A *maqam*, or shrine of a village saint. Up until the late 1920s, saint shrines were abundant throughout Palestine as sites of pilgrimage and prayer (Canaan, 1927:2) Sur Bahir's shrines and religious sites included: Sheikh Dawary's djami; Omar ibn al-Khattab (17) (now the old mosque of the neighborhood); es-Sh Neni (26) (now unknown); es-Sh Ismail (now known only as a neighborhood); and es-Sh Suwan.(22) (an existing cave, one part of the neighborhood called after es-Sh Suwan) (22); and the mosque/djami Omar ibn al-Hattab (17) (now the old mosque of the neighborhood).

10 Sur Bahir was considered a Jerusalem satellite village. The village is located in the first ring surrounding the city, approximately five kilometers from the city center. Its agricultural produce was sold in the city's markets. (Tamari, 1999:77-78).

11 Abu Aslah explains: "Say I would wish to go back to [agriculture]; it's not profitable. The yard [only] supplements the household income."

12 Local participation in the planning process is now recommended by the Israel authorities (Litzfield, 1994) for planning in the Arab sector, becoming a significant model for planning in Israel. Planning by assent, as central to the Palestinian tradition, is in fact participatory planning. Participation of the individual in the environment is also present in Palestinian building culture where habitation and building are negotiated and shared with the extended family.

Selected Bibliography

Gil Ayal, "Ben Mizrach vMaarav: HaSicha al 'HaKfar HaAravi' biIsrael," Teoria vBiqoret ["Between East and West: The Discourse on the 'Arab Village' in Israel," Theory and Criticism] (Tel Aviv: Van Leer Jerusalem Institute, Hakibbutze Hameuchad Publishing House, 1993).

Yehoshua Ben Arie, "Sanjak Yerushalayim biShnot HaShevaim shel HaMea Ha-19," ["The Sanjak of Jerusalem in the 1870s," Cathedra 36 (Jerusalem: Yad Izhak Ben Zvi, 1985).

Tawfiq Canaan, Mohammedan Saints and Sanctuaries in Palestine (London: Luzak, 1927).

Tawfiq Canaan, "Plant-lore in Palestinian Superstition," Journal of the Palestine Oriental Society 8 (1928).

Tawfiq Canaan. "The Palestinian Arab house—Its Architecture and Folklore (Jerusalem: Syrian Orphanage Press, 1933).

Ron Fuchs. "HaBeit HaAravi HaEretz Israeli: Aiyun miHadash" ["The Palestinian Arab House Reconsidered," Part 1 & 2, Cathedra 89-90] (Jerusalem: Yad Izhak Ben Zvi, 1998).

Stuart Hall, "The Work of Representation," in Representation: Cultural Representations and Signifying Practice (London: Sage Publications, 1997).

Yizhar Hirschfeld, Beit HaMegorim HaEretz Israeli biTqofa HaRomit Bizantit [Dwelling Houses in Roman and Byzantine Palestine] (Jerusalem: Yad Izhak Ben Zvi, 1987).

Wolf-Dieter Hutteroth and Kamal Abdulfattah, Historical Geography of Palestine, Transjordan, and Southern Syria in the Late 16th Century (Erlangen: Fraenkische Geographische Gesellschaft, 1977).

Ruth Kark and Michal Oren-Nordheim, Jerusalem and Its Environs Quarters, Neighborhoods, Villages, 1800–1948 (Jerusalem: Magnes, Hebrew University and Leicester University Press, 2002).

Yosef Jabarin and Hubert Law-Yone, Planning the Arab Towns in Israel (Haifa: The Technion, 1998).

Litzfieled Dalia, Litzfieled Netanel, Tohnit Mitar Gemisha Madrih LeThnon Ir Kayemet, Menhal HaTihnon Misrad HaPnim, [Flexible Statutory City Plan Guide for Planning Existing Town, Jerusalem Planning Administration Interior Ministry], 1994.

Trinh. Thi. Minh-Ha, Cinema Interval (New York: Routledge, 1999).

Trinh-Thi-Minh-Ha, Framer Framed (New York: Routledge, 1992).

Trinh-Thi-Minh-Ha and Jean-Paul Bourdier, Drawn from African Dwellings (Bloomington: Indiana University Press, 1996).

Michal Oren-Nordheim, "Ein Karem - Hitpathut HaShetah HaBanoy" ["Ein Karem - Developing of the Built Area"] (seminar work, Department of Geography, Hebrew University,1985).

James Reilly, "The Peasantry of Late Ottoman Palestine," Journal of Palestine Studies 10 (4) (1981).

George Lees Robinson, Village Life in Palestine (London: Longmans Green and Co, 1907).

Salim Tamari, Jerusalem 1948: The Arab Neighborhoods and Their Fate in the War, (Jerusalem: Institute of Jerusalem Studies El Bethlehem: Badil Resource Center for Palestinian Residency and Refugee Rights, 1999).

Shapira Yehotal, Israeliness and Space, A Case Study: Sataf: Representation and Other Spatial Possibilities as Subjective and Cultural Landscape (M.A. thesis, Faculty of Humanities, Hebrew University, 2004).

Hosh and Apartment

school

school

mosc

mosque

mosque

mosque

Arab Village
Sur Bahir (2005)

*case study
see next page*

school

chool

school

mosque

mosque

0 50 100 150 200 250 meters

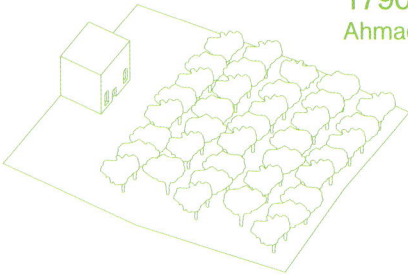

1790
Ahmad

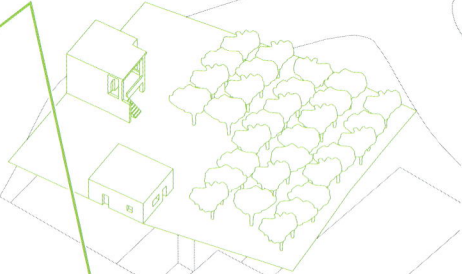

1920
Ahmad

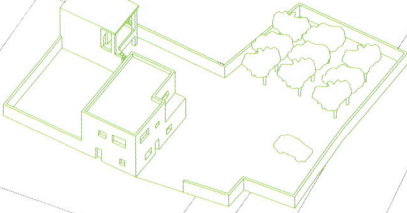

1960
Ismail

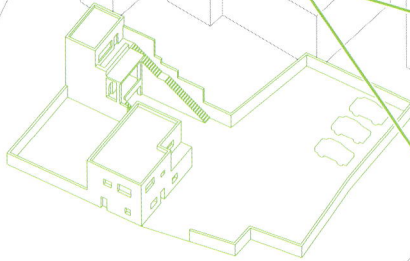

1968
Muhammed

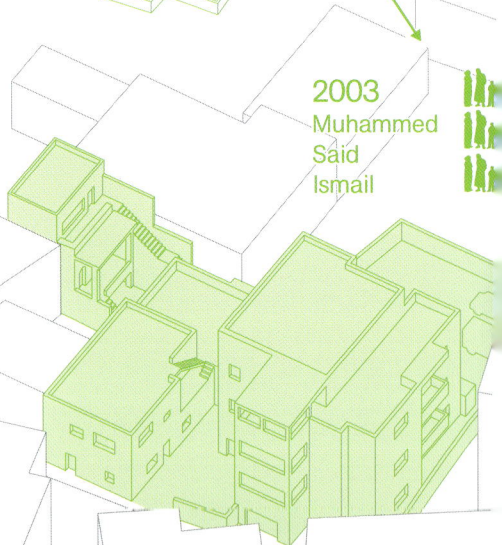

2003
Muhammed
Said
Ismail

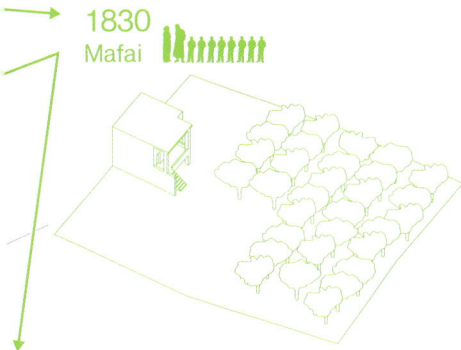

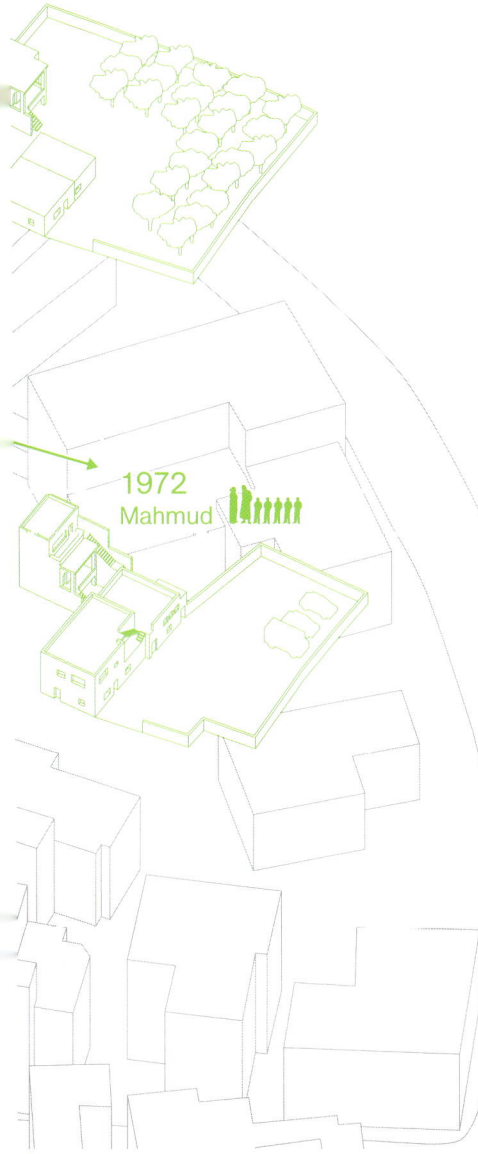

Growing House
Sur Bahir (1790-2005)

The traditional Palestinian family home is formed around a *hosh* (courtyard) shared by a multi-generational family. Ownership is passed on through patrilinear division and inheritance, serving as future generations' source of stability and security. The *hosh* system evolves gradually, based on a principle of slow growth. Little is ever demolished. Buildings are added, extended or upgraded in accordance with the spatial needs and economic abilities of the growing families. Over time, the *hosh* becomes dense and vertical, acquiring formal and architectural complexity. The biography of *hosh* and family are intertwined and its architecture reflects Palestinian cultural history where historical and modern building traditions persist simultaneously (for example, solid stone domes from Ottoman times were extended with rectangular masonry of the British Mandate period). Traditional solid limestone structures have been replaced today by cheaper stone cladding over modern reinforced concrete.

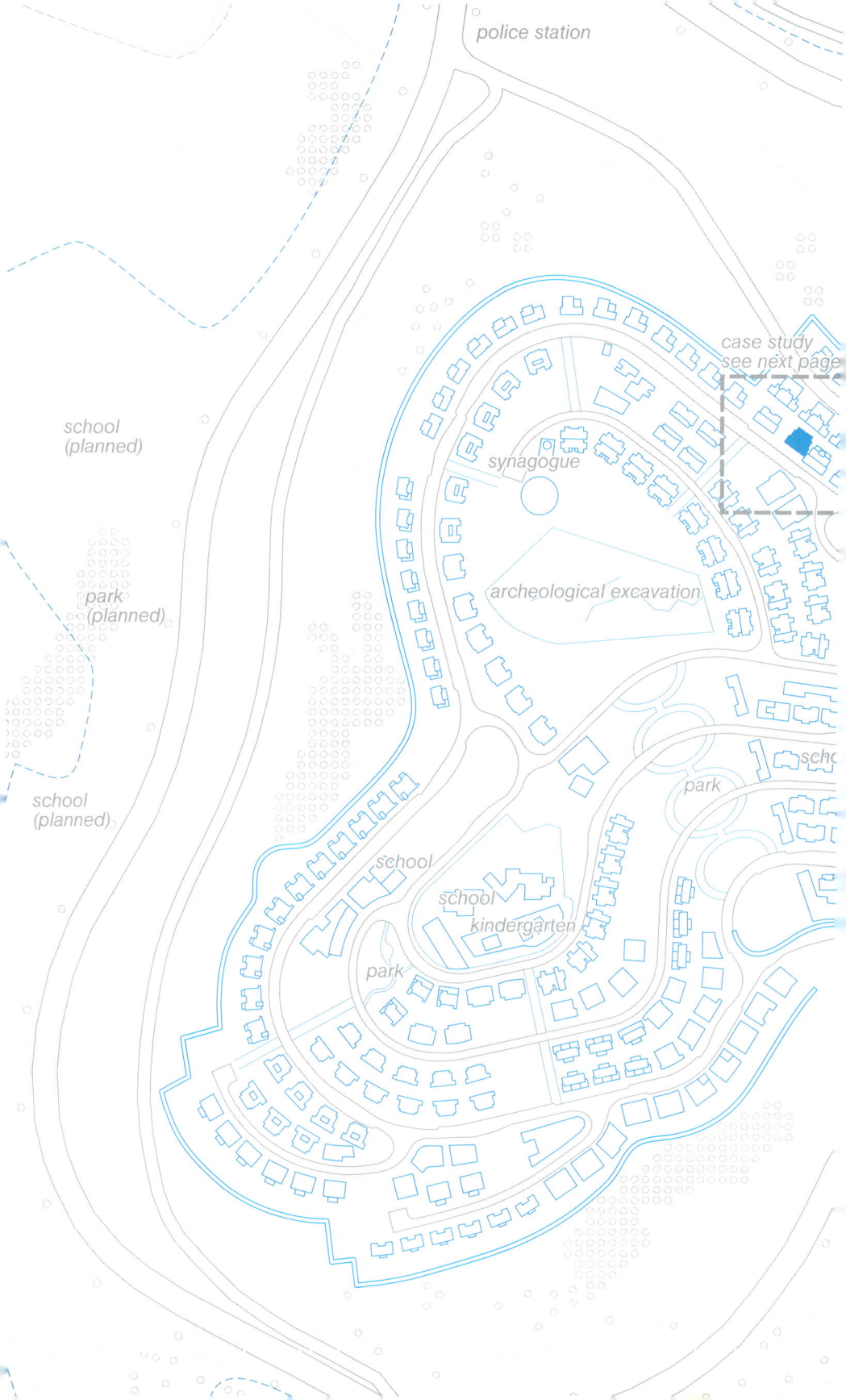

police station

case study
see next page

school
(planned)

synagogue

park
(planned)

archeological excavation

school
(planned)

scho

park

school

school

kindergarten

park

Jewish Settlement
Har Homa (2005)

kindergarten
(planned)

commercial center
(planned)

park

expansion area for Har Homa

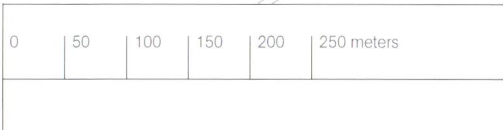

| 0 | 50 | 100 | 150 | 200 | 250 meters |

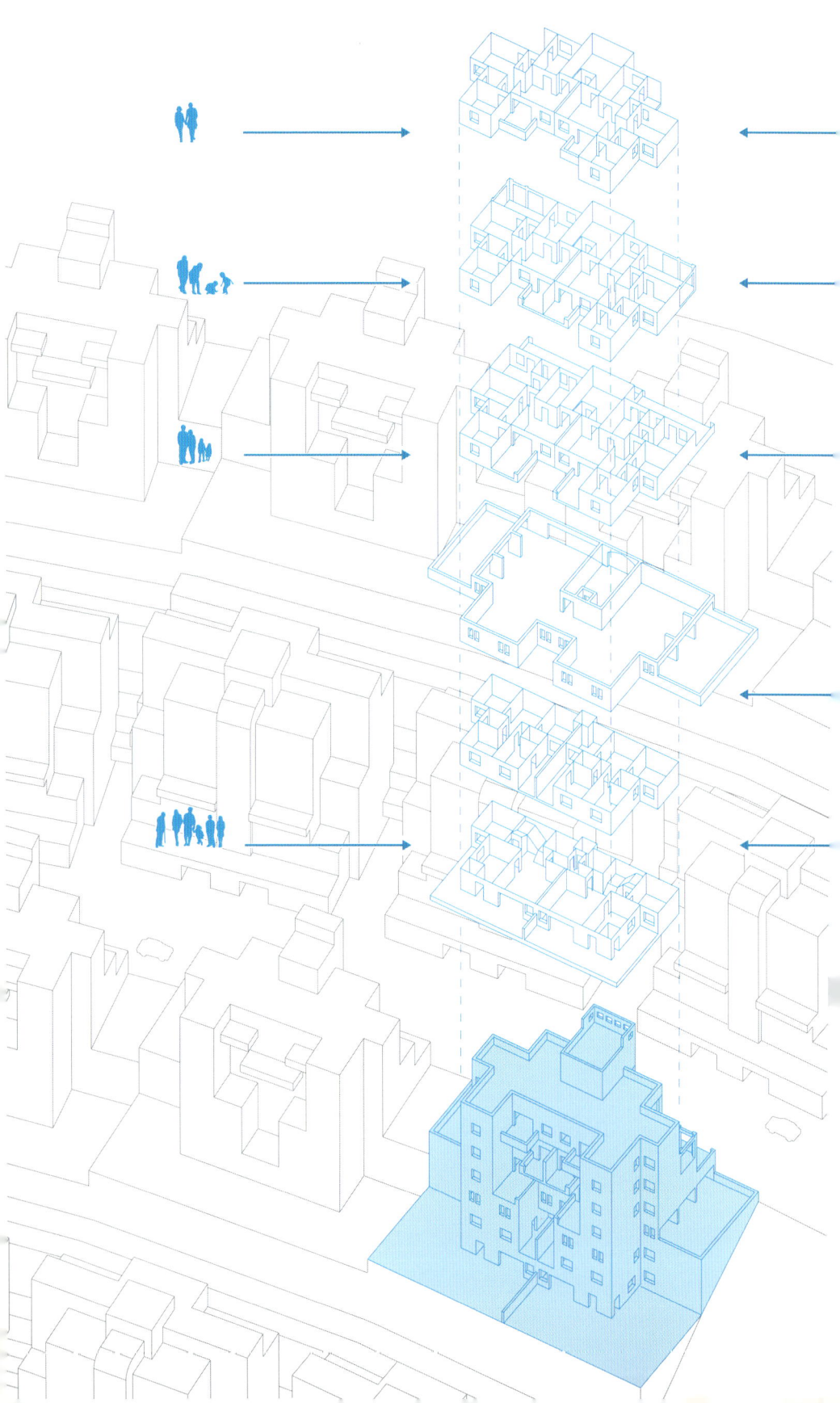

Instant House
Har Homa (2005)

The Israeli settlement of Har Homa is a state-initiated and subsidized housing project, accommodating in its first phase more than 10,000 inhabitants. Its layout and form follow a combined logic of security (circular with reduced access points at the hill's apex), standardized construction techniques (repetitive stacked units), accessibility by car (underground parking) and predicted market demands (size and layout of units designed for young secular middle class families). Following a tradition of western modernist planning, architects have assumed an authoritarian role in determining, in a single gesture, the entirety of the urban environment, from architectural form and detail to the design of public places, schools, commercial zones, etc. This approach allows little flexibility for adapting to residents' needs. Fast-track, top-down planning also serves the strategic political aim of rapidly establishing facts on the ground to secure territorial control.

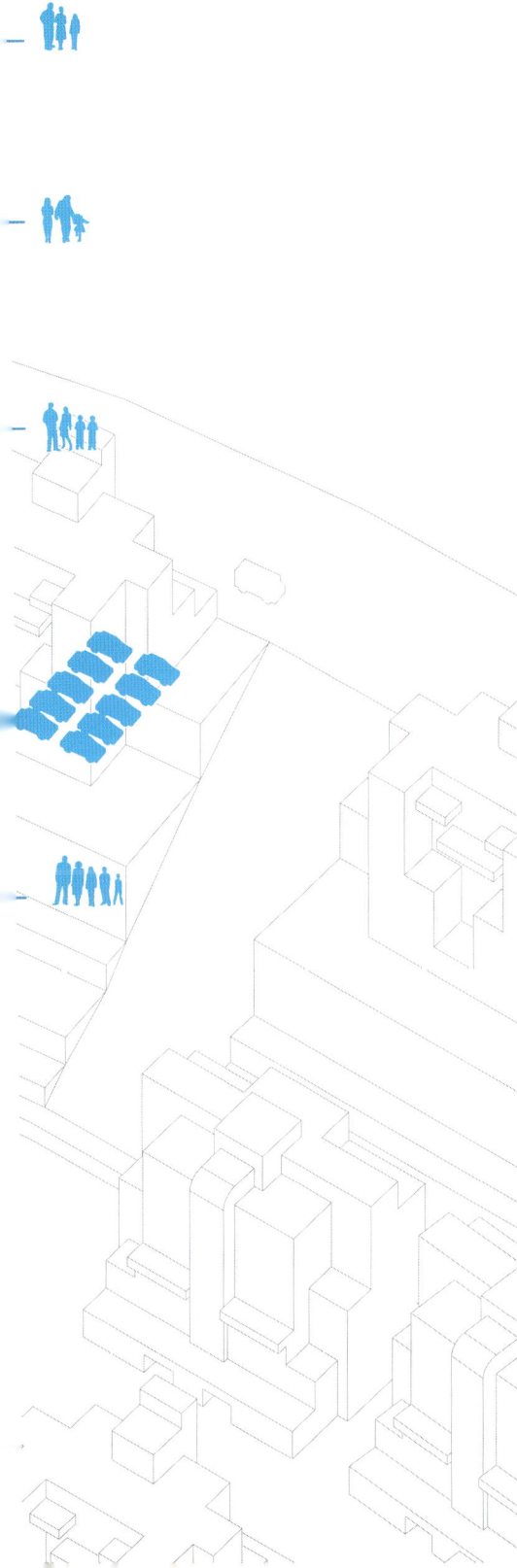

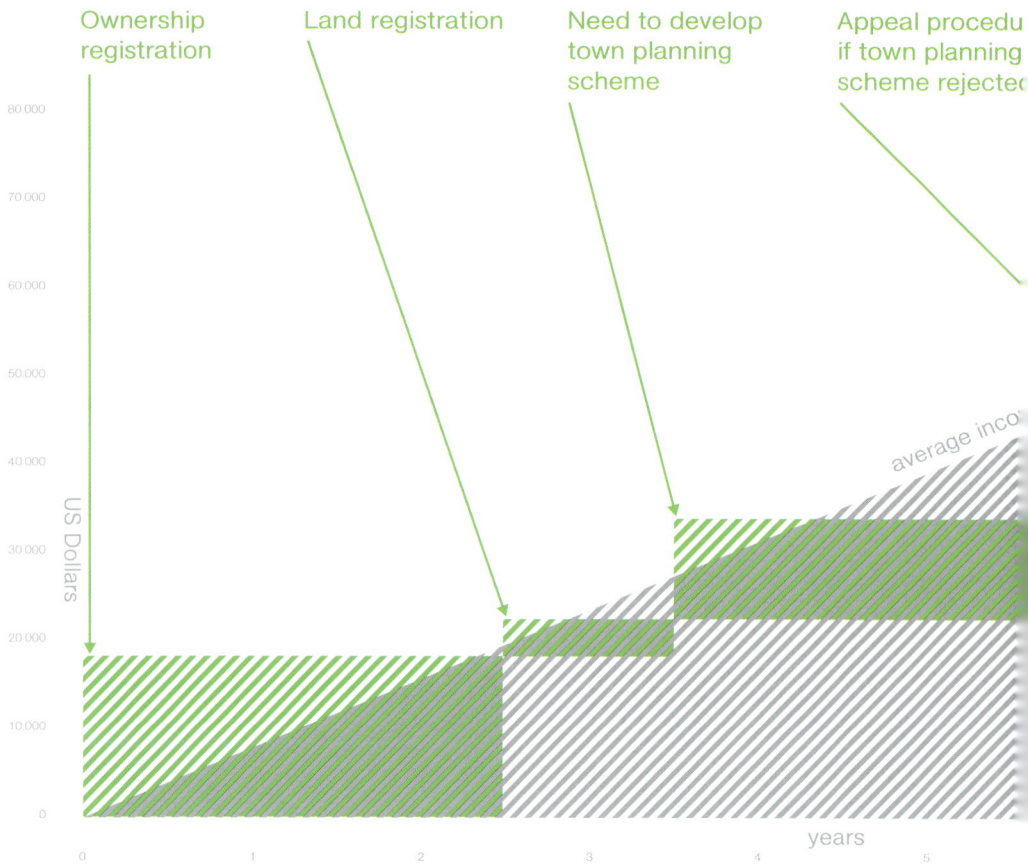

Ownership
registration

Land registration

Need to develop
town planning
scheme

Appeal procedu
if town planning
scheme rejected

average inco

US Dollars

80 000
70 000
60 000
50 000
40 000
30 000
20 000
10 000
0

years

0   1   2   3   4   5

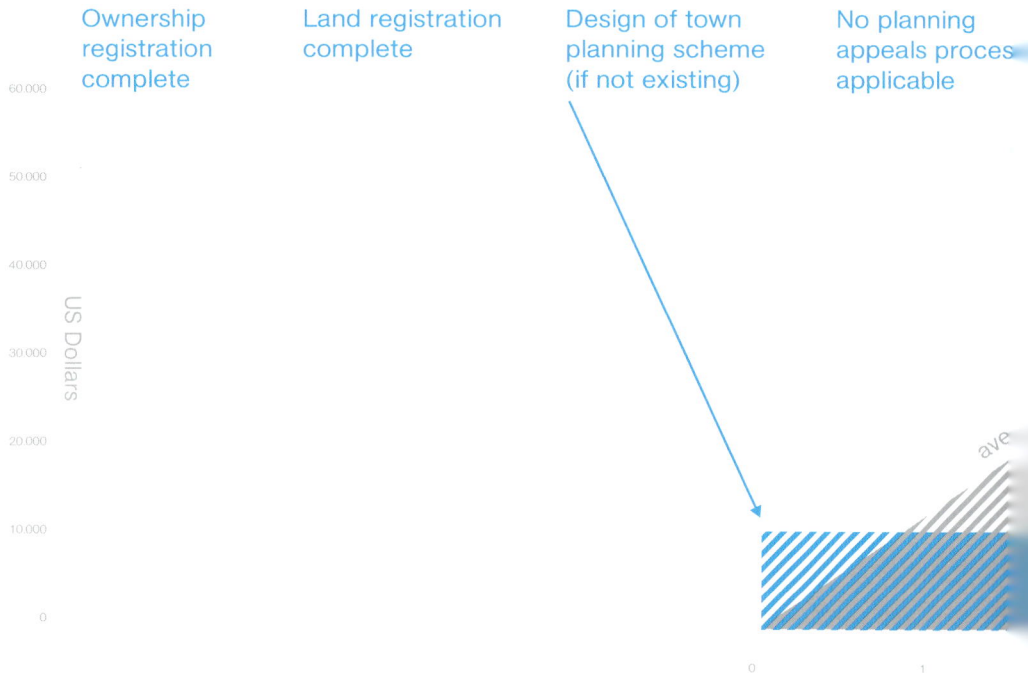

Ownership
registration
complete

Land registration
complete

Design of town
planning scheme
(if not existing)

No planning
appeals proces
applicable

ave

US Dollars

60 000
50 000
40 000
30 000
20 000
10 000
0

0   1

Building Process
Cost and Time

In Jerusalem, the production of urban space is strongly related to the political and judicative inequality that exists between Jewish and Arab citizens. While Jewish Israelis receive incentives to rent or purchase apartments in state-initiated public housing programs, Palestinians are both excluded from these programs and denied the right to build on their own land. Vast expropriations programs since 1967 have dramatically reduced Palestinian land reserves. In the remaining pockets of private land, Palestinians are subjected to a restrictive planning regime riddled with legal and financial hurdles. In many cases, property remained unregistered and outside municipal planning schemes. As a result, Palestinians resort to large-scale illegal building. According to Israeli estimates, more than half of Palestinian housing units in East Jerusalem have been constructed without building permits and thus are threatened with demolition, a policy that is not applied to illegal Jewish construction.

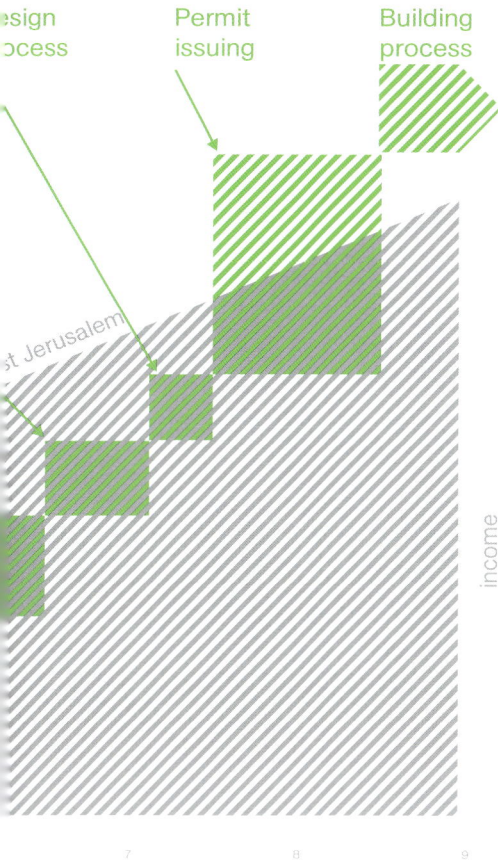

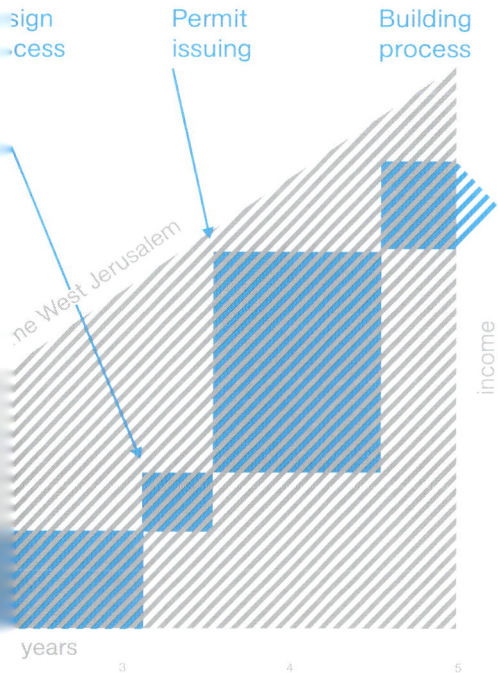

Design process

Permit issuing

Building process

East Jerusalem

income

7   8   9

Design process

Permit issuing

Building process

...ne West Jerusalem

income

years

3   4   5

Cost/duration for Palestinian landlords

Cost/duration for Israeli landlords

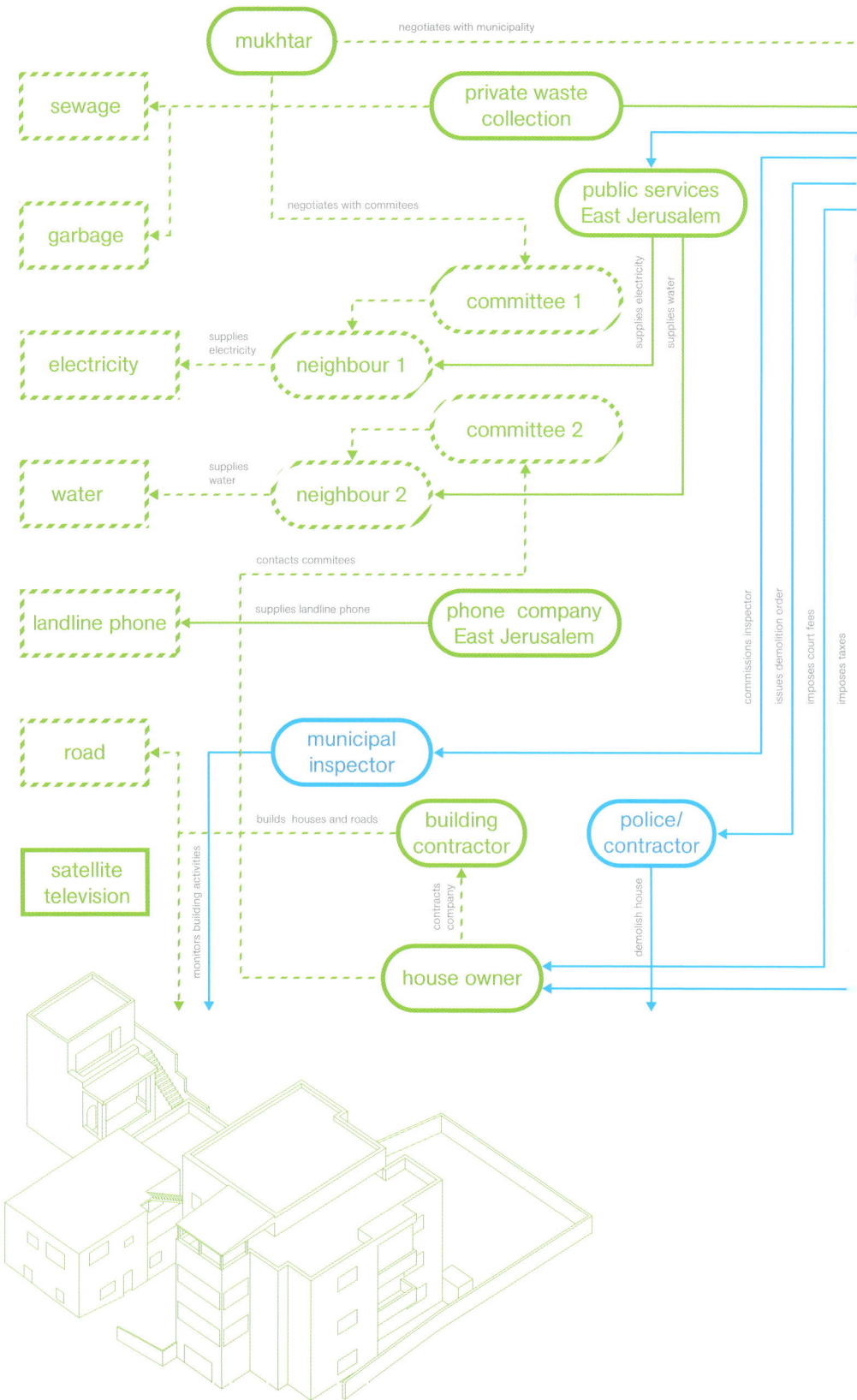

mukhtar — negotiates with municipality

sewage

private waste collection

garbage

public services East Jerusalem

negotiates with commitees

committee 1

electricity — supplies electricity

neighbour 1

supplies electricity

supplies water

committee 2

water — supplies water

neighbour 2

contacts commitees

landline phone — supplies landline phone

phone company East Jerusalem

commissions inspector

issues demolition order

imposes court fees

imposes taxes

road

municipal inspector

satellite television

building contractor — builds houses and roads

police/ contractor

monitors building activities

contracts company

demolish house

house owner

Construction Process Interaction

Palestinian and Jewish construction in East Jerusalem incorporate profound differences indicative of existing power relations. While Israeli settlements are state-initiated and subsidized housing projects, Palestinian construction is excluded from municipal investment. The owner of a dwelling built without a building permit for example relies on a complex, semi-formal family and neighborhood support system for constructing road extensions or tapping into existing water, electricity, or sewage networks, as well as conducting pragmatic negotiations with the Israeli authorities. Many Palestinians pay high municipal taxes on illegally-built structures in the hope of eventually legalizing them. For the same reason, illegally-built structures often follow Israeli building design criteria. Wherever possible, Israeli legal loopholes are explored: Palestinian municipal trash collectors or bus drivers frequently ignore the rules by servicing illegal buildings or areas outside the municipal boundaries.

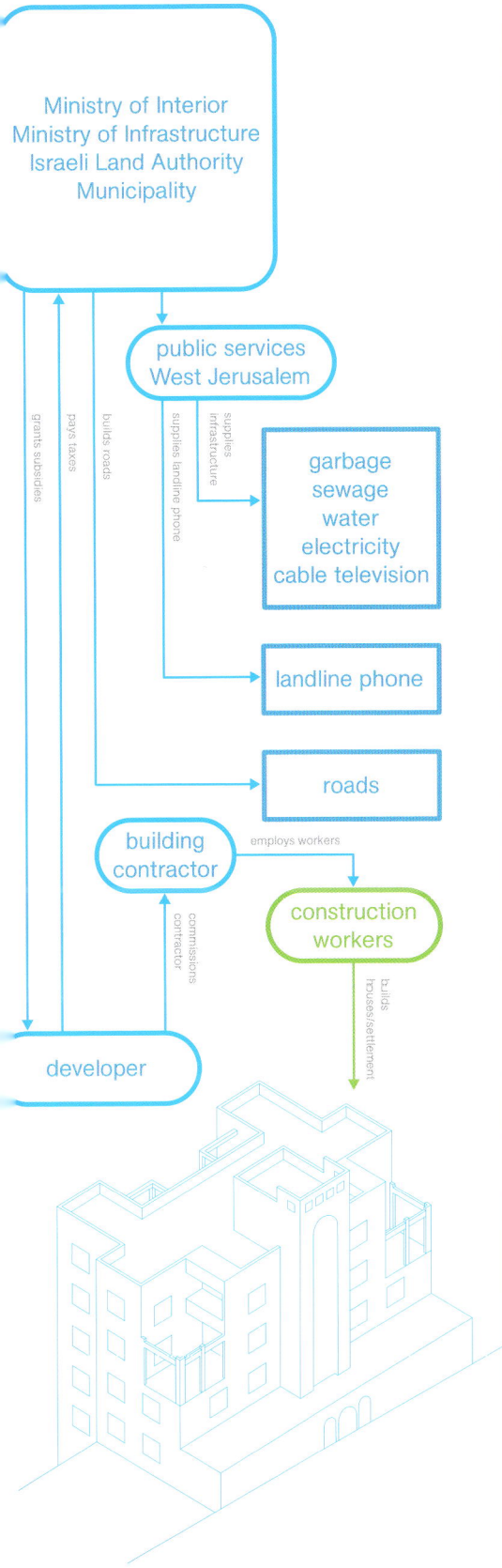

Ministry of Interior
Ministry of Infrastructure
Israeli Land Authority
Municipality

public services
West Jerusalem

garbage
sewage
water
electricity
cable television

landline phone

roads

building contractor

construction workers

developer

grants subsidies
pays taxes
builds roads
supplies infrastructure
supplies landline phone
employs workers
commissions contractor
builds houses/settlement

phon East	Palestinian actors
neig	Palestinian actors (Informal/ilegal processes)
mu ins	Israeli actors
landli	Palestinian infrastructures
wat	Palestinian infrastructures (Informal/ilegal)
landli	Israeli infrastructures

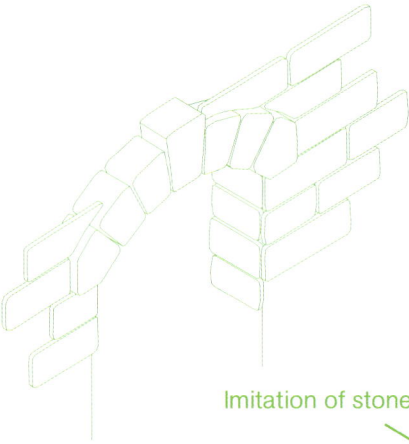

Imitation of stone arches

decorative crenellation

Imitation of vernacular building forms

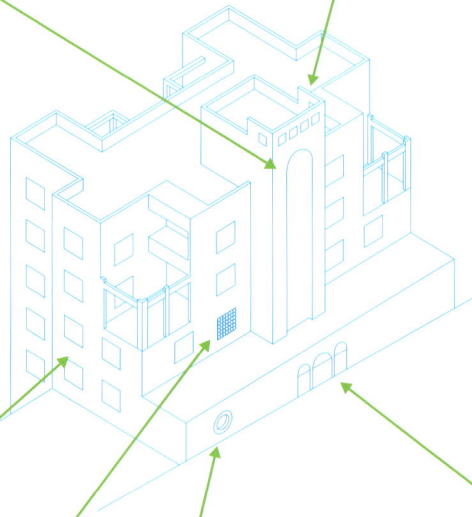

Mashrabiya

Imitation of circular
stone window

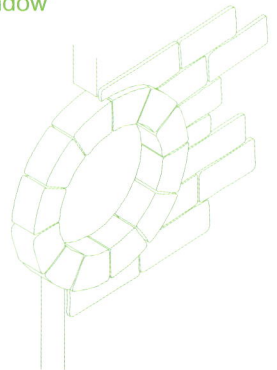

Sloped roofs
with shingles

Architecture
Adaptations

Beyond formal and cultural differences which
allow the immediate ethnic identification of
an Israeli or Palestinian home, Jerusalem
also shows how the presence of the other is
negotiated through architectural means. With
close examination, an ambivalent relationship
is revealed: Israeli buildings include elements
of Palestinian vernacular architecture—a rustic
stone finish, arched windows or the simulation of
age through design gestures. At the same time,
Palestinian homes are being modernized and
extended using western construction techniques
(built as compact, multi-storey dwellings with
tiled roofs) and equipped with Israeli appliances.
Here, the proximity to Israeli culture is resisted as
a colonial influence, and admired as a window
on modernity and Western lifestyles.

Transfer of modern
construction techniques

tation of rustic
ck works

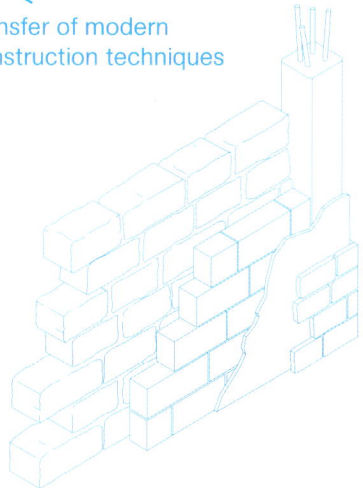

Concept and copyright

Tim Rieniets, Philipp Misselwitz

Sources

Project Grenzgeografien (International Peace and Cooperation Center IPCC Jerusalem, Bezalel Academy of Art and Design Jerusalem, University of the Arts Berlin, ETH Swiss Federal Institute of Technology Zurich), *Trilateral Student Workshops* (Jerusalem, 2003-2005).

BARRIERS LINKS

East Jerusalem's fragmented spatial units rely on an extensive infrastructure for access, supply, and protection. The Israeli-Palestinian conflict has produced a set of typologies that simultaneously connect and separate different spaces. A highway linking suburban settlements directly to the body of the city is also a barrier for Palestinians living along the road who have no access to it. Sixty kilometers of the Separation Wall/Fence in the Jerusalem area, justified to protect Israeli citizens from attacks, contorts through space, linking Israeli areas while slicing through the Palestinian socioeconomic fabric. More often, however, the strategic agenda creating barriers and gateways is hidden behind the seemingly benign objectives of urban planning. As a result, urban space becomes suspicious and insecure, fuelling bias and mistrust.

SPECTERS OF TERROR

Stephen Graham

New York: September 11, 2001; Madrid, March 11, 2003; London, July 7, 2005—the legacy and specter of catastrophic terror haunt the collective unconscious of Western cities in the early 21st century. Of course, terrorism in Western cities is nothing new. A long history of domestic terror campaigns in the West has been fuelled by subnational independence struggles or Left-Right ideological battles. But due to the scale of their operations, the culture of martyrdom shared by their volunteers, and the transnational diasporic character of the communities from which those volunteers come, Islamist terror networks and their imitators call into question the deepest underlying assumptions about Western urbanism.

Such attacks add further impetus to an already palpable militarization of urban space in many Western cities, fuelled by social polarization, urban sprawl, the proliferation of fortified enclaves, and an intensifying culture of fear. Moreover, these recent attacks have led to widespread calls, especially from right wing commentators, for the radical redesign of the physical, technical and social architectures of cities in order to fight the "new enemy within." After 9/11, for example, many US urban commentators called for an acceleration of sprawl and an end to skyscraper construction so that iconic urban targets were less likely to attract similar attacks. Across the major cities of the Western world, policy-makers addressing transport, immigration, urban design, architecture, community policing, and social policy have suddenly been forced to concern themselves with how their work might become "counter-terrorist."

But who exactly is this "enemy within"? And "within" what exactly does this alleged enemy exist? Can rethinking cities really prevent catastrophic terror attacks? And what might the possible dangers be in attempting to rethink urbanism so as to apprehend this "enemy"? In what follows, I will explore three key points that, I argue, need to be central to any discussion on the links between terrorism and contemporary Western cities.

TRANSNATIONAL URBANISM, TRANSNATIONAL TERROR

My first point is that terror attacks are, in their own way, horrific moments that reveal some of the complex dynamics of "transnational urbanism"—as Michael Peter Smith termed it (Smith, 2001). Such attacks reveal the porosity of Western urban sites to the transnational networks that crosscut and constitute them, as much as any global financial marketplace, cultural mediascape, tourist experience or commodity chain. Disaffected and radicalized Islamists, either directly

linked to transnational terror groups, or using TV and the Internet to imitate
the latter's tactics, become convinced that martyrdom will avenge Western and
Israeli military assaults on the everyday sites, spaces and lives of Muslim cities
and their residents. Internet sites help to propagate the extreme ideologies of
the martyrdom, dehumanization, and hatred needed to recruit potential attackers.
Be they second or third generation citizens of Western nations, or visitors with
temporary visas or immigration documents, attackers do not require access to
substantial military hardware. In their eyes, cities, particularly Western cities,
consist of and are constituted by an infinite number of "soft targets."

Thus, airplanes hijacked by a few terrorists wielding box cutters become
suicidal cruise missiles, which, when carefully flown into the world's largest
modernist structures, bring about devastation akin to a tactical nuclear attack.
The world's TV networks, zoomed in on Manhattan, provided the perfect form
of transmission for the terrorists' message as it broadcast the second plane's
impact "live" across the globe: you are our target and nowhere is safe. Invariably
crowded buses, subways and suburban trains provide confined spaces where
devastation, bloodshed, and media frenzy can be maximized. The very bodies of
the perpetrators become both perfect camouflage and perfect weapon, mingling
unnoticeably into the vast ebb and flow of the contemporary, globalized city.
Smart new technologies like the Internet and mobile phones provide triggers
(as with Madrid 3/11), as well as the means to plan and coordinate attacks, acquire
technical information on bomb-making, and deliver triumphant propaganda after
the fact. When extended to tourist sites of leisure and pleasure (as with the
two sets of attacks in Bali), the purpose is clear: to undermine notions of bodily
safety and security—an essential element of Western urbanism—and to promul-
gate the fear that the banal sites, spaces, and technologies of the Westernized
cityscape can erupt in orgies of death and destruction at any moment, regardless
of geographic location.

THE DILEMMAS OF URBAN ANTITERRORISM

My second point is that once people become radicalized to the point of committing
themselves to urban suicide attacks, the prospects of preventing those attacks
are limited. Improving the efforts of security agencies to generate intelligence
that would make it possible to intercept attackers before they strike, offers the
best immediate hope for undermining further attacks. Whilst there have been
some successes in this area, improving intelligence is extremely difficult. With
many attackers apparently imitating the broader ideologies and tactics of al-Qaeda
and their like, and attackers with Western citizenships volunteering for the job
(as with London 7/7), it is all too easy for attacks to be planned using readily
available materials and information without being detected. However, Western
police and intelligence agencies could certainly improve their coordination, and
gathering and exchange of information, thereby improving their chances of inter-
cepting attackers before they strike.

Major efforts are currently underway to reengineer strategic urban spaces and
infrastructures so that they are equipped with increasingly sophisticated surveillance systems. Many precedents apply here. The financial center of London, for

example, was wrapped in a "Ring of Steel" during the 1990s to counter IRA bomb attacks. Roads were closed and a "wall" of smart CCTV sensors was strung up around the area. These automatically scan for "abnormal" events such as stolen cars being driven in or cars driving the "wrong way" down a one-way street.

The post-9/11 surveillance surge may enable known terrorist suspects to be tracked more easily. "Defensive" urban design can help to minimize the damage of terrorist bombings on strategic urban spaces. For example, metal detectors can help to secure vulnerable buildings but there are no "quick fixes" and "silver bullets" when the population willing to commit terrorist attacks is utterly indistinguishable from the general population of a city or state.

Then there are the fundamental permeabilities and almost infinite complexities of contemporary cities. These inevitably undermine simple technical solutions to possible terrorist attacks. Technologies fail or do not work as intended. Systems always have blind spots. The human vigilance that backs up technologies wavers, a weakness that can be exploited by determined attackers. Moreover, the fact that the very fabric of a city is made up of what terrorists regard as "soft targets," makes it extremely difficult to defend against determined attacks that have reached the launching point. The hopes attached to emerging technologies, too, may be false. Face-recognition CCTV, for example, which is being heralded by military and security technology companies as a means to track known suspects, is only effective when people stand in line in decent lighting conditions and can be carefully scrutinized at what sociologists call "obligatory passage points" (in airports or sports stadiums, for example). In the jumble of city streets, with rapidly varying weather, light and facial angles—face recognition is rather ineffective.

Furthermore, the unplanned side effects of radical urban antiterrorist policies might be extremely damaging for urban life in the broader sense. Attempts to turn the *mêlée* of cities into a system of securitized points of passage where every person is observed, scrutinized and matched up to facial and/or other ID databases, could quickly make urban life untenable and intolerable. Successful cities, after all, are based on the freedom to move and interact, on the power of serendipitous contact and on the sheer creative capacity of dense and unpredictable mixture. The worry here, then, is that attempts will be made by governments (and the security-military-industrial complexes which have burgeoned since the advent of the "war on terror") to reengineer cities so that their porous, open and intrinsically fluid spaces and systems become little more than an endless series of securitized passage points (either visible or invisible). If this were to happen, the millennia-old tradition of urban anonymity would be sacrificed. The very vibrancy that marks all successful cities might simply be engineered away. Democratic civil liberties attained through social and political struggle over centuries might be abandoned in the name of "fighting terrorism." With the mantra of "security" creeping over every domain of public life and public policy—previously dominated by other concerns such as urban design, social welfare, immigration policy, transportation management and city planning—there is a real risk that with the excuse of stopping terrorists, the very processes of interchange, interconnection, privacy, political organizing, and the social and

18.6 km: outside Damascus Gate

democratic innovation that make cities livable, dynamic, creative, and successful, might be seriously undermined.

Chances are, though, that the effort to "securitize" every domain of public life might be hampered by an unlikely source: big business. Indeed, if borders and movement within and between cities were to be placed under an ever-intensifying armory of continuous checks and exclusions, the mobility and freedom required by transnational urbanism and global capitalism may also be severely undermined. Since 9/11, many US corporations have complained that they have suffered major losses by not being able to bring in employees, affiliates, recruits, and colleagues from around the world due to the extreme tightening of US national borders. But radical urban securitization strategies involve another major risk. The reliance of Western law enforcement and intelligence agencies on crude profiling techniques, which place citizen and resident Arabs and Muslims under extreme scrutiny, restriction and, in some cases, detention without trial, has in many cases served to deepen the sense of grievance, marginalization, and criminalization already felt in these communities. Coupled with the widespread demonization of Arabs and Muslims in Hollywood movies and mainstream Western media, many people living in Arab neighborhoods in Western cities feel like they have been living in a state of siege since 9/11. Facing rising racist violence, arson and murder, as well as increasing repression at the hands of security forces, many in such communities feel that they are branded as terrorists even though they condemn terrorist attacks and may have long been working to reduce the power of radical Islamist ideologies and recruitment networks.

ENDING THE CIRCLE OF ATROCITY?

In the end, then—and this is my third point—the only sustainable way of preventing catastrophic terror attacks against Western cities and their residents is to address the grievances which make it possible in the first place for radical Islamist ideologies and ideologues to successfully recruit and radicalize large numbers of activists and attackers. There is virtually no known history of technical or military assault successfully ending a terrorist campaign. In the long run, only political and geopolitical change, which address political and geopolitical injustices, can reduce the number of recruits and render violence illegitimate among those who might otherwise have explicitly or implicitly condoned it. Moreover, quasi-Imperial military assaults against cities or states allegedly harboring "terrorists" only result in the deaths of thousands of innocent civilians and—as even the CIA has admitted in the case of the US-UK invasion of Iraq—serve as massive recruitment aids to terrorist and insurgent groups.

Here a grim irony presents itself, one that urbanists are in a good position to spot. Terrorist acts against Western cities and their inhabitants mirror prevalent Western policies of inflicting catastrophic violence upon Muslim and Arab urban centers and their inhabitants. Of course, the means of delivering the violence could not differ more starkly: "smart bombs" and "cluster bombs" vs. the corporeal immediacy of the suicide bomber; laser and GPS targeting vs. lone perpetrators boarding a train, plane or bus; media-obsessed "shock and awe" campaigns orchestrated via satellite vs. low-grade propaganda web sites and grainy video footage of murdered civilians, "martyrs," and "victorious" attacks on "infidels." But both share deep similarities. Both strategies target the everyday urban spaces and systems of the "enemy" indiscriminately in order to project symbolic violence and coercive power aimed at mass media consumption. Both either deliberately try to kill as many innocent civilians as possible, or callously disregard the inevitability that many innocent civilians will die. Finally, on both sides, the complex social and cultural fabrics forged by the dynamics of transnational urbanism are systematically ignored so that such cities can be essentialized, demonized and dehumanized as preludes to violent attacks against them. Thus, state terror begets holy terror (and vice versa). A circle of atrocity emerges with both sides proclaiming themselves as righteous victims seeking revenge and justice through violence. And the everyday sites, symbols, and infrastructures of the city become the key targets of this new form of transnational, networked warfare.

The real challenge, then, is not to securitize cities against imminent terrorist attacks. Rather, it is to assert the power, strength, value, and inevitability of a mixed-up transnational urbanism in the face of both violent nationalist and imperialist projects and extremist religious ideologies. Only then might the racist foreign policies of Western states, with their catastrophic targeting of Muslim and Arab cities and their residents, and the reign of holy terror promulgated by al-Qaeda and their imitators, be eradicated.

The place to start is the crucially important acknowledgement that, in an intensely globalizing and urbanizing world, transitional urbanism will inevitably create cities, which are hybrid and infinitely complex jumbles of difference. (Graham (ed.), 2004) This leads to five concluding points. First, in this world, all notions of national, ethnic, or religious purity—including the crude and incendiary notion of an "enemy within" some putatively homogenous imagined community—amount to calls to violence. Second, all attacks against the urban everyday spaces of transnational, mixed-up cities will end in the killing and injuring of people from a vast kaleidoscope of national, ethnic, social, and religious communities. Third, in such a world, the only hope is a transnational civil society, which works to marginalize extremist and violent national, ethnic, and religious ideologies. Fourth, such a society can only be based on the key building blocks of the diverse and "mongrel" urban spheres that are key to our globalizing age. (Sandercock, 2003) And fifth, successful transnational cities can demonstrate that the diversities of this world can coexist with something akin to collective tolerance (or at least in a state where inevitable frictions and grievances need not spiral catastrophically into dehumanization and cycles of atrocity). Destroy and erode this crucial role of cities through over-zealous anti-terrorist campaigns in the West and Middle East, and the dance of death will only gain momentum.

Selected Bibliography

Michael Peter Smith, *Transnational Urbanism*, (Blackwell, 2001).

Stephen Graham (ed.), *Cities, War and Terrorism* (Blackwell, 2004).

Leonie Sandercock, *Cosmopolis II: Mongrel Cities in the 21st Century* (Continuum, 2003).

JERUSALEM: FROM SIEGE TO A CITY'S COLLAPSE?

Rassem Khamaisi and Rami Nasrallah

The issue of Israel's construction of encircling cement walls, fencing, patrol roads, and guard towers around Palestinian population centers, has headed the Palestinian-Israeli agenda for the past two years. Israel views the separation wall as a unilateral step intended to counter bombings against Israeli civilians and domestic insecurity. Israel's claims, however, that the wall was constructed for security reasons, does not constitute a political border, and serves as a temporary measure until the conclusion of an agreed-upon solution, are all merely pretexts to justify the wall's construction. In fact, the wall follows the June 4, 1967 borders in some areas, while penetrating deep inside the West Bank (ignoring the 1967 borders) to include Israeli settlement zones and vast open areas—effectively annexing them to Israel. The wall—or the "fence," as most Israelis prefer to refer to it, avoiding the word "wall's" negative connotations (in most built-up areas, the structure consists of a six to eight meter high cement wall, while in open areas the structure consists of a fence; there is no substantial difference between the two in security measures, surveillance, and operating patrols)—aims at separating Palestinians from Israelis in the process of expropriating a great deal of land. In Jerusalem and its surroundings, however, the wall separates Palestinians from Palestinians and amputates East Jerusalem from its direct environs, severing the city geographically and functionally from the rest of the West Bank, thereby terminating Jerusalem's centrality as a metropolitan center for the entire West Bank.

Most Israelis support the construction of the wall, saying it offers them security and psychological relief.[1] The reality imposed by the wall makes it hard to believe, however, that the structure will not become the eastern border of the state of Israel, and that its path will not unilaterally demarcate political borders, determining the area of the Palestinian state without negotiations over permanent status issues (access to water resources, Jerusalem as Palestinian Capital, return of refugees, etc.) established by the 1993 Oslo Accords. Palestinians point out that the wall constitutes one more annexation of Palestinian lands to Israel, and that the resulting isolation of the Palestinian population from the Israeli settlements and uninhabited Palestinian lands will be permanent. After all, historical experience has taught them that temporary borders, emerging for security reasons or to consolidate ceasefires, have later become concrete borders representing geopolitical terms of reference, even under international law.[2]

Here we will briefly overview the concept of the wall's construction, position, and ramifications in Jerusalem. This work is based on ongoing developments in the Jerusalem area, as well as interviews and surveys conducted to explore the wall's present and future consequences on Jerusalemite life, the possibility of reaching a political settlement based on a two-state solution, and Jerusalem's status under such a settlement.

BEFORE THE WALL WAS BUILT

The Arab-Israeli conflict has long been accompanied, since its evolution in the first half of the 20th century, by propositions to demarcate borders that "separate" the authentic Palestinian Arab population from the immigrant Jewish population.[3] The current structure underway is one more layer of physical differentiation.

Israel's 1967 occupation of the West Bank and Gaza, and the institution of direct military rule there, galvanized domestic calls for separation from Palestinians, expressed from the left as calls to end the occupation, and from the right as pressure to "disappear" the Palestinian population. The first Intifada (1987-1993) renewed these calls and finally resulted in Israel's willingness to accord the Palestinians autonomy as a step towards the possible establishment of a Palestinian state. The motive was both demographic and geographic; political and public voices sought to further entrench an overwhelming Jewish majority in Israel (Palestinians comprise some 20% of Israeli citizenry) without the threat of an expanding Palestinian population in the Occupied Territories. They recognized that continuing annexation and control of the Palestinian population would not preserve the Jewish majority for the long term.

But the most conclusive and widespread support for "separation" from Palestinians came after 1996. Bombings in Israeli cities by Palestinian suicide bombers raised the issue of physical separation from the Palestinians via establishment of a separation fence as one of the major means of achieving Israeli security, controlling Palestinian movement, and maintaining a Jewish demographic majority in the areas under direct Israeli control. By 2002, the physical components of separation had been drafted by a group of center-left former military leaders.[4] Their plan included substantial withdrawals from Israeli settlements in Gaza and the West Bank and drew the ire of the right wing, which saw any formal division of the broad religious concept of the Land of Israel as a concession. Eventually, however, right wing Prime Minister Ariel Sharon was convinced of both the need for drastic measures to halt the demographic threat, as well as the manner in which physical separation could be used to achieve further West Bank annexation, particularly in Jerusalem, and pursue the goals of the right.

The second Intifada, known as the al-Aqsa Intifada, broke out in the wake of failed Israeli-Palestinian negotiations at Camp David in 2000, and Ariel Sharon's provocative visit to Jerusalem's Haram ash-Sharif or "Temple Mount." Although negotiations did continue at Taba, these talks came to a halt in 2001 on the eve of the Israeli elections, just before the Labor Party's loss to Likud leader Ariel Sharon. The coming months would mark the bloodiest period of the uprising, capped by the Israeli army's invasion of Palestinian areas, including Palestinian West Bank

18.6 km: outside Damascus Gate

cities administered by the Palestinian Authority and placed under Palestinian security control (Areas A) in accordance with interim agreements.

Following the Israeli invasion, political figures calling for the establishment of a separation wall took center stage, and its implementation was popularized. In 2003, the plan was adopted by the government, when Sharon capitulated (despite his early opposition) to the idea's political popularity. Sharon's slogan became: if such a separation wall is imperative, then it must besiege Palestinians, rather than Palestinians using it to besiege Israel. This vision was fundamental in determining the path of the wall, which incorporated several crucial political principles.

First, the wall's path would be determined by its demographic goal: the route was to include the most Israelis, even those in Israeli settlements, and the smallest possible number of Palestinians. Second, its path would follow territorial lines in order to achieve the defacto annexation of any possible uninhabited lands. Third, the wall was to once and for all establish Israeli control over unified Greater Jerusalem, bringing West Jerusalem out of its marginal peripheral state, and replacing the concept of "unified Jerusalem" with that of Greater Jewish Jerusalem. Maale Adumim to the east and Gush Etzion to the south-west would become the new Israeli Jerusalem boundaries, stretching the city into the West Bank more deeply than ever before. Next, the wall, even as it separated the West Bank and Palestinians from Jerusalem, was to further incorporate the West Bank settlements and settlers within Israel by linking them to Jerusalem (now Greater Jewish Jerusalem) and facilitating their travel. Finally, the wall would bar Palestinian entry into Israel, including the flow of permitted laborers, which has slowed to a trickle since 1993, and which Israel has said will come to a complete halt by the year 2008.

THE WALL IN JERUSALEM

Inspection of the implemented and planned path of the wall in and near Jerusalem shows that the criteria guiding the establishment of the separation wall between Palestinians and Israelis in Jerusalem are different from those applied in the West Bank in general. In Jerusalem, the wall's path has not been guided by the 1967 Green Line (UN-administered armistice line between Israel and Jordan, 1948-1967), rather penetrating deep into the Occupied Palestinian Territories. The results mean the defacto annexation of all Greater Jerusalem settlement blocs, spanning an area of 10% to 16% of the West Bank. In essence, the wall concretizes the 1970s planning concept of metropolitan Jerusalem, which established roadways and services for highly populated settlements on the periphery of the Jerusalem municipality. National and regional traffic arteries are included on the Israeli side of the wall, facilitating travel between East Jerusalem settlements and Greater Jerusalem settlements, and linking them with West Jerusalem and central Israel. Gaps that lie between the Jerusalem-area settlements have been annexed to those settlements; Maale Adumim, for one, has been expanded so that its borders span over 53,000 dunams (1 dunum = 1000 square meters); its area now rivals that of Tel Aviv, and merges with the municipal borders of Jerusalem. The E-1 Plan, for which land has been prepared, will establish a settlement neighborhood north of Maale Adumim comprised of 3,500 residential units, West Bank police headquarters and a new Border Police base.

As such, Jerusalem's crucial and historic role as the West Bank's geographic and functional metropolitan center, already limited by Israel's checkpoint regime and closure policy (begun in March 1993), will dramatically recede. The wall will replace the checkpoints as a nearly impermeable means of controlling Jerusalemites' movement to and from their own neighborhoods, as well as the rest of the West Bank.

The long-term outcome will certainly be a reduction in the number of Palestinians who are Jerusalem residents, the separation of Palestinian existence from the Jewish metropolis, and the fragmentation and decline of Palestinian Jerusalem neighborhoods. Many Palestinian Jerusalemite neighborhoods within the municipal borders (Kufr Aqab and Samiramis in the north, Ras Khamis, and Shufat refugee camp and Dahiyat es-Salaam in the east) were placed out-

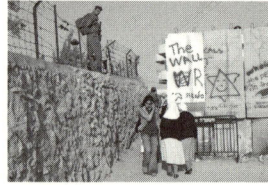

Informal checkpoint at Abu Dis before completion of the Separation Fence/Wall (photo: Jörg Gläscher, 2004)

side the wall in order to reduce the Palestinian population within the wall. These neighborhoods north and east of the Old City are inhabited by nearly 55,000 Palestinian Jerusalemites. In addition, an unknown number of Palestinian Jerusalemites (estimates lie at 40,000 to 60,000) continue to live outside Jerusalem's municipal border. Israeli policy is aimed at revoking these Palestinians' residency rights in the city and the wall will ease the Israeli goal of identifying and then stripping these Palestinians of their identity documents.

"CONCRETIZING" THE SIEGE OF PALESTINIAN JERUSALEM

Israel began constructing the wall north and south of East Jerusalem in 2002, building two segments, each ten kilometers long. This first phase was completed in July 2003. In the meantime, Israel began building three other segments east and northwest of the city, for a total length of 45 kilometers. Furthermore, in February 2005, the Israeli government approved the defacto annexation of Maale Adumim to the east of East Jerusalem by building a wall approximately 40 kilometers long around the settlement. Construction of the wall, by November 2005,[5] incorporated 12 border "gates" (for the entire West Bank) operated selectively on national/ethnic grounds: Israeli settlers are granted quick passage while Palestinians may only pass with a special permit and after rigorous checking.

The wall impacts Palestinians most directly, it is important to point out, because it is being built on Palestinian land. Approximately 536,200 dunams of previously confiscated settlement land lie to the west of the wall. Another 160,500 dunams of West Bank village land is partially or completely surrounded, on one side by the wall and on the other by a secondary barrier, and usually not made accessible to its landowners.

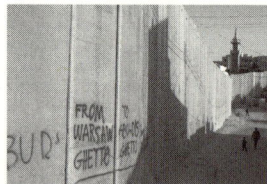

Separation Fence/Wall at Abu Dis (photo: Jörg Gläscher, 2004)

These areas alone total 12.4% of the area of the West Bank. Moreover, at publication time, another 205,350 dunams west of the wall was slated for confiscation with the approval of the Israeli government. This land grab aggravates the planning crisis that already exists in East Jerusalem (as part of the West Bank) and its hinterlands; residential expansion is forcibly concentrated and vertical, without proper planning, and without appropriate infrastructure, road networks, and coinciding open areas.

Otherwise, the wall is inarguably the most harmful change made to Jerusalem's social fabric since Israel occupied the city in 1967. It serves as a tool for fragmenting and dismembering Palestinian Jerusalem neighborhoods. For example, the wall runs straight down the center of the main road linking Ramallah with Jerusalem, beginning from Qalandiya refugee camp and ending in northern Beit Hanina. This portion of the wall separates Ar-Ram, Dahiyat al-Bareed, and northeast Beit Hanina from north Beit Hanina. Moreover, it severs Sheikh Jarrah, Ras al-Amud, Jabal al-Mukaber, and As-Sawahra al-Gharbiya neighborhoods from al-Ezariya, Abu Dis and Sheikh Saad neighborhoods. Beyond this physical disfigurement, the wall will stand between members of the same nuclear and extended family, and residents of the same town. As a result, Palestinian society, which is based on extended family relations, is facing a period of social fragmentation where relatives are unable to visit each other and the usual communal problem-solving will become more difficult.

Several years ago, Jerusalem's economy represented one-fourth to one-third of the entire West Bank market. Today, however, East Jerusalem within the wall is being transformed into a few fragmented neighborhoods affiliated with West Jerusalem and Israel. Simultaneously, the urban center and political heart that has developed unwillingly in Ramallah and al-Bireh competes with Jerusalem. The continuation of Jerusalem's isolation from its surroundings threatens any possibility that Jerusalem could become the capital of the Palestinian state. Moreover, the wall will undermine contiguity between the northern and southern Palestinian West Bank, replacing geographic contiguity with a transportation route. Israel plans to link the north and south West Bank with a road passing through an arid uninhabited area, thereby bypassing Jerusalem. No longer will West Bankers visit Jerusalem for leisure, medical treatment, pilgrimage, or even as a way-stop on to other West Bank sites. As such, the wall constitutes a geopolitical *fait accompli* preventing Jerusalem's development as a Palestinian economic and administrative center, weakening the city, and impoverishing its citizens (Brooks et. al., 2005). The city's urban elite may well choose to leave the city, further isolating Jerusalem's poor. Ultimately, security and social instability, increased poverty and crime can be expected in Jerusalem within the wall.

A POLITICAL PROGNOSIS

The constructed and planned segments of the wall in the Jerusalem area are intended to realize demographic objectives (ensuring a Jewish demographic majority in Jerusalem and the area annexed to it within the wall), territorial objectives (annexation of additional Palestinian lands for the free movement of Israelis and expansion of their interests), and "soft" ethnic cleansing (ensuring and consolidating Israelis' life fabric, while fragmenting Palestinians' life fabric and ultimately forcing Palestinians to emigrate).

The wall has been built in accordance with the specifications required for a formal border. It includes a wall, electric and barbed-wire fences, border patrol roads, and crossings that cannot be traversed without permits issued from the Israeli side. Israel has presented this wall as a temporary security barrier that can be dismantled in case of a political settlement with Palestinians. But the reality is very different: the immense investment in the wall, the considerations made in determining its path, and the settlement schemes accompanying it, intimate that the wall is an imposed permanent border fulfilling Israel's interests and contradicting the most basic human rights, let alone the Palestinian national right to establish their capital in Jerusalem in accordance with a peaceful two-state solution.

The wall is a geopolitical settlement imposed by Israel. It is the final phase of the separation process that began on the eve of the Oslo Accords with the erection of checkpoints isolating Jerusalem from its Palestinian environment. The wall will render it nearly impossible to conduct geopolitical talks concerning Jerusalem, or to make the city an open city with two capitals for two states—West Jerusalem as the capital of the State of Israel, and East Jerusalem in accordance with the 1967 borders as the capital of the future State of Palestine. In fact, it is possible to argue that, while the symbolic importance of Jerusalem formed a barrier to reaching a bilateral solution in the past, the new reality imposed by Israel, in the form of the wall and annexation of Greater Jerusalem, is a new physical barrier to the peaceful existence of two states.

1   Editors note: according to the Public Opinion National Security Survey 2004, conducted by the Jaffa Center for Strategic Studies (JCSS) 80% of the Israeli respondents supported the Separation Fence/Wall (see also: http://www.tau.ac.il/jcss/survey04.pdf).

2   For example, the 1949 truce line became known as the Green Line or the June 4, 1967 border, which is the border that partitioned Jerusalem into two parts: an eastern part under Jordanian administration and sovereignty, and a western part under Israeli sovereignty, which Israel proclaimed as its capital.

3   Editors note: for more on this subject, see the essay "Wall and Tower: The Mold of Israeli *Adrikhalut*," by Sharon Rotbard in this volume.

4   Additionally, in 2000 the government of Ehud Barak had drafted a plan for unilateral separation in case of the failure of the Camp David talks between Prime Minister Barak and Palestinian President Yasser Arafat.

5   While Israel had expected to complete the northern portions of the Jerusalem wall by the close of 2005, high court appeals by Palestinians living along the course of the wall slowed the process. At the time of publication, the Israeli defense establishment was fuming that delays had resulted in the completion of only one-third of the entire wall's length, far behind the project's target completion date.

Selected Bibliography

Robert Brooks et. al., *The Wall of Annexation and Expansion: Its Impact on the Jerusalem Area* (Jerusalem: The International Peace and Cooperation Center, 2005).

Rassem Khamaisi and Rami Nasrallah, *Jerusalem on the Map* (Jerusalem: The International Peace and Cooperation Center, 2005).

Yaacov Garb, *The Separation Barrier and Jerusalem's Arab Neighborhoods: Integrate or Separate but Don't Postpone* (Jerusalem: The Floersheimer Institute for Policy Studies, 2005).

BARRIERS, WALLS, AND URBAN ETHNOCRACY IN JERUSALEM

Oren Yiftachel and Haim Yacobi[1]

Some 1,200 kilometers of security fence/separation wall have already been built, consisting of 60-to-100-meter-wide complexes of trenches, barbed wire, tracking roads, and electronic fences in rural areas, and 8 meter high concrete walls in and around Palestinian towns and cities. Over 200,000 dunums (1 dunum = 1000 square meters) of Palestinian land are to be affected, i.e. expropriated, cleared, or declared "out of bounds" to West Bank Palestinians. The construction of this barrier, coupled with recent minor Israeli territorial withdrawals of late, constitute the State of Israel's latest attempts to manage the growing contradictions of its "ethnocratic" regime.

These contradictions, which erupted in full force during the al-Aqsa Intifada (since 2000), have moved Israel to unilaterally transform the landscape and further curtail Palestinian rights, including the right to develop. But Israel has also introduced limits to its own expansion, including the voluntary evacuation of the Jewish settlements of the Gaza Strip. These spatial and political "adjustments" are accelerating the process of "creeping apartheid" in Israel-Palestine.

A point critical analysts often overlook is the dialectical nature of spatial and political change. A "blind spot" of sorts leads many to portray the Palestinians chiefly as passive victims of Israeli aggression, both in the unfolding of local history and in the geographical transformation of the land. Yet Palestinian agency in general, and violent action in particular, play a major role in the shaping of Zionist-Palestinian spatial relations. This dialectic manifests as ever-radicalizing Palestinian resistance and ever-escalating Israeli oppression, causing ever-growing levels of human misery, mainly, but not exclusively, among Palestinians. This dialectic is asymmetrical, with the Jewish State yielding far greater military and economic power than its stateless Palestinian counterparts.

The barrier's route runs entirely through Palestinian occupied territory keeping the majority of Jewish settlers on the "Israeli side," effectively annexing 10-16% of the West Bank to Israel. When complete, it may or may not improve Jewish security, but it will have grave consequences for the Palestinians: some 210,000 people will be caught between the barrier and the Green Line (UN-administered armistice line between Israel and Jordan, 1948-1967), cut-off from their lands and their livelihood. Israel's intent to surround many settlements with a mini "security" barrier means that more Palestinian land will be illegally seized to protect settlements built on illegally seized Palestinian land.

ETHNOCRACY

Let us introduce the concept of "ethnocracy," which aptly describes regimes found in contested territories where a dominant ethnic group utilizes the state to further its expansionist aspirations, while maintaining the semblance of a formal democracy. Ethnocratic regimes are typified by high levels of oppression over indigenous, and (to a lesser extent) immigrant minorities. Indigenous groups and minorities, in turn, usually develop various forms of resistance around issues of land control and settlement, which often essentialize identities and polarize spatial and political systems further. Typically, gaps between the state's "democratic" self-presentation and persisting oppression develop into "fissures" within the ruling hegemony and destabilize the regime.

As with most ethnocratic projects, the Jews in Israel initially benefited greatly from territorial expansion. Until the late 1980s, identity, and economic and territorial goals reinforced one another. The Israeli conquest and occupation of the West Bank and Gaza, and the colonial settlements established in those territories, strengthened Jewish national identity and infused the expanding economy with a large pool of cheap labor and "free" land. Israel has used an effective double discourse. Domestically it has presented the Palestinian occupied territories as part of the "eternal Jewish homeland," thereby including Jewish settlers in those territories as full state citizens, despite the fact that they live outside the official bounds of the state. At the same time, internationally, Israel has presented the same occupied territories as "temporarily administered," thereby excluding their Palestinian residents from political participation, leaving them powerless to shape the future of their own homeland.

Like other ethnocratic regimes, Israel has begun to face the contradictions of its system. These surfaced with the suppression the first Intifada (1987-1993), and the resultant polarization between the Palestinian citizens of the state and the Jewish majority, and between religious and secular Jews, over the future of the Palestinian occupied territories and the character of the State of Israel. Given the depth of ethnocratic thinking in Israel and Jewish fears fed by a history of persecution, the effects of renewed Palestinian violent resistance, together with anti-Jewish rhetoric, calls for the "liberation of the whole of Palestine," and the specter of Palestinian refugees returning to Israel proper, have been potent, if predictable. Since the second Intifada (2000-2005), most Israeli Jews have closed ranks, stigmatized the entire Palestinian population as "terroristic," legitimized public debate on "transferring" Palestinians from their homeland, and shifted politically to the nationalist Right.

The Israeli public, especially the mainstream middle class, has demanded major changes. Seeking to maintain the illusion of a "normal" democratic state while maintaining control of Palestinian areas, they have demanded "security" and renewed economic growth while keeping the Palestinians voiceless and powerless. There have been dissenting voices, i.e. calls for a genuine end to the occupation and a return to sincere negotiations, but they have been outweighed by racism and chauvinism.

The state's response: construction of the separation barrier. Begun as an initiative of the Zionist Left (promising to combine territorial withdrawal with security), the separation fence/wall was cleverly hijacked by the ruling nationalist Right, which moved it eastward deep into Palestinian territory and away from the Green Line. This unilateral Israeli move is likely to generate more Palestinian resistance, subsequently strengthening the political Right, which feeds on a never-ending sense of hostility and siege.

URBAN ETHNOCRACY

Despite the relative openness of urban areas, their development in Israel/Palestine has been framed by an ethnocratic drive for Judaization. Similar to other sites shaped by the logics of reconciling ethno-nationalism with capitalism, ethnically mixed cities are characterized by stark patterns of segregation and ethno-class fragmentation within each national group. Mixed spaces are both exceptional and involuntary, often resulting from the spatial process of ethnic expansion and retreat, prevalent in contested urban spaces. "Urban ethnocracies," if you will, are settings where tensions characterize the interaction between a city's economic, planning, and ethno-territorial logics, producing sites of conflict and instability, and essentializing the boundaries of group identities and the zero sum nature of ethnic geographies.

JERUSALEM/AL-QUDS

Jerusalem/Al-Quds is a clear example of an urban ethnocracy. While the wall under construction in its midst is usually thought of as yet another manifestation of Israeli abuse of Palestinians human rights, it is also yet another manifestation of Jewish-Palestinian relations in the city since 1967. Walls have existed in Jerusalem/Al-Quds from the beginning of occupation, but were less visible, as the "stuff" they were made of were the "building blocks" of urban policy, planning strategies, and a rubber-stamp legal apparatus.

Palestinian Al-Quds was conquered by Jordan in 1948, and in turn by Israel in the war of 1967. In a move self-described as "unification," Israel unilaterally annexed large parts of the city and its surrounding villages. Since then, Israel has used its military might and economic power to relocate borders and boundaries, grant and deny rights and resources, shift populations, and reshape the city's geography to ensure Jewish dominance. Two complementary Israeli strategies in East Jerusalem have been the massive construction of an outer ring of Jewish settlements or "neighborhoods," which now house over half of the Jewish population of Jerusalem, and the containment of all Palestinian development, by denying building permits, carrying out house demolition, and prohibiting migration to the city through bureaucratic means. While Palestinian neighborhoods lack basic urban utilities and decent infrastructure, Jewish neighborhoods are fully serviced. Israeli roads and housing complexes have been shaped in the form of segregative walls, aimed at fragmenting the Arab city. These have led to the physical decline and urban stagnation of the Palestinian city, its severance from the Palestinian hinterland, and the exodus of Palestinian businesses northward and southward into the West Bank.

These transparent walls can also be found in Jerusalem's public and political spheres. Despite the bi-national character of Jerusalem/Al-Quds, urban governance has been completely dominated by Jews. Palestinians have been excluded from the city's decision making bodies—most notably City Hall—due to their refusal to accept the imposition of Israeli law and the distorted municipal boundaries of occupation. Israel would like the Palestinian residents of Jerusalem to see Judaization as "inevitable," a fact to be accepted passively as part of the modern development of the metropolis.

THE FENCE/WALL IN JERUSALEM/AL-QUDS

The fence/wall under construction in Jerusalem/Al-Quds will include most of the areas annexed by Israel in 1967 (an illegal annexation according to international law) but also areas beyond the municipal boundaries which Israel would like to annex "de facto," such as the "neighborhoods" of Pisgat Zeev and Har Homa and the settlements of Male Adumim and Givat Zeev. Palestinian areas within Jerusalem's municipal boundaries, such as Shufat Refugee Camp and the villages of Anata and Kufr Aqab, will be excluded from the fence/wall, causing some 40,000 Palestinian residents of Jerusalem to lose their Jerusalemite status. These spatial and demographic distortions aim to reduce the city's Palestinian population significantly.

For many years, Jerusalem was the social, cultural, and economic link between the northern and southern West Bank. Checkpoints, and now the fence/wall, are forcing West Bankers to use alternate routes such as the infamous and perilous Wad an-Nar (Valley of Fire/Hell) road to the east of the city. This has turned Jerusalem from a thriving (albeit occupied) Palestinian metropolis into a ghost town that not only no longer serves the West Bank, it can barely serve its own surrounding villages.

Israel's geopolitical and demographic impositions have redefined the city. The "known" division of West Jerusalem (the part controlled by Israel since 1948) and East Jerusalem (the part occupied by Israel since 1967) is no longer evident. The city is transforming as the fence/wall is forming another borderline altogether. It seems that Jerusalem's future is being decided by Israel before any negotiations between the two peoples who claim the city as their political and spiritual capital, have even begun.

ABU DIS

The village of Abu Dis is a case in point. Abu Dis is a suburb of East Jerusalem located two kilometers from the Old City. With a total area of 28,232 dunums, the separation wall will sever it from some 6,000 dunums (1 dunum = 1000 square meters) of agricultural lands, causing a significant blow to its economy. During the 1990s, Abu Dis gained centrality as a flourishing commercial center, but also as a political hub where the Palestinian Authority's offices related to Jerusalem were established. At one stage of the Israeli-Palestinian "peace process," Abu Dis was considered as a possible symbolic "alternative" to East Jerusalem as the capitol of the Palestinian State. Abu Dis is also home to Al Quds University, which, with a student body of some 4,000 men and women, is an important intellectual and professional community institution. The local population of Abu Dis (11,672) nearly doubles with the daily influx of students, teachers, and staff.

In October 2003, Israel began constructing a wall from Der Salah village southeast of Jerusalem northward toward Abu Dis and eastward toward Ezariya. This 17-kilometer-long section of the wall has turned a 10 minute commute into a 1-2 hour expedition. In Abu Dis, the wall has been built straight through the center of town, creating what graffiti artists/activists have aptly called a "Ghetto." The majority of the residents of Abu Dis and its surrounding villages have Israeli IDs which, in principle, entitle them free access to Jerusalem.

Many Israelis have argued that the escalation of violent struggle in the form of terror attacks on civilian targets required a radical "solution" in the form of a "security wall." However, in its current form, the wall supports the process of "creeping apartheid" more than it serves as a physical safeguard. In Abu Dis the wall separates some 35 households from their immediate families on the other side. Of these families, ten hold West Bank IDs, though their house falls on the "Israeli side" of the wall. It remains to be seen whether they will be granted Israeli IDs, or will be forced to relocate to the "Palestinian side" of the wall, fulfilling Israeli wishes to control the demographic "balance" between Jews and Palestinians in the city.

In Abu Dis, the wall runs between and alongside houses denying residents' access to their relatives, but also to daylight. Several houses along the wall's route have been issued demolition orders. The army has advised homeowners to take up the matter with the Jerusalem municipality, and the municipality, in turn, has offered to buy the houses from their Palestinian residents. Naturally, the homeowners have refused to sell and petitioned the courts instead.

The wall is taking its toll on the socioeconomic fabric of Abu Dis as well. With its once thriving commercial/political/academic district effectively cut in half, it is losing customers, businesses are closing, students are dropping out, and unemployment is on the rise.

THE LONG AND SHORT RUN

In the long run, urban ethnocracy produces a deeply flawed and unsustainable urban order, generating conflict and instability. The political, social, and economic pressures created by the separation fence/wall will feed the frustrations of an already distraught Palestinian community in Jerusalem and escalate violence further. "Security" will not likely be the result in the short run, but apartheid most probably will.

1 We are indebted to the Israel Science Foundation for its financial support of our project: "The Emergence of a New Land Regime: the Transformation of Israel's Urban Legal Geography."

Selected Bibliography

Oren Yiftachel, "Ethnocracy and Its Discontents: Minority Protest in Israel," *Critical Inquiry* 26 (2000).

Oren Yiftachel and Haim Yacobi, "Urban Ethnocracy: Ethnicization and the Production of Space in an Israeli Mixed City," *Environment and Planning D: Society and Space* 21 (6) (2004).

Oren Yiftachel and Haim Yacobi, "Planning a Bi-National Capital: Should Jerusalem Remain United?" *Geoforum* 33 (2002).

THE POLITICS OF ROADS IN JERUSALEM

Shmuel Groag

The planning of roads in Jerusalem and its surrounding areas is an integral tool in the appropriation of physical space in eastern Jerusalem. This essay will examine the existing and projected road system from two perspectives. First, a comparison will be made between the Palestinian neighborhoods in East Jerusalem and their contemporaries in the western part of the city. Second, we will examine the network of roads and traffic arrays in the Jerusalem metropolis. Put simply—who are those who move in this space and who are those who stand still?

Fundamentally, this task is based on the fact that planning not only addresses the aesthetics, beauty, and professional and technical organization of the environment and space, but also embodies politics in its broadest sense: the manifestation in open space of power relations between groups of interests. Even though West and East Jerusalem are formally "united," the division between them is evident in the physical condition of the roads, which are very poor in the east and fully developed in the west. The quality, size, and nature of each road, one might say, is a fair indicator of whether Palestinians or Israelis move along it.

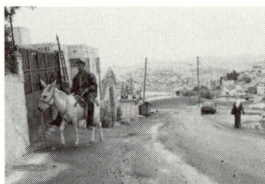

Main road at Jabal al-Muka-ber, East Jerusalem (photo: BIMKOM, 2003)

Bypass road near Bir Naballa (photo: Shmuel Groag, 2004)

The planning system in Israel, and in Jerusalem in particular, is a top-down system. In the Jerusalem area, the central goal of the system is to implement the principle of a united Jerusalem under Israeli sovereignty. As phrased by the planner of the previous (1978) master plan, architect Yossi Schwied: "The first and foremost principle in the planning of Jerusalem is to ensure its unity [through]...the building of the city in such a way that will prevent the formation of two separate national communities, in order to prevent the possibility of the city being divided once again on the dividing line between the two communities" (Btselem, 1995:35).

The existing and planned road system in the city is a tangible manifestation of this perception. Since 1967, planning policies in Jerusalem have spurred political and urban change with two goals in mind. On the one hand, policy has sought to disengage East Jerusalem from its metropolitan hinterlands in the rest of the West Bank, thus blocking any possibility of it becoming the capital of a future Palestine. On the other hand, planning policy has worked to create a Jewish metropolitan in all possible areas in the city and its surroundings, simultaneously expanding the brand name of "Jerusalem" beyond the original municipal borders into the West Bank.

A CAPILLARY ROAD SYSTEM

A comparison of road system typology in the Palestinian neighborhoods of East Jerusalem with that of western neighborhoods reveals that the eastern region is served by a very sparse road system based on old rural roads and without the various types of roads required for urban development. The eastern neighborhoods function without a major urban axis from which it is possible to develop public institutions and commercial centers, or out of which new residential neighborhoods might grow, similar to the existing model in West Jerusalem.

Currently, the roads in Arab neighborhoods are also in poor physical condition, most of them without sidewalks and infrastructure systems. Only some 10% of the Jerusalem municipal budget goes to infrastructure and services in Arab neighborhoods (30% of the city's population).[1] This official neglect of East Jerusalem's infrastructure is raised every single year, and the reply given by all mayors to date has been that improvements would require a titanic amount of money, and hence special governmental allotments. These never arrive, and the development gap grows. While new Jewish neighborhoods in the west, as well as those constructed by the Housing Ministry in the east, were built according to sophisticated plans that allocate public space for public roads and passages, most of the Palestinian neighborhoods in the east remain—territorially and structurally—seventeen traditional villages that surrounded Jordanian East Jerusalem.

The aged road system in these villages, all of which are located on hilltops and separated by ravines, was broadly based on a central road running along the top of the mountain crest. Alongside this road, built-up areas developed organically and moderately in scattered clusters, according to familial ownership. The lack of roadway development and municipal investment in Palestinian neighborhoods is one component of a policy intended to limit Palestinian urban development, expansion and demographic growth. The underdevelopment policy in East Jerusalem neighborhoods is identical to that underway in Arab locales within Israel. There, too, the central planning bureaucracy designs and implements development and building systems in new Jewish communities, but ignores the development of infrastructure in Arab neighborhoods, where the land is privately owned and there is no large-scale real estate enterprise. In opposition to this ethnocentric planning policy, organizations such as Bimkom are increasingly demanding the formation of a "civic" planning policy that neutralizes the national component and addresses area planning needs objectively, and on the basis of the assumption (also partially imaginary) that planning decisions should derive from planning rights, which are among the broader human rights. In the Israeli reality, where economic and national interests dictate planning priorities, this vision is but a distant dream.

MOVING AROUND IN "GREATER JERUSALEM"

The settlement project extending from Gush Etzion in the south to Givat Zeev in the north, and from Betar in the west to Maale Adumim in the east, has been dubbed "Greater Jerusalem." Sophisticated new highway systems incorporating bridges and tunnels connect these settlement blocs to West Jerusalem, bypassing Palestinian neighborhoods. Today all of this land formerly on the Jordanian side of the 1948 lines is located on the Israeli side of the series of walls, barbed wire, fences, and patrol roads (the Separation Wall) that Israel is constructing in the West Bank.

Roads, as taught in all architecture schools, are the basis, the skeleton, of every urban plan. In a parallel metaphor, they are comparable to the vascular system, the network supplying blood to all areas of the body. Central roads are the traffic arteries, secondary roads are the veins, and local roads serve as capillaries. The city center is the heart of the urban area, and bypasses are required to reroute traffic blockages.

Hence, while the western city has been opened to its Jewish satellite neighborhoods, East Jerusalem has been truncated and cut off. The Abu Dis road that formerly served as the main access road to East Jerusalem from the Dead Sea has been turned from a central traffic route to a cul-de-sac. The main road running from the northern to the southern West Bank from Ramallah to Hebron through Jerusalem (Road No. 60) is currently closed to Palestinian traffic, serving the Jewish population in Jerusalem and nearby settlements exclusively. The development of high-speed traffic systems for the exclusive use of Jewish settlers is prominent in the whole of the West Bank, where all major roads are located (as per the Oslo agreement) in Area C, under full Israeli control (Btselem Report, 2005; Efrat, 2002). Often these highways run through difficult topography, causing damage to the landscape and Palestinian agriculture.

But the detachment of East Jerusalem from its Palestinian metropolis is not achieved solely through lack of planning or nondevelopment of roadways. It is an integrated policy that incorporates the removal of Palestinian official markings and cultural centers from the eastern side (such as the closing down of the Orient House, the long-time Jerusalem address for Palestinian nationalist organs) and the restricting of Palestinian West Bank residents from the city (even those who want to pray at its holy sites). The prohibition of non-Jerusalemite Palestinians from entering the Jerusalem city boundaries has been an expanding process, one which began in 1991, before the Oslo agreements between Palestinians and Israelis. To visit the city, West Bank Palestinians are required to request a permit to enter Jerusalem from the civil administration (a cover name for the military commander) in the West Bank, and this permit must be presented at military barriers set at the city's eastern entrances. Permits are only afforded to those of a certain age, marital status, and with a "clean" security file, and applications can be turned down for any unstated reason. They are usually given solely for daylight hours and span only a number of days at a time. Alternately, Palestinians carrying West Bank identity cards can attempt to steal "illegally" into Jerusalem territory, risking arrest and monetary fines.

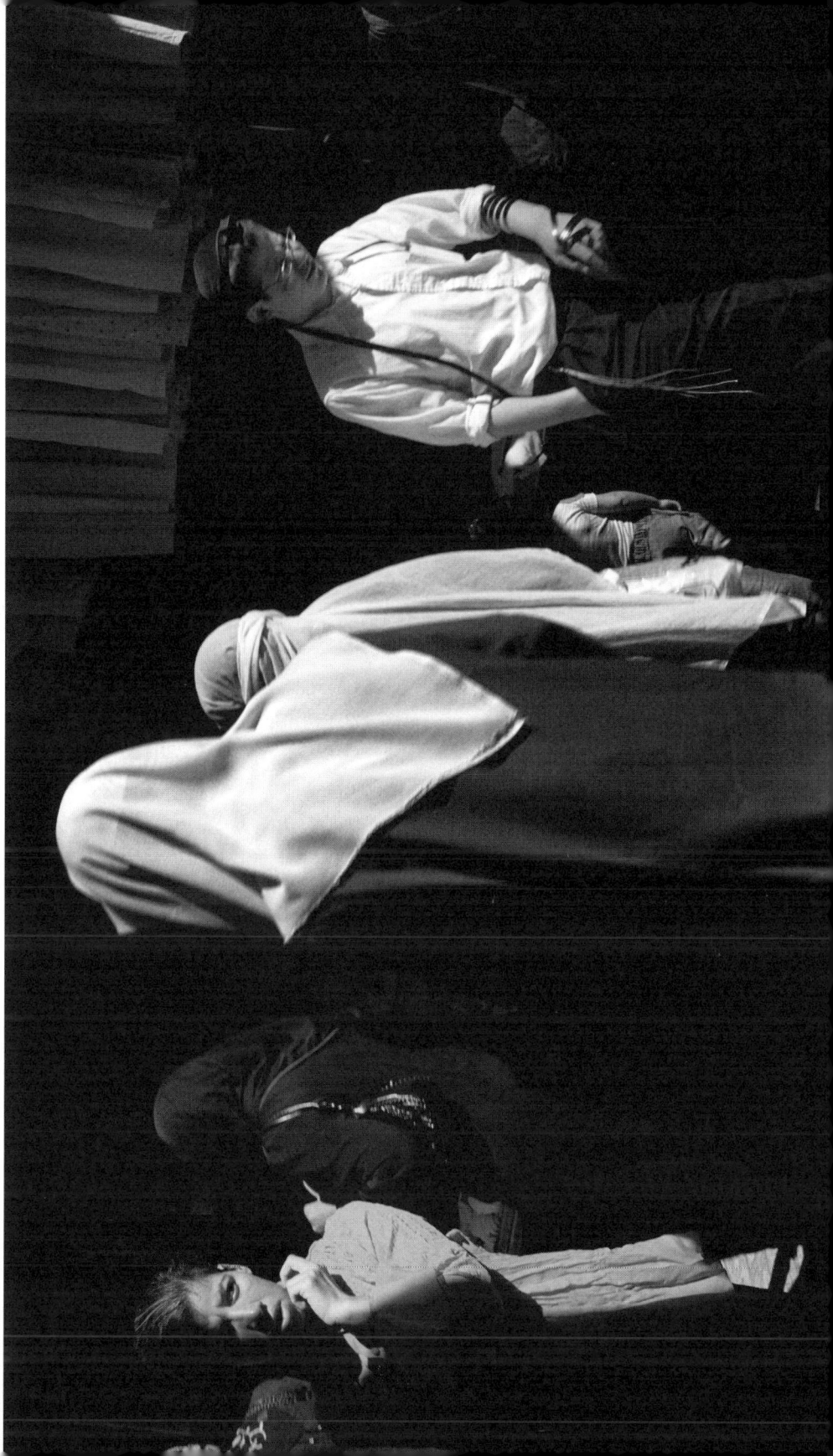

19.0 km: Old City

Today this policy is being "perfected" by the Separation Wall under construction on the edges of Jerusalem's municipal boundaries (which twists and turns to avoid incorporating large Palestinian populations on the city's hinterlands). Eventually, this barrier will make it impossible to enter the Jerusalem area with cars and merchandise. The city will be surrounded by five control centers where merchandise will be transferred into Jerusalem in a "back-to-back" process, where trucks meet for the transfer of goods but never leave their respective areas (similar to the existing passages between the Gaza Strip and the State of Israel). Hence the relative freedom of movement previously enjoyed by Arabs of East Jerusalem to enter and leave the rest of the West Bank will also be constrained.

The destruction of East Jerusalem and the transformation of its neighborhoods into culs-de-sac are also destroying West Jerusalem. In the western part of the city, which is currently expanding towards the green lungs of the Jerusalem mountains, a new traffic array is planned, incorporating a western ring road in the Beit Zayit and Mevasaret Tzion areas, to connect to the new access road coming from Beit Shemesh (Road No. 39), and to the traffic array entering into the urban area under construction near Moza and Lifta. This traffic array, in combination with the fast train being built to Tel Aviv, is awakening public disputes, one over environmental damage and another concerning Jerusalem's urban character as the largest and most scattered city in Israel. West and East Jerusalem are like Siamese twins, one of them receiving excessive nourishment, while the other is systematically suffocating. Despite the relative growth of West Jerusalem, the economic decline of East Jerusalem is degenerating its Siamese twin. Even flashy, expensive transportation projects such as the light-rail train will not revive the degenerating urban center of West Jerusalem.

MOVING BELOW AND UNDER REALITY

On the eve of the Six Day War in 1967, Naomi Shemer wrote the song "Jerusalem of Gold." The songwriter, a deeply-rooted *sabra* (native-born Israeli) from the Jordan Valley, described the Old City and East Jerusalem as vacated of humans ("The market square stands empty"). The roadways to Jerusalem are also described in the song—this time not as empty but as untrafficked. ("And no one goes to the Dead Sea through Jericho") These lines in the song that has almost become Israel's new national anthem regard the eastern city and the roads leading to it as empty—inasmuch as they are empty of Jewish visitors. But the metaphor of "the empty land" and "the invisible Palestinian" is not only literary; the absurdity in Jerusalem, is the way in which metaphors and images are turned into operative action: a distortion of time and space perpetuated through the road system.

Zigmund Bauman, in his book about globalization (1998), describes a worldwide process of strong populations gaining unlimited mobility and a free flow of capital, while weak populations gradually become enclosed in their domestic spaces. Conditions in East Jerusalem and the West Bank are a tangible example of this process. The development of neighborhoods and settlements in the "Greater Jerusalem" area has also introduced sophisticated and multileveled traffic systems. In order to enable the direct access enjoyed by residents of these neighborhoods and settlements to the sources of the occupation and the city center, residents of Palestinian neighborhoods and towns have been closed in. In constructing the traffic systems leading to settlements such as Gush Etzion and Maale Adumim, Israel invested unprecedented amounts of money in bridge systems and wide, state-of-the-art tunnels passing below and above the Palestinian areas and, in fact, below and above the Palestinian reality, which Jewish residents do not even want to see.

One example of this can be found on Road No. 443, where the Palestinian town of Bir Nabala is hidden from those who cross the bridge above it by an array of concrete walls painted with rainbows and blue empty skies. An imagined orientalist view of reality replaces the panorama of the actual community, all the while masked by the argument that such a wall is necessary to guard the security of passing travelers. In the Bethlehem-area Jewish settlement of Gilo, a similar wall was constructed, ostensibly to protect residents from gunfire, and painted with an "improved" landscape of nearby Palestinian Beit Jala.

THE EASTERN RING ROAD

One of the largest Israeli transportation projects ever, and a case study for the concepts described above, is Jerusalem's Eastern Ring Road (Plan No. 4558). This 15-kilometer-long highway will pass through the most underdeveloped eastern neighborhoods, which house approximately one-third of the Palestinian residents of Jerusalem (some 65,000 people). This highway will be facilitated by tunnels and bridges, more or less on the edge of Jerusalem's municipal territory, between the Palestinian neighborhoods that are inside Jerusalem and those that lie to the east of the city, such as Ezariya, Abu Dis, and az-Zaim.

Bimkom was asked by the affected Palestinian communities to assist in their formal objections and to check all related planning documents (Paden, 2005). An examination of the reasons given for this sophisticated road revealed that they are not merely transportational—for example, completion of the traffic ring that already exists in West Jerusalem—but also geopolitical. The planned road will serve as a kind of patrol and border road, defining Jerusalem's municipal boundaries in conjunction with the Separation Wall. The implicit assumption is that this road will help prevent division of the city and the transfer of Palestinian neighborhoods to the Palestinian Authority in the event of substantive political negotiations.

The mainstream Israeli argument over this road focuses on how much the related financial investments actually serve the Israeli interest. Only a tiny aspect of the argument addresses the impact Palestinians will feel from this massive infrastructure project, even though—like the settlement roads in the West Bank—this road will also pass above and below their neighborhoods and dissect them like a highway, rather than a major urban artery serving the neighborhoods themselves. The goals detailed by the road's planners were mainly the creation of a fast-moving traffic array to connect the southern settlements (the Gush Etzion area) with those in the east (Maale Adumim and the E-1 area), and from there on to the north (Adam, Geva Binyamin) without clogging the city center.

The road's development necessitates the expropriation of 1,250 acres of privately-owned lands from East Jerusalem Palestinians, and the destruction of 43 buildings in the Jabal al-Mukaber neighborhood alone. The width of the

area impacted by the highway, as much as 200 meters, will further entail new
construction limits on buildings standing alongside it, not to mention certain damage to agricultural lands and sensitive natural resources. The blueprints as they
stand will disconnect the neighborhoods through which the road passes (there
are minimal entries and exits incorporated for the neighborhoods), as well as
dissect an existing array of roads.

Bimkom has submitted objections to the construction of this ring road,
emphasizing that it will not serve the neighborhoods it passes through, nor contribute to the development of urban areas, public institutions, and residential
neighborhoods, as its plans are limited solely to the construction of the roadway.
The plan does not propose alternative compensation, for instance, which would
allow a landowner, whose agricultural land was expropriated or damaged, to build
in a commercial development or residential area. Instead, Bimkom demanded
that the proposed plan become a lever for the urban development of the entire
East Jerusalem area, and that the plan be altered to minimize injury to private
landowners. The objection suggested an alternative, for one, that construction of
supporting beams along the road could prevent the expropriation of agricultural
lands currently allocated for the work process alone.

ONE-WAY MOBILITY

For Israelis, West Jerusalem before 1967 was a quiet, sleepy capital city at the
end of a no-exit highway commonly called the "Jerusalem Corridor"; to them,
it was a city centered around government offices and the Hebrew University.
Since 1967, the Israeli planning system has resolved to invert this metropolitan
process—i.e., to turn expanded Jewish Jerusalem into an urban metropolis, while
simultaneously turning Palestinian East Jerusalem into a closed and degenerated
neighborhood at the end of a cul-de-sac.

The development of this ring road, as a fast highway and patrol road alongside
the Separation Wall that seals Jerusalem, will hinder the possibility of developing
the local road system in East Jerusalem and adapting it to that of a modern and
progressive city. Additionally, it will reinforce the trend of Israeli spatial domination
over the whole Jerusalem metropolis, strengthening connections between the
Jewish settlements near Jerusalem and the city itself.

Palestinian movement is at a standstill. The Separation Wall is dramatically
slowing traffic flow into East Jerusalem. While previously unregulated admission
into the city supplemented regulated admission, the Wall is intended to achieve
complete control over all entrances and transitions. As previously noted, the
historic road running towards the Dead Sea from Abu Dis has been completely
blocked. The main road between Jerusalem and Ramallah has been bisected
lengthwise and turned from a four-lane thoroughfare into a two-lane road, only
be severed in its middle by the Separation Wall. Since the concrete barrier in
this section is exposed to those traveling along the road, its built elements were
reduced from a height of eight meters to a height of 6.5 meters, in a "mini wall"
model. (Petitions entered by the Palestinian residents, accompanied by Bimkom's
advisory brief, to abolish the wall or enable additional entrances through the wall
were rejected by the Israeli Supreme Court.)

Thus, a situation has been created in which East Jerusalem is gradually being closed in, and unlike other cities in the world where traffic systems are being enlarged and improved, the number of entrances into East Jerusalem is being purposefully minimized and its roads made narrower and narrower. If these roads are blood vessels, the veins leading into the city are being blocked at an actual risk of gangrene to its limbs.

In total, Jerusalem's road array—both existing and planned—can be read as a graph of political and planning realities in the city and the West Bank. The massive physical changes brought about by this system do not alter the essential problem that Jerusalem is a divided city. Theoretically, a solution might lie in the separation of the Siamese twins, or in finding a political resolution that enables cooperation based on principles of equality and freedom of movement.

---

1   The roads that were developed were generally for tourists and foreigners looking out on the "storefront" of the local landscape. Almost 90% of Jerusalem's sewage pipes, roads, and sidewalks are found in West Jerusalem; entire Palestinian neighborhoods have yet to be connected to a sewage system and do not have paved roads or sidewalks.

Selected Bibliography

Btselem, *A Policy of Discrimination: Land Expropriation, Planning and Building in East Jerusalem,* Comprehensive Report (May 1995).

Btselem Report, "Forbidden Roads," *http://www.btselem.org/english/publications/summaries/ 200408_forbidden_roads.asp* (accessed December 21, 2005).

Elisha Efrat, *Geografia shel Kibush [Geography of Occupation]* (Jerusalem: Carmel, 2002).

Zygmunt Bauman, *Globalization: The Human Consequences* (New York: Columbia University Press, 1998).

Yael Padan and Nili Baruch, "Bimkom Planners for Planning Rights Report, Eastern Ring Road," *http://www.bimkom.org/communityView.asp?projectId=35* (accessed December 21, 2005).

ARIJ, "Roads Circling Jerusalem," at *http://www.arij.org/paleye/road45/* (accessed December 21, 2005).

THE H₂O FACTOR

Jane Hilal and Sandra Ashhab

In arid areas such as the Middle East, conflict over scarce water resources appears inevitable. All the major regional river systems and many regional aquifers—no less those contested by Israel and Palestinians—cross national borders. Since Israel controls the Jordan River, groundwater has become the only possible water resource for Palestinians. Still, Israel insists on exploiting the majority of groundwater reservoirs, leaving Palestinians with a severe shortage. For Israel, control of this water is a crucial element of its geostrategic planning. "My view of Judea and Samaria [the West Bank] is well known," said then-infrastructure minister Ariel Sharon in 1998, "The absolute necessity of protecting our water in this region is central to our security. It is a non-negotiable item." (Boston Globe, 18 October 1998).

Following the 1967 War and Israel's occupation of the West Bank and Gaza Strip, Israel imposed restrictions on Palestinian water use and declared the lands located alongside the Jordan River closed military areas. Thus commenced Israel's steady appropriation of aquifer-rich areas for Jewish settlement expansion, a process, which has resulted in deep inequalities in local water use. Currently, Israel is exploiting about 82% of the annual safe yield of West Bank's groundwater basins to meet 25% of its water needs. By comparison, Palestinians consume 18% of the basins' annual safe yield.

The Israeli National Water Carrier unilaterally diverts the Jordan River water flow from Lake Tiberias to the dry Negev desert, without consideration for other riparian parties, including Palestinians. This has caused a drop in the river waters flowing into the Dead Sea. As a result of this (and mineral mining by both Israel and Jordan), the Dead Sea has sunk to dangerous levels, threatening the Dead Sea environment and diminishing its unique ecosystem.

Water consumption in the Gaza Strip now amounts to 100-110 mcm or million cubic meters per year. Taking into account the assumed natural inflow (a natural annual recharge rate of 60 mcm), the Gaza aquifer is heavily overexploited. This over-exploitation has continued for decades, beginning during the period of Egyptian administration between 1948 and 1967 (Shawwa, 1993:26) and after the Israeli occupation in 1967.

The Gaza aquifer is the only renewable resource available for supplying drinking water to the overpopulated strip. But the dramatic overexploitation of the groundwater is causing seawater intrusion (freshwater is extracted and seawater takes its place), rendering the water nearly undrinkable. In some areas, water salinity in Gaza is as high as 500 mg to one, twice the salinity level recommended by the World Health Organization (at 250 mg to one) (PHG, 2004:43). Israeli water policies are not only causing Palestinian thirst, but harming the environment—probably irreversibly.

WATER AND THE PEACE PROCESS

Israel recognized Palestinian water rights when it signed the Oslo accords (see article 40 in Oslo II). But the details of these rights were to be negotiated in subsequent permanent status negotiations. To date, however, no negotiations have been held; the issue of Palestinian water rights is expected to be one of the most fractious issues on the table.

In the interim, it was agreed that the future needs of Palestinians in the West Bank area measured 70 to 80 mcm of fresh water annually. It was also agreed that a stopgap measure to raise Palestinian domestic water availability during the interim period was to supply them with an additional 28.6 mcm. The Palestinian Authority would supply 19.1 mcm per year through the drilling of new wells, whereas the remaining 9.5 mcm per year was to be supplied by Israel (Israeli Ministry of Foreign Affairs, 1995:87). Regrettably, not all of this water has reached Palestinians; nor has the amount allotted proven sufficient to meet the population's expanding needs (PWA, 2003:19).

Since its occupation of the West Bank and Gaza Strip in 1967, Israel has granted Palestinians only a few permits for the digging of new water wells. All of these were restricted to domestic use. New water wells for agricultural purposes in the West Bank were also restricted to three permits. In addition, Israel policy of metering all Palestinian wells was another means of restricting quotas on Palestinian water utilization. In 1997 and in order to honor the Palestinian commitment of providing 19.1 mcm per year of newly supplied water resources, coordination was necessary within the framework of the joint Israeli-Palestinian-American Committee agreed upon by the Joint Water Committee (JWC) on water production and development-related projects. A project was initiated, commencing in July 1997. Six monitoring wells between 300 and 700 meters in depth, and six pairs of water supply wells between 350 and 850 meters in depth, were to be constructed in the Hebron, Bethlehem, Jenin, Nablus, and Ramallah areas. Within the framework of JWC, the Israelis had given the Palestinians proposed locations, but not permission, for 11 well sites for constructing Palestinian wells. These proposed wells were to be located in Hebron, Bethlehem, and East Jerusalem to tap the Eastern Aquifer System. According to the working plan of the project, the wells were to be completed within 18 months of initiation. By the year 1999, only two permissions had been granted to construct two wells in the Hebron-Bethlehem area in the Herodion well field. It was only in 2003 when Israel gave additional permission for the construction of six new wells, two of which were eventually supplanted in the plans by existing wells. Moreover, and in violation of the signed agreements, Israel has only supplied 12 mcm of water per year of the additional 80 million to which it committed itself.

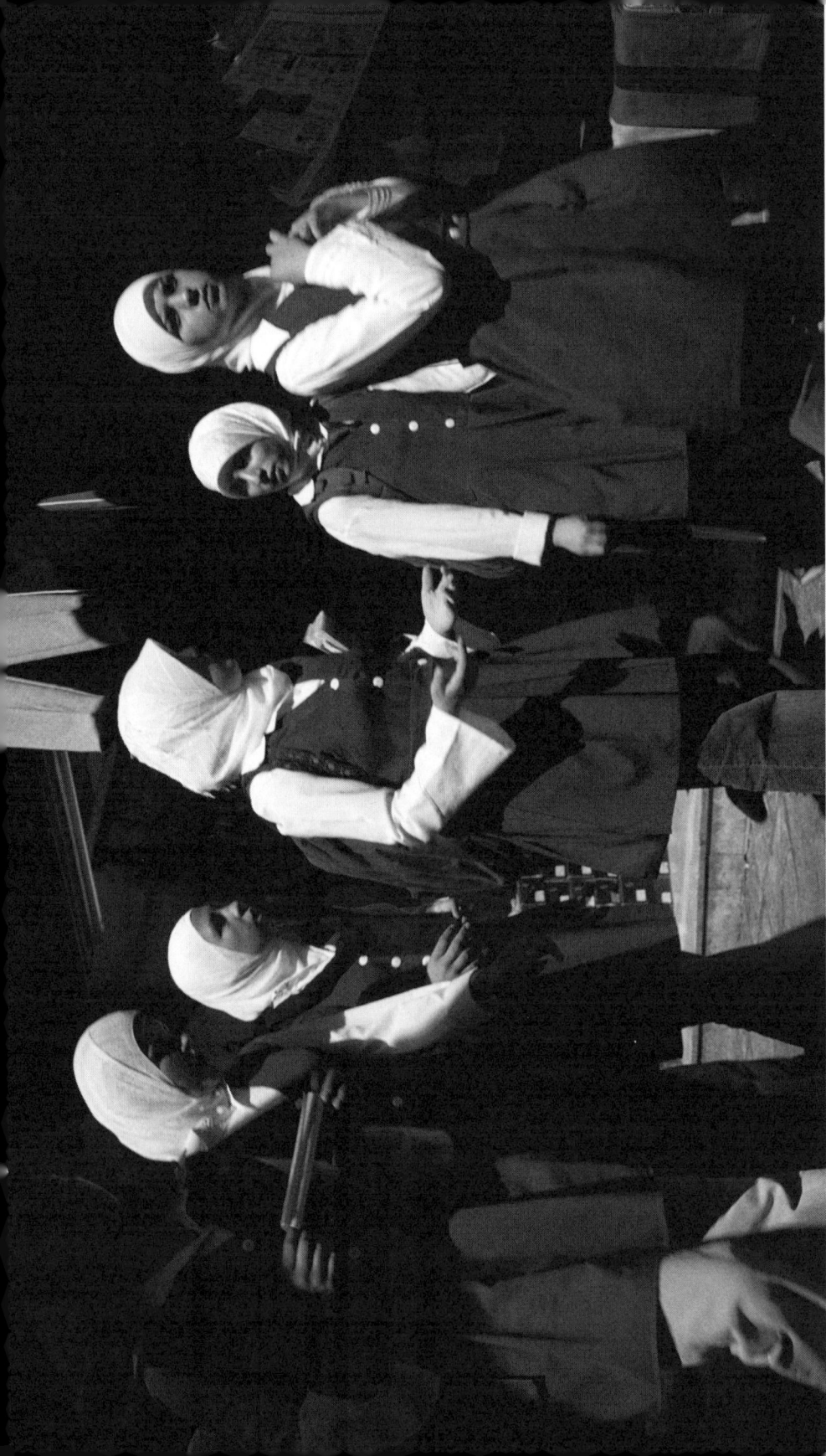

Palestinians are therefore forced to reconsider the Oslo II agreement and estimations of their water requirements for the future. They must also demand immediate and serious negotiations for their water rights to the Jordan River waters and the West Bank aquifers, particularly the western aquifer shared between Palestinian Authority and Israel. Currently, Palestinian consumption from this groundwater resource's safe yield does not exceed 6%.

INEQUITABLE ALLOCATION OF WATER RESOURCES IN THE JERUSALEM DISTRICT

The management of shared water resources in the region should ideally be inte-grated for their protection and sustainable use, with mutual recognition of each party's water rights. Water allocation and management between Israel and the Palestinians, however, is a projection of the larger conflict—it is defined by Israel's denial of Palestinian rights and continued resource colonization. Conditions in the Jerusalem District, where infrastructure is divided between the city's west and east, are representative of the issues at hand.

Although Palestinian East Jerusalem's water distribution infrastructures were built and/or repaired by the Israeli municipality after 1967, they remain consist-ently underdeveloped in comparison with those in West Jerusalem and the East Jerusalem Jewish settlements. The disparity in public services and infrastructure provided by the State of Israel to Jewish neighborhoods and Palestinian communi-ties in East Jerusalem is conscious and systemic. Former Jerusalem mayor Teddy Kollek confirmed this with brutal honesty: "We said things that were just talk, and carried them out. We repeatedly promised to give the Arabs in the city rights equal to those enjoyed by the Jews in the city—it was all empty words...For Jewish Jerusalem, I accomplished something over the past 25 years. For East Jerusalem ...Nothing. Cultural centers? Zilch. Yes, we provided them with sewage and we improved the water delivery system, but why? For their benefit? To make their lives better? Not at all. There were a few cases of cholera there, and the Jews panicked that it might come their way, so they improved the sewer system and the water system against the cholera" (Shragai, June 5, 2000).

Until 1967, East Jerusalem was supplied with water by the Jerusalem Water Undertaking (JWU, a private Palestinian water distribution company located in Ramallah). After the 1967 War, the Israeli Jerusalem Municipality connected the waterworks in east and west Jerusalem. In 1968, the offices, pipelines, and equipment of the JWU were confiscated and transferred to the Jerusalem munici-pality (Abdul-Jabar and Mir, 1998:101).

The Jerusalem municipality, as it was redefined by Israel after 1967, includes 1,032 kilometers of water pipeline snaking through the city (Jerusalem municipality website, November 20, 2005). On average, this equals one kilometer of pipe for every 600 Jerusalem residents and covers West Jerusalem, East Jerusalem, Jewish settlements in East Jerusalem, and other West Bank lands annexed by Israel to Jerusalem municipality. But the condition and size of the pipelines serving the Palestinian and Jewish communities are far from comparable. From 1967 until 1983, temporary gravitational lines of two inches in diameter were installed in some East Jerusalem Palestinian communities on the backbone of the Jordanian system, pending the development of comprehensive road, water, and sewage plans. Those plans never materialized, and piping was simply added on request and according to the availability of funds. In 1983, larger diameter pipes (12 to 16 inches) were installed, replacing the smaller network, as part of a decision to begin to replace the water system (Abdul-Jaber et al, 1998:114). But less than 30% of the upgrade plan has been carried out. Even today, there remain some rural Palestinian Jerusalem neighborhoods with no running water (PWA, 2003:5).

While Israel remains the main supplier of water through its national water corporation Mekorot Water Company Ltd., the water management in Jerusalem is divided between three main bodies: the Israel municipality (Gihon Company), the Jerusalem Water Undertaking (JWU), and the West Bank Water Department (WBWD). Gihon is responsible for managing both water and sewage for most of the Jewish areas inside the borders of the Jerusalem municipality (barring a few exceptions to be discussed later). The JWU supplies water to some Palestinian parts of the Jerusalem area, mainly its northern suburbs. Within the municipality boundaries, the JWU supplies Beit Hanina and Qalandiya refugee camp. It also supplies some villages outside of the municipal boundaries. To meet this demand, the JWU utilizes the Ein Samia wells east of Ramallah, augmented by water purchased from Gihon and the Mekorot Water Company (CDM/Morganti, 1997:25).

The WBWD, in existence since 1967, was an official governmental body, transformed by the Israeli Civil Administration into a sort of public department with responsibility for operating bulk water facilities. Protocols were signed by Israel relinquishing the WBWD to the Palestinian Authority in 1996, but the Palestinian side refused to sign this document because it did not include the return of thirteen West Bank wells confiscated by Israel in 1978 (Jass, 2004:1). Today WBWD supplies water to as-Sawahra as-Sharqiyya and al-Sheikh Sa'd (also called as-Sawahra al-Gharbiya), which both lie within Jerusalem's expanded municipal boundaries. It also supplies many villages within the Palestinian Jerusalem district.[1] (PWA, 2003:17).

In 1967, several days after the war, Israel and the United Nations Relief and Works Agency for Palestinian Refugees in the Near East (UNRWA) signed an agreement through the Israeli Ambassador to the United Nations, Michael Comay, and UNRWA Commissioner General Lawrence Michelmore. The agreement stated that Israel would, at its own expense, supply water to the refugee camps at public water points. Since 1989, however, Shufat refugee camp has been disconnected from the water network. The Israeli military government and Gihon ordered the disconnection after disagreements over water costs. Moreover, the Palestinian village of Ezariya is also in dispute with the Israeli municipality over water prices. By way of punishment, the village endures frequent reductions in water supply ordered by the Jerusalem municipality.

The underlying commonality of this complicated division of labor is that all three companies buy their water from the Israeli Mekorot Water Company. Each system, however, has a different pricing plan, which leads to very different prices for Israeli and Palestinian customers, to the disadvantage of the Palestinians, who end up paying higher water rates (New Israeli Shekel (NIS) 4 in Bethlehem as compared to approximately NIS 3.4 in Israel). This also influences the overall rate of water use (Palestinians use 81 m³ per year per capita while Israelis use 250 m³ per year per capita). In addition, these differently managed systems are distinguishable by their physical characteristics. For instance, inside the Jerusalem municipal boundaries, homes serviced by the Gihon Company (particularly Jewish neighborhoods) never have reserve water tanks on their roofs, simply because water is generously supplied all year round. Neighborhoods serviced by the JWU or WBWD, however, are easily recognizable by the large black water tanks on each and every roof (Abdel-Jaber, 1998:30).

In a 1999 strategic planning study, the Palestine Water Authority (PWA) indicated that the Jerusalem District would continue to depend on the Mekorot Water Company for the district's water supply even after the year 2020. It is clear that the PWA does not expect to have control of Jerusalem's wells before the year 2010; the frozen state of negotiations offers no reason to refute that prediction. Still, the PWA plans to supply 98% of Jerusalem's population with potable water by the year 2020. To achieve this target, the PWA is developing deep wells with pumps operating an average of 20 hours per day during regular consumption months and 24 hours per day during peak demand.

WATER AND THE SEGREGATION WALL

The intent of Israeli strategic planning is to control as many water resources as possible. Israel's construction of a series of walls, fences, patrol roads, barbed wire barriers, and guard towers running through Jerusalem's neighborhoods and the West Bank also incorporates an aspect of water resources confiscation.

In the northern part of the West Bank, 31 artesian wells have been isolated on the Israeli side of the Segregation Wall.[2] These wells tap the western basin of West Bank aquifers, with an annual discharge of 4.3 mcm; as such they represent 16% of the Palestinian share in the western aquifer. Palestinian agriculture depends a great deal upon the various springs that bubble up throughout the West Bank. The Segregation Wall has isolated 33 springs on its western (i.e. Israeli) side. In the eastern area bordering the Jordan River, a region that may also be blocked by the Segregation Wall in the future, there are 105 artesian wells and 30 springs that are used by Palestinians living in localities located within this slice. There is no doubt that the Segregation Wall will sever Palestinians from important water resources, at the very least making it more difficult to access these wells

Ethnic roofscapes: small white water tanks and solar heating plates are typical for Jewish areas, large black tanks signify Arab areas where they ensure basic water supply during frequent shortages (photos: editorial team, 2006)

and exacerbating already "dry" conditions. Further, it appears that this exercise of control is nonnegotiable. Israeli officials have indicated that the equitable sharing of water is a goal Palestinians shouldn't even dare dream of. "I recognize needs, not rights," Israeli water commissioner Meir Ben Meir noted in a meeting

with Palestinian negotiators. "We are prepared to connect Arab villages to Israel as well, but I want to retain sovereignty in hand."

To summarize, Israel controls, manages, and sells water to the Palestinians, including East Jerusalemites, on its own terms and without due regard for their needs. As a result of Israeli policies, Palestinians utilize 259 mcm per year to supply 3.6 million Palestinians in both the West Bank and Gaza Strip (including Jerusalem) with their domestic, industrial, and agricultural needs. By comparison, 6.8 million Israelis are utilizing 1,831 mcm per year. Broken down per capita, this is an annual difference of three times.

Colonization is usually perceived as a technique, taking shape at the surface of contested territories. Settlements, road infrastructures, fences, and barriers are the visible products of the struggle over territorial and demographic control. On the other hand, the control of resources such as water remains invisible at first and thus overlooked by the public as well as local and international media. Yet as argued in this article, the control over this "invisible layer" not only influences access, pricing politics, and living conditions, but also has very concrete physical consequences, determines the layout and position of settlements, and influenced the planning of the Segregation Wall. Colonization of resources is adding a third dimension to the geopolitics of the Middle Eastern conflict and a just solution over their distribution is a precondition for a lasting peace.

1   According to the Palestinian Authority, the Jerusalem District is one of 11 districts of the West Bank covering an area of 353.67 square km. The Jerusalem District is comprised of 49 localities in addition to two refugee camps (Qalandiya and Shufat) and 34 illegal Israeli settlements with an estimated Israeli settler population of 288,044.

2   Editor's note: Separation Fence/Wall in Jerusalem and the West Bank.

Selected Bibliography

Qasem Abdel Jaber et. al., *Wells in the West Bank: Water Quality and Chemistry* (Palestine: CMS Ltd., 1999).

Boston Sunday Globe, October 18, 1998.

Clean Development Mechanism (CDM)/Morganti and The West Bank Municipal Services Project, "Comprehensive Planning Framework for Palestinian Water Resources Development USAID and PWA (Task 4)," *report for the Water Resources Program*, Morganti (1997a).

Peter Glieck, "Basic Water Requirements for Human Activities: Meeting Basic Needs," *International Water* 21 (2) (1996).

Israeli Ministry of Foreign Affairs Report (1995).

Mohammad Jass, "International Forum on Food Security under Water Scarcity in the Middle East: Problems and Solutions," *West Bank Water Department Report* (2004).

Palestinian Hydrology Group, *WaSH Monitoring Report* (2004).

Palestinian Water Authority (PWA) Report (1999).

Palestinian Water Authority (PWA) Report (2003).

Malin Falkenmark and Carl Widstrand, "Population and Water Resources: A Delicate Balance," *Population Bulletin* 47 (3) (Nov. 1992).

Isam R. Shawwa, "The Water Situation in Gaza," in *Water: Conflict or Cooperation. Israel/Palestine: Issues in Conflict, Issues for Cooperation* 2 (2), ed. Gershon Baskin, 2nd ed. (Jerusalem; Israel/Palestine Center for Research and Information [IPCRI], 1993).

Mobility and Immobility

Contiguity

Haifa

Nazareth

Hadera

Tel Aviv

Ashqeton

Jerusalem

Dead Sea

Beersheba

Contiguity and Fragmentation
Israel and West Bank

Movement inside the West Bank is based on
two nearly completely segregated road systems superimposed on each other. After the
Oslo Accords and the establishment of limited
Palestinian self-rule, Israel begun to invest in
bypass roads which linked the most important
settlements with Israel proper. Most settlers now
no longer needed to drive through Palestinian
towns and villages, and were able to maintain
a suburban lifestyle working in Israel but living
in the occupied territories. After the al-Aqsa Intifada, Palestinians were barred of many of these
roads; entrance and exit points were sealed.
Palestinian traffic was left to use an old road
system punctuated by checkpoints.

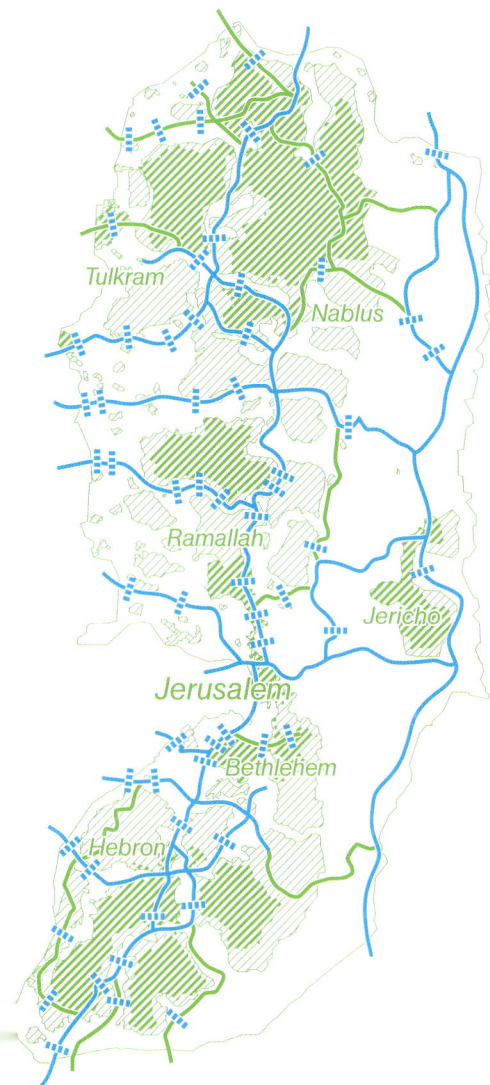

Tulkram

Nablus

Ramallah

Jericho

Jerusalem

Bethlehem

Hebron

Contiguity

		Israeli main roads
	●	Israeli settlements
	◯	Israeli cities
		Oslo Area C (full Israeli control)

Fragmentation

		Israeli main roads
		Checkpoints
		Oslo Area A (full control of the Palestinian Authority)
		Oslo Area B (Palestinian civil control, Israeli military control)

0   10   20   30   40 kilometers

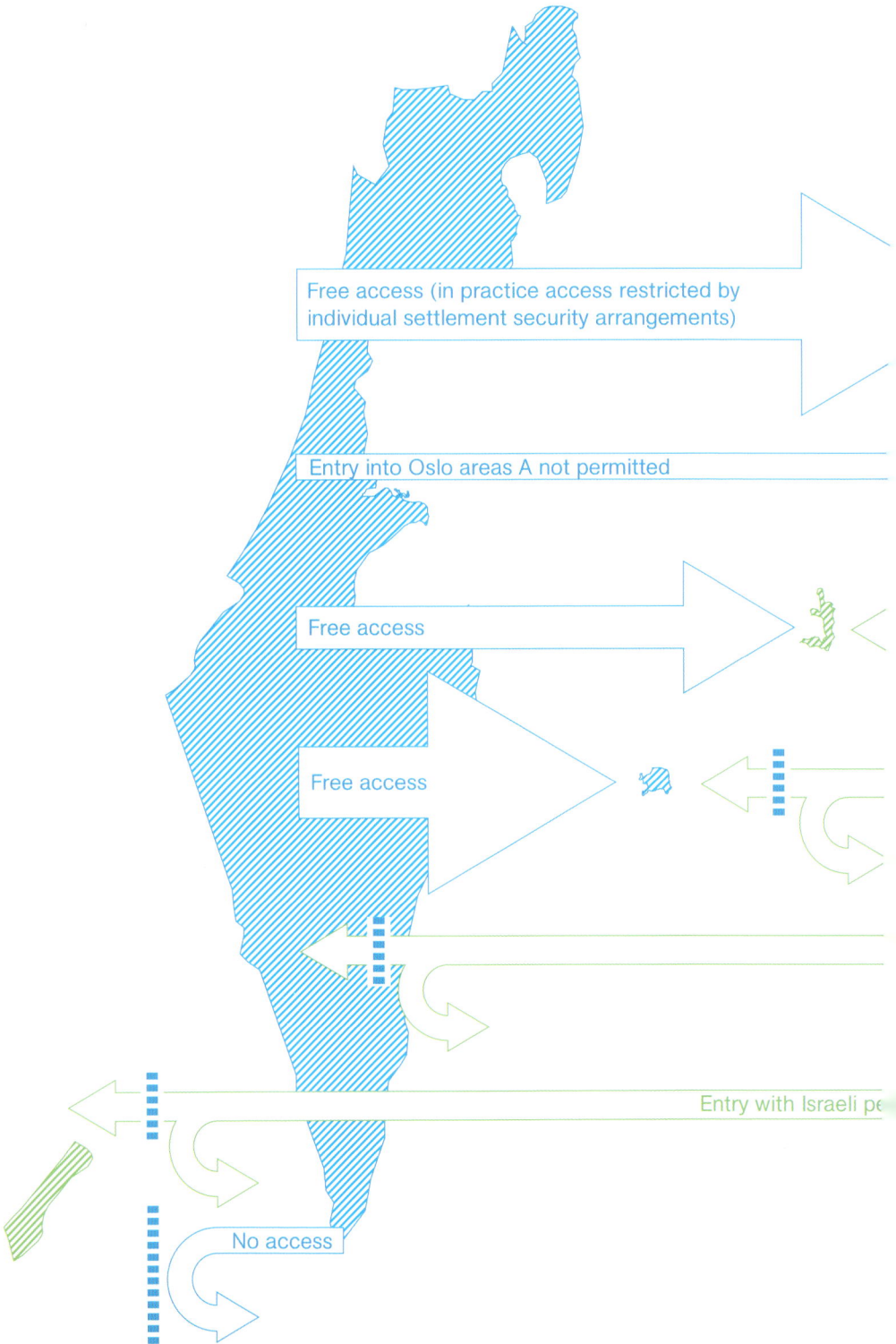

Free access (in practice access restricted by individual settlement security arrangements)

Entry into Oslo areas A not permitted

Free access

Free access

Entry with Israeli pe

No access

Settlements (Area C)	West Bank (Areas A/B)

Movement Restrictions
Israel / Occupied Territories

Restrictions on movement have become one of the most effective tools used in enforcing Israeli occupation of Palestinian territory. As a consequence of Oslo-sanctioned territorial fragmentation, Palestinians are exposed to a complex and constantly-changing regime of travel permits and checkpoints, while thousands of settlers travel freely to Jerusalem and Israel on bypass roads. Traffic between the West Bank and Gaza is at a complete standstill; few Palestinians are issued work permits for Israel, or access permits to work, study, seek healthcare and so on. Israelis are barred by the Israeli Army from entering Palestinian administerred territories. Security fears and a persisting Arab boycott prevents most Israelis from travel to the surrounding Arab states.

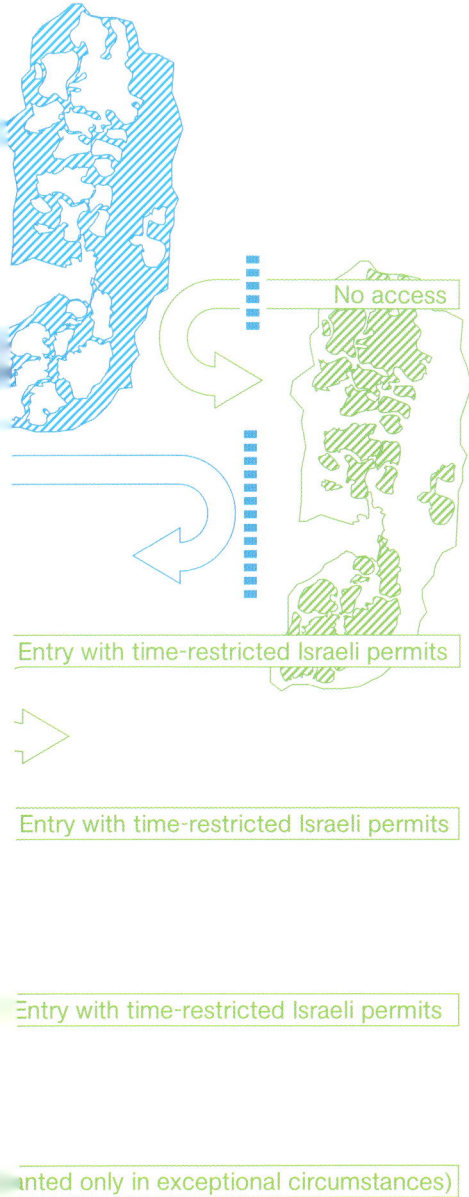

No access

Entry with time-restricted Israeli permits

Entry with time-restricted Israeli permits

Entry with time-restricted Israeli permits

Entry with time-restricted Israeli permits

anted only in exceptional circumstances)

	Access
	Access refused
	Checkpoints

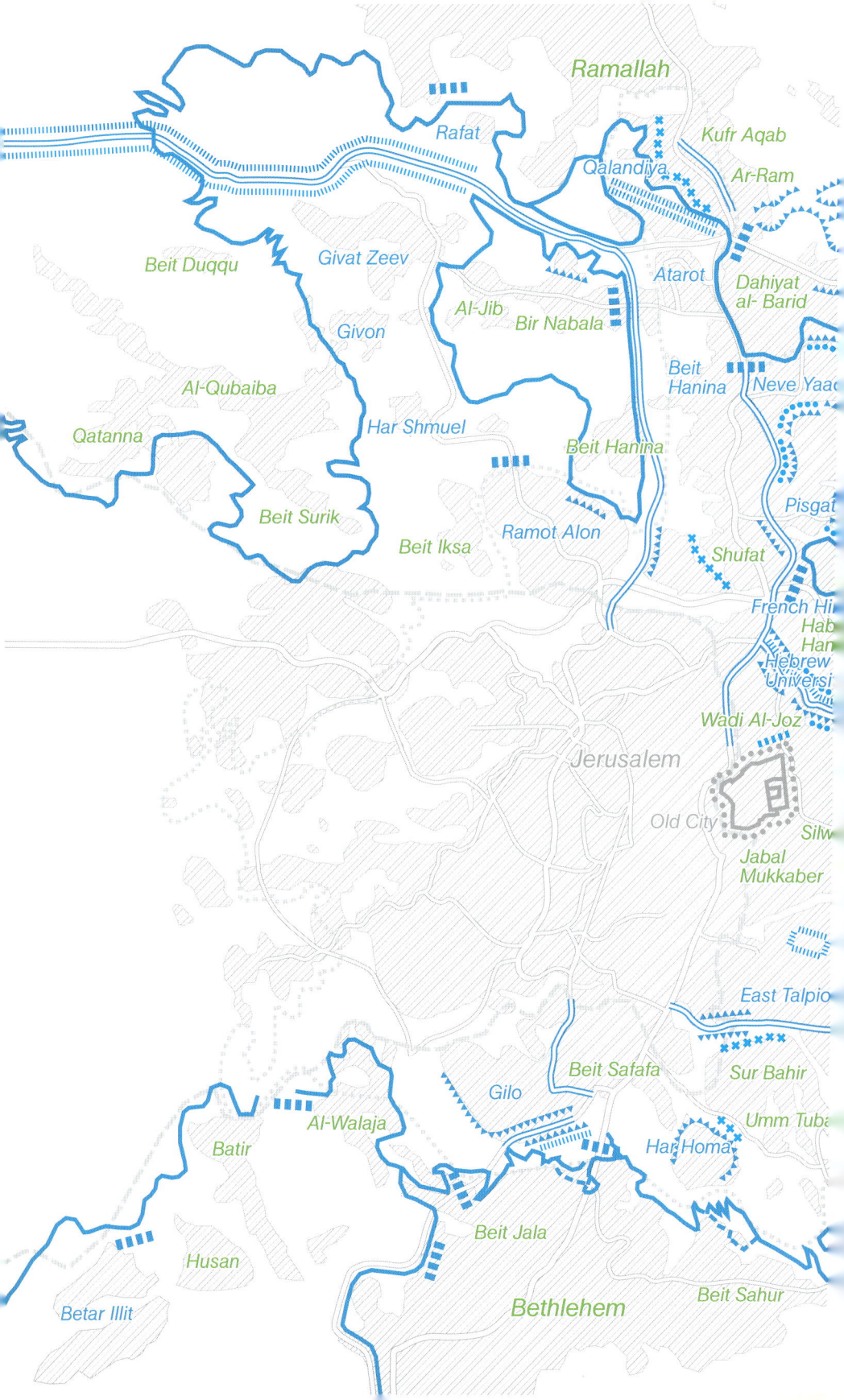

Ramallah

Rafat

Kufr Aqab

Qalandiya

Ar-Ram

Beit Duqqu

Givat Zeev

Atarot

Dahiyat al- Barid

Al-Jib

Bir Nabala

Givon

Beit Hanina

Neve Yaac

Al-Qubaiba

Har Shmuel

Beit Hanina

Qatanna

Pisgat

Beit Surik

Ramot Alon

Shufat

Beit Iksa

French Hi

Hab

Han

Hebrew Universi

Wadi Al-Joz

Jerusalem

Old City

Silw

Jabal Mukkaber

East Talpio

Beit Safafa

Sur Bahir

Gilo

Umm Tuba

Al-Walaja

Batir

Har Homa

Husan

Beit Jala

Beit Sahur

Betar Illit

Bethlehem

Frontiers
Jerusalem (2005)

Despite the physical intimacy of Palestinian and Israeli Jerusalem, their differing urban systems are separated by identifiable physical buffer spaces and barriers such as walls, fences, roads, dikes, slopes, plantations or valleys. This array of frontier typologies obstructs and limits visual or physical contact. While Israeli government maintains the rhetoric of a "unified city," its planning policies encourage the increasing fracturing of the urban landscape along ethnic territorial lines, which helps to limit Palestinian growth and allows for the easy severing of all linkages between the communities in times of security alerts. The Separation Wall/Fence is the most extreme of these typologies. It not only separates Israelis from Palestinians, but slices the Palestinian socioeconomic and cultural fabric between villages annexed into Israeli Jerusalem, and their West Bank hinterlands.

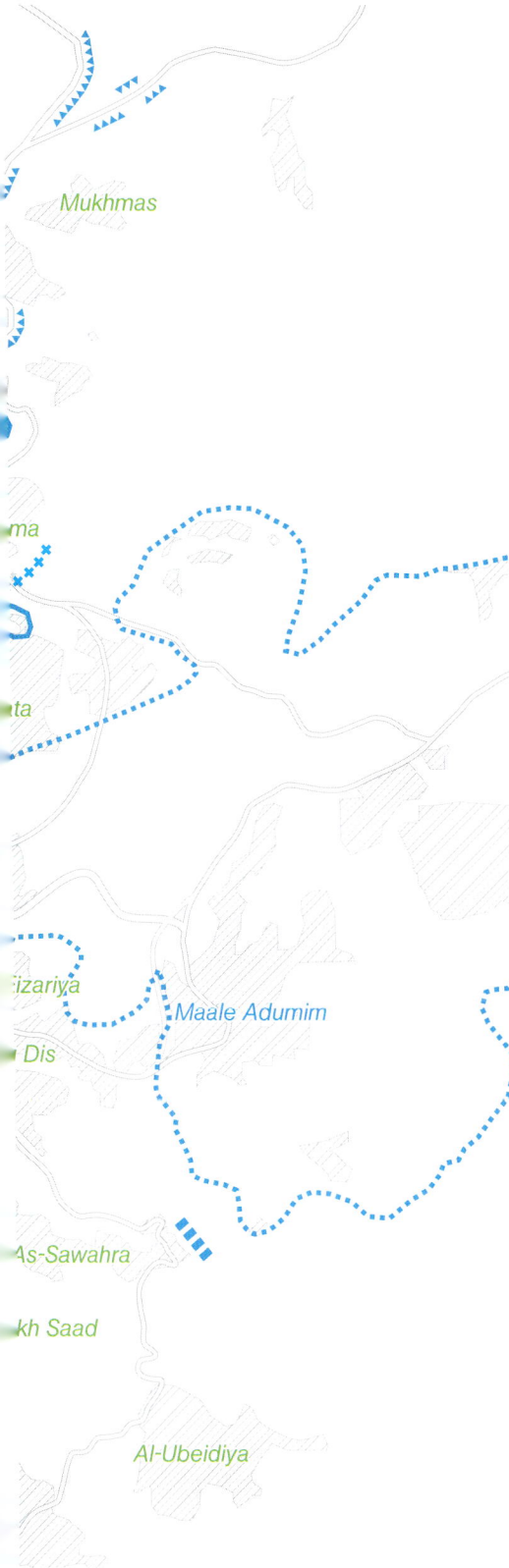

Mukhmas

ma

ta

izariya

Maale Adumim

Dis

As-Sawahra

kh Saad

Al-Ubeidiya

	Separation Fence/Wall
	Separation Fence/Wall route subjected to further complotition
	Fences
	Roads
	Topography
	Waste lands
	Public green
	Checkpoints

0   1   2   3   4   5 kilometers

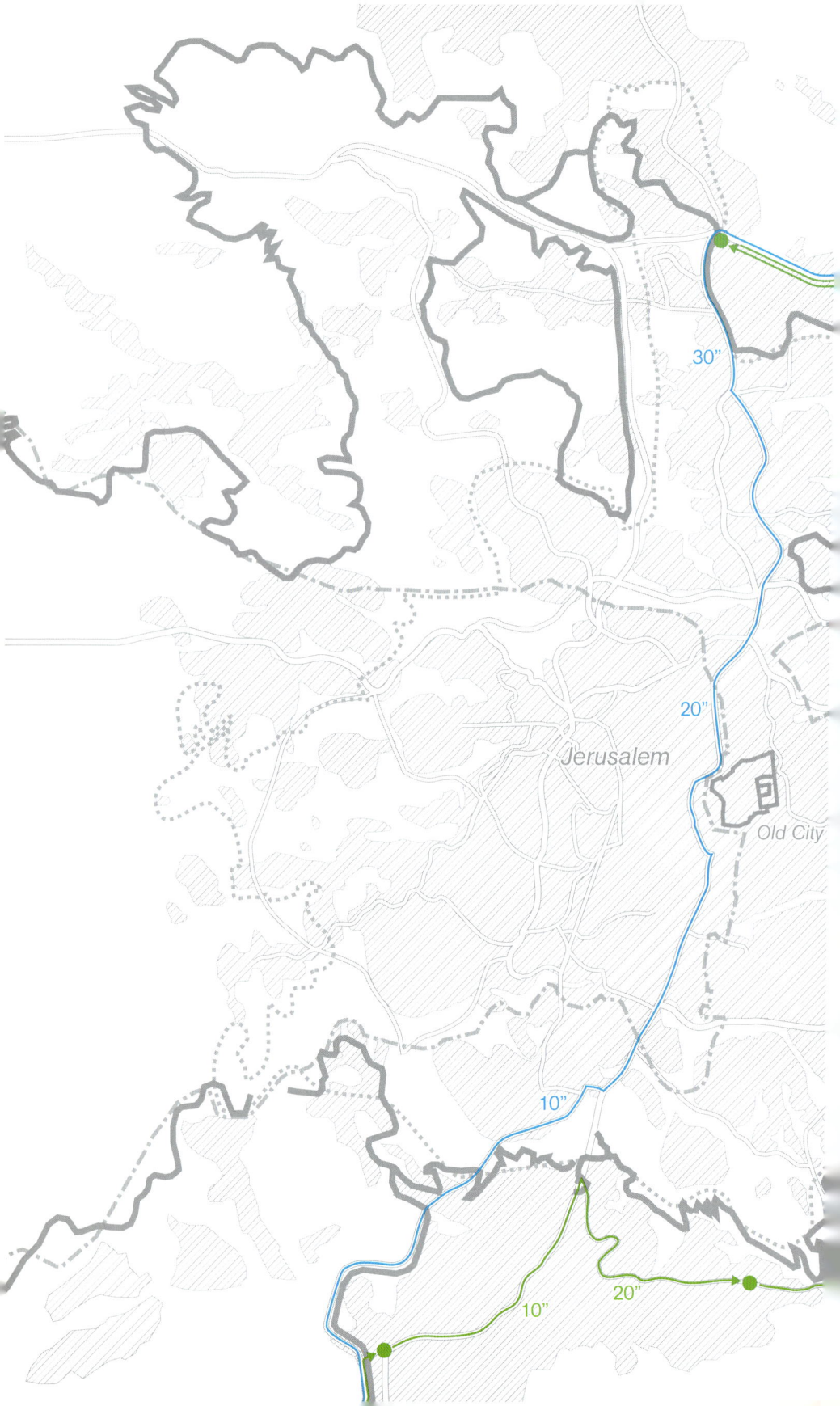

Jerusalem

Old City

30"

20"

10"

10"

20"

Exemplary Travel Routes
Jerusalem (2005)

While Israeli settlers continue to use the fast arterial highway system of Road 60/Road 1, which connects Jerusalem with the northern and southern parts of the West Bank, this route's central Jerusalem section has been closed to West Bank Palestinians since 2000. Barring medical emergencies or rarely-issued work permits, their access to the city is denied. This documented example of the route between Bethlehem and Ramallah shows how Palestinian travellers are forced to take a lengthy detour across the hilly desert mountains, a route frequently interrupted by military checkpoints. The formal overland bus system has collapsed and private vehicles are often prohibited, making informal private Ford transit drivers a flexible and cheap travel alternative which links several transportation hubs along the route.

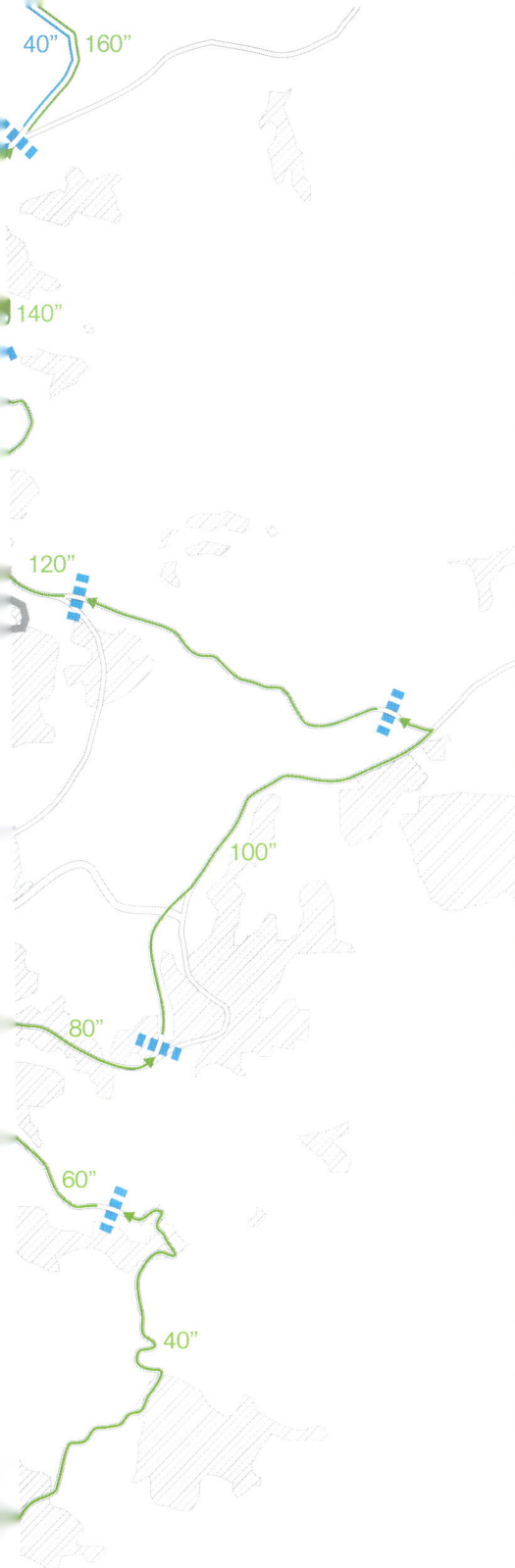

	Separation Wall/Fence
	Palestinian travel route (example)
	Israeli travel route (example)
	Mini bus hubs
	Checkpoint

0   1   2   3   4   5 kilometers

40" 160"
140"
120"
100"
80"
60"
40"

Road Systems
Sur Bahir / Har Homa (2005)

The morphology of road patterns in Sur Baher and Har Homa indicates both cultural differences between Israelis and Palestinians and their asymmetrical access to public resources. The settlement is served by a convenient inner city highway, a linear system, which includes signage and hierarchical control systems and relies on a high levels of planning and maintenance.
In contrast, the road system in Sur Bahir evolved over centuries in parallel with the changing needs of the local villages. As an open capillary road system, it reflects close linkages between the communities and their agricultural hinterlands. It is non-hierarchical and can be extended and adjusted with ease. The lack of signage, sidewalks, and repair reflect a lack of municipal investment. The limited points of crossover between Israeli and Palestinian road systems are indicative not only of fears and mental barriers dividing the communities, but also allow easy control through Israeli military checkpoints.

Palestinian roads

Israeli roads

Temporary checkpoints

0 | 100 | 200 | 300 | 400 | 500 meters

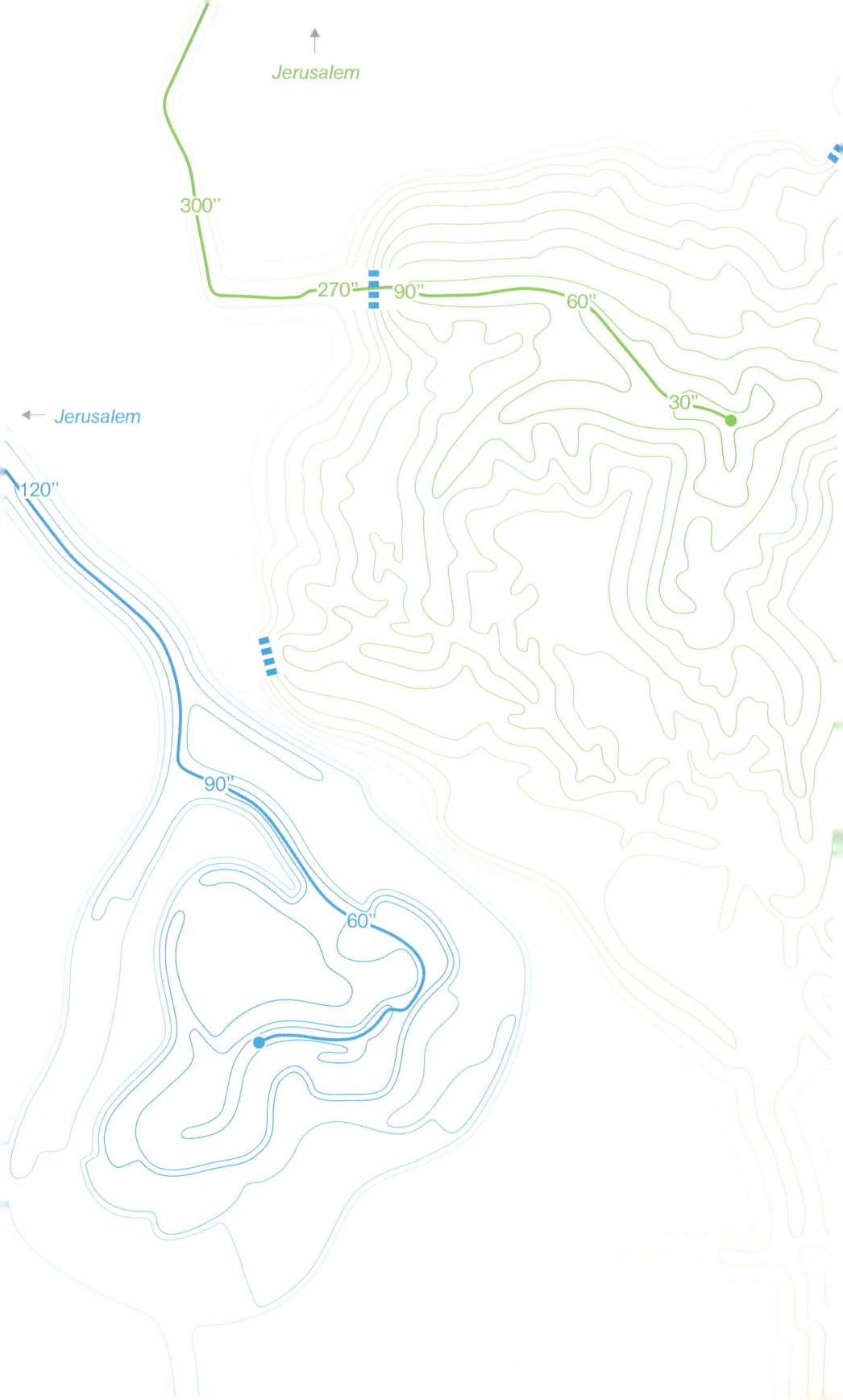

Jerusalem

300"

270" 90"

60"

30"

Jerusalem

120"

90"

60"

Travel Speeds
Sur Bahir / Har Homa (2005)

Measuring travel speed and efficiency of car
access indicates the fundamental qualitative
differences between Israeli and Palestinian road
systems.

	Palestinian travel route (example)
	Israeli travel route (example)
	Travel time Sur Bahir (30 seconds intervals)
	Travel time Har Homa (30 seconds intervals)
	Temporary checkpoints

| 0 | 100 | 200 | 300 | 400 | 500 meters |

Frontiers
Sur Bahir / Har Homa (2005)

Settlement and village have a different, even
oppositional relationship to the surrounding
landscape, which is indicative of cultural differences and the dynamics of the conflict. A heavy
retaining wall system has been designed to
protect the introverted settlement of Har Homa,
whose rounded perimeter evokes the military
logic of minimizing contact with the outside.
A single access road guarded by a police station
connects the settlement with its surroundings.
Engagement with the landscape is reduced to
panoptic views, made possible by staggered
building arrangements. In contrast, Sur Bahir's
boundary is highly permeable, providing numerous access points for villagers travelling to
their agricultural land holdings. The distinction
between built-up area and landscape is blurred.

	Buildings
	Trees
	Slopes
	Retaining walls
	Access

0 | 100 | 200 | 300 | 400 | 500 meters

Concept and copyright

Tim Rieniets, Philipp Misselwitz

Sources

Project Grenzgeografien (International Peace and Cooperation Center IPCC Jerusalem, Bezalel Academy of Art and Design Jerusalem, University of the Arts Berlin, ETH Swiss Federal Institute of Technology Zurich), *Trilateral Student Workshops* (Jerusalem, 2003-2005).

United Nations, Office for the Coordination of Humanitarian Affairs (OCHA), *Closure Maps* (2005).

MONUMENTS
NO-MAN'S-LANDS

Wherever Israeli and Palestinian urban fragments collide, a host of frontier spaces exists—territories of fear and anxiety, hostile wildernesses, and buffer zones that shield each community from the other. Given a closer look, these sites reveal ambivalence. Contradictory elements of traditional agricultural landscape and its decay are juxtaposed with green areas orchestrated as parks or monuments. The rural has been replaced by the suburban, the agricultural by the decorative. Garbage dumps and neglected olive groves alternate with pockets of a highly engineered and aesthetic (yet often equally deserted) landscape. This micro-landscape mirrors the spatial quality of the sprawling Jerusalem conurbation at large. Its discontinuities embody the tensions and contradictions of a landscape that has been urbanized rapidly under conditions of intense conflict. They are symptoms of a hidden fight over identity, ownership, and aesthetic domination of an otherwise banal-seeming suburban landscape.

BARING LIFE

CITIES, MILITARY VIOLENCE, AND THE POLITICS OF REPRESENTATION

Derek Gregory

The question "In what way does the living being have language?" corresponds exactly to the question "In what way does bare life dwell in the polis?" (Giorgio Agamben, 1998:8)

The exclusionary matrix by which subjects are formed requires the simultaneous production of a domain of abject beings. ...The abject designates here precisely those "unlivable" and "uninhabitable" zones of social life which are nevertheless densely populated by those who do not enjoy the status of the subject, but whose living under the sign of the "unlivable" is required to circumscribe the domain of the subject. (Judith Butler, 1993:3)

ORIENTALISM, OBJECTIVES, AND OBJECTS

Edward Said identified two moments in the operations of modern Orientalism. In the first, "the Orient" is conjured as a space of the exotic and the bizarre, the monstrous and the pathological: "a living tableau of queerness." In the second, "the Orient" is summoned as a space to be disciplined through the forceful projection of the order that the first presumes it to lack: "framed by the classroom, the criminal court, the prison, the illustrated manual" (Said, 1978:41, 103). I want to highlight the continuing connection between epistemological violence—in particular the epigraph that, with exquisite irony, prefaces Said's critique: Marx's admonition that "[T]hey cannot represent themselves; they must be represented"—and the corporeal violence of the "war on terror."

The US-led wars in Afghanistan and Iraq, and their opportunistic extensions in occupied Palestine and elsewhere, claim to project military violence from the space of reason into spaces of unreason. This cartography is sustained through three imaginative geographies that make those other spaces "Other" by mapping them in highly particular and partial ways.

Strategy	Register	Space
Locating	techno-cultural	abstract, geometric
Inverting	politico-cultural	wild, savage
Excepting	politico-juridical	paradoxical, topological

These renderings have such acutely material consequences that they can be described as *performances of space*. The second and third strategies reinforce one another to produce precisely those "unlivable" and "uninhabitable" zones that Judith Butler identified so presciently. "Inverting" works primarily in a politico-cultural register to produce a wild and savage landscape stalked by marauding bands of barbarians. "Excepting" works primarily in a politico-juridical register to produce a paradoxical space, whose contortions can only be conveyed through a topology, the haunt of "shadowy 'third things' lodged between animal and human," placed by the force of law outside the protections of the law (Gilroy, 2003:261-76).

These tropes are commonplace in the sphere of Orientalism where so much of the "war on terror" is orchestrated. But how can such maps show the cities on which Orientalism's martial fury is focused? If cities are the pivots of civilization, as a long tradition of Western political thought insists, then how can military attacks on Kabul and Qandahar, East Jerusalem and Jericho, Baghdad and Basra, be sustained without compromising the very cartography of violence on which the "war on terror" is based? How can the existence of such places be made to commensurate with their habitation by barbarians and "third things"? The answers, I suggest here, turn on the first strategy, which locates cities like these within an abstract, geometric space that makes them not only become military objectives but also *objects*. To understand how this works, it is necessary to examine how this strategy, like the other two, activates a series of profoundly colonial dispositions.

CITIES, CONFLICTS, AND COLONIALISMS

The history of cities is also, in part, the history of war. The two—the destruction of the one by the other—have marched in lockstep throughout recorded history. Ryan Bishop and Gregory Clancey have identified an abrupt break in the bleak tattoo from Mesopotamia to modern Iraq, however, from a world in which "whole cities were destroyed and their inhabitants slaughtered" to one in which "urban sacking was sporadic and constrained" (Bishop and Clancey, 2003:64). This rupture, they say, was brought about by the Napoleonic wars. In turn, I would argue that this is an excessively generous reading minimizing revolutionary France's repeated assaults on cities. It turns a particularly blind eye to Bonaparte's butchery at Jaffa in March 1799, an episode bookended by the bloody reprisals taken by the occupying French army against insurgents in Cairo in October 1798 and again in April 1800. For Said, of course, the French occupation of Egypt marked the threshold of a distinctively modern form of Orientalism, and in fact Bishop and Clancey concede that "Europeans continued to raze African and Asian cities," but "the destruction of cities became a show at the periphery" in spaces pitched outside the space of the modern. Monsters were loose in the *demi-monde* and would only be cowed by spectacular displays of violence. These colonial lessons were eventually repatriated to the Western metropolis, and then later reexported to the global South for, as the authors observe, "the colonial city was the paradigm for the city-as-target that has dominated the military imagination in the twentieth century" (Bishop and Clancey, 2003:68). By identifying three ways in which the contemporary strategy of "locating" reactivates that colonial paradigm, I want to show that this has continued into the twenty-first century.

TARGETS AND THE GEOPOLITICS OF VERTICALITY

Eyal Weizman has shown how the Israeli encirclement, occupation, and dispossession of Palestinian lands has been effected through what he calls a "politics of verticality," (Weizman, 2002) and Stephen Graham has both generalized and radicalized this as a "geopolitics of verticality" (Graham, 2004:12-19). Graham means this to convey the US predilection for high-level warfare waged on cities in Afghanistan and Iraq. During the first phase of the attack on Afghanistan in 2001, for example, news management worked to restrict reporting on the ground. The intent was to make those held responsible for the attacks on the Pentagon and the World Trade Center appear as nothing more than locations on a grid, letters on a map: notations in an abstract space. Weeks before they took to the skies, pilots had flown sorties over "Afghanistan," a high-resolution three-dimensional virtual space, produced through a mission rehearsal system called Topscene that enabled pilots to visualize their approaches to designated targets. It was so "life-like" (or death-like, depending on your point of view) that "Afghanistan" was virtually interchangeable with Afghanistan. Time and time again, the media merged with the military in their reification of this techno-cultural imaginary. In the weeks preceding the invasion of Iraq, for example, press and television reports were dominated by satellite imagery and the reduction of Baghdad to a city of targets. "Get a satellite-eye's view of Baghdad," *USA Today* invited visitors to its website. The *Washington Post*'s interactive instructed viewers to "roll over the numbers to see what targets were hit on which day; click to read more about the targets."

Aerial bombardment originated in colonial warfare, but these contemporary strategies are colonizing in a much more insidious sense. They depend on abstractions to produce the illusion of an authorizing master-subject who asserts, through the unyielding geometries of linear perspective, both visual mastery and violent possession. They deploy a discourse of objectivity—so that elevation secures the higher Truth—and a discourse of object-ness that reduces the world to a series of objects in a visual plane. Bombs and missiles then rain down on coordinates and letters: on K-A-B-U-L but not on the city of Kabul, its innocent inhabitants terrorized and their homes shattered by another round in the incessant wars, choreographed by superpowers from a safe distance. The result—fervently desired and carefully orchestrated—is optical detachment.

"Remote as they are far from 'targets'," Zygmunt Bauman observes, "scurrying over those they hit too fast to witness the devastation they cause and the blood they spill, the pilots-turned-computer-operators hardly ever have the chance of looking their victims in the face and to survey the human misery they have sowed" (Bauman, 2001:11-28). Just like Mr. Barrow who ventured into "the land of the Bushmen" in the early 19th century and reported sighting not the Bushmen but merely "scratches on the face of the country," so do these images reveal scars on the face of the country but never scars on the faces of those injured and killed there (Pratt, 1985:119-43).

The various viewing publics produced by this voyeuristic spectacle are themselves complicit in the process of effacement. The week Saddam's statue was toppled in the center of Baghdad, new maps of the city were published by newspapers and magazines. "Targets" were replaced by "neighborhoods," and it turned out that these were inhabited not by tyrants, torturers, and terrorists—as one might have expected—but by doctors, architects, shopkeepers, children: people very much like you and me. How loudly would the war-drums have sounded had maps like these spiraled through the public sphere in the months and weeks before "shock and awe" was unleashed?

GEOMETRIES AND THE POLITICS OF URBAN WARFARE

In his influential meditations *On War*, published in 1832, Clausewitz argued that "the geometrical element" was indispensable at the tactical level but had been greatly exaggerated at the level of strategy. Urban warfare confounds these distinctions, however, and the "war on terror" has mobilized a series of geometric imaginaries to structure its operations in "urbanized terrain" (a term-of-art that craftily reproduces those geometric emphases). In September 2002, the US Joint Chiefs of Staff issued their *Doctrine for Joint Urban Operations*. The prospect of an imminent invasion of Iraq had produced nightmare scenarios of urban warfare: unlike Afghanistan, Iraq is densely urbanized and the Iraqi regime insisted it would take the fight to the streets. On the pages of the *Doctrine*, the city appeared as an object-space—a space of envelopes, hard structures, and networks—that posed a series of geometric challenges to be met by geometric responses. Although much has been made of the close cooperation between the US military and the Israel Defense Forces, the horrifying US assaults on Fallujah in April and November 2004 mobilized the most solid of geometries, leveling vast areas of the city. In contrast, a senior IDF (Israeli Defense Forces) officer in Tel Aviv told me (also in November 2004) that the key to urban warfare was a more forensic "deconstruction" of "the spatial grammar of the Arab city"—and his models were Derrida and Deleuze.

Here, too, the ground is prepared using simulations. There are close collaborations with Hollywood set designers and FX-technicians to construct mock "Arab cities" for troops to rehearse their roles, and collaborations with videogame designers and filmmakers to produce virtual scenarios. For example "one square mile of tightly-nested buildings," which, according to an executive from game company Forterra Systems, is "reminiscent of Baghdad...which Army soldiers all over the world [can] roam simultaneously." Projects like these dissolve the boundaries between the military and the public. *Full Spectrum Warrior* emerged out of these collaborations and is available in both commercial and military versions so that, as one journalist noted, you can now walk into a games store "and get a taste of what it is like to manage troops under Arab fire" (Thompson, 2004; Slagle, 2004). Not surprisingly, in the weeks before the invasion of Iraq, American and British media reproduced the same imaginary (a beta-version, as it were) with remarkable fidelity: "Inside Iraqi cities, military operations would be vastly more complicated... From sewers to rooftops, cities are multilayered, like three-dimensional chessboards, creating endless opportunities for ambushes and snipers... 'Urban warfare is close, personal and brutal,' says an Army report. 'Tall buildings, sewer and storm drains, allow unobserved shifting of forces, and streets become kill-zones'" (Tyson, 2003).

Here, too, graphics dramatized the likely scenarios of urban warfare. In endless cutaways and Flash presentations, US troops were shown moving purposefully through a shell-torn landscape of buildings, streets, and alleys. Yet in most
cases, the only human figures to be seen were those of the troops themselves.
Helicopter gunships swooped low over the streets and alleys, tanks raised their
barrels and swiveled their turrets, patrols fired round after round. There were
explosions, smoke, flames—but no sign of Iraqi troops, insurgents, or even a
civilian population.

This hollowing-out of the city has two rhetorical effects. First, it repeats the
familiar colonial gesture of *Terra Nullius*, but transposes it to the city, which
similarly becomes a vacant space awaiting possession. The city's very emptiness
works to convey a right to be there to those who represent it thus. Second, it
decorporealizes the city, which becomes a space, permeated with violence, yet
without a body in sight. If the city can be so readily reduced to a space of objects,
it is scarcely surprising that death is made to disappear into "collateral damage."

LABYRINTHS AND THE GEOGRAPHIES
OF MILITARY OCCUPATION

The "war on terror" permits no clinical distinction between military offensives
and military occupations, but military occupation cannot be conducted in the
language of targets and geometries alone. The city must still be represented
as a spatialized object. One of the first tasks assigned to the engineers who
accompanied the Napoleonic expedition to Egypt was to draw up a detailed
map of Cairo (and one of the first objectives, of the insurgents, was to sack the
house of the engineers and make off with their surveying instruments). But
military occupation makes it plain that cities are more than object-fields, and
military research organizations have had to come to terms belatedly with the
people who live in them. A steady stream of military-technical conference presentations from 2000 through 2002 complained that while "civilian populations
can have a profound effect on a crowded battle space," existing military simulations provide "little representation" of them. But "representation" was made to
carry a particular charge. Several research groups are currently working on the
development of crowd modeling capabilities for the US military, for example,
and their graphics work is state-of-the-art; yet their generative assumptions
mimic the shop-worn behavioral geography of the 1970s. The city is imagined
and animated as a series of physical paths and object-tracks.[1] There is little
or no recognition of the city as a cultural space, permeated with meaning and
effect, so that the simulations provide a techno-cultural echo of Said's epigram:
"They cannot represent themselves; they must be represented." Those who
live in these cities are not allowed a cogent voice of their own, but are reduced
to crowds and mobs. Even research directed toward creating "artificially intel-
ligent virtual characters that can interact with humans using natural language,"
who "will understand the situation" and "act as members of the local population," relies on an abstract behavioral model rather than a substantive cultural
geography. The difference between the two is considerable, as the CEO of
Forterra Systems reveals when he fantasizes about a world in which "friendly

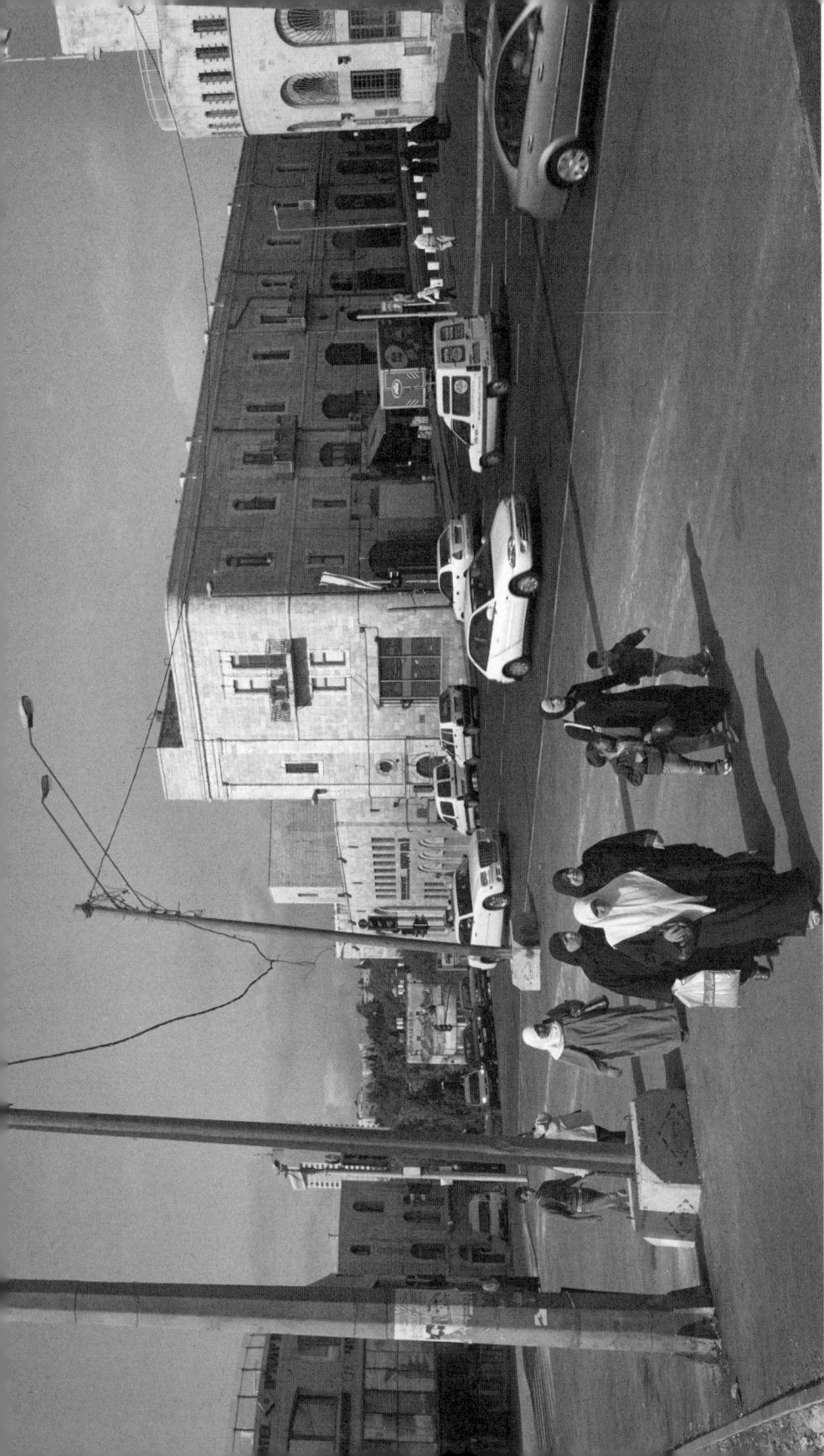

20.6 km: Jaffa Street

Iraqis could log on and take part in a virtual mob scene, complete with abuse hurled in Arabic" (Verton, 2005).

There are some signs that the military has followed contemporary urban theory into its own cultural turn, recognizing however —as that same IDF officer told me—"the need to conduct cultural voyages into different territories," in order to conceptualize "the logic of the Other." In 2004, the Combat Studies Institute inaugurated its series of "Occasional Papers on the Global War on Terrorism" with an extended essay on military operations and the Middle Eastern city (there's apparently only one of them) (DiMarco, 2004). The survey, by the author of the *US Army's Field Manual 3-06 on Urban Operations*, opens with a review of several descriptive urban models that, while technically less sophisticated than computer animations, at least do not reduce cities to grids and lattices. Instead, there is considerable emphasis on the *places* through which cultural meanings are activated and negotiated, and on the *protocols* through which they are established. There are discussions on the sacred geometry of the mosque and the conduct of its welfare activities within the local community; the neighborhood and the codes through which privacy is maintained; and the home as a place which "no person [should] enter uninvited."

But these cultural affordances turn out to be mere preliminaries to their abrupt reversal. Mosques must be monitored and may be "isolated" from the community ("as a last resort") by "shaping operations." Neighborhoods are mazes of narrow streets, alleys, and culs-de-sac—difficult to navigate and even harder to enter by surprise. But these same characteristics "make isolating specific objectives from reinforcement and preventing the escape of targeted enemy forces easier." Similarly, "effective population control techniques" can be implemented through "well-placed checkpoints," and armored bulldozers can "maximize mounted movement" through these close quarters. Inward-facing courtyard homes "are more secure from rapid seizure and search," but this simply "changes the TTP (tactics, techniques and procedures) for those charged with attacking, defending, seizing or searching these types of residences" (Dimarco, 2004:23, 32, 36-7).

The result is a sort of *Doppelgänger* geography, in which claims from more or less conventional urban studies are reversed by the priorities of military occupation. Any city would be made strange by such an analysis, but Arab cities are made doubly strange. They are rendered as inherently deceptive, places where nothing is ever as it seems, opaque spaces that conceal as much as they reveal, labyrinths designed to trap the unwary. Those who inhabit them are thus axiomatically alien, irredeemably other, because even in "normal" circumstances these are not normal cities.[2] They speak not only from positions of power and privilege but from a single (and singular) space of reason. There is a telling passage towards the end of the survey, where poverty is sutured to political radicalism and resistance. "Insurgents use the grievances of the urban poor to garner recruits, support and sanctuary," so that "a key to countering terrorists and insurgents based among the urban poor is removing their grievances" (DiMarco, 2004:53, 60). True to the traditions of colonialism, it is poverty, ignorance, and manipulation by malcontents that provokes insurgency; military occupation can never see itself as a legitimate cause for rebellion.

CITIES, CIVILIZATIONS, AND CIVILIANS

These various modalities direct urban warfare to two hideous ends. On one hand, they severely reduce and even annul the "right to the city" that has been celebrated by European and American political theory for centuries. The apotheosis of this terrible project of reducing cities to targets is urbicide, which destroys the material basis for urban life (Graham, 2004:192-213). On the other hand, these models pare back the lives of those who somehow survive in these shell-torn and bomb-blasted landscapes, to what Giorgio Agamben calls "bare life." At best, they are a spectral presence, traces that flicker across the geometricized spaces of the city, avatars in the virtual spaces of simulations: spaces produced and performed under the sign of their colonial masters, who observe but rarely listen. Their deaths are not only uncounted—who can forget the callous claim that "We don't do body counts"?—but also unaccountable. They are placed out-side language, outside political representation, and their voices, like their bodies, have no place in these monotonic, abstract spaces (Agamben, 1995). Abstract they may be, but these spaces have a very precise and racialized geography. For the Pentagon has identified the "broken cities" of the global South as the "key battlespace of the future." As the "war on terror" pursues its enemy into these cities of deadly night, then, as Mike Davis suggests "[T]he poor peripheries of developing cities will be the permanent battlefields of the twenty-first century.... Night after night, hornet-like helicopter gunships stalk enigmatic enemies in the narrow streets of the slum districts, pouring hellfire into shanties or fleeing cars. Every morning the slums reply with suicide bombers and eloquent explosions. If the empire can deploy Orwellian technologies of repression, its outcasts have the gods of chaos on their side" (Davis, 2004a).

Against this bleak prospect, I want to insist on the connections between cities, civilizations, and civilians, and to place my faith in something other than the gods of chaos. Part of my argument, it should be clear, concerns how these cities are represented in analytical and experiential terms. But we must also look to the representation of the people that live in them in political and legal terms. The civilian is a figure of recent date (and not only in military simulations). In English, the word originally—and ironically—meant one who studied civil law, but the Oxford English Dictionary traces its "fashionable" meaning as "a nonmili-tary person" to the late 18th and especially 19th centuries, when the term was closely tied to Britain's colonial enterprise in India. In international law, whose genealogies are no less invested in colonialism and imperialism, the figure is of even more recent date. In 1899, the convention with respect to the laws and customs of war on land (Hague I), (reaffirmed in Hague IV, 1907) prohibited the bombardment of undefended towns; the rules of aerial warfare, drafted at the Hague in 1923, proscribed "[A]erial bombardment for the purpose of terrorizing the civilian population, of destroying or damaging private property not of mili-tary character, or of injuring noncombatants." In 1938, the League of Nations unanimously affirmed that the bombing of civilian populations was forbidden by international law and called for new regulations to protect them; and in 1949, the Fourth Geneva was addressed explicitly to "the protection of civilian persons in time of war."

Some politicians insist that these legal protections are out of date because that they have no purchase in the "war on terror." I am convinced, on the contrary, that they do; and given the colonial templates, which frame so much of its military violence, this is scarcely surprising. But the law is not a deus ex machina, chaotic or otherwise. It is (and must be) the site of political struggle. For, if the gray zones of the "war on terror" continue to expand then, like the fate foreshadowed by Foucault for that other invention of recent date, the human subject, the figure of the civilian may soon be effaced as well. As I completed this essay, I discovered that entering "civilian" in Google's search engine generated, as its first entry, the webpage for Iraq Body Count.

1   See for example, Petty (2004: 483-493), Nguyen (2005: 55-64). For a comparison with cognitive-behavioral modeling in geography, see the discussion on the 'theater fire problem' in Wolpert & Zillman (1969: 91-104) "The sequential expansion of a decision-making model in a spatial context."

2   DiMarco acknowledges that many cities in the region have substantial modern (read: "normal") districts, but he argues that these neighborhoods pose military challenges no different from those of any other modern city: force can be brought to bear on them quickly and directly. The burden of his analysis thus falls on the "traditional" city, only to leap over the modern rings of development towards the periurban "squatter settlements and shanty-towns."

Selected Bibliography

Giorgio Agamben, *Homo Sacer: Sovereign Power and Bare Life*, trans. Daniel Heller-Roazen (Stanford: Stanford University Press, 1998).

Zygmunt Bauman, "Wars of the Globalization Era," *European Journal of Social Theory* 4 (2001).

Ryan Bishop and Gregory Clancey, "The City-as-Target, or Perpetuation and Death," in *Postcolonial Urbanism: Southeast Asian Cities and Global Processes*, eds. Ryan Bishop, John Phillips, and Wei Wei Yeo (New York: Routledge, 2003).

Judith Butler, *Bodies that Matter: On the Discursive Limits of Sex* (New York: Routledge, 1993).

Mike Davis, "The Pentagon as Global Slumlord," *http://www.tomdispatch.com/index.mhtml?pid =1386*, accessed April 19, 2004.

Mike Davis, "Planet of Slums: Urban Involution and the Informal Proletariat," *New Left Review* 26 (2004

Mike Davis, "The Urbanization of Empire: Megacities and the Laws of Chaos," *Social Text* 22 (4) (2004).

Lt. Col. Louis A DiMarco, "Traditions, Changes and Challenges: Military Operations and the Middle Eastern City," *Combat Studies Institute, Occasional Papers (Global War on Terrorism)* 1 (Leavenworth: Combat Studies Institute Press, 2004).

Paul Gilroy, "'Where Ignorant Armies Clash by Night': Homogeneous Community and the Planetary Aspect," *International Journal of Cultural Studies* 6 (2003).

Stephen Graham, "Vertical Geopolitics: Baghdad and After," *Antipode* 36 (2004).

Stephen Graham, "Constructing Urbicide by Bulldozer in the Occupied Territories," in *Cities, War and Terrorism: Towards an Urban Geopolitics*, ed. Stephen Graham (Oxford: Blackwell, 2004).

Derek Gregory, *The Colonial Present: Afghanistan, Palestine, Iraq* (Oxford: Blackwell, 2004).

Q. H. Nguyen, F. D. McKenzie, and M. D. Petty, "Crowd Behavior Architecture Model Cognitive Design," in *Proceedings of the 2005 Conference on Behavior Representation in Modeling and Simulation (BRIMS)*, Universal City, CA., May 2005.

Mikel Petty, et al,. "Developing a Crowd Federate for Military Simulation," in *Proceedings of the Spring 2004 Simulation Interoperability Workshop (SIW)*, Arlington, VA, April 2004.

Mary-Louise Pratt, "'Scratches on the Face of the Country': Or What Mr. Barrow Saw in the Land of the Bushmen," *Critical Inquiry* 12 (1985).

Edward Said, *Orientalism* (London: Penguin, 1978).

Matt Slagle, "Urban Warfare on a Sound Stage," *CBSNews.com*, December 20, 2004.

Clive Thompson, "The Making of an X-Box Warrior," *New York Times*, August 22, 2004.

Ann Scott Tyson, "Block to Block Combat," *Christian Science Monitor*, January 17, 2003.

Dan Verton, "Simulating Fallujah," *Computerworld* (January 31, 2005).

Eyal Weizman, "The Politics of Verticality," *Open Democracy* at www.opendemocracy.net. 2002.

J. Wolpert and D. Zillmann, "The Sequential Expansion of a Decision-Making Model in a Spatial Context," *Environment and Planning* 1, (1969).

COLONIZATION BY IMAGINATION

ON THE PALESTINIAN ABSENCE FROM THE LANDSCAPE[1]

Issam Nassar

While debate on the wall that Israel is erecting around the Palestinian communities of the West Bank has taken various forms—legal, economic, humanitarian, and political—one by-product of the wall has yet to be seriously examined: the effect it has on one's imagination of the Other. The issue of seeing, or, in our case, not seeing the Other may not be of enormous consequence in the short run, but there is no doubt in my mind that it will have serious long term effects. After all, fighting an obscure, invisible enemy demonized by pundits and politicians alike, entails less guilt and ill-feeling on the part of the attacking soldiers regarding the pain they inflict in the course of modern warfare. In this essay, I trace a history of "unseeing" the Palestinians as a means to deny their claims to the land.

Boaz — in reference to the biblical field of Boaz in the Jerusalem-Bethlehem area (unknown photographer, The Collection of the Library of Congress, USA)

The first instance of Palestinian visual absence in modern times "appears" in the first photographs taken of Palestine in the 19th century, shortly after photography was invented. The first photographers came to Palestine from Europe in December 1839. In the decades that followed, dozens of European (and other) photographers imaged Palestine quite extensively. A striking feature of these early European photographic representations of Palestine is that the country's native population rarely appears in them. Instead of an inhabited space with villages, towns, and a social, cultural, political, and economic life, Palestine was reduced to an empty landscape that corresponded with the stories of the Old and the New Testaments. For some reason, this process of "biblification" necessitated leaving the local population outside the frame.

The absence of Palestinians from most of these photographs attests to the fact that they were also absent, on some level, from the European consciousness of their photographers. Palestine was reduced to a backdrop upon which the biblical story could be substantiated, rather than recognized as a real place in the real world—attesting to real histories other than the Judeo-Christian narrative. The American photographer Edward L. Wilson, who photographed Palestine in the 1880s, corroborates this point. In an article in *Century Magazine*, Wilson actually stated that the peasants he encountered near the Sea of Galilee were "repulsive [and] entirely out of harmony with the character of the Land." (Davis, 1996:87)

It is interesting to note that even photographers who were favorably impressed by the people of Palestine avoided including them in their photographs. The Scottish photographer John Cramb wrote of his disappointment at not being able to photograph the women of Bethlehem, whom he found quite striking. Reporting on his 1860 journey to Palestine, he wrote: "The women of Bethlehem are generally fair and always beautiful. Every traveler remarks that... Sincerely did I regret the arrangement that denied me the pleasure of bringing home witnesses to the correctness of my judgment. But I was not expected to spend my time on such subjects, though I now think it a pity that I was so scrupulous in the discharge of my duty" (Cramb, 1861:388).

It seems that, like Cramb, other photographers thought their buyers would resent having photographs of important holy sites "desecrated" by the presence of Arabs, Turks, and Jews (Nir, 1985:135). This "amazing ability to discover the land without discovering the people" (Doumani, 1992:7), may very well have paved the way for the popular image of Palestine as "a land without a people," ostensibly lying in wait for "a people without a land"—as the Zionist slogan went.

Empty Street in Jerusalem's Old City (Eric Matson, circa 1900, The Collection of the Library of Congress, USA)

With time, Palestinians began to appear in photographs as exotic Orientals (sheiks, harems, Bedouins, clergy, etc.) and as contemporary illustrations of biblical ancestors. In both cases, the framing eye extracted the photographed subject from history and placed him or her in a context more relevant to Europe's relation to Palestine than to the lived reality of the depicted. Peasants were captioned with anglophile biblical names and classified into biblical categories to which European spectators could relate (Samaritans, Jews, Mohammedans, Saracens, etc.). When the "ethnographic" divide was not employed, "biblical careers" were introduced and images of fishermen, shepherds, and carpenters began flooding the tourist markets.

In other words, the European historical imagination cast a 19th century Palestine in a first century light, thus paving the way—through photography, travelogs, and later cinema—for the colonization, or better yet "reclamation," of the land by Europe and its agents. Although this imaging of Palestine and its inhabitants was largely Christian in nature, it was adopted by secular European Jews as well. By the turn of the 20th century, the Zionist Movement was a fully established political organization which had held several worldwide (read: Western) conferences, and established numerous ideological settlements throughout Palestine.

The Zionist imagination of Palestine introduced new sets of Palestinian images. Palestinians came in and out of portrayals of the land in early Zionist photography and cinema. Sometimes the Palestinian was part present as a shepherd— a would-be prototypical ancient Israelite. On other occasions, the Palestinian was altogether absent or represented as a hapless native incapable of self-representation. As the conflict between Jewish settlers and indigenous Arabs intensified, the essentialization of Palestinians took on new dimensions such as primitivism—images that bring to mind White North American settlers' depictions of Native "Indians." Over time, Palestinians were transformed into signifiers of senseless violence, cruelty, and terrorism.

It is important to bear in mind the colonialist-settler nature of the Zionist project, at least as far as the Palestinians are concerned. Jewish immigrants to Palestine were not expected, nor did they expect, to live among and mingle with the local population. Instead, they joined exclusive Jewish colonies in Palestine where natives were out of sight (and out of mind), save for the occasional passing shepherd. It should be of no surprise then, that the bulk of the immigrants who made up the *Yeshuv* (pre-State Jewish settlement) continued to nurture the dominant European notions they had about Palestine upon arriving there. When the Palestinians really did start to vanish from the landscape as a result of the 1948 war, many members of the *Yeshuv* hardly noticed what was happening to their already "invisible" neighbors.

Begin Road cutting through the village of Bir Nabala (photo: editorial team, 2005)

The events of 1948, which the Palestinians call *al-Nakba* (the Catastrophe) are central to the Palestinian historical narrative. Despite the fact that *al-Nakba* refers to countless incidences of death, destruction, expulsion, and exile, Palestinians conjugate it in the singular, as though it stood for a single event. In 1948 the Palestinians "disappeared"—more than two-thirds of the population was expelled from over 400 towns and villages—most of which were subsequently ruined—making the early photographic images of Palestine as "a land without people" look like a self-fulfilling prophecy.[2] As far as the Palestinians were concerned, Palestine was lost after 1948: the village was erased from the map, the city was colonized and its name often changed, the house was someone else's, and the fruit trees were locked behind barbed wire fences. The disappearance of Palestine was also an issue in areas that remained under Arab control: East Palestine became the "West Bank" and was incorporated into the Hashemite Kingdom of Jordan, and Gaza and its environs became the "Gaza Strip" under Egyptian rule.

The "disappearance" of Palestine and the resultant "loss" of Palestinian identity at the hands of the newly-established State of Israel, did not necessarily mean that the Jewish population of the state was fully aware of what had occurred. Indeed, it would have been "unnatural" had the Palestinian catastrophe been fully noticeable, since the Palestinians were largely absent from the Zionist purview to begin with. The fact that Israel enacted policies and laws that delegitimated and outlawed expressions of Palestinian national identity made this blind-spot of Israeli consciousness all the more acute.

The Israeli negation of the existence of Palestinians as a people with political rights led the state to support traditional, reactionary elements within the Palestinian community. Those Palestinians who remained inside the territory that became the Sate of Israel (some 150,000 in 1948) were renamed "Israeli Arabs" and categorically fragmented into a number of religious and communal groupings. After the 1967 Israeli occupation of the West Bank and Gaza Strip, the Palestinian population was called "the Arab residents of the administered territories of Judea, Samaria and Gaza." The Israeli policy of encouraging "traditional" as opposed to political leadership was consistent with the European colonial view—which the Israelis adopted wholesale—that Arabs, as natives, were incapable of practicing democracy.

On the rhetorical level, Israel found it useful to highlight the Arab identity of the Palestinians, especially of the Palestinian refugees in the surrounding Arab states. Turning pan-Arab discourse on its head, if the refugees were simply "Arabs," then they were already in the Arab world—where they "belonged"! Taking this skewed logic even further, Israeli propagandists argued that Arabs were not native to Palestine, but had migrated there as late as the 1930s, thanks to the economic growth spurred by Zionist immigration, investment, and development.

Meanwhile, the Palestinians, both as individuals and as a national movement in formation, were rising from the ashes of the 1948 trauma of dispossession and dispersion. It would take another two decades before "Palestinian" would become a "legitimate" political identity represented by the PLO (a process that entailed a great deal of internal and external debate).

Gradually, this reemerged Palestinian identity gained international legitimacy and was legally recognized by the State of Israel with the signing of the Oslo Declaration of Principles in 1993. The "peace process," with all its faults and deficiencies, did make Palestinian national and political symbols present in the eyes of the Israeli public. The previously outlawed Palestinian flag was decriminalized, and Palestinian cultural, political, and economic national institutions were established in the occupied territories. This legitimization was perhaps the most positive of all the agreement's provisions, which otherwise reflected the weakened position of the Palestinian national movement. After a series of political and military defeats: the expulsion of the PLO from Lebanon in the early 1980s, the collapse of the Soviet Union in the late 1980s, the Iraqi defeat in the first Gulf War, and the decline of the first Intifada popular uprising in the early 1990s—the Palestinians had little bargaining power left.

However, the "peace process" launched at Oslo failed, and Israeli settlements proliferated both during the process and since. The Palestinian residents of the occupied territories, who were recognized as a people with (certain) political rights, found themselves confined to a few besieged Bantustans while "bypass roads" (highways really) built at the height of the process to connect the settlements with Israel, now enable Israelis to travel throughout the land without having to encounter a single Palestinian. These bypass roads, coupled with the "closure" barring Palestinians from entering Israel, have rendered the Palestinians invisible once more, which, it seems, makes attacking them that much easier. Are we witnessing 1948 all over again?

It's hard to say. There are, however, some similarities. For one, keeping Palestinians out of sight and out of mind; for the first time in decades, there is no serious discussion of a viable Palestinian future. Rather, Israelis are debating the "peaceful expulsion" of Palestinians. Coined "transfer," this debate has a footing in academic, political, and journalistic circles. One might argue that the fence/wall currently under construction around the Palestinian communities of the occupied territories is a manifestation of the idea of "transfer," a reminiscence of sorts for "a land without people"—especially when some of the walls have been painted with imaginary pastoral landscapes void of people, when in fact they conceal populated Palestinian urban centers. The wall not only keeps Israelis, and especially Palestinians, from moving about freely, it hides present-day Palestine from the Israelis on their side of the wall, and historical Palestine from the Palestinians on their side of the wall. This is not to suggest that Israelis will forget the Palestinians altogether, but that nonseeing is a definite step towards psychically denying and repressing something's existence. By barring Palestinians from accessing their former homes in Israel (and barring Israeli civilians from accessing Palestinian refugee camps, for example), Israelis will not have to reckon with the consequences of 1948.

The question Israelis are not asking themselves is: "What does this wall hide?" Were we to imagine the establishment of a Palestinian political entity, no matter its parameters, this entity would undoubtedly open unto the Arab world at its eastern borders. When this happens, hopefully sooner than later, will the fence/wall separate the Palestinians from the world, or isolate the Israelis from their surrounding environment in the Middle East?

1   An earlier version of this essay appeared in *Remapping the Region: Kultur und Politik in Israel/Palästina*, O.K books 2/04, Folio Verlag, Vienna, 2004

2   I am borrowing the image of a Palestine that disappeared as opposed to having been occupied from Elias Sanbar in his book Falasteen 1948 al-Taghyeeb, translated into Arabic by Kazim Jihad (Beirut: al-Mousasa al-Arabuyah lil-Dirasat w al-Nashr, 1987).

Selected Bibliography

John Cramb, "Palestine in 1860; Or, A Photographer's Journal of a Visit to Jerusalem," *The British Journal of Photography*, No. X (November 1, 1861).

Beshara Doumani, "Rediscovering Ottoman Palestine: Writing Palestinians into History," *Journal of Palestine Studies* XXI, (2) (Winter, 1992).

Issam Nassar, Photographing Jerusalem: *The Image of the City in Nineteenth Century Photography* (Boulder: East European Monographs, 1997).

Yeshayahu Nir, *The Bible and the Image* (Philadelphia: University of Pennsylvania Press, 1985).

David Ron, *Arabs and Israel for Beginners* (New York: Writers & Readers Pub., 1993).

Ralph Schoenman, *The Hidden History of Zionism* (Santa Barbara: Veritas Press, 1988).

Edward L. Wilson, "In Scripture Lands," quoted in John Davis, *The Landscape of Belief* (Princeton: Princeton University Press, 1996).

COMMON GROUNDS
THAT EXCLUDE

Amir Paz-Fuchs, Efrat Cohen-Bar

The irony expressed in Robert Frost's *Mending Wall* line: "good fences make good neighbors," seems to have been lost on many readers who have opted to take it literally. Presumably, these readers thought that Frost was suggesting a counter-intuitive and, thus, thought-provoking idea: that a fence, which appears to separate, may actually bond by allowing parties on both sides to develop their autonomous lifestyles and interact on mutually agreed grounds. It is now accepted that Frost was, in fact, mocking the rhetoric that rationalizes division and segregation as preferable to unity and solidarity. Indeed, the opening line of the poem, "Something there is that doesn't love a wall," is key to understanding its final phrase, quoted above.

It is important to continuously call into question the motivations behind the physical constructions that make up our lived environments. Just as good fences may not make good neighbors, the current situation in East Jerusalem shows us that common grounds, in the form of national parks, normally envisaged as encouraging interpersonal and intercommunal connections, can be cynically exploited as a means to disenfranchise communities and advance spatial domination.

Such an assertion should be made with caution, as it may play into a conservative worldview which idealizes private property and posits that property as such can not be commonly held. This view has been popularized as "the tragedy of the commons" (Hardin, 1968). Refuting such claims is an important "progressive move" (Wu and Turner, 2004) because common property, at least ideally, creates a legal platform for access to all individuals, irrespective of race, citizenship, financial ability, and so forth. Private property rights refer to a "bundle of rights" that include, *inter alia*, the owner's ability to limit access to, and control the use of, their property by means of practices which, were a state agency to do so, it would be accused of blatant discrimination on the aforementioned grounds. Hence, from one's private property rights, it is possible to infer a strong power to exclude. Indeed, it has been argued that "excludability… is a conceptually necessary feature of [the] property claim" (Grear, 2003:37). If unchecked, the power of exclusion could be threatening to "fundamental values of community and democracy" (Gray and Gray, 1999:15) and lead to the conclusion that common property is a contradiction in terms.

In a more sophisticated reading, however, rights of use may be distinguished from ownership, and the ownership of land may be subject to the rights of common use. (Ciriacy-Wantrup and Bishop, 1975:715) It should be made clear that common property is not "everybody's property." Moreover, "contrary to widespread belief, common lands are private and not public property" (Juergensmeyer and Wadley, 1974:376). However, public authorities may designate certain lands as common, thereby restricting the owner's ability to exclude others from his/her land and, intentionally or not, creating the physical grounds for interaction and inclusion.

Exclusion is, perhaps, "the major social phenomenon of our day" (Rosanvallon 2000:46). Until quite recently, it was not uncommon for municipalities to employ laws that mandated racially segregated zoning patterns (Dubin, 1993:744-778). The recognition that the legally enforced physical separation of individuals of different races, ethnicities, or religions is incongruous with liberal thought has necessitated the modification of such practices.[1] Some authors have suggested interpreting social exclusion as unequal access to rights, and social inclusion policies as a way to reduce disparities (Gore, 1995:22).

Wary of the degree to which social exclusion practices may or may not be accepted if submitted to public scrutiny, they have been cloaked quite brilliantly in the city of Jerusalem by policies normally meant to bring individuals and communities together. In recent years, the Nature and Parks Authority (NPA) has worked hand in hand with the Jerusalem Municipal Council to plan and proclaim new national parks in and around Palestinian East Jerusalem. Before this effort began, open areas in East Jerusalem were designated as "green areas," and, apart from the area surrounding the walls of the Old City, which was deemed an area of unique historical, archeological, and scenic value, no area was designated as a national park. The shift came with the planning of the Emek Tzurim national park on the western slope of Mount Scopus. Despite administrative and legal objections on the part of the residents of the Sheikh Jarrah and Wadi Joz neighborhoods, the area was proclaimed a national park in 2001. This success encouraged the NPA and the Jerusalem Municipality to take the scheme to other neighborhoods. A plan for a national park on the eastern slope of Mount Scopus, between Issawiya and A-Tur, is currently under consideration by the Local Planning Committee (a necessary legal hurdle prior to proclamation).

Similarly, there is a declared intent to plan a national park in the Al-Bustan neighborhood of Silwan, a Palestinian village at the south-eastern edge of the Old City. This area, currently built, is home to over 1,000 people. The proclamation of a national park in the neighborhood would necessitate the demolition of scores of homes, and procedures for the destruction of 88 houses are underway (36 demolition orders have already been submitted for authorization) on the pretext of illegal construction, a phenomenon to be elaborated upon further on. What explains this sudden proliferation of national parks?

Over the past 38 years, since Israel occupied East Jerusalem and its vicinity in 1967 and subsequently annexed it to the Municipality of West Jerusalem, demographic concerns have dominated Jerusalem's development policies. The principle at work has been that a significant Jewish majority[2] be maintained. To realize this objective, new Jewish neighborhoods were built in East Jerusalem, while no similar provisions—including the expansion of existing neighborhoods—were made to Palestinians in East Jerusalem, let alone in West Jerusalem. Jerusalem's development policies have given incentive for Jews to come to, or remain in, the city, while Palestinians have been encouraged to leave it.

22.6 km: Hebron Road

The fact that planning is regarded as a neutral tool shrouded in a professional jargon of "concerns" has made it possible for planners to serve, wittingly or unwittingly, a development policy guided by ethnic, national, and religious domination. What makes development possible or impossible is the designation of land. Appropriate planning balances various interests and, guided by community needs, designates land for housing and common use in accordance with predictions for population growth. Inappropriate planning "may be employed as a 'subtler' device in pursuit of segregation" (Dubin, 1993:762) or forced migration.

From the outset, Israeli planning in East Jerusalem has chosen to designate limited space for Palestinian housing whilst leaving considerable space for common grounds or "green zones." This has been accomplished in one of two ways. First, after expropriating some 25% of the land in East Jerusalem for the construction of Jewish neighborhoods, only about 50% of the remaining Palestinian lands were planned at all, and the remaining "unplanned" areas defaulted to their British Mandate era designations as open rustic or agricultural landscapes. Second, the areas that were planned also included sizable "green areas"—well beyond the community's needs. Thus, in the current plans for East Jerusalem, about 35% of the land is designated for preservation as "open landscape" and in one extreme case, the neighborhood of Jabal Mukaber, the area designated as "green" reaches almost 70% (Bimkom, 2005).

Due to the demographic aims they are meant to advance, it is not surprising that these common grounds have remained undeveloped, with no landscaping to speak of. Nor have they fulfilled their purpose of preventing the expansion of Palestinian housing. Due to basic housing needs, "illegal" construction is rampant in East Jerusalem: there are an estimated 15,000 housing units built without permission. Paradoxically, sweeping restrictions on residential development have undermined the possibility of preserving the green areas that warrant it. The tendentious agendas guiding planners have led them to lose sight of the need to distinguish between valuable common grounds and areas that could be designated for residential use. In light of the municipality's failure to meet its formal objective of preserving common grounds for the benefit of the general public, and its failure to realize its informal objective of reducing the Palestinian population of Jerusalem, it has come up with a new mechanism for securing Jewish national, ethnic, and religious hold on the land: the NPA.

The National Parks, Nature Reserves, and Memorial Sites Act (1998) provides that once a plan designating an area as a national park has been certified, no construction in the area will be permitted without the authorization of the NPA. Once the said area has been proclaimed a national park (by the Minister of Interior), all other designations or uses of the area are overridden, though property rights held prior to the proclamation, remain in tact.

The NPA is vested with considerable powers. As noted, any construction in the designated area requires permission from the NPA. Moreover, once a proclamation is made by the minister of interior, the NPA enjoys additional powers, including the ability to remove "unlawful" residents (who may be property owners) from the area. The NPA may charge entrance fees that limit access to those individuals and families (including property owners) who can afford to buy the entry ticket. Lastly, the activities that these individuals and families may undertake are restricted. The director of the NPA may appoint overseers with police powers, including the power to detain, search, seize, destroy, and inter-rogate. These "inspectors" would be entrusted with ensuring that "illegal" acts, which might harm the national park, are not committed. Such acts range from destruction of park property to posting a sign, from picking vegetation to graz-ing, and are punishable with as much as three years in prison. Such extreme powers may be deemed necessary to preserve landmarks of unique historical, archeological, architectural, or scenic value—which is what national parks are categorically supposed to do. It is questionable, however, if they can be justi-fied as a means to preserve urban green areas whose sole purpose is to prevent housing construction.

Neighborhood parks and open spaces are an important feature of any city. They constitute the physical grounds for interaction between dog owners, joggers, senior citizens, children at play, tourists, and so forth. The decision to designate an area as green, notwithstanding the fact that it may be private property, is not uncommon. In doing so, the property owner's right of control and use are (usu-ally) taken into account. At times, the municipality may choose to use its power of eminent domain. Simple put, this is "the inherent power of a governmental authority to take privately owned property, especially land, and convert it to public use, subject to reasonable compensation for the taking." (Black's Law Diction-ary, 1999:541) Such taking is exercised when it is likely to be permanent, e.g. for the paving of roads and, in the case of national parks, when the owner refuses to devote the ground to acceptable uses (Sax, 1977:243). However, expropriation usually entails compensation.

The decision to designate an area as a park may conflict with an owner's property rights. If private property is conceptually linked to exclusion, an author-ity may decide that certain goods cannot be held as private property because the social cost of exclusion is too high: [C]laims of 'property' may sometimes be overridden by the need to attain or further more highly rated social goals... the law of human rights... the furtherance of constructive interaction, purposive dialogue and decent (or 'moral') communal living" (Gray, 1991:281).

However, both premises: that the municipality has the community's best interest in mind, and that compensation is due and thus granted, are inopera-tive when it comes to the designation of Palestinian lands in East Jerusalem as national parks. First, the issue of compensation: the general rule, under section 197 of the Planning and Construction Act (1965), is that the owner of land deval-ued by planning, and not by expropriation, is entitled to compensation, subject to section 200. Section 200 states that land will not be deemed harmed by a plan if the damage to it is not unreasonable under the circumstances, making it unjust to compensate the owner.

In East Jerusalem much of the land is designated as "green," making it difficult to demonstrate devaluation in a compensation claim.[3] Furthermore, ownership is notoriously complex in East Jerusalem. The British Land Settlement Ordinance (1928) sought to limit the phenomenon of collective ownership (musha)—the most common form of ownership in 19th century Palestine—since it led to fragmented land holdings. However, only 5,200,000 dunums (1 dunum = 1000 square meters) were settled under this system, including most Jewish-owned land (Peretz, 2000:18). Israel adopted this incomplete land registry and had no incentive to impose a modern bureaucracy that would facilitate legal claims on an individual basis. The result is that most of East Jerusalem's private land has not been legally registered through the land registry office, a fact that keeps many property owners from being able to undertake legal construction projects on their lands, and will likely impede their ability to seek compensation upon future redesignation.

The process taking place in East Jerusalem today is rather exceptional. The local authority is, upon its own initiative, foregoing control of lands within its jurisdiction, despite the fact that these could bear significant tax revenues, should they be rezoned as residential or commercial districts. The assumption is that a national authority will be less attentive to the needs of the local community than a local authority would be. When transferring Palestinian lands to an Israeli national authority, the Jerusalem Municipal Council is displaying flagrant disregard for the well-being of its Palestinian residents.

Few things could be more insensitive and exclusionary than the confiscation of land in and around Palestinian East Jerusalem for the purpose of national parks. Section 1 of the National Parks, Nature Reserves, and Memorial Sites Act explains that a national park is an area designated, *inter alia*, to "...memorialize values that are of historical, archeological, architectural or scenic importance." (section 1) If we understand nationalism as a constructed, rather than "natural," identity (Jackson and Penrose, 1993:11), the rationale for bringing the NPA into the picture could not be more transparent. National parks in Israel celebrate and reinforce Israeli "identity" and "tradition," and the national park planned for Silwan—including the house demolitions it will entail—is a prime example. The fact that in West Jerusalem, where there is clear justification for proclaiming national parks, city officials repeatedly cave in to real-estate interests, demonstrates that, where Israeli sovereignty is not in question, capitalism supercedes "values of historical, archeological, architectural or natural importance." Where the conflict is at its most acute, planning is the refuge of the patriot. This, if anything, is the true tragedy of the commons.

1   To the extent that physical barriers which encumber the inclusion of people with disabilities in the social environment had to be addressed. See, e.g., the *American with Disabilities Act* PL 101-336; the *Israeli Equal Rights for People with Disabilities Act* (2003); HCJ 7081/93 Botzer v. Maccabim-Reut Municipal Council 50(1) 19.

2   From the occupation of East Jerusalem in 1967 to the present, the share of the Jewish population in Jerusalem declined from 74% to 67%. Originally, the government decided on a minimum ratio of 70%-30% in favor of the Jewish population. This barrier has been bypassed and, at the moment, seems unrealistic. See *Statistical Yearbook for Jerusalem 2002-2003* (Jerusalem Institute for Israeli Studies, December 2003) www.jiis.org.il/main-findings-eng.pdf

3   Another argument against compensation is that national parks protect the environment and thus prevent harm to the "natural *status quo* of the environment" *Just v. Marinette County* 201 N.W.2d 761, 768 (1972); see Circiacy-Wantrup and Bishop 726.

Selected Bibliography

Bimkom, *Comments for the Jerusalem Local Plan 2000* (forthcoming, 2005), www.bimkom.org.

Siegfried Ciriacy-Wantrup and Richard Bishop, "'Common Property' as a Concept in Natural

Resources Policy," *Natural Resources Journal* 15, (1975).

Jon Dubin, "From Junkyards to Gentrification," *Minnesota Law Review* 77, (1993).

Elishar v. Regional Planning Committee, Central District, Civil Appeal 4390/90, 47(3), 1990.

Euclid v. Amber, 272, U.S., (1926).

Charles Gore, "Introduction," in *Social Exclusion*, eds. Gerry Rodgers, Charles Gore, and José Figueiredo (Geneva: ILO, 1995).

Kevin Gray, "Property in Thin Air," *Cambridge Law Journal* 50, (1991).

Kevin Gray and Susan Gray, "Private Property and Public Propriety," in *Property and the Constitution*, ed. Janet McLean (Oxford: Hart Publishing, 1999).

Anna Grear, "A Tale of the Land, the Insider, the Outsider and Human Rights," *Legal Studies* 23, (2003).

Garrett Hardin, "The Tragedy of the Commons," *Science* 162, (1968).

Peter Jackson and Jan Penrose, "Placing Race and Nation," in *Constructions of Race, Place and Nation*, eds. Peter Jackson and Jan Penrose (London: UCL Press, 1993).

Julian Juergensmeyer and James Wadley, "The Common Land Concept: A 'Commons' Solution to a Common Environmental Problem," *Natural Resources Journal* 14, (1974).

Don Peretz, "Problems of Refugee Compensation" in *International Conference on Palestinian Refugees*, (UNESCO, 26 April 2000), http://domino.un.org/UNISPAL.NSF/)/3f2d0e281fbf38578525 669e5005 4ed17?OpenDocument.

Pierre Rosanvallon, *The New Social Question* (Princeton: UP Princeton, 2000).

Joseph Sax, "Helpless Giants: The National Parks and the Regulation of Private Lands," *Michigan Law Review* 75 (1977).

Diana Wu and Robin Turner, "Recognizing and Eradicating Racism in Environmental Commons" (paper submitted to the International Association for the Study of Common Property, 2004), www.iascp2004.org.mx/downloads/paper_431.pdf .

Rachel Leah Jones

A professor of history from Bayit Va-Gan took his family for a picnic in a
quiet pinewood near Giv`at Shaul, formerly known as Deir Yassin. It was not
too cold to be in the shade and not too warm to build a fire, so the professor passed on to his son camping skills he had acquired in the army. They
arranged three square stones in a U, to block the wind, leaving access on
the fourth side. They stacked broken branches on top of twigs on top of dry
pine needles. He let his son put a match to it. [...] The professor did not talk
of the village, origin of the stones. He did not talk of the village school, now
a psychiatric hospital, on the other side of the hill. He imagined that he and
his family were having a picnic, unrelated to the village, enjoying its grounds
outside history.

Oz Shelach, Picnic Grounds: a Novel in Fragments[1]

One day I happened upon it. In the middle of a no-man's-land—a rough diamond
shaped valley carved from two would-be "green lines" that split at the source
in Jabal al-Mukaber and come together again in Abu Tor—a maze. I knew what
it reminded me of, in fact, I thought it was the
real thing, albeit too polished. Suspicious, I con-
tacted the planners (or the planters): the Jewish
National Fund (JNF). The JNF official in charge
of planning identified the area as the "Forest
of Peace," and referred me to the now-retired
regional director responsible for creating the
park and designing its various attractions.

Road sign (photo: Rachel Leah
Jones, 2005)

The "Forest of Peace," relayed the former
regional director, was conceived and planned as a children's forest by and for
"the children of Israel." Apparently, children around the (Western) world donat-
ed funds for its planting and construction, receiving in exchange certificates of
merit for playing their part in making the desert bloom.

The park was designed with an "international orientation," explained its planner, "on the eve of Jerusalem's 3000 year anniversary." It was meant to serve
tourists from abroad as well as the residents of the city. Aware that the park was
planted in an area between a Jordanian boundary and an Israeli boundary, the
objective was to turn this Palestinian "no-man's-land" into "every-body's-land."

Conceptualized as an interplay between past and future, each "attraction"—and the park is full of these—was designed as a time tunnel with eight "gates" that function as a lookout point unto a world of content. These include: "Fore-fathers" (e.g. a view of Mount Moriah where, speaking of children, it is said Abraham intended to sacrifice his son Isaac), "Judges," "Prophecy," "Return to Zion," "the National Home," "Israeli Sovereignty," "the Unification of Jerusalem" (e.g. a view of Mount Scopus where the Hebrew University of Jerusalem stood severed from West Jerusalem between 1948-1967) and "Peace." Universal themes indeed...

At the center of this theme park a "Museum of the Child" was to be erected, where "the story of the Land of Israel" would be told through its children: Abraham the child, Muhammad the child, etc. But this, perhaps the more international portion of the park, was never completed, as the eruption of the second Intifada stopped the flow of tourists to Israel and the flow of Jews to East Jerusalem—where the forest is located.

Forest of Peace, Jerusalem
(photos: Rachel Leah Jones, 2005)

But what about the maze? "People come to a park," continued the planner, "for three reasons": to get away and change environment, to rest and recreate, to enjoy the wonders of the place. One such wonder is a large red jungle-gym pyramid. "We wanted to reference worldwide imagery, like that of Egypt," explained the planner. The philosophy guiding planning for children, he added, is to provide a material basis that will stimulate kids to transcend time and place, or in lay terms: make-believe. So what about the maze? "I had nothing to do with planning the maze," the planner finally admitted, "a different department did, and I have no idea what it's for."

The "Forest of Peace" is frequented, as far as I could tell, only by Palestinian picnickers. What did the maze remind them of? Ruins. What did they understand from it? That Israelis like ruins. No more, no less. What kind of ruins did they remind them of? Just ruins, any old ruins. What did they remind me of? Destroyed Palestinian villages—the kind Israeli planners of national parks and forests grew up picnicking on throughout the country, and not only on the rubble of the village of Deir Yassin across town. The kind the anonymous planner of this maze must have thought his or her children needed in order to have the ultimate picnic experience. After all, how could we have a picnic without enjoying its grounds "outside" history?

And what did I find at the end of the maze, at the heart of the matter? A carousel. What can you see from the carousel? Spinning fragments of make-believe Palestinian vernacular architecture; stone walls, adorned with traditional ventilation holes that whirl the past into a continuous present, and round again.

1   San Francisco: City Lights Books, 2003. Reprinted with permission of author and publisher.

IMPRISONED BY DREAMS

SUR BAHIR AND HAR HOMA AS IMAGINED
AND ACTUAL LANDSCAPES

Naama Meishar and Yehotal Shapira

And in a slumber of trees and stone
Imprisoned in her dream
Is the city which dwells alone
And a wall is in her heart.

Shemer, 1974

These lines of "Jerusalem of Gold," a canonical Hebrew popular song, were written by Naomi Shemer before the 1967 Israeli occupation of the eastern part of the city. In this essay, we will argue that Israel's settlement policy in East Jerusalem cannot be explained purely by exposing the underlying geopolitical agenda of control over the city's territory and demography. Over and above strategic and military considerations, we want to bring to light the deap-seated dream which imprisons the city. This dream—as in Shemer's verse—equally comes to life through the implementation of planning policies.[1]

Likewise, when dreams move into this realm of truth, they become a kind of "phantasm." Plato's use of the Greek word "phantasma" helps us to explain the creation of landscape and experience. In the allegory of the cave, Plato describes a group of people imprisoned in a cave from childhood. Behind them a fire glows, and since they cannot turn their heads to see it, they perceive the shadows on the wall in front of them as reality. These glancing shadows are named "phantasmas" by Plato. The fetters that tie his prisoners are prejudices, fears, and ideologies, which prevent them from seeing reality.

This essay will explore how Israeli phantasms shape landscapes in the implementation of planning policy and through daily life, thus preventing any possibility of sustainable existence. In phantasm-driven planning, landscapes play a role in the spatial collision of east and west Jerusalem, enflaming the national conflict while economically and culturally weakening both Israelis and Palestinians. Familiarity with these phantasms and the manner in which they are embodied may enable real contact and reciprocal, unmediated perceptions of reality. As such, we will focus on Israeli phantasms and how they impact Israeli planning and everyday life.

To begin, the landscape is more than spatial syntax incorporating a set of symbols, or a representation of hierarchical social relations, but an actual cultural process (Mitchell, 1994:1). "Landscape does not simply mirror or distort 'underlying' social relations," writes Seymoure, "but needs to be understood as enmeshed within the processes which shape how the world is organized, experienced and understood, rather than read as its end product" (Seymoure, 2000: 214). These landscapes-in-formation participate in a two-way process: they construct subjects, who then go on to reshape the landscapes, thereby reinforcing their means of identity validation.

This essay addresses the landscapes of two neighborhoods—Har Homa, turned almost overnight from a wooded hill (Jabal Abu Ghneim) into a crowded settlement, which is continuing to spread eastwards;[2] and Sur Bahir, previously a rural agricultural village whose building culture has changed over hundreds of years from habitated caves to homes situated on family lands in urban density.[3]

LANDSCAPES AND ISRAELI PLANNING IN SUR BAHIR

Two Israeli government plans are currently in the works for Sur Bahir. The first is the nonstatutory Outline Plan for Southeast Jerusalem, and the second is an amendment of the Detailed Statutory City Plan for Sur Bahir.[4] We shall address the former, which will also impact the latter.

The Outline Plan proposes neighborhood tourism development, including bicycle paths connected to the wider Jerusalem system, large numbers of bed and breakfast in-home units, and an emphasis on open-space development (Kimeldorf, July 10, 2005). "It is impossible that the same rules that apply to the planning of open areas in the Israeli building fabric will apply to the fabric and culture of the Palestinian neighborhood," the Outline Plan's landscape architect tells us (Krugliac, September 7, 2005). She argues that the Palestinian residents have a need to get out in the open with the whole extended family, advocating several large (six dunam [1 dunum = 1000 square meters]) parks incorporating a variety of activities for different age groups. She goes on to note, "We have located areas of this size in the neighborhood that are interesting as *observation points overlooking wadis* [emphasis ours]. These areas are not free of ownership but they are free of use." Further, Krugliac is under the impression that Sur Bahir representatives thought compensation could be negotiated if these areas were appropriated for public use (Palestinians usually do not accept compensation schemes as part of their rejection of Israel's occupation of these areas). According to the Outline Plan, these parks overlooking *wadis* will be connected to a regional pedestrian path system, which will preserve traditional *wadi* agriculture and connect Sur Bahir and Har Homa. The planning for this *wadi* path system integrates local agricultural commerce, as a means of strengthening the community and encouraging women to engage in home-based economic activity.

These planners truly feel that they have acted professionally and for the benefit of the residents. Further proof of this was visible at a meeting of the planning team for the Outline Plan for Southeast Jerusalem which took place on the June 6, 2005. Here the creators of the Outline Plan conveyed their professional opinion that it should be possible for Sur Bahir residents to build beyond the Jerusalem Ring Road (where local landowners had initiated the independent planning scheme No. 9838 by Ayala Ronel for existing buildings, and No. 8876 by Metropolis planners for dense new buildings), which is widely perceived as a means of limiting construction in this area.[5] The expansion beyond the road would be crucial, since housing in Sur Bahir is divided among families who do not trade in land, subsequently putting at a disadvantage families stuck with land falling outside (east) of the Ring Road. Nevertheless, these opinions were rejected by architect and city engineer Uri Shitreet. He accepted and approved only existing buildings that had been rejected by the Regional Committee.

The phrase "a city dwells alone," coined by Shitreet, is the phantasm on which he bases plans to define the eastern boundary of the built-up territory of Sur Bahir as sitting smack against the eastern Ring Road. Beyond that road, according to his vision, there will be only open landscape areas. The Biblical verse from which this phrase is borrowed says, "the [Jewish] people shall dwell alone... and shall not be reckoned among the nations" (Numbers, 23:9). Many houses east of the designated planning line have been issued with demolition orders.[6] Heaps of debris stagnate throughout the neighborhood, rising as painful landmarks of the one-sided nature of governmental and planning involvement. Some officials contend that it will be possible in the future to allow building to the east of the Ring Road, but this eventuality should be postponed until the territory delimited by this road is more densely populated. This is proposed as a means of "educating" residents into the housing density, characterizing an urban profile. Thus planning policy is applied to Sur Bahir, instead of rising out of that community's needs and aspirations.

On this landscape, the bicycle routes and bed and breakfast units stand out in their irrelevance. They are derived from the phantasms of "peace" and a "unified city." Hassan Abu Aslah, head of the Village Development Committee, compares these enterprises—in light of the existential housing shortage in East Jerusalem neighborhoods—to the act of selecting attractive paint for the banister of a building whose foundations have yet to be laid. Sur Bahir residents label the plan discriminatory in that it does not resolve their desperate need for housing. Currently almost no tourists come to this neighborhood, particularly Jewish visitors. Even so, another planner on the municipal team described the village representatives as "smiling" when the tourist enterprise was presented. The villagers' politeness and the planners' misreading of this reaction is indicative, once again, of the planners' limited understanding of the residents' real needs. The Outline Plan only increases the neighborhood's building capacity by 11% and does not relieve the immediate distress caused by a lack of building permits.

The phantasm of "peace" implicit in the Outline Plan blurs the fact that hiking (itself a kind of civilian surveying) is mainly a deeply ideologized Israeli Jewish pastime (Selwyn, 1998: 12).[7] The specter of Jewish hikers climbing the wadis into Sur Bahir, buying Palestinian agricultural products along the way, is unrealistic in the current political situation. Are the village residents interested in this prospect? Such a planning vision further fortifies Israeli tendencies of becoming "acquainted" with Palestinian culture solely on the culinary level, and reinforces the exoticization of Palestinians and Palestinian society.

Ironically, "It would have been possible to carry out a left-wing 'Peace Now' demonstration at a convention of Ministry of Housing planners," architect and landscape planner for Har Homa, Elish Hausman, observed on July 13, 2005.

Hausman described the planners' sighs of relief when the authorities instructed them to freeze their planning commissions for the Jewish settlements in the Occupied Territories. The reason given for their participation was prosaic: "There was no alternative; we had to except these jobs in order to keep our firms." Thus the desire to maintain social and economic hegemony drives these planners to cooperate with discriminative colonial planning that contradicts their supposed moral values.[8] (As Jewish Ashkenazi Israelis who do not live in the area under discussion, we too are aware of our contested position.[9])

In fact, landscape architect Krugliac had not actually discussed the possibility of expropriating the lands with the landowners themselves. Unfortunately for landowners, some of them had initiated and paid for an independent planning scheme of their own (Plan No. 10133 by Ayala Ronel). "This initiative allocated private land for public needs according to the quantitative standards dictated by the Israeli authorities," says architect Ronel. "But once they had seen this plan, the Outline Plan creators made sure that their land use allocations [such as the hilltop parks] were inserted into the private plan" (Ronel, 2005). In the final analysis, the panorama observation points constituting the basis of this park system were an insurmountable obstacle to the implementation of an agreed-upon and sustainable plan initiated by the citizens themselves.

Furthermore, the constitutive panorama perspective ("looking out" over the wadis) does not bear in mind these landscapes' symbolic meanings for the residents of Sur Bahir. The landscape as seen from Sur Bahir is incessantly changing. Heavy machinery is busily erecting another section of Israel's Separation Wall,[10] thereby disconnecting Sur Bahir from neighboring Palestinian communities and from lands owned by its residents, as well as adding an arbitrary hulking Israeli presence to the landscape. Furthermore, as seen from Sur Bahir, Har Homa construction actually appears as another wall. The facades of the structures are uniform and successive, with openings resembling narrow slits below fourteen-story-high buildings protruding like sentinels. The entire Har Homa system rises as one from the topography, founded on an unbroken strip of six-meter-high supporting walls that sever the neighborhood from the surrounding environment. With the next stages of Har Homa construction to the east, the neighborhood's size will be quadrupled. The gaze of the elevated homes of present and future Har Homa will capture the facing southern view from Sur Bahir. Har Homa landscape characteristics visible from Sur Bahir include pavements shaded by plants, well-maintained roads, and orderly parking spaces. But the observer knows that none of these exist in his neighborhood. Thus, the Outline Plan dictates that the residents of Sur Bahir will spend their leisure time encountering the aggressive Jewish wedge, which for them is a landscape of ongoing domination, expropriation, and discrimination.

LANDSCAPES AND ISRAELI PLANNING IN HAR HOMA
Har Homa's architecture and open space system is spatially oriented outwards, towards distant landscapes. From the neighborhood garden plots, it is possible to view Beit Jala, Sur Bahir, Beit Sahur, and the expanse of the desert. The neighborhood's central public space is a grandiose gesture towards the view. It is a

strip running vertically, dissecting Har Homa's radial construction around the mountain. A double symmetrical stair system, reminiscent of the flights of stairs found in Italian Renaissance gardens, forms a vertical axis connecting the bottom of the neighborhood, at the foot of the mountain, with a pre-Har Homa, stone Palestinian house built next to a cave on the mountaintop.

The residents, like the contractors, wish to maintain this gaze to faraway landscapes and are apprehensive that the view will be blocked following the neighborhood's expected eastern expansion. Resident Osnat shared her feelings with us, "[B]efore coming here I lived in a village; it is important for me to have a view. We can see out to the section between Sur Bahir and Beit Sahur, and to Herodian. One pays for that view, for the desert landscape."

It is our argument that the centrality of the landscape view comes at the expense of everyday well-being. Har Homa's southwest garden plot is built with a strong 7,5% inclination in most areas to enable the open view. The inclination minimizes the garden's recreational possibilities, and children cannot play ball here since the ball always rolls down the sloping grass towards the road.

"These garden plots are annoying, they are crowded and there is not enough room to move around here," Osnat told us as she ran around the playground after her infant daughter. "The playground is unsuitable for the little ones and there are not enough grassy areas, basketball courts, or bicycle paths. The children play football in the large apartment balconies or in the private courtyards of the ground floors."

The dominance of this "gaze" at the expense of the open environment is also visible in the organization of the central open space. The height difference between its foot and head is sixty-four meters, creating a gross inclination of 37%, which creates hostile conditions for the planning of a central garden (Raz, 2000:22). Furthermore, the grand open area is dissected horizontally by four neighborhood roads and vertically by eight high supporting walls, resulting in a number of flat narrow levels. The doubling of the flight of stairs has caused an additional, internal horizontal dissection of each terrace. Sports facilities and wide grassplots have no place in this terraced, open space. The dramatic and expensive design gesture is ultimately no more than a collection of small garden plots, leaving the neighborhood—contrary to the Ministry of Housing's instructions—without any significant open areas (Lerman, 2000:100; Raz, 2000:98).[11] Osnat, like many of her neighbors, leaves Har Homa to use parks in the city, a choice which, in effect, alienates her neighborhood. Her act expresses a protest at the ineffectual planning, but also transforms her home into a suburb.

The constant and ever-present outward gaze distances Har Homa residents from lives taking place outside their compound-like neighborhood, turning the neighbors into a landscape drawing visible only through observation corridors. Osnat's opinion about this detachment explicates the ever-present phantasm of "walls"—their origins and how they are perpetuated. "We can't go really far downhill," she says. "When we came here there was an army troop below us. There are no walks in the *wadi*, even though we are the type of people who hike a lot. Sur Bahir does not interest us as a place to visit."

The phantasm of Jewish "ancestral rights" to the land is constructed by designing unsuitable open spaces facing—and dominating over—what is perceived as an ancient landscape representing the stories of the Bible. This gaze further enflames the national conflict over right of possession and native ownership (Mitchell, 1994:28-29). Yoel Berkowitz, Har Homa resident and editor of the local paper, declared in a newspaper interview, "[W]e are Jerusalem's safety belt. It is a type of mission; we are here with intention and purpose" (Winer, May 15, 2004).

Visual unification in Har Homa is based on the phantasm of the "Israeli melting pot" (the "gathering of the diasporas" or *"Kibbutz Galuyot"*), which prevents representations of multiculturalism within the national boundaries. The residents of Har Homa belong to many different Jewish ethnic groups, among them Mizrahim. Still, the open public spaces include no representations of customary non-Ashkenazi architecture and preferable vegetation such as fruit trees or herbs. Religious Mizrahi Jews' use of aromatic plants in Saturday evening Havdalah[12] ceremonies is ignored in the public landscaping. Further, poverty in design variation characterizes Har Homa's two gardens, which employ identical building materials, and recreational equipment made by the same commercial company. The goal of unifying Jewish ethnic groups nationally, in order to gird them against the Palestinian Other, dominated the planning of public housing in the 1950s and 1960s (Kallus and Law-Yone, 2000:161).[13] This move has now been reenlisted in architectural practices and private enterprise along the expanding Israeli frontier.

THE VIEWER AND THE VIEWED

Spaces and landscapes in Har Homa and Sur Bahir develop separately but simultaneously, according to their relative influence, and in response to the neighboring space. "A city dwells alone" is the phantasm used to maintain Jerusalem's "green belt" periphery, which equally serves to deny Sur Bahir of the right to decent housing and environmental self-determination. Some Israeli planners mean well, but are actually cooperating with a discriminatory official mechanism, and have no awareness of the phantasms on which they base their blueprints. Their designs remain detached from the difficult every day, deaf to residents' protests, and void of the mutual participation and learning required for neighborly relations.

In Sur Bahir, the crowded village center is spreading to the hilly ranges, and its agricultural hinterland has become homogeneous, incorporating only olive groves. These groves are increasingly essential for the future, promising both land market values and land national values. But it is this same landscape which is used by the observer from Har Homa to constitute the phantasm of "ancestral land," i.e., Jewish land currency constructed from the past. The Har Homa experience of exaltation through the distant gaze comes at the expense of available, sufficient, everyday open spaces. The importance of the docile hilly landscape seen from Har Homa, evidenced both in architectural structures and residents' priorities, stands in direct opposition to Har Homa's aggressive gesture in the view seen from Sur Bahir and other area neighborhoods and villages.

Thus, the phantasm of "ancestral landscape" turns the landscape viewed from Har Homa into a validation tool of the settling act. The ideas transmitted by this distancing contradict the actual scene, that of a Palestinian people with historic roots in the land who have developed their own villages, and validated their ownership through their very existence in the area.

Nowadays Palestinians plant olive trees in the *wadis* as an inexpensive means of proving ownership. In the garden plots of Har Homa, olive trees are planted for ornamentation and as a Jewish symbol. Palestinian writer Raja Shehadeh has critiqued the transformation of the olive tree into a phantasm-like symbol in Palestinian culture as a result of Israeli colonization. "Sometimes when I walk through the hills… unconsciously enjoying the feel of the hard earth underneath my feet, of the smell of thyme, of the hills and trees around me—I catch myself looking at an olive tree. As I observe it, it changes its nature and becomes a symbol, the symbol of the *samdeen* [steadfast ones], the symbol of our loss. From that moment on, the tree has been stolen from me" (Shehadeh, 1982:91).

Perhaps it will be possible to return that which has been robbed—a fertile place unmarked by phantasms of conflict. This can only happen through an awareness of the mutual gaze, an understanding of the presence of phantasms in the creation of distant and close landscapes, and a new view of difference as a chance for cultural diversity and acknowledgement.

1   We do not intend here to depoliticize the discourse on settlements in East Jerusalem, nor argue for the naiveté of the planners. Rather, we believe that understanding these phantasms can help to explain how architects cooperate with a discriminatory planning policy by engaging in an apparently depoliticized discourse on planning which masks these agendas.

2   Har Homa is home to 10,000 residents. Israel, in its national effort to create a Jewish demographic majority in a "united" city and thus preclude a Palestinian capital there, develops wedges of Jewish settlement on expropriated Palestinian land. In the case of Har Homa, 30% of the neighborhood lands were expropriated from Jews; 10% had been purchased by the Jewish National Fund (JNF) before 1948, and the rest was Palestinian private and absentee property. The plans for Har Homa were drafted in only 18 months (Kolker, August 30, 2005). Its construction, was the subject of an intense Palestinian and international campaign.

3   Official planning in Sur Bahir has created a severe housing shortage for its 12,000 residents, like that in other Palestinian neighborhoods.

4   *Arab as-Su'ahra Detailed Statutory City Plan No. 2683a* enables 37.5% construction per dunam (two housing units). Nearly 70% of the lands are categorized as open landscape areas, and 61.4 % as areas that otherwise cannot be use for building (Ir Shalem, 1999: 38-41). Another relevant plan is *Sur Bahir Detailed Statutory City Plan* - 2302a and 2302b, prepared in the 1980s and approved in 1999. The plan enables construction (two stories high) on 50 % of each dunam in the village center, and 25 % in the hinterlands. The neighborhood residents consider both plans discriminatory and inappropriate for their real demographic needs.

5   The Internet site of the Authority for the Development of Jerusalem writes: "The Eastern Ring Road that will bypass the city from the east will serve as an urban-metropolitan road and as an interurban road for the benefit of the Jerusalem metropolitan residents."

6   These number in the dozens, according to the committee's estimation.

7   Around Jerusalem, Palestinians are forced to walk a great deal around the military checkpoints and barriers that deter them from reaching Jerusalem for work, study, and medical treatment.

8   Many other Israeli architects choose not to plan settlements in the occupied territories.

9   *Ashkenazim*, Jews originating from Central and Eastern Europe countries, shaped Zionism before it was realized, and was the dominant group in Israel from the beginning of the twentieth century. This elite group subordinates all other ethnic, religious, national, and class groups living in Har Homa and Sur Bahir: Palestinians, Jews that immigrated to Israel from Arab and Muslim countries (*Mizrahim*), orthodox religious Jews (*Haredim*), and Russian immigrants.

10   The series of walls, barbed wire, fences, patrol roads, and lookout towers that comprise Israel's Separation Wall runs right through East Jerusalem, putting key physical interests and open land on the Israeli side of the boundary, and large Palestinian populations (even those carrying Jerusalem identity cards) on the West Bank side.

11 It is all the more necessary owing to the neighborhood's distance and detachment from the city, being connected to the city by one road, "an 'Areb-rein Road' that creates not a city but a settlement, which does not contain urban life" says Ofer Kolker Har Homa master plan architect (interview, August 30, 2005). A neighborhood of this size has to have a ten to twenty dunams open neighborhood space, which has to include many land uses as sports facilities and lawns (Lerman, 2000:100; Raz, 2000:98).

12 A Jewish ceremony that marks the transition from the Sabbath to the workday, and from the holy to the secular.

13 Israeli Jews of low social-economic status were driven to settle in frontier settlements, such as Musrara, Mishkanot Shaananim, Katamonim, Gilo, and Maale Adumim.

Selected Bibliography

Ir Shalem, *Mizrah Yerushala'im Matsav Tihnuni—Skira Shel Tohni'ot BeMizrah Yerushala'im [East Jerusalem, a Planning Condition - Review of the Master Plans in East Jerusalem]* (Jerusalem: Btselem, 1999).

Elisha Hausman, interview with the authors, July 13, 2005.

Rachel Kallus and Hubert Law-Yone, "HaBait HaLeumi vHaBait HaIshi: Tafqid HaShikun HaTsiburi biItsuv HaMerhav" ["National Home/Personal Home: The Role of Public Housing in the Shaping of Space"], *Theory and Criticism* 16, (2000).

Avishai, Kimeldorf, interview in the office of Naama Malis with authors, July 10, 2005.

Ofer Kolker, interview with the authors, August 30, 2005.

Rina Krugliac, interview with the authors, September 7, 2005.

Edna Lerman and Raphael Lerman, *Planning Briefing for Land Allocation for Public Needs* (Tel Aviv: The Institution for Research and Development of Education and Welfare Institutions, 2000).

Naama Meishar, "Fragile Guardians: Nature Reserves and Forests Facing Arab Villages," in *Constructing a Sense of Place: Architecture and the Zionist Discourse*, ed. H. Yacobi (Aldershot: Ashgate, 2004).

W. J. Thomas Mitchell, "Imperial Landscape," in *Landscape and Power*, ed. W. J. T. Mitchell (Chicago: University Of Chicago Press, 1994).

Erez Raz and Ein-Dor Dalit, *Medadim vHanhayot laShtahim Ptuhim Iraniyim [Urban Open Spaces: Categories, Indexes and Planning Guidelines]* (Tel Aviv: Teva va Din, 2000).

Ayala Ronel, interview with the authors, 2005.

Tom Selwyn, "Landscape of Liberation and Imprisonment: Towards an Anthropology of the Israeli Landscape," in *The Anthropology of Landscape: Perspectives on Place and Space*, eds. Eric Hirsch and Michael O'Hanlon (Oxford. Clarendon Press, 1995).

Susanne Seymour, "Historical Geographies of Landscape," in *Modern Historical Geographies*, eds. Brian Graham and Catherine Nash (London: Longman Press, 2000).

Raja Shehadeh, *HaDerekh HaShlishit [The Third Way]* (Jerusalem: Adam, 1982).

Naomi Shemer, *Shirey Naomi Shemer [Songs of Naomi Shemer]* (Jerusalem: The Jewish Agency, 1974). [Hebrew].

Stuart Winer, "Beyond the Wall," *Jerusalem Post*, May 13, 2005.

CONFRONTATION
EXCHANGE

In Jerusalem, space is divided into that of "the self" and "the other," "us" and "them," resulting in islands of cultural containment and social exclusion. Wherever possible, the crossing of ethnically defined boundaries is avoided. But a complete physical disengagement is equally impossible: areas of contact and entanglement include involuntary encounters between Palestinians and Israeli soldiers at military checkpoints, but also more banal meetings. Opportunism supports a fragile web of economic relationships between Jews and Arabs. The proximity of contrasting social cultures and resources, the asynchronism of Arab and Jewish religious holidays, as well as the comparative salary gap have created economic possibilities for both. Despite a backdrop of fear, hate, and suspicion, there are casual and inconspicuous encounters at work, in hospitals, or shopping malls, which offer the opportunity to escape political posturing and declarations about a united/occupied Jerusalem.

CALIBAN IN QALANDIYA

TOWARD AN ANALYSIS OF A CHECKPOINT

Tamar Berger

At an internal checkpoint in Saxony, Michael Kohlhaas' calamitous trip is prompted by a missing travel permit. Kohlhaas, innocent and honest, becomes a suicide terrorist of sorts, after his long and arduous journey culminates in revenge. Could it have been otherwise? Martin Luther's character in the novel believes that Kohlhaas should have forsaken his quest for infinite justice and refuses to pardon him, though he does act on his behalf. And Kleist? As for Kleist, Kohlhaas could not have done otherwise; the souls of men interest him, not moral-political questions.

An Israeli soldier at the Qalandiya checkpoint, armed and equipped from head to toe, straightens the people in line. Indeed, the people have lined up as required, but not in a straight line. Discipline and order—the soldier unconsciously reenacts his military training—are the backbone of obedience. And the Kohlhaases usually obey. They maintain an appropriate distance from the soldiers who check their IDs and permits; they respond to the little head nods, hand gestures, or hollers that command them to approach; they open their bags and bundles and boxes; they keep quiet, hushing their restless, frightened children; and off they go.

Everyday thousands of Palestinians cross Qalandiya checkpoint, which connects Jerusalem with Ramallah and the northern West Bank: workers, schoolchildren, teachers, merchants, peddlers, porters, professionals, shoppers, students, civil servants, clerks, craftsmen, doctors, patients, and so forth. At rush hour, the line stretches into the hundreds. They arrive in Ford Transits, yellow taxis, and buses. They cross a distance of several hundred meters from one end of the checkpoint to the other, on foot. Regulations at the checkpoint change from time to time, sometimes at midday, with no early warning.

For a long time, those wishing to cross were required to have special permits in order to do so, and sometimes even an extra special permit to validate an existing one. At times, one's address and age were enough to guarantee safe passage. Changing rules are built into the checkpoint.

Qalandiya checkpoint was erected in March 2001, several months after the outbreak of the al-Aqsa Intifada. A couple of soldiers were stationed to inspect passing cars. A few weeks later, it was deserted, only to be manned again—this time by more soldiers clad with watchtowers, concrete blocks, and plastic dividers to manage traffic. By the end of 2001, the checkpoint had spread across a few hundred meters, and included five lanes, a high fence separating vehicles from pedestrians, and sniper positions. Since then, it has transformed extensively—at times even requiring its dismantling (physically that is, never functionally) in order to revamp it. In its present state, it has seven narrow electric rotating passages that enable unprecedented control over the people who move through them. Soon, the checkpoint will be integrated into the elaborate complex of fences and walls running up and down and across the West Bank.

Fichte wrote about "internal boundaries." These being the first, original, and natural boundaries of states, i.e., of those who share a common language and are joined to each other by invisible natural bonds that constitute them as an inseparable whole. Fichte's nationalist conception of the romantically organic is typically 18th century. (Since then, nationalism has been severely undermined—deteriorated according to some, restored according to others—while other frameworks, both wider and narrower, both social and cultural, have developed alongside it (or instead of it). These frameworks being new and different variants of the same whole to which Fichte refers.

In one sense, Qalandiya checkpoint is an external border: it stands a few kilometers south of Jerusalem's northern municipal line. This is in the formal sense by way of a unilateral decision on the part of an occupying power marking a would-be national boundary. But this border is empty of real content, violence and imposition aside, because it brutally undermines the natural or "internal border," as Fichte would have it. Qalandiya separates men, women, and children from their homes, families, workplaces, schools, clinics, stores, and favorite cafes.

Why was the municipal line drawn exactly there? The logic is the same as the nihilistic logic of the settlements: one that expropriates, uproots, imprisons, deports, negates, erases. The very logic that leads—in places where it is impossible to make Palestinians physically vanish—to the severance of mixed areas into separate Jewish and Palestinian spaces.

The location of Qalandiya checkpoint—at the southern edge of the northern West Bank on the way to the settlements of Ofra, Beit El, and Sebastia—expresses desire. Israel's desire for land, for its Hebrew past, for unending genesis; a basic Zionist desire. The Declaration of Independence—the textual distillation of decades of Zionist practice—expresses it clearly. In a giant leap over two thousand years of vivid Jewish experiences in various lands back to a brief moment in time when the Hebrew people enjoyed territorial sovereignty in their land, they ascended, built, created, and made the desert bloom, as the primal, constructivist, modernist terminology epitomized by the term "pioneers" would have it.

But between the good-old-land and its remastering, stand the Palestinians (hence the need to redeem it)—its keepers for hundreds of years who worked it, built on it, walked upon it. "I traveled to the Land of Israel, and walked upon its sands. And here, the first man I came across who greeted me with "Salaam Aleikum!" was an Arab. With a black beard just like my father's. So I got to thinking: a man like this has been here for many a generation," wrote Avoth Yeshurun.

And here, where the violent invasion of a foreign body results not only in domination over the existent, but is also an encounter of sorts, I would like us to pause for a moment.

The checkpoint belongs, if you will, to the family of inbetween places. Inbetween places are characterized by the liminal, the borderly, the nonplace, the hybrid—though none of these describe inbetweeness in full.

It is liminal (in Victor Turner's sense) in that it is intermediary, it leads from one state to another, and yet has distinctive attributes of its own. Though the checkpoint lacks one of liminality's most salient features: its liberating dimension.

The checkpoint is a border site. First, because officially—albeit unilaterally—it demarcates (more or less) the northern boundary of (annexed) Jerusalem. Second, because of its duality of inclusion and exclusion, it simultaneously undermines and confirms identity. But border alone is an insufficient description of the checkpoint.

The checkpoint is a nonplace (or heterotopia, no-place), in that it renders mechanical the process that takes place there, in the anonymity it produces (crossers are no more than ID cards, document bearers), and in the tight surveillance it entails. Though the concept of the nonplace (in all its variants) does not point at a single source of authority and power, but rather at a Foucauldian diffusion of power, and at the checkpoint, power relations are perfectly clear.

The checkpoint is, arguably, a rather hybrid place. The term hybridity, borrowed from biology, defines the state of existence of two separate yet interdependent identities. In other words, a state of "also and also" rather than "either/or" or "and/and." It is not the pluralism of separates, nor is it the exclusion of binaries, but a mutual osmosis that does not forsake distinctive identities altogether. In nature, it is a state of coming into being, of non-permanence.

Claiming hybridity in the context of the checkpoint may appear strange: for what better example is there of a classical colonialist binary: ruler vs. ruled, powerful vs. powerless, foreign vs. local, military vs. civilian?

However, a deeper look reveals a more complex picture. It turns out that both sides are enmeshed, reflected in each other—far more than it would appear. Hybridity finds expression in the complicated relations between solidity and fluidity at the checkpoint, both physical and social. Solidity and fluidity constitute what I call the "hybrid focus" of the checkpoint, the place from which the elaborate relations found in it stem.

Despite the validity of this definition, and the fact that, in my view, one can employ it without losing sight of oppression, defining the checkpoint as an inbetween place—a broader more general definition—enables us to discuss the above characteristics, both physical and social.

It is very difficult to describe a checkpoint. As a place of passage, it is evasive by nature. It is inherently impermanent. It is modular, flexible, and adjustable according to differing military-operational needs, all of which clarify to the Palestinians with seeming randomness how provisional their lives are.

In terms of function and structure, all checkpoints are the same. Their basic form is linear, marking a course of passage from one point to another, and a few permanent stations where one is routinely stopped and checked. The lanes are demarcated by concrete railings, and at times are partly covered. This linearity is often broken by a perpendicular line, that of the checkpoint: a row of improvised horseshoe-shaped concrete cubicles, where the checker who checks the crossers'

IDs is stationed. I should add that the process described is not merely physical, but also emotional, a gradual approach to salvation.

Checkpoints are made out of massive yet movable materials, namely concrete and steal. Contrasted with this massiveness, one finds the amorphousness of mud, puddles, dust, dirt, garbage, barbed wire, tin roofing.

Further down the checkpoint, are the peddlers. Selling their goods at improvised stands made of plywood and corrugated tin, offering anything from falafel to poultry at the larger checkpoints. An area Palestinians call "the duty free," these stands are reestablished as regularly as they are brutally dismantled.

No checkpoint has clearly defined boundaries. Diffuse and dynamic, they overlap with their surroundings in myriad ways. Their outer boundary lengthwise is marked by the end of the line of cars leading up to them, a line that can stretch hundreds of meters, or the edges of the makeshift markets they spawn. Nor are their horizontal boundaries very clear.

They can be hermetically sealed or open to varying degrees of human "flow." They permit as much as they prohibit. They can be a place of humiliation, revenge, sadistic cruelty, recruitment of collaborators, but also of subversion and disdain, for getting to know the enemy, for training suicide bombers.

The first thing noticeable at Qalandiya checkpoint is the mayhem and movement. The honking trucks, the rattling diesel taxis, the wailing ambulances, the speeding military jeeps, the traffic jams, the stream of pedestrians and peddlers, the checkpoint line itself. This is the fundamental dissonance in a place where discipline and order are the core concerns.

I will not expand on the binary hierarchical nature of the checkpoint at this stage, assuming this is clear to anyone who has eyes with which to see and ears with which to hear. Indeed, at the heart of the checkpoint stands an occupying, oppressive, armed, threatening soldier in the way of an occupied, oppressed, disempowered civilian.

The structure of the checkpoint, as described above, makes this relationship clear. At the checkpoint, power-drunk arbitrariness, indifference, cruelty, humiliation, and violence reign supreme over obedience, insult, injury, and anger. The terms "fascist temptation," "laziness," "viciousness," "denial of humanity," and "speaking in the plural" drawn from Albert Memmi's impressive colonialist dictionary, are redefined day in and day out at Qalandiya.

One would suppose that for the Palestinians this means subjugation and survival. A deeper look at the checkpoint also reveals a certain degree of agency, a place of Palestinian power and Israeli weakness, a place of resilience, even defiance. The Palestinians defy the brutality of the checkpoint with their very presence—passive in appearance, pacifist in practice, self-controlled and civil, as they traverse a threatening, humiliating obstacle that forces them to contend with great physical duress (terrible cold in winter, rain, puddles, mud, heat in summer, dust, etc.). A place meant to instill fear and resignation, but they neither give up nor give in.

They take roundabout routes, sneak across the checkpoint, or insist on trying their luck head on. Some are caught, their IDs are confiscated, and are punished with long detentions, but they keep coming back.

The checkpoint gives expression to other modes of resistance: armed struggle (setting off an explosive device) and violent struggle (stoning a Jerusalem municipal garbage truck). This includes child stone-throwers, though it must be noted that the latter's encounters with the army come in waves, usually after an action taken by Israel, such as the assassination of Hamas leader Ahmad Yassin, the killing of Qalandiya Refugee Camp resident Arafat Ibrahim Yaaqub while drinking his morning coffee, or the construction of a wall around the south-western side of the camp. The army's reaction is lethal at worst and vicious at best: tear gas, rubber bullets, live ammunition. Five children in the camp have been killed by IDF (Israeli Defense Forces) fire in the current Intifada. But the kids are not afraid. They provoke the soldiers, approaching them within meters, calling to them in mimicry, "Come on! Let's see if you're a man!"

Mimicking (in Homi Bhabha's sense), and thus also resistant, is the behavior of the Tanzim activists who strut through nearby Qalandiya Refugee Camp in IDF uniforms, so authentic-looking, that the only thing which discloses their true identities are the black masks hiding their faces.

And then there are the other kids, the chewing-gum and trinket sellers, who half hustle half loiter, crossing the checkpoint this way and that, running between the soldiers legs, imitating them to their faces, getting chased away but reappearing time and again.

Resistant are also the mocking expressions on the faces of a group of exhausted laborers coming home from work, who watch a cluster of awkward equipment-laden soldiers waddle like ducks back from a man-hunt in the nearby quarry, returning empty-handed. Now, at the end of the day, the look on their faces is relaxed, resilient.

Resilient are the bribes offered to soldiers—a phone card, dope, cigarettes.

Resilient are also the peddlers, continuously expelled, who return to vend the latest fashions, fresh produce, or cold refreshments to passersby.

And no less resistant are the Ford Transit drivers who organize ad hoc to regulate the mayhem of the checkpoint, making it possible to function more or less "normally" in a place whose raison d'etre is running interference in the normalcy of life (Rema Hammami of Birzeit University describes the development of this informal system at the Surda checkpoint north of Ramallah).

Resistance, though perhaps not that which is violent, is by and large unorganized. It is measured in its cumulative effect, and adds up to undermine the sharp distinction between sides. It brings to mind Michel de Certeau's distinction between strategy, which is the domain of the powerful who possess a place and perspective of their own (e.g. a watchtower or the sites of a rifle) and tactics, which is the "art of the weak," those who are limited by the givens of place and time.

The soldier, for his part, is not only exerting force, he is also fortifying himself. The concrete walls, the fences, the gates, imprison him as well. His state-of-the-art gear is also cumbersome and restrictive. His eight hours of duty get him soaked to the bones on a winter's day, and cause him to stink to high heaven under the blistering sun, something his "subjects" confirm by holding their breath as they pass him by. The soldier sees his likeness reflected back to him in two senses: as his counterparts in age, class, look, and as the objects of his oppressive actions. The only way to settle this internal conflict is to deny and harden; to repress feelings, to negate affinities. But as that which has been denied tends to do, it lingers just beneath the surface.

The disruption of the binary also has to do with the spectrum of people who cross Qalandiya. The soldier witnessing a silver-haired professor from Birzeit pass before him, or a Ramallah pediatrician with his medical bag, or a student at al-Quds University wearing the latest tight jeans, cannot but—due to age, class or look—feel somewhat inferior to them. He has to work hard to restore his perception of them as a nondistinct mass of "Palestinians." Their signifiers deconstruct the great Palestinian "monolith" in his head, evoking instead the complexities of the Israeli experience, with which he is all too familiar.

In Shakepeare's *The Tempest*, Caliban—"a savage and deformed slave," says to his master, Prospero, the expelled Duke of Milan: "You taught me language, and my profit on't / Is I know how to curse. The red plague rid you! / For learning me your language."

It is the beginning of the 17th century, and postcolonial thought must wait for its predecessor, colonial thought, to sprout, grow, and flourish. But Caliban's words—after ridding them of their Eurocentric undertones—formulate the power of the oppressed; a power at the heart of which lies, among other things, the adoption of the oppressor's tools so as to undermine him, and the unavoidable affinity between oppressor and oppressed that no degree of denial can undermine. Prospero's might and magical powers, it must be remembered, stemmed from Caliban's knowledge.

Since autumn 2004, when the above text was written, a new checkpoint was conceived alongside the old one. Due to be completed in autumn 2005, it will continue to function as the main point of passage between Jerusalem and the northern West Bank. While the new checkpoint far exceeds its predecessor in size, mass, and order, interestingly it is no less provisional in structure and material. It links up to the maze of fences and walls intended to "Judaize" the area around Jerusalem by severing the city from its eastern environs and annexing maximum land and minimum people. Blockade, suffocation, provisionality. We are doomed, so it seems, to live this way for years to come.

ON THE IMPORTANCE OF THUGS

THE MORAL ECONOMY OF A CHECKPOINT

Rema Hammami

For almost three years, from March 2001 through December 2003, the final leg of a commute between Birzeit University and Ramallah, both located just north of Jerusalem, meant a one- to two-kilometer walk across the Surda checkpoint.[1] Commuters would disembark from transit vans that jammed both ends of the no-drive zone. Skirting rubble and concrete blocks, they tripped down the valley, holding their breath as they passed the Israeli soldiers, before finally trudging up the incline to the vans on the other side. Thousands made the walk every day. In the morning, the flow of fashionably dressed students on their way to the university crossed the flow of villagers heading into Ramallah for work and the services that can only be found in a city. In the afternoon, the pattern would repeat in reverse. Refreshments and groceries could be purchased along the way from peddlers or makeshift stands called "the duty free."

On the worst days, trigger-happy soldiers suddenly prohibited pedestrian traffic, leaving students and villagers stranded on the opposite side of work or home. More commonly, soldiers would drop in at the checkpoint for a few hours to toy with the droves of walking commuters, stopping all—or a select few—for interminable identity card and baggage checks. Often they would "organize" the drivers and peddlers by ramming their vans or stands with their jeeps. In those three years at the Surda checkpoint, three Palestinians were shot to death by the Israeli military, another two died in accidents among the crush of vans, at least one man died of a heart attack as he was wheeled across on a stretcher, two babies were born behind a rubble mound, and untold numbers of young men were beaten by soldiers, often in full view. No one has counted the numbers injured at the futile demonstrations staged to clear the checkpoint away.

During the same 2001-2003 period, the UN Office of the Commissioner for Humanitarian Affairs documented the near-constant presence of more than 600 army checkpoints and roadblocks strangling communities throughout the West Bank.[2] But in the last 18 months of its existence, Surda, often the sole point of transit for goods and West Bank citizens and entering and leaving the city, became a strategic nexus within this larger web of closures. Surda also became a magnet for dispossessed workers from throughout the West Bank, seeking to earn a good living from the thousands of commuters passing through the checkpoint every day.

During the second *intifada* (from 2000), neither the Palestinian Authority nor political groups have provided the population with the frameworks of mass organizing
that were so crucial to civic resistance in the 1987-1993 Intifada. Instead, the military thrust of resistance organizations has primarily condemned the majority to
the role of audience. At the same time, Israel's use of collective punishment during
2000-2004, resulting 60% of the population living in poverty, has been more total,
and more savage. But collective punishment gives rise to collective experience and
meaning. Checkpoints, ironically, have become the "public spaces" of this Intifada;
it is at places like Surda where most Palestinians have a constant and direct confrontation as members of the collective with the Israeli occupation. It is at, and in
relation to, checkpoints that the society has developed new meanings of resistance
and ad hoc forms of civic organization. The emergent ideology of civic resistance
is a variation on the old nationalist theme of *sumud*, or steadfastness. In the 1970s,
sumud meant refusing to leave the land despite the hardships of occupation; now
it connotes something more proactive. Its new meaning, found in the common
refrain, "*al-hayat lazim tistamirr*" ("life must go on") is about resisting immobil-
ity, refusing to let the army's lockdown of one's community preclude school or
work. The collective memory of how years of general strikes during the first Intifada backfired, helping to destroy businesses and the education of a generation
of schoolchildren, has led schools, universities, and workplaces to adopt "stay-
ing open" as their rallying cry. In so doing, they helped establish the collectively
understood, but individually achieved, daily resistance of simply getting there.

Checkpoints do not merely thwart mobility; they also create immense chaos.
It is not simply that goods cannot reach the market, or students their schools,
but that the circuits are shattered through which social relations flow, which
make commerce and education possible. Initial attempts to recreate these circuits
are individual and ad hoc, but over time, informal systems begin to emerge. In
Palestine, in the absence of mass organizations, networks of informal sector
workers have stepped into the gap. Thus, the unlikely symbols of the new steadfastness are not "national institutions," but rather the subproletariat Ford van
drivers, whose semicriminal bravado is summed up by ubiquitous Nike "No Fear"
stickers emblazoned on their rear windshields. Derided even now as a menace
on the roads, these drivers exemplify the uprising's ethic of getting through anything, by any means, to anywhere. This same thuggish hypermasculine subculture
has provided the informal systems, which have made "getting there" possible.
Thuggishness (*zar'aniyya*) has become a crucial force for everyday resistance and
organizing at checkpoints—not just to deal with crowds and traffic jams but also
to deal with the thuggishness of soldiers, given immense operational leeway in
dealing with the civilian population.

THUGS AGAINST CHAOS

Palestinian mass transit is dominated by privately owned Ford vans that can
legally carry seven passengers and are licensed to work on a set route under a
local taxi office. Within a week of the Surda roadblock's appearance, the army
also blocked the two possible detour routes for vans traveling between Birzeit

and Ramallah (which became known as al-Jawwal and al-Mahkama checkpoints). So van drivers blazed new trails across nearby agricultural tracks, but the terrain would not allow for the creation of a final detour route into Ramallah. The Fords were forced to drop off and pick up passengers at whichever end of Surda checkpoint they had reached, instead of completing the route. For months even this system remained ad hoc, because the road was often "half open," with soldiers allowing one lane for both directions of traffic. The massive traffic jams that ensued finally led many commuters to walk through the checkpoint, rather than wait senselessly for hours in a vehicle.

The system was in total disarray. While registered Fords continued to assemble at their official stands at the end of each route, independent cowboys were showing up to spirit away the licensed drivers' passengers and livelihoods. The Birzeit drivers, the largest group of drivers in the area, eventually acquiesced to the new reality and began to group at the checkpoint, their old organizer Abu Ahmad at the helm. But the checkpoint remained a lawless frontier. They needed a thug.

Ziad, in his late 30s, is a driver from Birzeit village. Like most men his age, he had worked in construction inside Israel until the permit system imposed during the 1990s forced him to look for work closer to home. With the compensation pay from his former Israeli boss, he bought a secondhand, eight-seat Mercedes and began to ferry passengers on the Birzeit village university line. When the roadblocks appeared, Ziad seized the new situation and began to work the off-road *wadis* (Arabic for "canyon") and tracks forged between besieged villages. It was dangerous and grueling, but the money to be made was far better than that on his regular route. Then a better opportunity arrived. Courted by the Birzeit drivers to organize their line, Ziad first went to Jalazun refugee camp, just over the hill from the checkpoint, to solicit the backing of local Fatah activists. With their help and his own brand of persuasion, the flow of Fords gained some rhythm.

The Ramallah side of the checkpoint posed different problems as the number of vans had to be increased. To meet the need, drivers stepped in, whose licensed routes had been severed elsewhere. On the Ramallah side of the checkpoint, the Ramallah governor and the municipality was able to wield some clout. He appointed two organizers, one for the vans and another for private taxis. Then the check point al-Jawwal was sealed, and the drivers who had been serving that checkpoint, the majority from Jalazun camp, descended upon the Ramallah side of Surda. The new competition snarled traffic and heated tempers. ("You know, in Jalazun—well, we have our own way of dealing with things," said Abu al-Abed, the al-Jawwal organizer from Jalazun.) Eventually, the governor hammered out a deal between the warring drivers, setting a quota of vans from each village (but giving the highest quota to Jalazun) and putting the old organizer Abu al-Abed in charge.

Ziad and Abu al-Abed were able to take control of either side of the Surda roadblock because they had tough reputations, but also because they had local weight and backing (hence the governor's calculated decision and Ziad's quest for the right support). The hard-nosed character of both is typical for the culture of resistance, which has made refugee camps the front line of each Intifada and produced the collective ability to fight and win turf wars with neighboring communities—in this case over the limited resources offered by a checkpoint.

Checkpoints have caused crushing joblessness, yet simultaneously created the one growth area of the economy. For 15,000 shekels ($3,500), an unemployed youth can buy a used Ford and exploit the public's need for transportation, unhindered by the weakened Palestinian National Authority. A main role of Ziad and Abu al-Abed was to keep these unfair players away, or, as time went on, to allow them a small quota when extra vans were needed at the end of rush hour.

Controlling drivers with permits could often be more complicated. The Surda checkpoint blocked the road at a narrow point between a steep hillside and a drop to the valley below. It was a great challenge to squeeze enough vans onto either side of the checkpoint to handle the thousands of commuters, while at the same time allowing the vans to load, turn, and move out quickly without creating gridlock, particularly at rush hour. Drivers were often tempted to bypass the queue of up to 150 vans in order to get their turn sooner and thus make more runs, a practice described as "stealing a turn."

If controlling the vans was a balancing act between being tough on drivers but keeping them working, coping with the soldiers was much more tendentious. Vans and taxis were forced into a constant game of cat and mouse with army patrols. Occasionally, when no soldiers were in sight, drivers needing to get their cars to the other side would drive at breakneck speed through the rock-strewn openings left for the exclusive use of army jeeps. Those caught risked being beaten or having their cars smashed. The lucky ones would only have their keys and identification cards confiscated for the day. The soldiers eventually learned that Ziad and Abu al-Abed were responsible for organizing the drivers. "When they would take the keys and IDs and leave the drivers without work, they couldn't be bothered to look for the owner," commented Ziad. "So they would come and throw [the confiscated items] on me, because I know all the drivers."

It was more ominous for the organizers when soldiers tried to implicate them in the soldiers' own obsession with pushing the drivers back from the rubble mounds that marked the no-drive zone—conflicting with the drivers' interest in scooping up exhausted pedestrians. When faced with the soldiers' demands that he force the drivers' back, Abu al-Abed would simply disappear from the scene. Ziad has a similar story. "A soldier called me over and said to tell the drivers to move up. I said to him, 'Listen, do I work for you as an employee?'" The soldier confiscated Ziad's ID. "It was winter and I sat in the rain for three hours. The soldier tells me, 'Now you've been taught a lesson.' I told him, 'Nevertheless, you call me again, I'm not going to answer. It's not my job.'" Both Ziad and Abu al-Abed preferred the soldiers to go about their business directly.

HUMAN POWER

Transportation across the no-drive zone was also needed for goods and for people who couldn't walk. During the period when one lane was open, trucks carrying Israeli goods to Palestinian markets could get permits to drive through. But even before Surda was fully closed to vehicles in the summer of 2002, the small businesses, farmers, schools, builders, travelers with luggage, and university students returning from the holidays all needed a solution. It arrived in the form of porters with three-wheeled wooden pushcarts.

Among workers, porterage is considered one step above begging. The majority of long-term porters working in the Ramallah market come from the villages around Hebron, the poorest area of the West Bank, and sleep at the market throughout the week. Comparatively, working at Surda was a modest step up. But, once again, with the closure of al-Jawwal checkpoint, guys from Jalazun showed up with carts. The original handful of Hebronites could not defend their territory against the five men from Jalazun, but with greater human traffic now passing through Surda, there was work enough to go around.

A sample of what porters carried across the checkpoint on one summer morning suggests how crucial they were: meat from the slaughterhouse in Birzeit, fresh mulberries, packaged foods for a supermarket, glasses and plates for a houseware shop, fabric for a tailor, luggage, wood, cans of white paint, a glass showcase, a stone-cutting machine, a car engine—not to mention the day's edition of al-Quds newspaper. The flow of meat, wood, and vegetables into the city crossing the stream of industrial and consumer goods going to the villages attested to the interdependence between Ramallah and its hinterland—a relation-ship the checkpoint nearly shattered. But porters also ferried people across—children too small to walk the two kilometers, yet too large to be carried; the sick and elderly whose wheelchairs couldn't navigate the rubble; six dialysis patients from the villages; and, on several occasions, people wounded at the checkpoint itself. That porters were allowed to operate at a number of checkpoints bespeaks the army's sordid logic of permissible mobility. Wheels were all right, as long as they weren't motorized.

FOUR LEGS

But the moral economy of the porters, who were relatively accommodating to newcomers, began to take its toll. At one point, their numbers had reached 35. To compensate for declining income, they doubled the fare from five to ten shekels. When the no-drive zone doubled in length, they doubled the rate again. Commuters and merchants started to complain and the governor intervened. Falling income hit the married porters hardest; a wooden pushcart cost only 600 shekels and too many people were getting into the business. Three of the older married porters from Jalazun decided to take a chance on the logic of permissible mobility and invested in a horse and carriage.

Horse-drawn carts had been tried and turned back by the soldiers at the al-Mahkama checkpoint, and at first, the same thing happened at Surda. Shrewdly, the porters-cum-carriage drivers waited for the platoon to change, since the new soldiers would be none the wiser. With the horse-drawn cart, Moustapha and his partners knew they could corner the market on the morning transport of sheep carcasses from the Birzeit slaughterhouse destined for butcher shops in Ramallah. "The meat needed seven pushcarts. That's 70 shekels. With the horse, we could carry it in one load for 20 shekels."

Two months later, most of the older married porters were working horses and a number of farmers from nearby villages had also moved in. The original horsemen had carried mostly heavy, unmanageable loads such as building materials and large machinery and had not deeply damaged the porters' market. But, once again, increased numbers led to declining income, this time on an initial investment of some $1,700. It was only a matter of time before one universally-derided carriage driver began to carry people, cutting deeply into the porters' trade.

Then in July 2003, everyone was swept out of business by the opening of the Surda and Ein Areek checkpoints—the grand achievement of the US-sponsored "road map." When Surda was closed again to traffic five weeks later, the horsemen and the porters negotiated an agreement, aided by the new configuration of bull-dozed mounds marking the no-drive zone. It was agreed that a customer would be offered the option of crossing the checkpoint in a horse-drawn cart with other riders for six shekels, but only to traverse the distance between the two mounds. For ten shekels, a customer could take a pushcart around the mounds, thus moving his goods all the way from a van on one side to a van on the other. The porters had little leverage to extract this deal; the horsemen's generosity came from the responsibility they felt towards their relatives, friends, or neighbors.

A LIMINAL ZONE

In the final period when Surda was the hub of movement between the north and south West Bank, there were roughly 25 porters, 18 carriage drivers, as many as 400 vans, and another 30 small taxis working the checkpoint. In addition, there were the peddlers, whose numbers averaged about 30 in good weather, and as many as 70 during Ramadan. On any given day, up to 540 people were making a living off Surda. That number does not take into account the service sector that sprang up to feed and quench the thirst of the checkpoint workers—the coffee vans, cigarette sellers, drink sellers, kebab stands, and blacksmiths for the horses.

This new market was not lost on the communities affected by the checkpoint. The October 2003 reclosure hit them hard, while providing a boon to checkpoint workers. "I got sick of it," remembers Moustafa. "The work was going well, but I was ready to drop it because there wasn't a person passing who didn't say 'Exploiter! You're the ones that are keeping the checkpoint closed.'" Abu al-Abed sums up the problem: "With the checkpoint there was suffering for everyone, but you had 10% benefiting and 90% losing."

The checkpoint had taken men from the margins and provided them with public roles that were central to the society's survival. But the checkpoint workers, while equally victims of the sanctions regime, had found a way to turn that source of dispossession into a livelihood. In addition, their ability to work at the checkpoint was dependent, if not on the soldiers' permission, at least upon their indifference. Porters and van drivers ultimately became caught in a liminal position between the lines of oppressor and oppressed, exploiter and exploited, that were so clearly drawn at the checkpoint.

While the workers did not want to cooperate or be seen to be cooperating with the soldiers' dirty work, at the same time, they could not afford to openly confront them. In the first 18 months of the checkpoint's existence, before the labor infrastructure had developed, the university organized three large demonstrations against the checkpoint. Each resulted in the army simply worsening the existing regime. Still, spontaneous demonstrations were planned by students and young men, whose constant harassment brought them to a breaking point. These moments of collective resistance created deep dilemmas for checkpoint workers. Hurled stones and rampaging soldiers threatened not only bodies, but vans, peddler stands, and stock. The checkpoint might be completely sealed—not even allowing pedestrians to cross—for an afternoon or even a few days. On these days, workers complained that kids letting off steam were damaging the collective interest. "Nothing is going to happen to the jeep—it is protected," noted Ziad, But "the next thing you know, the soldiers are firing bullets, breaking more windshields." The class difference between demonstrating students from the university, and the subproletariat of van drivers and porters, accentuated the latter's contention that middle class kids, who "do not know how to fight properly anyway," were simply creating a mess for travelers or the working poor.

But Ziad's willingness to sit in the rain for three hours, rather than give the soldier rights over him, attests to the workers' everyday resistance. Often these were individual confrontations when soldiers stepped over an invisible line, of what workers saw as permissible, within the rules of dominator and dominated. Examples include the heroic story of the coffee vendor who kept choosing to let soldiers destroy his stand with a jeep rather than provide them with free coffee, or the young van driver who, for the sake of the rest, went and punched a soldier who had cursed their mothers. More significant resistance could be found in less dramatic, but tenacious everyday subversion of the checkpoint regime itself. At night, checkpoint workers stealthily pushed concrete blocks a few more inches apart to make way for horse carriages, or trampled the edges of new mounds of rubble so porter carts could pass. Through need and ingenuity, in a myriad of ways, they reclaimed the space of the checkpoint, from being a site of pure oppression and brutality, into one where livelihoods, social life, and even sociability could be recovered.

1   Editors note: this essay is a shortened version of the original published in *Middle East Report* 231, Summer 2004. It is part of the author's wider research on the impact of checkpoints; we have included it here as indicative of the checkpoint regime which currently dissects all of the occupied territories, including Jerusalem.

2   The Gaza Strip was subjected to a similar checkpoint regime, albeit one spanning wider spaces and not penetrating the large urban areas in which the Palestinian Authority operated.

Fear and Assertion

View of Har Homa as seen from Sur Bahir

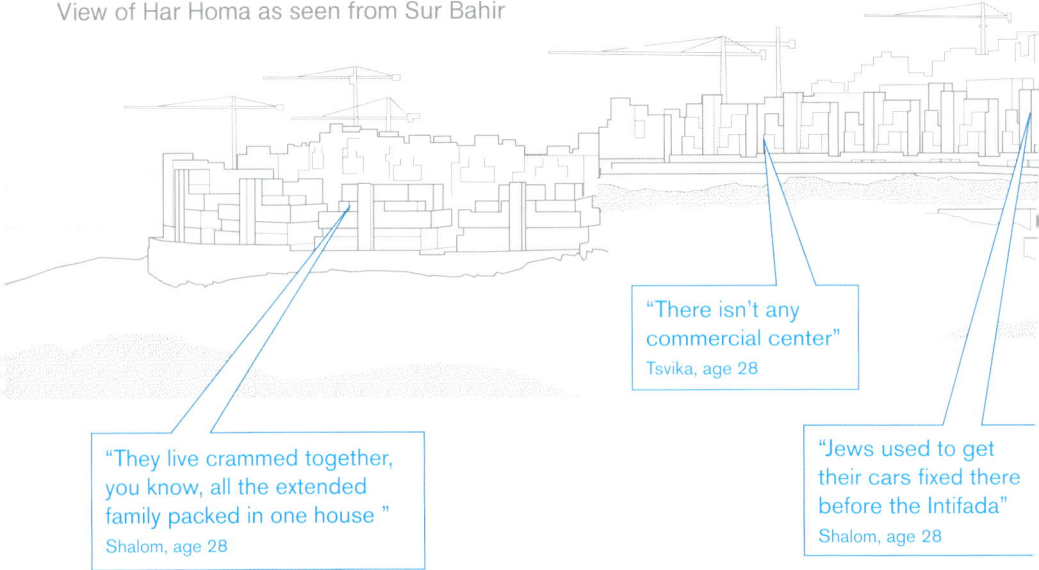

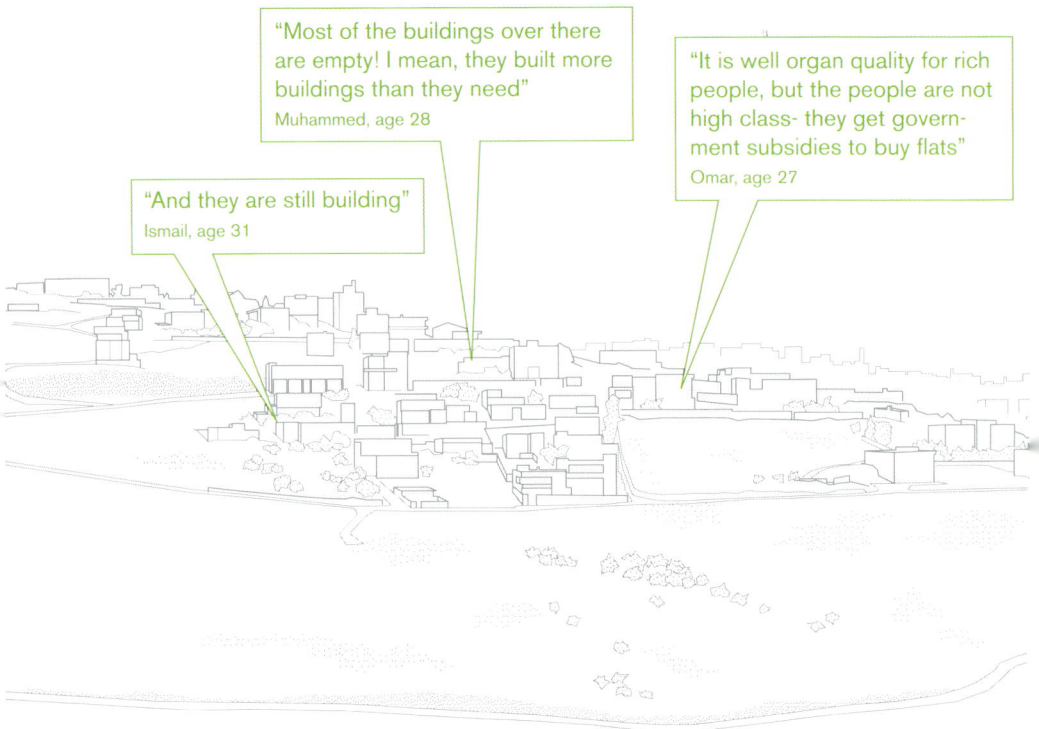

"There isn't any
commercial center"
Tsvika, age 28

"They live crammed together,
you know, all the extended
family packed in one house "
Shalom, age 28

"Jews used to get
their cars fixed there
before the Intifada"
Shalom, age 28

"Most of the buildings over there
are empty! I mean, they built more
buildings than they need"
Muhammed, age 28

"It is well organ quality for rich
people, but the people are not
high class- they get government subsidies to buy flats"
Omar, age 27

"And they are still building"
Ismail, age 31

View of Sur Bahir as seen from Har Homa

Projections
Sur Bahir / Har Homa (2005)

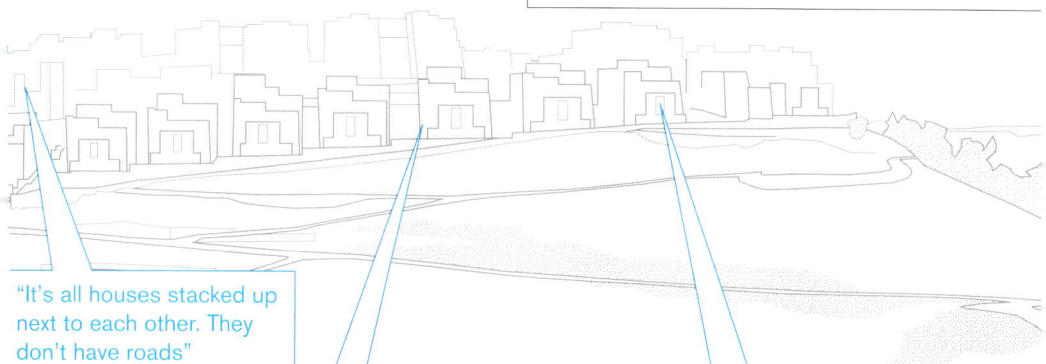

"It's all houses stacked up next to each other. They don't have roads"
Zev, age 32

"I don't know how many they are – I don't go there"
Kfir, age 31

"This whole area was a natural forest once"
Racheli, age 29

They have services in the center of the neighborhood and they have everything they need"
Sami, age 37

"There are approx. 4,000 people- they will reach 1,000,000!!"
Rassem, age 35

e this kind of itecture. It is e well"
, age 35

"Very rich American Jews buy these apartments"
Said, age 22

"The Israeli army has soldiers camping in the valley"
Omar, age 33

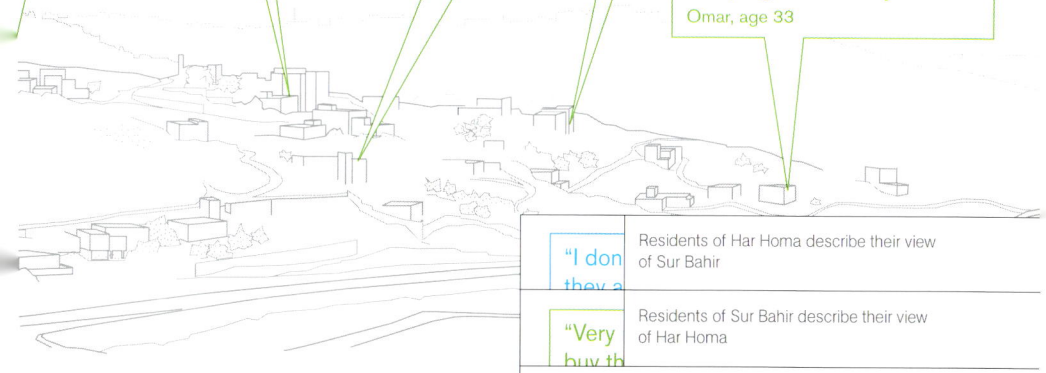

| "I don they a | Residents of Har Homa describe their view of Sur Bahir |
| "Very buy th | Residents of Sur Bahir describe their view of Har Homa |

Sur Bahir
Tsur Bahir

Jabal Abu Ghneim
Har Homa

Visible and Invisible
Sur Bahir / Har Homa (2005)

The gaze across a narrow valley is the only means of contact between most villagers and settlers, and both Har Homa and Sur Bahir are thus part of an ambivalent and complex game of hide-and-seek. The monumental fortress-like posturing of Har Homa seeks to induce fear and respect, while its streets and public spaces remain sheltered from the perceived hostile surroundings. Sur Bahir's residents express their contempt for their neighbor by turning their back on Har Homa, discarding domestic and building rubble or discarded cars in the open space as if to spoil the view. Camouflaged in the hilly terrain of south-east Jerusalem, everyday life in the village remains sheltered from the gaze of the settler, building inspector, soldier, or policeman.

●	Exemplary viewpoint in Sur Bahir
●	Exemplary viewpoint in Har Homa
▨	Areas visible from Sur Bahir
▨	Areas visible from Har Homa

0 | 100 | 200 | 300 | 400 | 500 meters

Sur Bahir
Tsur Bahir

Har Homa
Jabal Abu Ghnaim

Light
Sur Bahir / Har Homa (2005)

The gaze across a narrow valley is the only means of contact between most villagers and settlers, and both Har Homa and Sur Bahir are thus part of an ambivalent and complex game of hide-and-seek. The monumental fortress-like posturing of Har Homa seeks to induce fear and respect, while its streets and public spaces remain sheltered from the perceived hostile surroundings. Sur Bahir's residents express their contempt for their neighbour by turning their back on Har Homa, discarding domestic and building rubble or discarded cars in the open space as if to spoil the view. Camouflaged in the hilly terrain of south-east Jerusalem, everyday life in the village remains sheltered from the gaze of the settler, building inspector, soldier or policeman.

Illuminated minarets

| 0 | 100 | 200 | 300 | 400 | 500 meters |

Sound
Sur Bahir / Har Homa (2005)

Sound is an omnipresent medium, which crosses physical or mental barriers of segregation.
The soundscape of Har Homa and Sur Bahir fus-
es both realities into an uncanny and complex
whole, amplified by the echoes in the narrow
valley. The sound of the *muezzin* (loudspeaker)
penetrates at times of prayer from all sides into
the private flats of Har Homa. The shooting
range of the Israeli military sends echoing noises
through Sur Bahir's valleys and the sound of
vehicles and heavy construction on both sides
form permanent background noise. At night,
young villagers turn on Arabic pop music full
volume as they cruise through the no-man's-
land between settlement and village.

	Cars
	Construction machines
	Muezzin
	Military shooting range
	Arab music (car radio)

0   100   200   300   400   500 meters

الجِهاد Jihad
سبحان الله Prais
Glory be to Allah
حماس Hamas
خ أحمد ياسين
الله أكبر Allah is great
Ha

حقق الانتخابي
حافظوا على النظافة Keep cleanliness
Start
و قسما أن نواصل المسيرة على درب الشهداء
We swear to follow the martyrs
الله أكبر و لله الحمد
الله محمد• القدس لنا Jerusaelm is ours
القدس لنا• الله أكبر• رمضان كريم• أذكر الله الحمدلله
Ramadan is benevolent
Mention Allah, praise be to Allah
تح + حماس
ف خية•للشيخ أحمد ياسين القدس لنا الشهيد محمد عيد
Jerusalem is ours, Martyr Muhammad Eid
A thousand salutations to Sheikh Ahmad Ya

ه - محمد• فتح الموت للعملاء الغرباء
Death to foreign collaborators
Fatah Allah - Muhamm
مبروك• Congratulations
قرىتنا Let the flags of victor
القدس عاصمة الدولة الفلسطينية
شاء من شاء و أبى من أبى
Jerusalem is the capital of the Palestinian state,
regardless of who accepts and who refuses
أذكروا الله Remember Allah
لفتح Regarc
حماس- فتح ياسر عرفات• لنا القدس
Yassir Arafat Hamas - Fatah Jerusalem is ours

عيد الجهاد القدس عروس مهرها الدماء Marty
Jerusalem is a bride whose dowry is blood
أذكروا الله Remeber Allah
فلسطين الله أكبر
Palestine Allah is great
فلسطين Palestine
و ما بكم من نعم فمن الله
Whatever blessing you have it's from Allah
كاكين In the
و من يتقي الله يجعل له مخرجا
And for those who fear Allah; he prepares a way out
الإسم و العنوان حماس و الإخوان
The name and place: Hamas and the Brotherhood
كل عام و أنتم بخير
May you be well every year
حماس Hamas
لا اله الا الله There is no God bu
الله أكبر Allah is great
ت
حماس Hamas
القدس لنا حماس
Jerusalem is ours Hamas
شرون هنا Sharon is here

הר-חומה: Har Homa:
חומת שמואל Shmuel's Wall
גם אני מתחבר: I am also related
גוש קטיף והשומרון Gush Katif and the Shomron
הטרנספר לא יעבור The transfer (disengagement) won't work
העם עם גוש קטיף The nation is Gush Katif
יש לנו אהבה והיא תנצח We have love and it will win
שימרו על שכונה נקיה! Keep the neighbourhood clean!
حماس Hamas
גוש קטיף לנצח נצחים Gush Katif forever
גם אני מתחבר: I am also related
فتح Fatah
יום שמח God Day
גוש קטיף והשומרון Gush Katif and the Shomron
יהודי לא מגרש יהודי A Jew does not evict a Jew
גוש קטיף לנצח נצחים Gush Katif forever
יהודי לא מגרש יהודי A Jew does not evict a Jew

מושחתים נמאסתם
We're fed up with your corruption

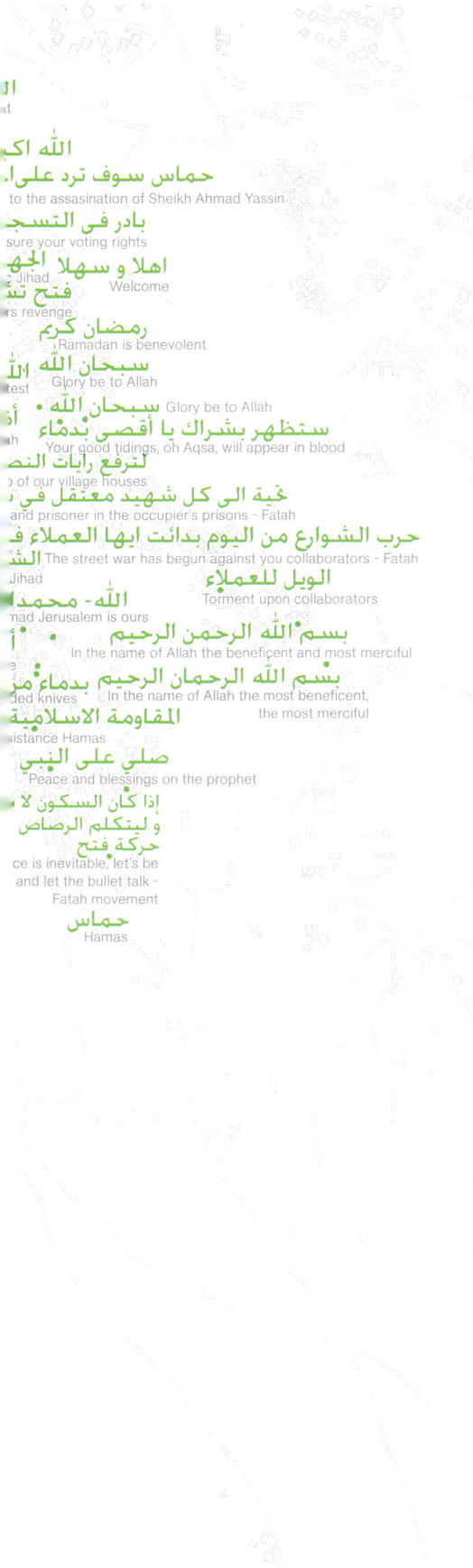

Graffiti
Sur Bahir / Har Homa (2005)

Politics and everyday life are fused as political graffiti, stickers and posters are sprayed or glued in public spaces. Declarations and messages, whether violent, aggressive, racist, defiant, or even sceptical, are written in Hebrew or Arabic, aiming to rally the local population. While graffiti displayed in Sur Bahir is predominately aimed against the Israeli occupation and in support of a Palestinian capital in Jerusalem, graffiti in Har Homa largely defends the aims of the Israeli settler movement.

الله اك
حماس سوف ترد على
to the assasination of Sheikh Ahmad Yassin
بادر فى التسج
sure your voting rights
اهلا و سهلا الج
Jihad   Welcome
فتح تث
r's revenge
رمضان كريم
Ramadan is benevolent
سبحان الله ال
est   Glory be to Allah
سبحان الله • أ
ستظهر بشراك يا أقصى بدماء
h   Your good tidings, oh Aqsa, will appear in blood
لترفع رايات النص
o of our village houses
حية الى كل شهيد معتقل فى
and prisoner in the occupier's prisons - Fatah
حرب الشوارع من اليوم بدائت ايها العملاء ف
الش   The street war has begun against you collaborators - Fatah
Jihad
الويل للعملاء
الله - محمد   Torment upon collaborators
nad Jerusalem is ours
بسم الله الرحمن الرحيم
أ   In the name of Allah the beneficent and most merciful
بسم الله الرحمان الرحيم بدماء م
ded knives   In the name of Allah the most beneficent,
المقاومة الاسلامية   the most merciful
istance Hamas
صلي على النبي
Peace and blessings on the prophet
إذا كان السكون لا
و ليتكلم الرصاص
حركة فتح
ce is inevitable, let's be
and let the bullet talk -
Fatah movement
حماس
Hamas

| سطين Palestine | Palestinian graffiti |
| חומה- Har Hom | Israeli graffiti |

0 | 100 | 200 | 300 | 400 | 500 meters

POLICE PATROLS
Frequent police patrols along major roads

FLYING CHECKPOINTS
Periodic control of Palestinian traffic

PEDESTRIANS

SHOP KEE
Informal sta
observers

ISRAELI PATROL ROUTE

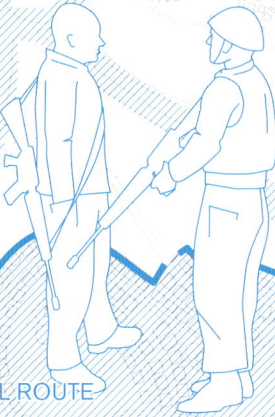

MOBILE PHONES
Passing-on warnings of patrols or road closures

MOSQUES AND COFFEE HOUSES
Permanent information exchange

ISRAELI PATROL ROUTE

SOLDIERS, POLICE, SECURITY COMPANIES
Stationary control of public spaces and surroundings

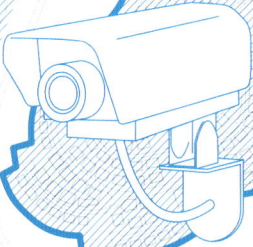

FLOODLIGHT
Illumination of open areas at night

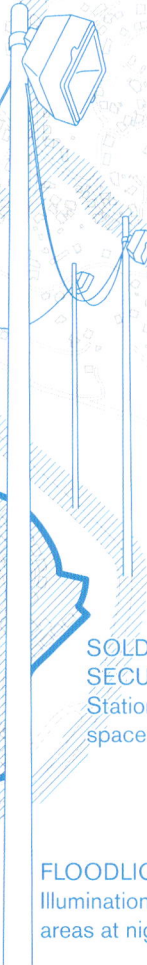

VIDEO CONTROL

Control
Sur Bahir / Har Homa (2005)

MINARET
LOUDSPEAKERS
Important announcements

:DESTRIANS
ssing-on of
ormation

ISRAELI PATROL ROUTE

SCHOOL CHILDREN
Information exchange

The ambient fear which overshadows civilian lives has led to an inflation of security measures and control systems on both sides. But strategies employed by Israelis and Palestinians differ fundamentally. In Har Homa, control and security are part of a formalized system aimed at detecting individual intruders: Frequent patrols by Israeli security forces or private security companies, or advanced technical equipment such as CCTV or flood lighting, reinforce architecture and planning based on strategic security concerns. In Sur Bahir, villagers resort to an informal system of control, mainly directed against the incursions of police or military or feared building inspectors. This system is based on cooperation and flow of information between individuals: mosques and shops became semi-institutionalized nodes of an early warning system that relies on mobile phones, loudspeakers, or messages passed through gestures.

SEPARATION FENCE/WALL
Fencing, barbed wire, movement
sensors, and patrol roads

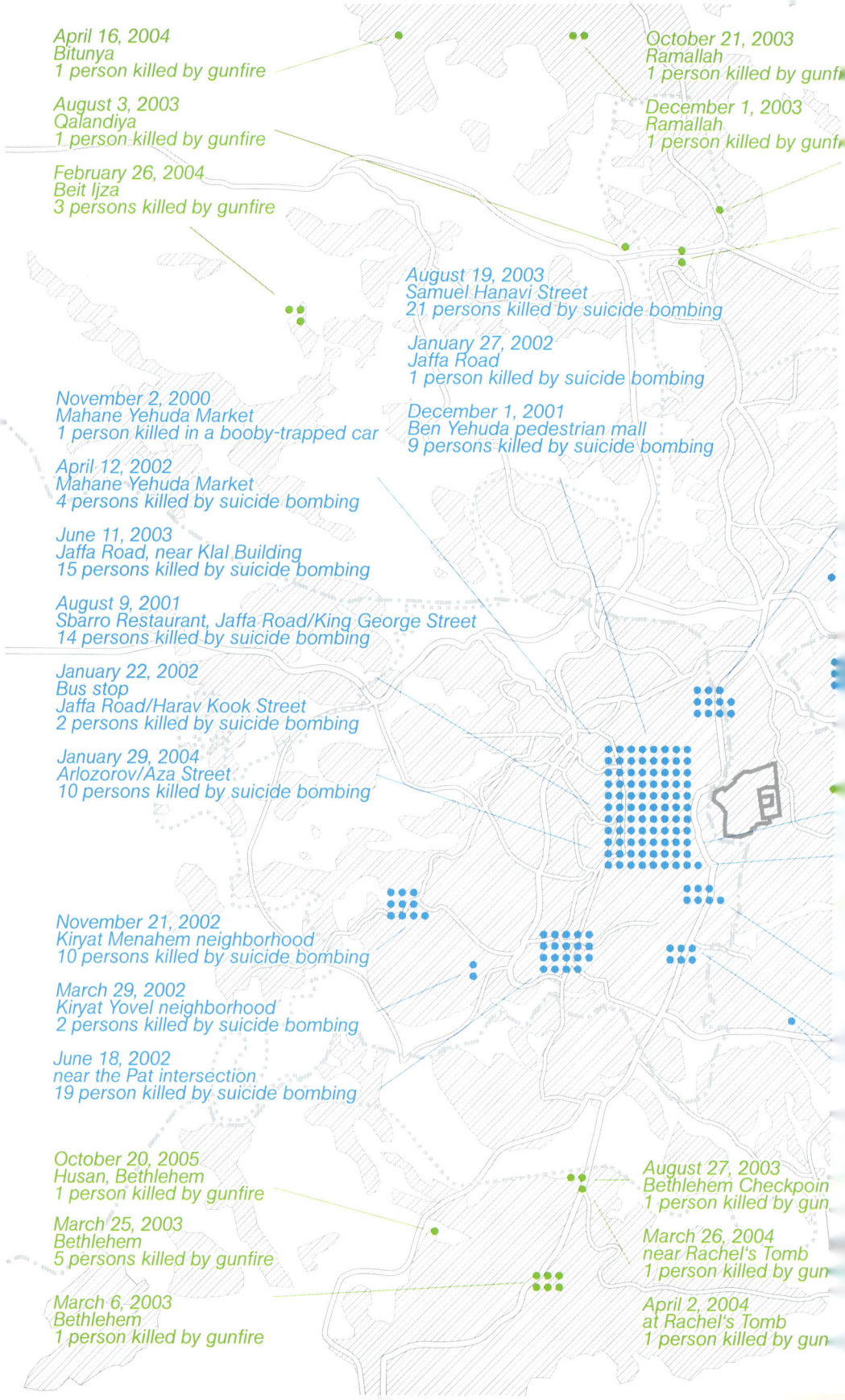

April 16, 2004
Bitunya
1 person killed by gunfire

October 21, 2003
Ramallah
1 person killed by gunf

August 3, 2003
Qalandiya
1 person killed by gunfire

December 1, 2003
Ramallah
1 person killed by gunf

February 26, 2004
Beit Ijza
3 persons killed by gunfire

August 19, 2003
Samuel Hanavi Street
21 persons killed by suicide bombing

January 27, 2002
Jaffa Road
1 person killed by suicide bombing

November 2, 2000
Mahane Yehuda Market
1 person killed in a booby-trapped car

December 1, 2001
Ben Yehuda pedestrian mall
9 persons killed by suicide bombing

April 12, 2002
Mahane Yehuda Market
4 persons killed by suicide bombing

June 11, 2003
Jaffa Road, near Klal Building
15 persons killed by suicide bombing

August 9, 2001
Sbarro Restaurant, Jaffa Road/King George Street
14 persons killed by suicide bombing

January 22, 2002
Bus stop
Jaffa Road/Harav Kook Street
2 persons killed by suicide bombing

January 29, 2004
Arlozorov/Aza Street
10 persons killed by suicide bombing

November 21, 2002
Kiryat Menahem neighborhood
10 persons killed by suicide bombing

March 29, 2002
Kiryat Yovel neighborhood
2 persons killed by suicide bombing

June 18, 2002
near the Pat intersection
19 person killed by suicide bombing

October 20, 2005
Husan, Bethlehem
1 person killed by gunfire

August 27, 2003
Bethlehem Checkpoin
1 person killed by gun

March 25, 2003
Bethlehem
5 persons killed by gunfire

March 26, 2004
near Rachel's Tomb
1 person killed by gun

March 6, 2003
Bethlehem
1 person killed by gunfire

April 2, 2004
at Rachel's Tomb
1 person killed by gun

June 6, 2004
Qalandiya Checkpoint
1 person killed by gunfire

September 14, 2003
Atarot, airport area
1 person killed by gunfire

December 9, 2003
Atarot, near the airport
1 person killed by gunfire

March 2, 2002
Beit Yisrael neighborhood
11 persons killed by suicide bombing

October 17, 2001
Hyatt Hotel
1 person killed by gunfire

July 31, 2002
Hebrew University
Mount Scopus
5 persons killed by suicide bombing

November 9, 2005
East Jerusalem
1 person killed by gunfire

March 21, 2002
King George Street
2 persons killed by suicide bombing

March 9, 2002
Moment Café
Aza/Ben-Maimon Streets
10 persons killed by suicide bombing

May 9, 2004
Abu Dis, Al-Quds district
1 person killed by gunfire

February 22, 2004
Liberty Bell Park
7 persons killed by suicide bombing

August 19, 2003
Cafe Hillel, German Colony
6 persons killed by suicide bombing

February 8, 2002
East Talpiot promenade
1 stabbed to death

Attacks
Jerusalem (2000-2005)

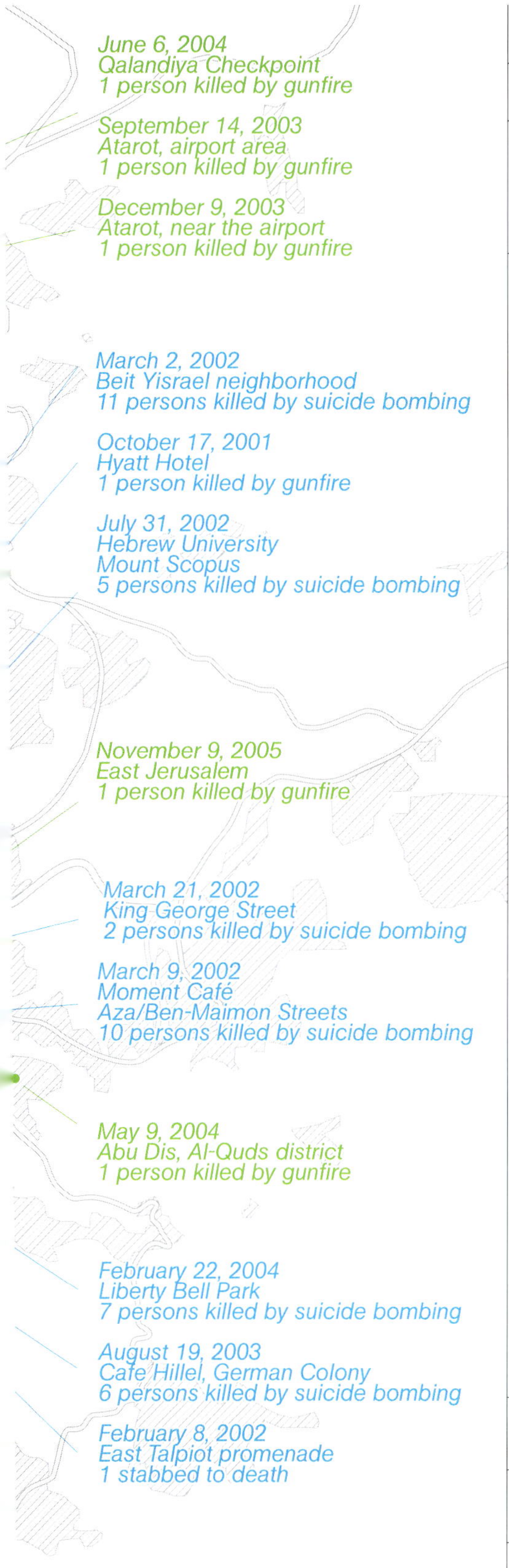

The most dramatic clashes of the Israeli-Palestinian conflict have unfolded in the urban realm, which has radically changed the production and use of urban space on both sides. Be it through Israeli military incursions or targeted missile assassinations, or through Palestinian suicide attacks, the conflict can erupt at any moment anywhere, claiming the lives of civilian bystanders. Omnipresent fear has led to the introduction of large-scale security measures in Israeli cities and outside every public area or institution. Palestinians live in persistent fear of falling unintended victim to Israeli military operations or settler attacks. Since the beginning of the al-Aqsa Intifada, violent deaths include:
3,345 Palestinians killed by Israeli security forces;
44 Palestinians killed by Israeli civilians;
683 Israeli civilians killed by Palestinians of which 228 (mainly settlers) were killed in the occupied territories and 455 became victims of suicide attacks in Israel.
309 members of the Israeli security forces were killed in clashes with Palestinians.

Palestinian casualties

Israeli casualties

0 | 100 | 200 | 300 | 400 | 500 meters

Concept and copyright

Tim Rieniets, Philipp Misselwitz

Sources

B'tselem - The Israeli Information Center for Human Rights in the Occupied Territories, *Israeli civilians killed by Palestinians in Israel,* http://www.btselem.org/english/statistics/Casualties.asp (Jerusalem, 2006).

B'tselem - The Israeli Information Center for Human Rights in the Occupied Territories, *Palestinians killed by Israeli security forces in the Occupied Territories,* http://www.btselem.org/english/statistics/Casualties.asp (Jerusalem, 2006).

Project Grenzgeografien (International Peace and Cooperation Center IPCC Jerusalem, Bezalel Academy of Art and Design Jerusalem, University of the Arts Berlin, ETH Swiss Federal Institute of Technology Zurich), *Trilateral Student Workshops* (Jerusalem, 2003-2005).

OF FEAR, CONTACT, ENTANGLEMENT

Irit Rogoff

Borders, to paraphrase Jacques Derrida, serve to establish the limits of the possible. Therefore, while borders that have been expanded, stretched, revised, or interrupted may produce a temporary sense of satisfied achievement with regard to an expanded field of possibilities, in reality they continue to establish those limits, albeit behind slightly redrawn lines. Every activity surrounded by a borderline, be it national identity or disciplinary identification, puts a parallel logic of division and containment into practice. There has been much cultural, artistic, and theoretical production surrounding borders—most of it focused on trying to inhabit the border in a way that refuses divisions between its mythical status and its pragmatic effects, which, of course, characterize the activity of every border. However, for all its playfulness and strategic irreverence, none of this work has been able to eradicate the limiting function of the border, to unravel it conceptually and destigmatize its cultural and civic affects.

In thinking about borders, it seems important to explore an array of terms and concepts that work against the division and containment inherent to any borderline, terms through which we might go beyond the xenophobic or provincial to tolerance and acceptance. I would much rather explore the possibilities contained in thinking of ourselves as caught up in an endless process of "contact," making it difficult to reproduce the historical periodizations or cultural/geographical divisions, which, when breached, dramatize insular politics in order to promote a sense of threat. Simple historicizing often proclaims that this or that group arrived amongst us at this or that historical moment as a direct result of a rupture, conflict, or disaster. Thus, the influence of this culture on that culture is dated from the moment a particular and dramatic encounter took place, and we are provided with a justification or a legitimizing narrative for its occurrence; we are assured that it only happened because something extraordinary took place.

Conversely, we might say that we have always been in contact, always been deeply entangled; that Mar Thomas was converting Hindus to Christianity on the Malabar Coast in the fifth century, that Arab navigators were charting the Indian Ocean in the eigth century, that spices and diseases and languages were shipped back and forth, to and from Europe from the 12th century onward, that travelers have always told tales of faraway places, that the beat of African drums underscored world music long before we had numbers to name our centuries. It would seem that the periodizations, which counter pose more recent arrivals in relation to native populations who have seemingly "always been there," aim to constitute a rupture or a surprise, and that these, in turn, aim to ensure that we perceive contact as painful, as an invasion that will somehow shift the terms of our lives.

CONTACT

I do not have a working definition for "contact." What I do have are explorative ideas about why someone like me might be attracted to the concept in its different formulations, as well as to the possibilities it unfolds. In referring to myself, it is not my geographical biography that is of relevance, but rather my intellectual one, for what interests me are analytical models in which a condition in the world and the conditions in our intellectual work collide and dance. That is, the breaching of boundaries occurs spatially, in the real spaces of our world, as well as in the cognitive procedures and possibilities currently open to us. This exploration will take the form of a circuitous route that shifts from notions of "contact" to notions of "entanglement" to notions of the "terroristic." Each of these concepts will take the form of a breach in the boundaries of division and containment.

We all know there are vast arrays of xenophobic prejudices that refuse to acknowledge that Westerners—myself included—are not the arbiters and inventors of either progress or modernity, but simply those who have the power to produce themselves as such. The counterpart of this fearful binary of "us" and "them," i.e. the desire to be inclusive and welcoming, to romantically embrace the differences that arise in our midst, is equally problematic in its lack of reflexivity, for it assumes Western culture is infinitely elastic and expandable. But contrary to its own self perception as revisionary (here I would include both cultural institutions and analytical critiques), the endlessly expansive inclusiveness practiced by so many Westerners is actually premised on an uncritical notion of Western plenitude, on the untroubled ability to simply add "others" without losing a bit of one's "self," on the romantic belief that we can simply add other histories to the narratives of modernism and its various crises and collapses over the past 30 years.

What is so disturbing about this additive model, besides the obvious fact that it ignores the conflict between hegemonic and marginalized cultures, is that it leaves intact the illusion of expansive plenitude at the heart of the West's cultural project. Therefore, it assumes the possibility of change without loss, without alteration, without remapping the navigational principles by which we have traditionally made our way through the cultural terrain.

Contact might facilitate getting around the binary of hostile and violent refusal to accept cultural difference on the one hand, and its overenthusiastic counterpart of naive embrace on the other. In this context, I employ the term following Mary Louise Pratt, who coined the term "contact zones" to describe "social spaces where disparate cultures meet, clash and grapple with each other, often in highly asymmetrical relations of domination and subordination; colonialism, slavery, plantation culture etc" (Pratt, 1992:6-7). "Contact zone" is adapted from the linguistics' notion of "contact language," which refers to the improvised languages that develop among speakers of different native tongues who need to communicate with one another continuously, usually in the context of trade.

Initially called "pidgin," these languages came to be called "Creole" when they developed native speakers of their own—those born into the hybrid tongue. Like "contact zone" societies, such languages were commonly regarded in the West as chaotic, barbarous, and unstructured.

"Contact zone" is an attempt to invoke the spatial and temporal copresence of subjects, previously separated by geographic and historical disjuncture, whose categories now intercept. "Contact" emphasizes "the interactive and improvisational dimensions of colonial encounters which were previously described by models of subordination and domination. It allows for copresence, interaction, interlocking understandings and practices often within radically asymmetrical relations of power" (Pratt, 1992:6-7). "Contact" has come to mean a fusion of high and low, here and there—in which it is no longer possible to separate out the strands, or establish traditional hierarchies.

FUSED TERRITORIES

An early example of fused territories operating as much psychically as territorially are Palestine-EY (EY stands for Eretz Yisrael, the Land of Israel). This was the last and perhaps also the first time the two entities were hyphenated in the postal designation of the British Mandate. The British Empire, stretched to its limits by the immense efforts of World War II, started the decolonization process with its withdrawal from India, but was essentially at a loss as to what to do with this particular set of natives: on the one hand, Zionist zealots fuelled by modernist visions of socialist nation-building coupled with refugees/survivors from the war in Europe, and on the other hand, a regional people whose national identity spanned from Greater Syria to Egypt.

Britain was, at the time, a new interloper in the Eastern Mediterranean, having brought to an end an Ottoman rule of some 400 years, a rule said to have declined the region into benign neglect, treating it as nothing more than province with some important trade routes and a few holy sites, but with not much else of interest—certainly not as a source of revenue, or technological innovation, etc. This perceived state of stagnation has been critically revisited by Ottoman scholars as a Eurocentric depiction of "Oriental laziness" to justify the colonial takeover of the Middle East. Nevertheless, the British Mandate staged this conquest as a "modern" order replacing a "premodern" one.

The moment I am referring to, is a moment in which everything was coming into being, a Deleuzian "becoming" in which an empire was defined as modern, a Palestinian people came into political formation, and a Zionist state was conjured into reality. Looking back from the 21st century, none of the above are entities to be viewed with nostalgic, except perhaps the hyphen between the words Palestina-EY. That hyphen stands for the moment when confused British policy allowed for a fusion—at the level of a linguistic sign—of these two entities. In hindsight, it stands for that which Edward Said had long called for: a secular binational state in an area inhabited by both peoples. Instead, we have an ongoing war between two concepts: borders established and reestablished daily by an existing state, and ambient fear mobilized by an aspiring state, in order to counter these borders' claims to immutability.

What is it, then, that refuses and denies the legitimacy of "contact," as both theory and condition of entangled lived relations? What provides the stoppages and blockages that keep "contact" from coming into being? Obviously, borders and boundaries are high on the list of the operational logics we must counter, in order to produce "contact" as our lived reality.

AMBIENT FEAR

From its inception as a state, Israel has insisted on establishing itself within boundaries, naming them, moving them, negotiating in the name of borders that one forgets from one week to the next. Israeli public rhetoric is inculcated with an endless array of borders that have become the hallmark of border hysteria. These state borders also serve as a line of division between so-called "legality" and "illegality," and thus produce a terroristic breach—an act which punctures the sacred sphere of the law, and is therefore positioned outside of it as "out-lawed." In turn, the State of Israel as an aggressive occupying power becomes the would-be victim of incursions into its self-proclaimed spatial integrity.

In a situation where fears can no longer be contained to borders, borders themselves become fear; not that which contains it, guards against it, segregates its aggregate components—but the material of fear itself. In places of extreme conflict, borders are reconstituted daily. Reflecting yesterday's agreements or good will, they move with astonishing speed at the first sighting of that which needs containing at a moment's notice. Borders are movable feasts of fear, and increasingly impotent efforts are made at staving off that fear by arming, for-tifying, and fixing borders. As Jean Luc Nancy writes, "nowhere then is there war and everywhere there is tearing apart, crumpling down, civilized violence and the brutalities that are mere caricatures of ancient, sacred violence. War is nowhere and everywhere, related to any end without any longer being related to itself as supreme end" (Nancy, 2000:108).

TERRORISTIC

At present, it seems important to insist on boundary-free entanglements in which we cannot split into origins and hybrids, but rather begin to understand that we have always been part of a performative mixing. Those who have studied decolonization, anti-colonization, and transnational migration know that the history of the terroristic well precedes the abrupt "break" the United States and its allies have tried to create in the aftermath of 9/11. Therefore, the final notion I want to invoke in a theoretical attempt to provide possibilities for unthinking the logic of boundaries, division, and containment, is the notion of the "unbounded." This is related to the notion of ambient fear and the fact that borders cannot do all that they are mobilized for. The terroristic, being neither an act of terror-ism nor the "war on terrorism," constitutes a breach in the dominant—whose own violence is masked by a set of intricate and articulate logics that operate in the name of "freedom," "democracy," "globalization," etc. The terroristic can be thought of not as a series of violent acts, not as a moment of rupture or the articulation of disenfranchisement, but as the possible production of a breach that might allow for a counter logic to emerge.

The inadequacy of borders at restraining or staving off the new forms of mobile
threat currently termed "terrorism," has become glaringly obvious in the wake
of recent "terroristic" acts in various parts of the world. The aim of terrorism,
argues Nikos Papastergiadis, is "to disperse fear into the whole environment: to
make anxiety ubiquitous and unlocatable" (Papastergiadis, 2003:2-3). After 9/11, fear
of the Other could not be contained within a single territorial entity or confined
to a place of origin. Fear was ambient, and initially the war was not to be fought
against an enemy with a conventional army, but against the concept of terror.
The original American code name for the battle was "Operation Infinite Justice,"
later substituted to "Enduring Freedom" because as Muslim clerics pointed out,
only God could execute infinite justice. The boundlessness of the "war on terrorism" had chilling implications, not only for the ambiguities of place and identity
in global politics, but because a world with infinite terror implies that vigilance
and war will never end.

Confrontation
Exchange

At the end of the conference "Cities of Collision" for which this paper was
drafted in 2004, after several days in West Jerusalem, I visited Ramallah, where
the casual presence of posters, produced largely by the al-Aqsa Martyrs' Brigades,
function like an urban wall paper of terroristic detritus. The saturated presence
of these posters struck me as one of those moments that translate the grandi-
osity evoked by the word "terrorism" to minute gestures of engaging the possible, which I think of as "potentiality" (Agamben, 1999:177-184). In "potentiality"
we are poised on the cusp of "I Can/I Cannot," suspended between the possible
and the impossible without reaching an impasse. Here, fear is translated into
multidimensional daily reality, far from the rhetorical bombast that has constituted Western politics since 9/11. Within this spatial framing, the murderous
intentions attributed to the gestures and messages that appear on those posters, become, once they are translated back into context, the everyday language
of resistance. As in "potentiality," the gesture's meaning is not dependent on
its outcome, but rather on its drive. Instead of the spatial polarization of borders, we find on Ramallah's streets the spatial complexity of multifunctionality,
a space that is at once civic, mobilized, and commercial; the space of political
entanglement, in which the legal and illegal cohabitate.

Selected Bibliography

Janet Abu-Lughod, *Before European Hegemony: The World System 1250-1350 AD* (Oxford University
Press, 1991).

Giorgio Agamben, "On Potentiality," in *Potentialities: Collected Essays in Philosophy* (Stanford
University Press, 1999).

Jerry H. Bentley, *Old World Encounters: Cross Cultural Contacts and Exchanges in Pre-Modern Times*
(Oxford University Press, 1993).

Mary Louise Pratt, *Imperial Eyes: Travel Writing and Trans Culturation* (London and New York:
Routlede, 1992).

Jean Luc Nancy, *Being Singular Plural*, (Stanford University Press, 2000).

Nikos Papastergiadis, "Ambient Fears and the New Authoritarianism" (unpublished lecture, 2003,
courtesy of the author).

THE SOFTER SIDE OF COLLISION

Yaakov Garb

I was driving with Samir, a Palestinian taxi driver from East Jerusalem, past a small family hotel in West Jerusalem, whose ad hoc synagogue my father sometimes attended. The hotel reminded Samir of a certain period in his life. It began when he was stopped by a *Haredi* (Jewish ultra-orthodox) woman near Sabbath Square. She sat in the back. They talked. Then they joked. Then he booked into this hotel. "I came out of the shower, and she was on the couch. We started fooling around. Then I almost had a heart attack—her head came off in my hands!"

As opposed to most religious women, who simply cover their hair in public, in the strictest ultra-orthodox communities women shave their heads, over which they wear a scarf or a wig—which is what had come off in Samir's hands. He wasn't expecting this. "She was bald, Yaakov, completely bald! But what a bombshell. We carried on, and really liked each other, so we met again, and then again, quite regularly. For half a year we kept meeting. I started to get scared that her people would find out and come after me, so I broke it off. But she was great."

I was new to Jerusalem when I heard this story in the late 1990s, and discounted it as a delightful and outrageous anomaly. As I continued to live in the city, however, I kept hearing and seeing things that crossed the ethnic, religious, and national lines many of us have come to hate. These stories were no longer anomalous but evidence of a hidden shared life. Away from the posturing and political declarations about a united/occupied Jerusalem, everyday passions, kindnesses, mischief, and creativity weave us together—more than anyone dares to acknowledge. I share some of these stories because they are what make life in Jerusalem livable, even enjoyable, for me. But I also want to suggest that they are indicative of a different kind of life, the kind that has been, is, and could be possible.

My stories center around East Jerusalem taxi drivers (and Samir in particular) who introduced me to this mixed-up world where two Jerusalems come together.

Over half the taxi drivers in West Jerusalem are East Jerusalemites, mostly operating Arab-owned cabs. Indeed, several of the larger companies are Arab-owned or co-owned—a Jewish partner having been added to lubricate relations with the authorities.

Think about it. What other opportunity do young Palestinian men have to circulate unobstructed around the city? There are none more mobile than those who make a living by roaming. And not just in West Jerusalem. They swing back and forth from West to East (eat lunch; give the wife a lift; pray at the mosque), effortlessly crossing the lines that govern most people. And there are also long distance trips to other parts of Israel and the West Bank (settlers often prefer Arab drivers who know how to "handle" themselves in the Occupied Territories). What other Palestinians move through Jewish space unhindered, in command, on duty? Who else spends their 10, 12, 14 hour days conversing with Jews in an unstructured, anonymous, and intimate way, bracketed by the clean start and clear finish of a given ride—if both parties so wish? Where else does the Arab in such encounters possess a modicum of authority—behind the wheel, often of a late-model Mercedes few passengers could afford?

You have to be pretty "together" to be an East Jerusalem taxi driver. Your Hebrew must be good if you are to thrive (and if good enough to pass for a North African or Middle Eastern Jew—all the better). You need to pass the taxi driver certification course, get a commercial license, have an accountant, and stay out of trouble. The latter can be difficult when a hard-to-please client's complaint to the Ministry of Transportation places you under the presumption of guilt, because of your dual ethnic and occupational inferiority. Many drivers own their vehicles—a big capital investment that feeds one or more families. These are kept running, in top shape, often 24 hours a day in two 12-hour or three 8-hour shifts. Among Jews, a taxi driver is seen as someone who lacks alternatives, whereas it is a fairly well respected job in East Jerusalem.[1]

CROSSING LINES

I began with Samir and his ultra-orthodox lover not (just) as prurient gossip about a community assumed to be "above such things," but because there is something so hopeful about a simple human frustration reaching across bound-aries—far across boundaries—to be met.

Ironically, in such cases, it is precisely distance which is at play: ultra-orthodox men and women regard dalliances with non-Jews as less sinful. Indeed, as some ultra-orthodox men explain to their taxi drivers on the way to the red light district of North Tel Aviv, the Diamond Exchange in Ramat Gan, or the "escort institutes" of South Jerusalem, the Jewish prohibition on extramarital sex does not apply if their partners are non-Jews. I doubt they suspect the extent to which their wives and sisters are enjoying this loophole (and for free!), or would appre-ciate Samir's deft recycling of their Talmudic logic as he playfully introduces this exemption to ultra-orthodox female passengers who may not be aware of this finer point of religious law.

Another driver also told of ending his affair with a religious Jewish woman, indeed one living in a hardcore political settlement near Jerusalem. This was not for fear, however. "After a while, when I saw how serious it was getting, I told her that it was not fair that I go home to my wife at the end of the day and she goes back to an empty house. I told her she had to find a man she could marry. She protested, but I encouraged her, and eventually she did. She still calls me all the time, to talk, or for advice. We've stayed friends."

This was relayed to me by way of explanation for a call that came in on the speakerphone while I was in the taxi: a consultation about visiting family that just couldn't wait. I can vouch: this was a real relationship, respectful, mature, not sleazy. Others are more usurious, I am sure, but that runs both ways.

Setting aside the ethics of these infidelities, there is a lot of clandestine consensual cross-national mingling going on in Jerusalem. I doubt there is a reasonable looking Palestinian driver on the road for more than a couple of years who has not been approached by an ultra-orthodox or other Jewish woman at some point in his career (and more than a few have acquiesced). Because Jewish law prohibits one from being alone with an adult non-family member of the opposite sex, this is the only chance ultra-orthodox women, many of whom marry in their late teens or early 20s, have of interacting informally with men. And, apparently, they take advantage of it when needed. But it's not just Jewish women. Sometimes the passenger is an Arab woman, though an affair within the Palestinian community is much more risky, sometimes even fatal.

I joked with Samir once about how many Jewish kids he may have unknowingly sired, and that one of them, now old enough to be in the army, could stop him at a checkpoint. We laughed, wondering if they would recognize each other. What we were really laughing at, of course, was the messy muddle beneath Jerusalem's surface.

Samir's son is of a more casual generation than his father: jeans, T-shirt, sunglasses. He has his father's charm, but of Israeli, not Jordanian vintage. He often stayed with his Russian immigrant girlfriend in the Jewish town of Beth Shemesh, until he entered into an arranged marriage with an East Jerusalem girl. Recently, I stopped with him to buy some soda at an East Jerusalem shop where a wild male finch in a cage was chirping away. The owner explained that he was trying to "marry" it with two domesticated female canaries. If a female likes the finch's voice, she will start nesting, and the two can be put into the same cage. If they have offspring, the fledglings will learn their wild father's tunes and zest for singing, but inherit their domesticated mother's much stronger voice—which is what makes them so valuable, albeit infertile. A female finch, I am told (by men), will never accept a male canary. You cannot put them in the same cage, and she would never, "in a thousand years," let him mount her.[2] The finch, a native species which the laws forbids to capture or own, is expensive, around a thousand shekels, and a male's value is increased by his proven ability to produce hybrid offspring. I asked Samir's son how you say "hybrid" in Arabic. *Banduk*, he told me with relish.

The cheap trick of starting with sex to address ruptures in Jerusalem's oppressive dividing lines should not downgrade or sensationalize the phenomenon. There are more sedate and sanctioned forms of mingling as well: social visits, exchanged favors, loans, joint business ventures. It starts with asking the Palestinian gardener if he wants a glass of water or a cup of tea, or two coworkers at the bus company appreciating each other's style, and then . . . humans are humans, after all.

But if I did start with mingling across gender lines[3], let me be provocative: beneath the violence, distrust, and ethnic enclaving, is there not some racial fear (on both sides) of what might happen in this cohabited city (and country) if the barriers fell? We'd be all over each other! All the dietary, temporal, and other purposeful asynchronizations of Jewish law, which seem designed to make social mixing difficult, no longer guide the majority of the Jewish population. Strategists of Jewish

29.6 km: view from Har Homa to main access road

survival worry about the demographic threat in Israel and the assimilation threat abroad. But what if the barriers were reduced to a point that allowed for assimilation with fellow Semites right here in our own back yard?[4]

Our pasts were fluid, and I suspect our futures could be too. Years after meeting him, a friend from East Jerusalem mentioned in passing that his ancestors were Syrian Jews who converted to Islam when they moved to Hebron during the time of Saladin. I was amazed, he was nonchalant. "Yes, sometimes when I do something stupid or make an astute financial decision my friends tease me and call me a Jew." I mentioned this to another friend, a Jordanian originally from the Hebron area, who knows Hebronite families well. "That's right," he confirmed, "the Shweiks have done well for themselves in business," and then he listed off the names of several other Palestinian families known to be formerly Jewish. "In fact," he continued, "my great grandmother on my mother's side is Jewish, you know. She was a Jewish girl orphaned in some battle, whom my great grandfather adopted and later married. Whenever he got annoyed with her he would call her *bint Yahoud* (daughter of a Jew). It was only years later that I learned that this was not just an epithet."

PLAYING WITH LINES

Lines are a very serious thing in Jerusalem. The separation barrier is as blunt and concrete as you can get. If government inspectors (these days Palestinian citizens of Israel from Abu Ghosh) find you in a home in Ezariya or Ar-Ram, rather than at your declared address within the municipal lines, as little as a kilometer away, you can lose your Jerusalem ID, i.e. your ability to work, visit family, or claim the national insurance benefits you have been paying into for years. Fears are real: Jerusalemites do get stabbed, shot, blown up, arrested, and tortured. I've seen my friends' kids cower the first time they heard me speak Hebrew in their East Jerusalem homes ("Dad, why is the soldier here?"). At the height of the bus-bombing period, with the kin of three schoolmates buried, my 12 year old niece matter-of-factly asked her mother to help her draft a will ("What's better, Yaakov, that I tell her not to or help her do it?")

The ability to play with, and thus soften, these facts of life is what I want to talk about.

Samir also had a lover in a settlement near Jerusalem. Once, his colleague dropped him off there after her husband left for work. Coming back some hours later, Samir had to take a bus. This was at the height of the bus-bombing period. Samir is dark and mustachioed. Boarding the bus, he greeted the driver with a smile "to put him at ease." The bus, half full, looped through the settlement to pick up people before heading to Jerusalem. At the first stop after Samir got on, many people got off. At the next stop, the remainder got off. As the bus left the settlement for Jerusalem, only Samir and the driver remained. So he went and chatted with the driver, suggesting that the bus company hire him to ride the bus regularly, since all the fearful passengers who got off had already paid their fare, and would need to pay again when they got on the next bus. Samir told me this story, because at this time Jews were also hesitant to get into taxis with Arab drivers. Once, after a potential client's qualms were dispelled by the fact that

I was already seated in the cab, I offered to rent Samir my reassuringly Ashkenazi face and ride along during his shifts.

Nonsensical suggestions, of course, but somehow a way for people to talk about fears and place ourselves on the same side of these concerns,.

Both reinforcing and eroding such prejudices, Akram, another friend from Hebron, gave me a half-serious standing offer after the first couple of bus-bombings. "If you ever get on a bus and see an angry Arab man with a coat, get off right away and take a taxi, take even two taxis, I will pay for it." It was impossible for Akram to come to my wedding, as the closure was in full effect, but I was touched when he offered to send money to hire extra guards at the event. (In fact, Samir showed up early to circle the periphery "and make sure the grounds were properly secured").

Operating an Arab-owned and almost entirely Arab-staffed taxi company in an increasingly edgy and vengeful West Jerusalem is tricky business. The 70 or so Arab drivers at the station I use, all communicate with each other over the radio in Hebrew, and have Hebrew work names with addresses to match. "Ami from French Hill" might be Amer from adjacent Isawiya; "Avraham from East Talpiot" is assumed to be more palatable than "Ibrahim from Sur Bahir," across the valley. I once overheard a radio conversation (in Hebrew), in which a pseudo-named Arab dispatcher sent a pseudo-named Arab driver to pick up a real-named Jew-ish client, and told him to give the woman a fair price. "Of course," the driver said, using the phrase Jews sometimes use to express brotherly largesse, "*kulanu yehudim!*" (We're all Jews!)

Once Samir took the wife of Rabbi Aryeh Deri from their Har Nof home to a meeting. (Deri was then the political leader of the Shas party whose North Afri-can and Middle Eastern Jewish electoral base had shaken up Israeli politics). She needed a phone to check the address, and Samir, who appreciated Deris boldness and considered himself a *Shasnik* of sorts, had a color sticker of Deri on the flip panel of his mobile phone. "What's this?" Deri's wife asked when he handed her the phone. "Our Rabbi," he answered, deadpan, using the Hebrew insider term of affectionate deference. They laughed together, across lines, at lines.

More calculatingly, when checkpoints were less stringent, Palestinian drivers would put right-wing stickers on their cars to increase their chances of getting waved through quickly (I imagined, perhaps wrongly, that they must have had some satisfaction at the hidden meaning of slogans like "Hebron: Ours Always and Forever"). At the time of writing, there are those who tie the orange anti-Gaza-disengagement ribbons on their antennas, to increase their chances of picking up clients who are afraid of Arab drivers. (This for some reason, unlike the stickers, is frowned upon by some Palestinian drivers as "going too far").

With his looks, Samir, who works at a station staffed by both Arabs and Jews, could never pass as a Jew, and would not, therefore, think of trying. He uses humor rather than camouflage to reassure his clients. Often by making their fears explicit: "Come on, get in, ordinarily I would kidnap you and take you to Ramallah, but I don't have time this evening."

He has also been known to make good use of Jewish fears. One day, he had a big self-satisfied smile when I got in his cab: "You'll never guess what happened.

There's a round I do every night picking up workers from a factory. And there's a shortcut I take in Givat Shaul. It's a one-way street going the wrong way. Only 15 meters, but it saves ten minutes. I have two passengers in the car. A police car signals for me to stop. I think to myself, 'I can't afford a 1000 shekels fine and 10 penalty points on my license.' As the police officers approach I tell my passengers in Arabic, 'Hold tight, I need to play a little here, everything will be OK.' They're regular clients from East Jerusalem, workers whom I take home. So I meet the police halfway and say softly, 'Guys, I saw your patrol and came right to you. You've got to help me. These two passengers got in, and I have a funny feeling about them. Please check them out.' [This was just after a well-publicized incident in which a suicide bomber reached his destination by taxi]. So the police check their IDs. They come back to me and say, 'It's OK, they've checked out fine.' I say, 'Are you sure? It's your responsibility!' They thank me for my vigilance, shake my hand, and wish everyone were as alert as I am—a model citizen. And off we went."

"I wasn't afraid that they'd rough up my passengers, they were policemen in blue uniforms, not border patrol thugs. I said to myself, 'the fine would be 1000 shekels. If the passengers get beaten, I'll give them half that sum, say 250 each...'"

While Samir is an expert at dispelling people's fears, even inverting them to his own benefit, his eldest son was the lucky beneficiary of an entirely uncalculated inversion. Samir was in his Islamic period when the child was born, and wanted to call him Khomeini. When he went to register the boy at the East Jerusalem branch of the Ministry of Interior, where the lines between ministry officials and *Shabak* (GSS, General Security Services) officers are rather blurry, he was told he could not register such a name. He argued with the GSS officers, and in the end reached a compromise: he would name his son Iran. He did not realize it at the time, but Iran is very similar to Eran, a common Jewish Israeli boy's name, and was even spelled the same. So the child grew up with a name in his ID card, which enabled him to mingle with Jews more freely than most. Samir recalls how upset Eran/Iran(Khomeini) was when his his Jewish friends were drafted, and he could not join them, especially the ones enlisting in commando units. "When they came home from their bases for the first time," Samir's son told me proudly, "they let me hold their guns and showed me how they worked." Over time, however, he saw less and less of them.

SO WHAT?

What do they amount to, these stories? Some irrelevant humanistic weeds sprouting at the edges of the unrelenting concrete of occupation? Do they just barely ease the brutality of ethnic, religious, and national divisions, or do they actually reveal (or lay the ground for) something different, something more important?

I myself sometimes get annoyed at the theoretical romanticization of "everyday resistance," and wonder at the political efficacy of peasants who fart while bowing at the passing lord. Why tell these stories, as charming as they might be? After all, don't the exceptions described prove that distance and separation are the rule?

Perhaps I am naïve, but these stories strike me as the hidden rule of everyday coexistence and hybridizations, temporarily occluded by circumstance. Maybe Samir had to break off his affair, but somewhere in Mea Sharim there is a woman who remembers him, and perhaps not just with guilt. And for the 100 broken affairs there will be ten fond memories, and perhaps one couple who live out their rule, as Alegra Bellow and Jabara Rahil did when they met in the Mahane Yehuda market and eloped in 1929, at the height of Jewish-Arab tensions, eventually moving to Ein Karem, leaving behind heartbroken parents, but also a chain of descendents from East and West Jerusalem who share a mother, grandmother, and great-grandmother.

I have not asked Samir whether he thinks these everyday breaches amount to anything. I doubt it would be a productive line of questioning. But perhaps something he told me indicates his attitude. "There's this one Jewish driver at our station that hates Arabs. I don't know why. He just hates us. But he likes me. He doesn't know why. He says to me, 'Samir, I don't know why I like you, but I like you.' So last night when he said this, I responded, 'It doesn't matter whether you like me or hate me, because either way, we've taken your work.' I was joking with him. I said, 'Tell me, did you occupy East Jerusalem or did we occupy you?' He seemed baffled. I asked, 'Can you sleep with an Arab woman?' 'No.' 'Do you walk around the Arab markets freely?' 'No.' I told him, 'I shop on Jaffa street, I go wherever I want. I eat in your restaurants, sleep with your women, and take your work. I think it was we who occupied you in 1967.'

"Oh," says another Palestinian driver to whom I relayed this conversation, "Those are just Samir's philosophies."

You decide.

1   This disparity is actually a problem because salaries for unskilled jobs in West Jerusalem are significantly higher than salaries for skilled jobs in East Jerusalem. Gifted young men are tempted to prefer the former, overtraining for the latter. Women, however, do carry on studying, and it is not uncommon for a husband to have barely finished high school while his wife holds an academic degree.

2   Certainly, there are less Arab (especially Muslim) women who marry Jewish men. However, since I interact mostly with Palestinian men and not Palestinian women, I don't know what stories women tell each other.

3   Same-gender mingling across national lines are another, more complicated phenomenon, deserving of its own treatment. The city's gay bar, recently torched, is perhaps the one genuinely nationally-mixed bar in the city. I am told that for many years there was tacit refuge from persecution given to Palestinian gay men joining their Israeli lovers.

4   You will always hear of mixed couples in any large town, Jewish or Arab. I am always pleasantly surprised by the low-key acceptance of these.

5   The reference is to an epigraph in: James Scott, *Domination and the Arts of Resistance*: Hidden Transcripts (New Haven: Yale University Press, 1990).

6   Moshe Amirav who interviewed families on both sides tells the story in: Amirav et al, *Ein Karem: Voyage to the Enchanted Village* (Jerusalem: Keter, 2004).

INTEGRATION, SEGREGATION, AND CONTROL

FUNCTIONAL EVERYDAY JEWISH-ARAB RELATIONSHIPS IN JERUSALEM

Michael Romann

The contested city of Jerusalem is no doubt an extreme case of a polarized urban environment. Israel considers Jerusalem unified in political terms, yet Palestinians have rejected the 1967 enforcement of Israeli law, jurisdiction, and administration over East Jerusalem and continue to boycott key Israeli political institutions. Daily reality, in turn, reflects the persistent social, economic, and spatial divisions between the Jewish and Arab communities. Different ethnic identities are clearly marked and there is no space allowed for a mixed Jewish-Arab identity. Indeed, far-reaching patterns of segregation between members of the two communities affect almost all aspects of everyday life. At the same time, daily (mainly economic) interaction and exchange are also common. This is particularly the case in the labor and consumer markets; it relates to certain business transactions, and is most apparent where Jews and Arabs share public services.

Several questions arise in view of this diverse reality. First, to what extent have the two sectors undergone actual or functional integration? Second, where do the two communities interact and what do those interactions look like? Likewise, where are the communities segregated and what is segregation's appearance? Finally, to what extent can these patterns be attributed to political antagonism, different cultural norms or economic inequalities? Precisely because East and West Jerusalem were entirely separate between 1948 and 1967, we have a unique opportunity to trace and evaluate the processes of integration in the city's institutional and economic domains.

Just after the Six Day War in 1967, a first survey of the implications of social and economic reunification was conducted (Romann, 1968). Follow-up surveys were conducted during the late 1970s and early 1980s, considering the gradual process of integration and adaptation between these two largely distinct economic arenas (Romann, 1984). The importance of political and cultural (more so than economic) components in these changing patterns of interaction soon became apparent. Accordingly, subsequent research was diverted, and in addition to analyzing employment opportunities, commodity prices and the like, field observations were incorporated into the research. This evidence ranged from comparing the contents of tourist shops or the conduct of taxi drivers in the two city sectors, to analyzing relations between Jewish and Arab employees in a Jewish hospital or in the common municipal slaughterhouse of Jerusalem (Romann & Weingrod, 1991).

It is suggested here that the extreme case of Jerusalem as a polarized city is expressed not only in patterns of segregation, but also in specific modes of integration. In particular, ethnic identity is a determinant factor, reflected by specific and varying modes of intergroup versus intragroup interactions. There are two overall explanations for this. First, Jews and Arabs alike strive to control their territorial and economic assets, but are also anxious to preserve the ethnic "identity" of their economic entities by following cultural norms. Second, their respective abilities in this regard are largely determined by fundamentally unequal political and economic power relations, which are ultimately expressed in asymmetric patterns of transactions across the ethnic divide.

SEGREGATION VERSUS INTEGRATION

Despite the official Israeli rhetoric of Jerusalem as a unified city, the predominant condition is one of segregation. Spatial segregation is not confined to Jewish versus Arab residential quarters, as is generally the case in ethnically mixed cities, but is farther manifested in separate but parallel business centers. The Jewish and Palestinian sectors maintain parallel public transport facilities and separate chambers of commerce, as well as dozens of other professional organizations, from hotelier associations to blood banks. Finally, a basic distinction between the two sectors persists in the legal sphere, since Israeli law and municipal decrees (such as certain labor and building regulations) have not been fully applied to East Jerusalem. The existence of different commercial holidays and the use of Hebrew versus Arabic on shop signs in the two city regions is one among many visible indications of separation.

At the same time, daily encounters and interactions between Jews and Arabs are likewise multiple and visible, especially regarding the labor market, where about one-half of the entire Arab work force of East Jerusalem regularly crosses over to employment in the Jewish sector. While they are mainly employed in manual occupations or construction, Arabs also occupy certain clerical or professional positions in Jewish hotels, hospitals, and various municipal and public services located in West Jerusalem. In addition, Arabs often cross over to West Jerusalem for specialized professional or public services (legal advice or medical care, for example). Major shopping centers emerging on the Jewish side are equally and visibly frequented by Arab customers.

Jews, for their part, used to visit the Arab side in great numbers, particularly the tourist attractions located in the Palestinian part of the Old City. In addition, Arab shops and workshops in East Jerusalem were an accessible alternative on weekends and Jewish holidays when shops in West Jerusalem are closed. During the first Intifada and successive periods of violence in Jerusalem, a phenomenon was apparent. Whereas Jewish visits to "the other side" dramatically declined due to heightened fears, Arabs, by contrast, continued to frequent West Jerusalem despite the risks involved and Palestinian calls to boycott Israeli markets.

Besides these more obvious economic interactions across the ethnic divide, other less visible or quantifiable exchanges developed on an entrepreneurial level between firms and institutions. Business relationships are common, where mostly Jewish establishments supply the greater part of commodities and business services to the Arab sector. Arab workshops, for their part, are often engaged as subcontractors by Jewish construction and manufacturing industries. These exchanges extend from the financial world to the underworld.

In sum, overall economic interaction reflects accessibility and the relative advantages offered by each sector. Yet, no simple distinction can be drawn between areas of integration and aspects of segregation. Separate dual labor markets in each region persist alongside extensive employment relations. Despite extensive exchanges of goods and services, Arabs do not usually advertize in Jewish newspapers and visa versa. In fact, functional interactions between the Jewish and Arab sectors rarely reflect the full potential of economic opportunity and spatial proximity.

MODES OF BEHAVIOR

As a general rule, where inter-sectoral relations have been established, they can be characterized as "low level" interactions, in that they tend to avoid aspects of visibility and permanence. No formal, visible and binding partnerships between Jewish and Arab entrepreneurs were observed. The integrative significance of extensive Arab employment in the Jewish sector is moderated by the fact that relatively few Arabs have risen to white-collar work or management positions over Jewish workers. Jewish individuals and firms frequenting Arab shops or engaging Arab workshops can be equally defined as "low level" interactions, due to their occasional and temporary nature.

Economic relations between the two sectors are often associated with particular modes or terms of exchange. In particular, a kind of "ethnic price factor" is usually implied in both labor and consumer interactions. Jews engage Arab occasional labor, or acquire Arab products and services in East Jerusalem, under the implicit condition that they are cheaper compared to available Jewish alternatives. The difference involved might vary. Some Jews will not buy a pair of shoes in the Arab market if they are only 10% cheaper; others, however, will frequent car repair shops or even East Jerusalem dentists, since they charge far less than the norm in West Jerusalem. This was further exemplified by the fact that Arab workers engaged in similar occupations in both sectors—as unskilled labor, drivers, or hotel waiters—are willing to accept far lower wages and social benefits within the Arab sector compared to those they receive in the Jewish sector. Indeed, ethnic identity is always an intervening and relevant factor to the modes of exchange.

Mutual interactions in the business community often require an intermediary or "broker." Arab entrepreneurs use association with a Jewish firm, or engage Jewish professionals—engineers, architects and particularly lawyers—to obtain contracts in the Jewish sector or appeal to Israeli officials. In one revealing example, Arab individuals said they preferred to take their driving lessons with Jewish driving schools in order to increase their chances vis-à-vis the Israeli licensing authorities. A related mode of exchange might be called "disguised relationships"—many business transactions are conducted in such a manner that only one partner is publicly exposed when operating in his or her respective sector. Camouflage is essential when Arab manufactured goods—such as textiles, shoes, sweets, or paper and plastic products—are marketed in the Jewish sector.

Products are generally distributed under "Israeli" labels or neutral English brand names and rarely disclose their origin. Jewish entrepreneurs willing to open a business or, more particularly, seeking to acquire land in the Arab section also, as a general rule, engage an Arab straw man or employ camouflage tactics.

Some basic asymmetries in willingness and modes of interaction were also observed. For example Arabs regularly travel on Jewish buses on routes where Arab buses are also available, whereas Jews always avoid taking an Arab bus even if this is the best option. Comparing the types of tourist items exhibited in East and West Jerusalem souvenir shops is just as informative. In the Arab sector, alongside Christian and Muslim religious objects, all manner of Jewish religious and nationalist items, ranging from decorative stars of David to "Zionist" guidebooks and posters, are in full display. There are no comparable Arab or Christian symbols to be found in West Jerusalem shops, although many non-Jewish tourists frequent this part of the city. Likewise, whereas East Jerusalem Arab stores are abundantly stocked with the full range of Jewish-produced goods, most Arab products do not find their way into Jewish retail markets (one example being Arab cigarettes produced in East Jerusalem, but not distributed in the Jewish section of the city). Equally revealing is that although Arab entrepreneurs are willing on principle to open shops in West Jerusalem, particularly now that Jewish customers have become fearful of crossing into the Arab sector, this has never materialized. There are no legal or official restrictions involved, but rather a kind of social exclusion practiced by the Jewish sector. Generally, where purely functional interactions are concerned, Arabs are more often willing to conduct relations with Jews than vice versa.

THE ROLE OF IDENTITY

In an attempt to conceptualize functional relations between Jews and Arabs, it is useful to refer to Jerusalem's economic entities as having distinct ethnic identities. As we have seen, these distinctions remain total and unequivocal. Thus, ethnic identity can be applied not only to individuals and neighborhoods, but also to practically all firms, institutions, and products. It should be emphasized that such distinctions relate to the objective "internal" qualities of these entities, rather than subjective identification by outside observers. Foreigners, or even Jerusalemites, cannot always "tell" the ethnic identity of a Jewish or Arab passerby. Still, each passerby possesses an unequivocal identity agreed upon by both Jews and Arabs.

Looking into the question of how such identity is determined, we should first examine how parallel Jewish and Arab economic entities differ from one another. Empirical observation suggests that there are several such "differentiating variables," which could be defined in turn as "sectoral identity attributes." These can be classified under the following broad categories: identity of ownership, identity of customers, location, identity or origin of input and output, patterns of production and business norms, and finally, legal status.

A few examples will illustrate these distinctions. A Jewish business is, as a rule, Jewish-owned. It will mostly serve Jewish customers and be located in West Jerusalem or elsewhere in a Jewish neighborhood (whereas an Arab establishment will be Arab-owned, serving its respective customers and be located in the Arab sector of East Jerusalem). Jewish and Arab establishments will generally differ with respect to the identity of their employees and the origin of capital and might be distinguished by the kind of products or services they provide. Economic entities of the two sectors further differ, as already observed, with respect to employment conditions, professional affiliation, closing days and language spoken at work. Jewish firms will generally conduct transactions by means of legal contracts and make extensive use of the banking system, whereas Arab firms prefer mostly verbal agreements and cash payments. Finally, all of the above differences are often legally authorized or imposed through licensing, professional or business operation requirements, or even identity markings. Jewish and Arab taxis, for example, both freely circulate throughout the city but are nevertheless distinguishable by different identification numbers.

Obviously, economic entities in one sector do not necessarily possess all of the related attributes. In addition, these various attributes are not equally significant. Specifically, the origin of customers and input in production are not crucial factors. Arab establishments which serve mainly Jews, or Jewish enterprises employing mostly Arabs, do not lose their respective identities as a consequence. By contrast, ownership and location are determining factors, barring a number of informative exceptions. East Jerusalem public schools have been administered ("owned") since 1967 by the Jewish municipality, but have maintained their Arab identity because they continued to teach the Jordanian (and later Palestinian) school curriculum. In a similar vein, Jewish establishments located in the Arab zone, such as Jewish medical clinics, maintain their Jewish identities in the same way that an Arab taxi circulating in a Jewish zone remains Arab. As such, location does not constitute an "internal" identity marker. The massive location of residents or economic activities from one side on the "opposing" side is seen to change the identity of the territory, not of the entities themselves.

Comparatively, attributes such as "patterns of production" and "legal status" represent unequivocal determining factors. What basically distinguishes between Jews and Arabs are spoken language, consumption norms, and other culturally-related behavioral patterns visible in the modes of operation of an economic establishment. It is inconceivable that a place of business which uses exclusively Hebrew and is always closed on Jewish holidays would be part of the Arab sector.[1] Similarly, since legal status is often selectively applied on ethnic, cultural, or political grounds, it equally distinguishes between the two sectors. In polarized Jerusalem, even foreign-owned institutions (like Christian hospitals or the two parallel YMCA establishments) can be generally attributed a "Jewish" or "Arab" identity, mainly in accordance to their patterns of operation.

"TRANSACTIONS" IN IDENTITY

Functional interactions between the two sectors necessarily require the "giving up" of some aspects of identity and the adoption of attributes held by the other group. Thus, exchange can be carried out theoretically on alternative levels through ownership with a business partnership or organizational merge; through factors of production, where an establishment of one sector is sustained by the labor, capital, goods, or services from the other; through consumption, where establishments serve consumers from the other sector; and finally through location, where economic entities from one side locate on the "other side."

It appears that, since the various identity attributes differ in significance, both sectors prefer to conduct their relationships by involving those attributes that least compromise their identity. More specifically, precisely because dependence on the other sector's customers or factors of production does not endanger institutional ethnic identity, interactions are conducted on those levels. By contrast, because interactions involving ownership or location necessarily imply giving up sectoral economic or spatial assets, these are essentially avoided. In terms of the national conflict, preservation of identity is a priority.

THE ROLE OF POWER RELATIONS

The asymmetric patterns of relationship between the Jewish and Arab sectors can be attributed to the fact that the two sectors face an uneven degree of choice versus necessity regarding their interactions. Whenever exchange does occur, Arabs are the ones who generally need to pursue it, as compared to Jews who exercise a greater degree of choice in this respect.

This is particularly evident where patterns of interaction are determined by institutional jurisdiction. Since 1967, Arabs have been dependent on the Jewish sector for most state and municipal services. Because of its much smaller scale and more limited development, the Palestinian sector also relies heavily on the Jewish sector for essential economic functions, such as employment opportunities, most manufactured goods, and specialized services. By contrast, Jewish firms and consumers, even when applying to the Arab sector, generally have choices available in both sectors. Thus, the dominant majority sector generally has "first choice" in choosing domains of integration versus segregation, as well as the form and level of interactions. The Jewish sector is in a position to encourage labor and consumption, while opposing the location of Arab businesses or the marketing of certain Arab products within its territory. Jewish enterprises can choose to employ Arab labor directly or indirectly, and thus save on capital investments and social benefits. Arabs, on the other hand, are obliged and willing to take up any job offered by the Jewish sector, market the whole range of Jewish products, and more often put up with "low level" forms and terms of transaction.

Majority-minority patterns are also reflected in behavior. Most Arabs have become acquainted with Hebrew, while very few Jews learned to speak Arabic. Arab youngsters from East Jerusalem schools have been found to know West Jerusalem far better than the other way round. Arabs often must remain completely isolated all day in the midst of a purely Jewish zone (imagine a single Arab maintenance worker in a Jewish residential quarter or an isolated Arab patient in a Jewish hospital). Jews would rarely find themselves in a similar situation. It is in this context that the behavior of Jews and Arabs regarding transportation can be interpreted. Following 1967, the two parallel public transport systems were allowed to preserve their respective concession areas. But while the Arab companies remained restricted to purely Arab zones, the Jewish company was authorized to extend its lines to all requested destinations in East Jerusalem.

As a result, Jews can always take their own transportation mode; traveling on an Arab bus is an unfamiliar and seemingly dangerous endeavor. Arabs, who are often have to travel alone on a Jewish bus have a lower "deterrence barrier" and are willing to use Jewish buses even in East Jerusalem.

THE STRUGGLE FOR CONTROL AND IDENTITY

Access to political power and economic resources enables the Jewish majority to extend its control and better preserve its collective identity, as compared to the subordinate Arab minority. This is again reflected by the evolving patterns of functional interactions imposed by the Jewish sector. Thus, massive Arab employment or public services provision does not affect, as we recall, Jewish sectoral identity but rather enforces control. Jewish territorial control is preserved as long as Arabs cross over on a daily basis but do not locate their businesses permanently on the Jewish side.

At the same time, the Jewish administration compromised regarding Palestinian collective and cultural identity, generally allowing preservation of norms and institutions. Indeed, in the contested city of Jerusalem, both parties have faced essential dilemmas—political goals versus desirable interactions with the other side. But here again, the options reflect uneven power relations. While the Israeli authorities abstained from fully applying Israeli rule over Arab norms and collective identity, they could be uncompromising regarding various issues of direct political, territorial, and economic control. The Palestinians, for their part, were obliged to abandon some of their stated political goals for control, particularly in terms of functional economic relations with the Jewish sector. This was demonstrated during the first Intifada in the late 1980s with its emphasis on ending cooperation with the Israeli authorities and the Jewish sector. Palestinian attempts to resign from civil service jobs in the Israeli administration or to boycott Israeli products failed in practice due to existing majority-minority economic relations. In fact it was the Jews, who could and did more often "disengage" themselves than the other way round.

---

1   On the other hand, different cultural norms sometimes offer complementary opportunities for mutual exchange. Traditional Muslim women rarely visit Jewish commercial centers, while young Arab couples often meet in West Jerusalem cafes and cinemas, precisely because they are unable to do so in East Jerusalem.

Selected Bibliography

Michael Romann, *Saqr Khevrati-Kalkali shel Yerushalayim HaMiuhedet [An Economic and Social Survey of Reunited Jerusalem]* (Jerusalem: The Maurice Falk Institute for Economic Research in Israel, 1968).

Michael Romann, *Yahas HaGomleen ben HaMagzr HaYehudi vHaAravi biYerushalayim [The Inter-Relationships between the Jewish and Arab Sectors in Jerusalem since 1967]* (Jerusalem: The Jerusalem Institute for Israel Studies, 1984).

Michael Romann, *Hashpaat HaIntifada al Yahasay Yehudeem-Araveem biYerushalayim [The Impact of the Intifada on Jewish-Arab Relations in Jerusalem]* (Jerusalem: The Jerusalem Institute for Israel Studies, 1992).

Michael Romann and Alex Weingrod, *Living Together Separately: Jews and Arabs in Contemporary Jerusalem* (Princeton University Press, 1991).

CITY OF RIFFRAFF

CROWDS, PUBLIC SPACE, AND NEW URBAN SENSIBILITIES
IN WAR-TIME JERUSALEM 1917-1921

Salim Tamari

Between the time of Jerusalem's surrender to General Allenby's victorious army
by the Ottoman Governor Izzat Bey and Mayor Hussein al-Husseini (December
1917) and the commencement of the British Mandate (1920), Palestine experienced three years of administrative and legal flux.[1] Although British intentions
for the country were already defined by commitments to their French allies (in
the Sykes Picot Memorandum), and to the Zionist movement (as per the Balfour
Declaration), these commitments did not immediately translate into clear policies
on the ground. The bulk of the British military establishment in Palestine was
either hostile or ambivalent towards the prospect of a Jewish national home on
the grounds that it violated British promises to Sherif Hussein and his Syrian
allies, or—more importantly—because it provoked Palestinian-Syrian yearning
for independence and invited instability (Huneindi, 2003). But against those local
administrators and field officers who were clearly opposed to a Jewish national
home there stood a legion of philosemites[2] and supporters of Zionism, *including*
General Storrs, military commander of Jerusalem (Segev, 2000).

One often forgets that the British Mandate over Palestine occupied barely
three decades of the country's modern history. In scholarly literature and in
Palestinian popular imagination, the Mandate has acquired a colossal (if not mythical) reputation in the molding of modern Palestinian society and its destiny. A
quick list of its oft-cited achievements (and disasters) would make this point: the
creation of modern institutions of government, including a new civil service and
police force and a centralized national bureaucracy in Jerusalem; modernization
of the land code and taxation system; creation of a legal corpus to replace (and
supplement) Ottoman codes; conducting of a national census (1922 and 1931)
and the creation of the population registry; establishment of the rudimentary
features of citizenship and icons of unfulfilled sovereignty (currency, stamps,
passports); development of a modern secular educational system; and finally, the
construction of an infrastructure of roads and communication system, including
a broadcasting authority—Palestine Radio (1931). A major consequence of these
administrative changes was the separation of Palestine from greater Syria. All of
this happened in three short decades (less if we deduct the initial years, which
were years of military rule) and is shadowed by the Mandate's other major
legacy: laying the grounds for partition and the creation of the state of Israel
(Wasserstein, 1995).

The British are additionally remembered as architects of Palestine's urban planning, thereby establishing the modernity of urban space. This essay will question that legacy, problematizing the certitude with which a line has been drawn between two planning eras, that of the Ottomans and that of the British. A closer look at the period through the memoirs of Wasif Jawhariyyeh presents a rather different narrative. Jawhariyyeh's memoirs for the years following World War I—covering the Mandate period—significantly convey the spirit of emancipatory anticipation that engulfed Jerusalem (and Palestine) during these critical three years of military rule. Jawhariyyeh himself was maturing as a musical performer, and had reached an age where he was able to reflect on the future of Palestine and Jerusalem through the momentous events that he witnessed. He also occupied a strategic vantage point in these events as an entertainer for members of the city's notable elite, and as a ranking British civil servant in the country's capital. The memoirs of Ronald Storrs (1881-1955), based on his letters and diary, are at once elegant, informed, and acutely perceptive concerning Palestine's Ottoman and Islamic heritage. As such, they constitute an excellent exposition of the ideology behind the hegemonic liberal colonial discourse. Storrs' memoirs crisscross fruitfully with Jawhariyyeh's witty comments on the activities of the Pro-Jerusalem Society—Storrs' pet program for the preservation of the city's public monuments and architecture. The two narratives, Jawhariyyeh's and Storrs', present us with two divergent discourses—one native, the other colonial—on Jerusalem's modernity.

Conventional wisdom goes that the preceding Ottoman Empire made no contribution to urban planning in the Levant, and that it was the British who introduced the concept to Palestine. Here is what Ruth Kark suggests on the subject: "Until the end of the Ottoman period, there was no overall planning of the built-up area in Jerusalem. The Sublime Porte and the local authorities limited their operations to supervision. For security reasons a law prohibited the construction of any edifice beyond a distance of 2,500 cubits (about 1.4 km) from the wall of a city. Because of this restriction, Acre failed to expand beyond its walls until the turn of the century, and had the law been strictly obeyed in Jerusalem as well, the fate of that city would have been similar" (Kark, 1991:58-59).

But these Ottoman laws "were not strictly applied." The main provincial centers of the Ottoman Levant (Damascus, Beirut, Jaffa, and Aleppo) differed in the extent to which public spaces were planned. Jerusalem received planning guidelines of sorts after the passage of the Ottoman Municipalities Law in 1877, which regulated building permits, building materials, and the height of buildings (Khamaisi and Nasrallah, 2003:298). Historian Hala Fattah notes how "[t]he increased attention paid to the urbanization of Jerusalem, the spread of communications and the growth of the population forced the Ottomans' hand, so to speak. In the middle of the 19th century, the administrative redevelopment of Jerusalem was a key aspect of the Ottoman centralization of Palestine. As a result of the institution of municipal and administrative councils, Jerusalem's political life was revitalized" (Fattah, 1999).

Ottoman urban expansion schemes and city building regulations existed, but they were either haphazard or overwhelmed by construction activities undertaken by autonomous religious endowments, private parties, or international developers.

Kark suggests that even though "overall plans for the city of Jerusalem did exist during the Ottoman period...they were not implemented, even partially, until 1920" (1991:59). But it was on the basis of that Ottoman vision that many successive British planning schemes during the postwar transitional period (1917-1920), and the early Mandate, were built (Khamaisi and Nasrallah, 2003:296). It was against this background that Ronald Storrs introduced in 1918 the Pro-Jerusalem Society "to preserve the city's antiquities, develop modern cultural functions such as museums, libraries, theatre, etc., and foster the education and welfare of the city's inhabitants" (Gitler, n.d.:31). Storrs was able to assemble an impressive array of the city's ruling elite to constitute the council of the society. These included: Jerusalem Mayor Musa Kazim al-Husseini; the British director of antiquities; Mufti Kamil al-Husseini (and subsequently Haj Amin); the two chief rabbis; the Greek orthodox, Latin and Armenian patriarchs; the Anglican bishop; and leading members of the community (Storrs, 1937:322). One is struck again here by Storrs' vision of Palestinian society as composed of confessional elements joined to the local aristocracy (ayan)—a perspective that clashed frontally with the emerging national movement and its secularized intelligentsia.

Although Storrs was the key figure behind this idea and its execution, discussion of Jerusalem's early planning cannot ignore the participation of two innovative urbanists from the Mandate period, William MacLean and Charles Ashbee. MacLean, then town planner of Alexandria and Khartoum, was invited by Storrs in 1918 to introduce the first modern master plan for Jerusalem, which he accomplished in a record two-month period. His later achievements were groundbreaking. MacLean's plan "prohibited new construction within the boundaries of the Old City, mandated that the area around the walls be kept clear, and ordered the leveling of structures abutting the wall from the outside. New buildings, permitted only to the west and north of the Old City, would rise to a maximum height of eleven meters so as not to compete with the skyline of the Mount of Olives. Jerusalem was to be built of stone; industrial structures were banned" (Roman, 2001). In almost all of their features, these regulations were Ottoman in origin and British in implementation.

In terms of a conceptual paradigm for old/new Jerusalem's urban future, however, it was Charles Ashbee who provided the vision. Ashbee (1863-1942), a disciple of William Morris, belonged to a generation of socialist romantic thinkers who found themselves in the service of the British colonial enterprise. Although he was brought in by Storrs to survey and revive local handicrafts, his actual contribution was far more substantial (Storrs, 1937:323-326). Officially, Ashbee held the position of civic advisor of the city until 1922. In addition he was the secretary and main coordinator of the Pro-Jerusalem Council, the Pro-Jerusalem Society's administrative board. In these roles and through his close association with influential Storrs, Ashbee was deeply involved in proposing solutions to "the city's modern problems while conserving its ancient holy sights and unique character" (Gitler, n.d.:31).

Ashbee combined a romantic vision of the city's "oriental ideal" with a practical down-to-earth approach to the unique predicament of Jerusalem. In the Society's 1920 annual report, he defined the city's unproductive base ("riffraff

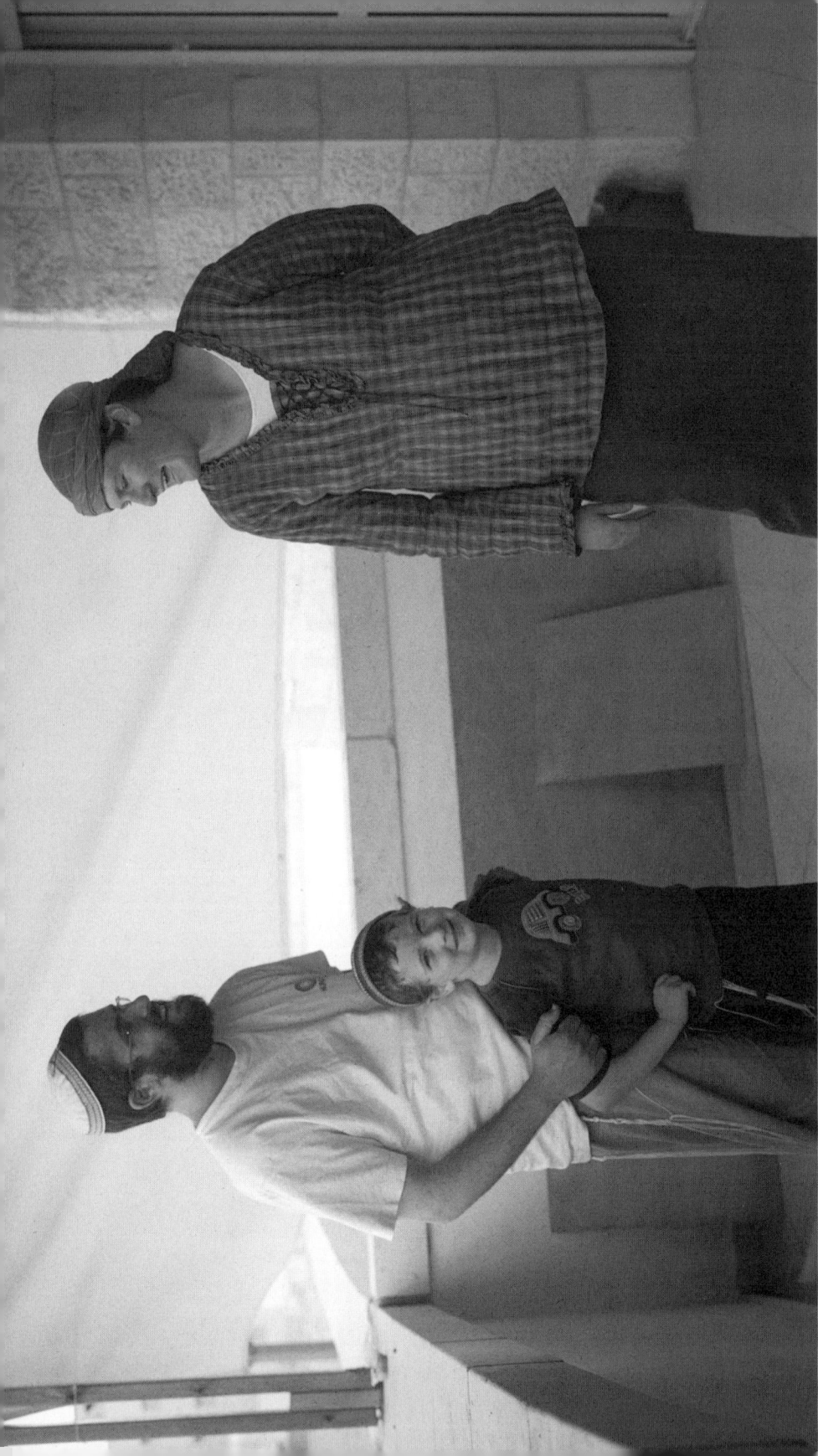

and priests," to recall Storrs) as the planner's main problem. He attempted
to overturn this "parasitic" occupational structure through the revival (and
introduction) of traditional crafts among the city's trades: weaving, tiling (with
Armenian ceramic experts brought in from Kutahia), and glassblowing (originally from Hebron). Among the projects undertaken and finished in this period
were the renovation of Suq al-Qattanin (the Cotton Market) in the Old City; the
tiling, alongside Waqf (Muslim endowment) authorities, of the Dome of the
Rock; the restoration of the ancient wall ramparts built by Suleiman al-Qanuni;
and the Citadel. All of these projects incorporated apprenticeships based on the
guild system. Storrs also set up an annual academy of the fine arts at the Citadel, which held exhibitions on Muslim art, Palestinian crafts, and town planning
(Storrs, 1937:326-327).

By sheer coincidence, Jawhariyyeh, who was toiling at the same period in the
Central Registry of the Military Government, caught the attention of Col. Storrs.
Jawhariyyeh's *oud* (lute) performances endeared him to the governor, who had
become fond of oriental music after his long stay in Egypt. Storrs then seconded
Jawhariyyeh to work as Ashbee's assistant in the Pro-Jerusalem Council.

In his position as secretary to Ashbee, Jawhariyyeh relates an incidence of
conflict between the architectural vision of the Pro-Jerusalem Society and the
Jerusalem Municipality. In 1901, the Ottomans had constructed a clock tower
inside Jaffa Gate during the tenure of Mayor Faidallah al-Alami to commemorate
the 25th anniversary of Sultan Abdul Hamid II's reign. The tower was designed
in the Baroque style by Jerusalem architect Pascal Affendi Sarofim, the municipal
architect at the time (Jawhariyyeh, 2004:49). When Ashbee became secretary of
the Pro-Jerusalem Society, he decided to remove the clock tower, since, according to Jawhariyyeh, "it did not fit well with the image of the historical wall."[3]
The tower was removed overnight despite protests from municipality officials.
Jawhariyyeh, however, concurred with Ashbee's aesthetics: "The design was an
elaborate hybridity of styles, and reminded me of Abdel Wahhab's Franco-Arab
music, although I must say that it should have been moved to another location,
perhaps in the vicinity of the new municipality by Barclays Bank" (2004:49). Years
later, Jawhariyyeh made a wooden model of the removed clock tower and the
adjoining plaza (also destroyed), for the benefit of those who wanted to see what
Ottoman Jerusalem looked like on the eve of the Mandate (Jawhariyyeh, 2004:50).[4]

Jawhariyyeh's diaries thus help us to rethink these changes in the urban landscape of Jerusalem, not only as the lived experience of a contemporary observer,
but also as a bridge rather than a rupture between Ottoman and English rule.
His observations undermine the notion that the Ottoman regime and the British
regime were opposites—one representing oriental despotism, the other modernity.

Here the presumed creation of these institutions of colonial modernity is seen
not as an innovation against the "decrepit" Ottoman system, but as an elabora-
tion on the foundations of Ottoman reforms (secular education, the civil service,
constitutional reform, urban planning). In certain areas, British political plans
constituted retrogression of the Ottoman system. This was the case, for example, with the confessionalization of quarters in the Old City, and enhancement
of religion as a marker of national identity. Jawhariyyeh reminds us that many

of the celebrated reforms of the Mandate administration were already in place before and during World War I. But the tragedies of the war, and conscription's poisoning of the relationship between the Ottoman rulers and their Arab subjects in Syria and Palestine, subsequently erased these features of Ottoman modernity from Palestinian collective memory.

Naturally, the British administration is recalled as the conscious instrument (through the Balfour Declaration) for the foundations of Palestinian displacement in 1948, and much of Jawhariyyeh's narrative is permeated with this under-standing (since he was writing in a later period). The hindsight largely explains his ambivalence about Jerusalem's liberation from the Ottoman yoke, even as Jerusalemites were dancing in the street, and as he and his brother Khalil were burning their Turkish military uniforms (Mana', 2003, 253-4).

Several writers have been able to retrospectively examine those years as a period of major restructuring in Palestinian and Syrian society. One contemporary observer refers to the radical impact that population movement and the war economy had on the normative aspects of daily life: villagers regularly coming to the city; young women attending school and removing their veils; the emergence of café culture; and the decline of religiosity in Nablus and Jerusalem (Barghouti, 2001:192-3). A derivative development of these normative changes was the decline of local affinities and the strengthening of Syrian and Arab nationalism.

CHAOS IN THE STREETS

Jawhariyyeh recalls these three transitional years as days of chaos—both in the country as a whole and in his private life, as if one condition mirrored the other. But the "chaos" is also seen here as a period of creative anarchy.

In his personal life, those were Jawhariyyeh's "precious" years of bachelor-hood before he settled down. They were also marked by the death of his patron, the mayor of Jerusalem, Hussein Effendi al-Husseini, after which Jawhariyyeh describes his condition as one of "vagabondage" (tasharrud): "I roamed around the city as if in a trance. I would spend all night partying, and then sleep all day, then spend another evening in neighboring villages of Jerusalem. I paid no attention to anybody or anything, and would only go home to change my clothes, sleeping mostly at my friends' homes until my body was completely depleted from intoxication. One day I am celebrating in the Bab Hatta neighborhood, and in the next morning I am having a picnic with the families of the top notables (ayan) in the city. Then I would have a "session" with some of Jerusalem's gang-sters (zuran and qabadayat) in a city alley" (Jawharriyeh, 2004:23). But these episodes of hedonism, lasting most of 1918 and part of the following year, reflected a mood, which engulfed the city as a whole. Jawhariyyeh depicts numerous episodes of public celebrations of freedom in the Old City streets, marked by musical processions and open consumption of alcohol. In one such fantasia involving hundreds of revelers, the celebrants started in Damascus Gate, moved out of the Old City through Musrara, to the Russian Compound, back into the Old City from Jaffa Gate, to the Austrian Hospice, only to finally end up in the Sheikh Rihan neighborhood of Mahallat al-Saadiyya (2004:41-2). "Why did we have these orgies of celebration the likes of which we have not seen since then?" he asks. Then proceeds to answer himself: "The people were hungry for a moment of release, after the years of humiliation, disease, hunger, and dispersal during the war and Ottoman despotism. When the British arrived we began to have a breath of freedom. Unfortunately our joy was short lived, for they brought us catastrophe which was several times more disastrous than the Turkish yoke" (2004:41-2).

These outbursts of street merriment were echoed during the years of military government in the mushrooming of local cafes and café-bars. They were places where Jerusalemites could meet at leisure, listen to gramophone music, drink araq and cognac, and smoke an arghileh. Two outstanding cafés from this period were Maqha al-Arab in Ein Karem (owned by Abu al-Abed Arab) which stayed open all night, and the Jawhariyyeh café bar (owned by Wasif's brother)—which featured live entertainment by visiting musicians from Cairo, Alexandria, and Beirut (2004:44-5).[5]

LIMINAL SPACE AND MILITARY RULE

The Jawhariyyeh memoirs shed significant light on the critical postwar years, when political ambiguity about the future direction of Palestine prevailed. These were the years of cultural liminality in Palestine, when the Ottoman system had collapsed militarily but the colonial system had not yet been ushered in. "We lived in a state of ignorance," Storrs later confessed, "and my word was the law" (Storrs, 1937:272-3). Under General Money's administration, all civil laws were suspended in favor of the military administration. Suddenly, in Palestine, according to Mandate historian Bayan al-Hut, there were no lawyers, no judges, no courts, and no newspapers (al-Hut, 1981:66). The northern regions of Palestine remained under Ottoman control in 1918, and the British were mobilizing resistance in the name of Sherif Hussein against the encircled Ottoman army. But even after Ottoman defeat and final consolidation of British rule, the borders between Transjordan, Lebanon, and Syria on one hand, and Palestine on the other, remained "Ottoman," with fluid boundaries and common cultural outlook. While the legal vacuum was filled in the countryside by a reversion to common law (al-qanun al-urfi) and tribal law, conditions in the large cities allowed appointed judges and senior administrators (British and Palestinian) considerable leeway in applying the law locally.

Another feature of this liminality was the porosity of the new borders with Lebanon, Transjordan, Syria, and Egypt, which still reflected Ottoman Greater Syria. In the summer of 1922, Jawhariyyeh goes on an excursion with his brother Khalil to Syria and Lebanon through the northern borders. The passage through Ras al-Naqura, which ten years later had become a formidable frontier post, is hardly recorded in the memoirs; it was as if one simply passed from one district to another (Jawhariyyeh, 2004:30). Three years later, Jawhariyyeh repeats the trip with his wife Victoria, again with barely any formal procedures (2004:161). The two stories illustrate the fluidity of frontier areas on the eve of the British and French protectorates' delineation of new state boundaries, which consolidated notions of citizenship, exclusion, and separation. The new regulations ended the period when northern Palestine and southern Lebanon were considered a subregion, a physical unit with shared cultural and social attributes.

The phasing-out of this border fluidity corresponded to the growth and consolidation in Palestine of the governing apparatuses of the colonial state: the army, the police force, the civil service, and the new legal system. Within every sector of the new state, the British had to balance a system of appointments that took into account both the native Palestinian population, and the emigrant Jewish population. But while native representation was individual and direct, incorporating social status and confession, Jewish representation was mediated through protracted negotiations with the Jewish Agency and Zionist executive. During the crucial formative stage of British rule, when the new civil administration was installed in 1920, Jewish representation was overwhelming, even though Jews constituted less than 12% of the population. Segev writes that "[t]he Palestinian Jews in senior positions were prominent principally during Samuel's tenure. Together with the British Zionists, they held key positions in his administration, complained Lieutenant Colonel Percy Bramely, the director of public security in Palestine. In fact, Bramely wrote, Samuel's was a 'Zionist-controlled government' (Segev, 2000:167).

Jawhariyyeh's two decades of work in the Land Registry provides a detailed record of how new laws were geared to facilitate the transfer of urban and rural property to the Zionists. This process included the abolition of the tithe and the werko[6] (both were Ottoman land taxes which garnered state revenue without regard to quality or productivity) and the institution of the new graded land tax based on land use, location, and quality. Finally, it included the expediting of the Land Settlement, whose main objective was a comprehensive cadastral registration of land plots to enhance and simplify the operations of the *Tapu* (Land Registry).

It is paradoxical, given his later nationalist credentials, that Jawhariyyeh was a critical instrument in this process of land alienation, initially unaware of its significance, and certainly unwilling to perform these tasks. But Jawhariyyeh's rendition of the process was typical of these early hedonistic years: passive resistance by delaying his work, bureaucratic sabotage, and creation of a jovial atmosphere of celebration in one of the most critical departments of the colonial government.

His mundane anecdotes satirizing the daily routine of the colonial bureaucracy draw a cumulative picture of the period's emerging liminal identity. Its main features were a legal vacuum filled by administrative fiat; a hedonistic street culture that celebrated the loss of tyranny, but filled it with new uncertainties; and porous borders that retained the texture of an older continuous Levantine (*Shami*) culture. What "cemented" these elements together was a strong sense of the local—of Jerusalem as the center of the country's shifting boundaries, and an anchor against the schemes engineered by the new colonial enemy amid a collective nostalgia for the "accursed" Ottomans.

---

1   This is a considerably reduced version of a longer introduction to the Memoirs of Jawhariyyeh Jawhariyyeh (Al-Quds al-Intidabiyyah fil Mudhakarat al-Jawhariyyah), 2004.

2   The reference here is to a number of colonial officials, including Churchill, Ashbee, and possibly Storrs, who held exotic views of European Jews, and adopted favorable attitude to the idea of "Jewish Return" to Palestine.

3   Henry Kendall refers to the incident: "permission was tactfully obtained to remove a hideous clock tower with dials showing the time according to both Western and Arab reckoning." He claims that the tower was erected to commemorate the 33rd, not 25th, anniversary of Abdul Hamid's reign (Kendall, 1948:8-10).

4   Fifteen years later, Professor T.F. Meisel, the Hebrew University archeologist, visited Jawhariyyeh and wrote glowingly about this model in an article published in the Palestine Post.

5   For more on this world, see "Jerusalem's Ottoman Modernity: The Times and Lives of Wasif Jawhariyyeh (Tamari, 2000).

6   The *werko* was originally a land and real estate tax levied on *zaamat* (*sipahis*, or feudal estates). With the abolition of feudal estates the werko became a land tax imposed by the state, together with the tithe. For details see, Moses Doukhan, "Land Tenure," in Said Himadeh, Economic Organization of Palestine, American University Press, Beirut, 1938:98-99.

Selected Bibliography

Omar Salih al-Barghouti, *al-Marahil* (Beirut 2001). Unpublished manuscript.

Moses Doukhan, "Land Tenure," in *Economic Organization of Palestine*, ed. Said Himadeh (Beirut: American University Press, 1938).

Hala Fattah, "Planning, Building and Populating Jerusalem in the Ottoman Period," *www.jerusalemites. org/jerusalem/ottoman/7.htm*, 1999.

Sahar Huneindi, *A Broken Trust: Herbert Samuel, Zionism and the Palestinians*, Arabic edition (Beirut: Institute of Palestine Studies, 2003).

Bayan Nuwaihid al-Hut, *al-Qiyadat wal Mu'assasat al-Siyasiyya fi Filasteen, 1917-1948 (Leadership and Political Institutions in Palestine, 1917-1948)* (Beirut: Mu'assasat al-Dirasat al-Filastiniyyah, 1981).

Inbal Ben-Asher Gitler, "C R Ashbee's Jerusalem Years: Arts and Crafts, Orientalism and British Regionalism," in *Assaph Studies in the Arts* 5, Tel Aviv University. (Undated).

Jawhariyyeh Jawhariyyeh, *Al-Quds al-Intidabiya fil Mudhakarat al-Jawhariyyah*, eds. Salim Tamari and Issam Nasar (Beirut: Mu'assasat al-Dirasat al-Filastiniyyah, 2004).

Ruth Kark, *Jerusalem Neighborhoods: Planning and By-Laws (1855-1930)* (Jerusalem: The Magnes Press, 1991).

Henry Kendall, *Jerusalem City Plan, Preservation and Development During the British Mandate, 1918-1948* (London: Her Majesty's Stationary Office, 1948).

Rassem Khamaisi and Rami Nasrallah, *The Jerusalem Urban Fabric* (Jerusalem: International Peace and Cooperation Center, 2003).

Adel Mana', *Tarikh Filasteen fi Awakhir al-Ahd al-Uthmani 1700-1918* (Beirut: Mu'assasat al-Dirasat al-Filastiniyyah, 2003).

Yadin Roman, "Jerusalem's Wall," *Eretz Magazine* (February, 2000).

Tom Segev, *One Palestine Complete* (New York: Metropolitan Books, 2000).

Najati Sidqi, *Mudhakarat Najati Sidqi* (Beirut: Institute for Palestine Studies, 2001).

Ronald Storrs, *Orientations* (London: Nicholson and Watson, 1937).

Salim, Tamari, "Jerusalem's Ottoman Modernity: The Times and Lives of Wasif Jawhariyyeh," *Jerusalem Quarterly File* 9 (2000)

Izzat Tannous, *The Palestinians: Eyewitness History of Palestine Under the British Mandate* (London and New York: I. G. T. Company, 1988).

Bernard Wasserstein, "The British Mandate in Palestine: Mythos and Realities," in *Middle East Lectures* 1 (Tel Aviv: The Dayan Center for Middle East and African Studies, 1995).

RE-IMAGINING JERUSALEM

A RETROSPECTIVE VIEW FROM CONTEMPORARY ISTANBUL?

Orhan Esen

How might Jerusalem's urban development have unfolded if ethnic conflict between Israelis and Palestinians had not become the dominant factor, and the resulting spatial segregation had not become the main feature of the built environment? Assume that, after the Ottoman Empire and British Mandate, a Jewish-Arab/Israel-Palestine state of two peoples had developed. Assume even further that a binational, Western-oriented, financial and cultural elite (similar to that in other parts of the outgoing and modernizing Ottoman Empire) held political and planning leadership roles, while the traditionalist sector of Jewish/Palestinian society (just in the early twentieth century) continued their patterns of life. Or that territorial independence had not been aspired for or attained, and the aforementioned social elite only exercised social and ideological dominance as carriers of the idea of modernity? How would the urbanistic careers of this elite and others have developed, if—in place of the national dichotomy between Israelis and Palestinians—a more complicated mesh of tension, dividing lines, and hybridization had arisen? In short: what would have resulted from Jewish-Palestinian urbanism in Jerusalem if different processes in the city had prevailed?

Take the city of Istanbul as an analogy for this speculative exercise. The interview with Meron Benvenisti and Salim Tamari in this publication suggests that, in the early modern times of the waning Ottoman Empire before the establishment of the nation state, Jerusalem and Istanbul (as other centers of the Ottoman Empire) were comparable urban areas. How did a city such as Istanbul develop similarly to Jerusalem? Both dissolved their inherited "Ottoman" diversity under the augury of competing nationalisms, instead producing new complex forms of segregation through migration and globalization processes. In both cities, historical ways of thinking and the urbanistic attitudes of an early modern elite were reproduced into new contexts—urban areas changed and transferred those new ideas into conceptual design. In that light, this essay[1] recounts the multi-layered socioeconomic and ideological cycles of "segregation" and "re-amalgamation" of Istanbul in the 20th century.

THE "SIMPLE DUALITY" OF OLD TIMES

Today's Istanbul is the site of a clear fault line between two "opposing" parties within the middle class. These two opposing camps each define themselves differently in their attitudes towards public space, their position in the mass media, and their view of this ideological battleground. On one side of the polarity are groups coming out of the *"post-gecekondu"*[2] environment. These milieus developed gradually from the waves of provincial migration that began 60 years ago, and now their inhabitants jealously cling to their acquired economic assets and positions. We could call these people the "rising new middle class." Politically, they seem to lean towards a kind of reformist conservatism, combining neo-liberalism with religious motives.

On the other side of the polarity is the „old," „established" middle class of Istanbul. This group could be said to represent "north Istanbulness" as a complex combination of mentality and collective action. The north Istanbulites think that they alone deserve the epithet "civilized" as heirs to the old, Occidentalist middle class values of the early modernization period. A great part of this group, however, has been forced to watch in desperation as better-skilled, new migrants conquer the economic and social fortresses which they attempted to scale in the 1990s.

The rising new middle class from rural origins, while skillfully exploiting the economic rent mechanisms of their new urban surroundings, has expressed its cultural origins with growing confidence. They have begun to wear turbans and hold barbecue parties and sacrifice rituals in urban public spaces, provoking negative feelings (even hatred) from the old, educated middle class, who were not as skilful in appropriating and using urban public resources.

This older class generally represents the losers of the 1990s, and was gradually driven to almost reactionary political stances. After the 1990s, in permanent economic crisis, the old middle class had difficulty in finding a place among the "dynamic" market forces of a growing metropolis and consequently lost their position. So they naturally identify the new rising middle class with the savage, "mafia-like" aspects of this new capitalism. Culturally, the essentially elitist north Istanbulites solve the problem of separating themselves from the newly wealthy by collectively labeling all *post-gecekondu* people with the notion of "varo," (meaning "outskirts") and thus identifying them as outsiders.

The word *gecekondu*, inherited from the 1950s, '60s and '70s and mainly positive, has gradually fallen out of use. In the 1990s, the media discovered the *varos* and promoted the term in its arguments about "distorted urbanization." The *varos* is what is not Istanbul; it is the incarnation of an unforeseen urbanization. The *varos*, with its chaos, is impossible to understand and penetrate. Those who can build illegally are just as likely to perform all kinds of other subversive actions. It is obviously notorious, a place where *civitas* comes to an end and where our security is no longer guaranteed, it is a no-go area.

This *varos* discourse reveals the collective unconscious of the old middle class, who use the term to emphasize the perceived poverty of the new settlements, and their own desire to avoid this fate. Their discourse is widely supported in the mass media. Its ambiguous use as a term describing both poverty and the threatening new middle class is possible because *post-gecekondu* Istanbulites reside in spaces still—or once again—intertwined with poverty. Such fine points are ignored by the northern Istanbulites, whose embedded cultural assumptions neglect important socioeconomic and political differentiations within this milieu.

In my article "Learning from Istanbul" (2005), I traced the mental and sentimental roots of this attitude back to the early period of modernization in

Istanbul in the second half of the 19th century. This was when the first spatial ruptures between upper and lower income groups occurred. With the social elite's movement from the old peninsula to Pera in the north of the city, an urban fracture opened up on the axis of Golden Horn, which quickly became an ideological break. In this period, a simple social duality emerged with decipherable spatial characteristics.

THE RISE OF GATED COMMUNITIES AFTER THE 1980s: SEGREGATION À LA ISTANBUL

During the second move of capital toward the north from 1950 to 1980, the upper and middle classes of the industrial-city-in-the-making settled along the axis between Taksim and Etiler. It was exactly in this intermediate era that the bourgeoisie made themselves out to be socially responsible, neither willing nor needing to isolate themselves. "Social Respect" was maintained by the lower classes inhabiting the classical *gecekondu* areas (no longer farmers, but not yet proletarians, they occupied the threshold between urban and rural). Separate cultures created a conventional framework with firm roles, within which everyone moved comfortably. In a society with production-based capital accumulation and values, everyone "knew" his or her place; desires were not unfurled as they were after the 1980s. At this time the old cultural dividing lines based on industrial production lost their validity; with the new wealth, the previous borders dissolved.

A highly visible section of this new, monied aristocracy originating mostly through successful financial speculation is, to a large extent, "uncultivated" from the viewpoint of the old urban middle classes. It is seen as not yet capable of differentiating itself through a separate "superior culture"—that is through a cool, distanced, bourgeois ("European") class behavior. In a society that has been "de-elitized," the inherited northern Istanbul discourse is too weak to develop an altogether new class position. So it remains for the nouveaux riches, who cannot set themselves apart through behavior, to distinguish themselves through material trappings: with jeeps, black sunglasses, and settlement walls in the Latin-American style.

The behavior of the lower classes in rejection of this segregation seems inevitable: tugging at and copying it, coming close to it, and further necessitating "hard" physical segregation by the upper classes. Origins, language, and behavior are distributed through the media and consumed, providing easy access. Reality shows starring members of the lower classes, and society shows where the new "uneducated" upper classes put themselves on display only serve to mirror each other. The new wealth is obviously not a result of performance and effort, and is not sufficiently legitimized; and both parties know this only too well. The new rich of today are yesterday's next-door neighbors. Thus, nothing speaks against a possible exchange of roles, except luck, good relations, rigor, and diligence.

In the late 1990s, the media landscape was flooded by a popular genre: the Mahalle television series.[3] These programs represent an unprecedented, sound, "traditional," Istanbul microcosmos. Even when involved in neat, quotidian conflicts, the poorer, petit bourgeois cohabitants always behave nicely to each other, mainly out of solidarity. Old boroughs with single-family houses such as Kuzgun-cuk, Samatya, etc.—relatively spared from the interfering hand of the *yapsat*[4]—are selected to portray Istanbul before 1945-1950. The story is ambiguously set in contemporary times, which is altogether an absolutely improbable time/space/action combination. The camera hardly moves; no undesirable apartment façades enter the picture. It captures the imaginary desires of a former (and impossible) but harmonious world: what would it be like if we and our city remained as we were in our childhood?

Interesting enough, the gated communities make exactly this infantile dream available for purchase. The known pioneer of these settlements, Kemer Coun-try, is marketed precisely thus: on the one hand, lamenting the harmonious old Mahalle, and at the same time, "selling" its re-establishment via an expensive, guarded, homogenous community on exclusive property. It is forgotten that 150 years ago, during their first migration to the north, the very ancestors of this Kemer Country clientele, turned their backs once and for all on the historical peninsula, and its socially heterogeneous Mahalles.

DISCERNING APPARENT AND REAL DIVISIONS

The "complicated" duality that prevails in the city in the 2000s is composed of two dissimilar dichotomies: first, a division subjectively experienced by different groups around the symbols of urban life and second, a conflict derived from the material production of urban space.

The first divide derives from the symbolic interpretation of public space. Described above, this ideological quarrel revolves around the lifestyles of the old and new middle classes. Both groups give the impression that they are poised to undermine each other for the sake of a greater presence in public space; each side's public presence, attitude, stance, material, and patterns of cultural con-sumption are apparently completely unbearable to its sociopolitical opponent.

However, it seems that these two groups have grown closer together, and have even become equals in the process of producing the built environment. In the area of architecture and methods of real estate exploitation, they increas-ingly copy each other. In other words, the old learn "the ways" from the new, and the new learn "the rules" from the old. Today, the production of small-scale *yapsat* capital is no longer distinctively different in either old "apartment build-ings" or new "*post-gecekondu*" surroundings. The urban structures of the old established central districts (for instance, Besiktas or Fatih) and the first wave of gecekondu districts (for instance, Zeytinburnu or Umraniye) were both founded with small-scale capital investments and are no longer visually different.

In the highly-publicized debate on conflicting lifestyles in public space, social trends, fluxes, and amalgamations are rather overlooked. Both middle classes form a large majority of the current urban population and share a public space that is incomparably widened and diversified relative to that of 1980. Mobility within urban space is now unprecedented. In the final analysis, the bipolar oppo-sition that emerges as harsh conflict and intolerance in ideological discourse is likely to eventually transcend itself to create the core values (derived from these new urban practices) of a "new Istanbul convention" for all middle classes.

ONGOING (AND UNSTATED) MATERIAL RUPTURES IN THE CITY

The second division relates to the restructuring of the urban environment and the role of new and rising capital investment groups. This phenomenon is in progress and its divisions are less fully articulated, although often touched upon, in the mass media. At its start in the early 1990s, new major investment groups were established in a city that had largely been created through small-scale investments. The islets these groups produced were "pasted" on top of the existing pattern. In the 2000s, this change came to public notice when the capital companies expanded their areas of acquisition. The ruptures that this process is sure to create will set the city's future agenda.

This process is marked by two trends; the first being the creation of new urban spaces, assuring the new upper income groups' spatial social segregation. (This trend flourished in the 1990s, and its consequences were widely discussed.) The second trend, which emerged only after the last economic crisis in 2001-2, is the transformation of large-scale construction and real estate investment for middle and lower income groups into a major means of capital accumulation. Rubrics such as "urban innovation," "earthquake-proof construction," and a return to "architectural identity," are used to justify a new capital accumulation process, in which funds from the middle classes are now being transferred to major construction companies.

In the Istanbul of the 1990s and 2000s, cars have become a major tool for differentiating urban space. New kinds of housing, working, shopping, and entertainment areas connect to each other through a network of highways—spaces of new urban geography attached to the old city map. The walls of the safe "gated communities" and the 4x4 jeeps, needed to progress through the "urban jungle," both made the new class more visible than the wealthy elites of the past, and more obviously separate from the rest of society. Two different public spaces have thus developed: one experienced by car, the other by foot. Each is associated with a different discourse, and—gradually—two separate communities.

This new separation, though visually manifest, was never the focus of the public agenda. Under the influence of the media, it was normalized without being subject to critical discourse. Such phenomena as the use of the turban or the sacrifice ritual in public space were emphasized in media coverage, while the problematics of a public space no longer accessible to pedestrians was hardly mentioned. The life of the vehicular-mobile, accessible to the public only by undergoing security checks, was sometimes a background in TV footage, but otherwise gradually driven out of the cognitive city map. The new life available for sale is socially justified as an individuals' decision to invest in private real estate. The nature of the public space thus created, however, is the subject of more subtle associations. Could it be that, failing to find a language for discussing this new division, the middle classes, instead, attack each other over superficial lifestyle debates?

SOME CLUES TO RETHINKING JERUSALEM

The social segregation within the northern section of the new city of Istanbul in the 19th century took place along topographic guidelines: the "better," cosmopolitan, and global society was established "above" on the ridge of Pera and to

the north toward Sisli continuing along the so-called "Grandes Rues." The equally
ethnically diverse simple folk, on the other hand, lived down in the valley (Esen,
2005b). This was during a time when Istanbul and Jerusalem shared the early
modern framework before the demise of the multiethnic empire. Similar to the
migration of capital in Istanbul to the north, the upper classes in contemporary
Jerusalem behaved similarly, leaving the Old City. At that time one could speak
(in both cities) of only a conditional and limited ethnic segregation. Inspired by
the French Revolution, the Ottoman state fought official appearances of premodern
segregation—i.e. rank based on ethnicity. These were to be relics found only in
the old part of Istanbul.

Hence, a new official construct was propagated: a multiethnic, multireligious
"Ottoman nation." Modern new cities under the guidance of bureaucrats, as well
as the internationally-networked trade and financial elite anticipated realizing
this ideal. A reproduction of ethnic-spatial segregation in the new Ottoman city
is therefore attributable to synchronistic centrifugal "nationalist" tendencies
within civil society, and not to official policy.

Premodern ethnic-spatial conditions were revived in interwar Jerusalem
through regressive British Mandate social policies, which reverted the early
modernization process. Interwar Istanbul, on the other hand, a shrinking city
now beyond global tendencies, fell under the influence of a newly created nation
state with its capital in Ankara. Certain groups, the Greeks above all, which
had acquired the status of "national minority," were already being disappeared.
Soon after national independence, an assimilation and/or emigration process
was supported by the state. By contrast, the newly founded Israel preferred the
politics of ostracism to coercive assimilation, to the extent that out-migration
(always and everywhere the first choice of nations in periods of establishment!)
through expulsion was not really effective.

As mentioned earlier, Istanbul's new complex dividing lines were reproduced
as a result of migration processes. A symptomatic attitude present since the
1990s in certain north Istanbul circles has been to lament the emigration of
minorities who somehow embodied urban values, while simultaneous complain-
ing about immigration from rural areas. The former ethnic heterogeneity of a
"manageable" large city is perceived as coherency, as a lost golden age, while
the newly developed metropolitan complexity is perceived as threatening chaos.
(The list of publicly stated desires runs the spectrum from forced deportation to
the reintroduction of internal identification cards, "like before.") But, the refrain
goes, the republican constitution, which guarantees freedom of choice of venue
of settlement ("freizügigkeit," or freedom of movement) as a fundamental human
right, "unfortunately" does not justify a legal apartheid regime on the Bosporus.
One available solution lies in voluntary isolation in gated communities, where
one can invest in a guaranteed non-change of the environment.

In Israel-Palestine, "English" segregation politics were the territorial starting
point for the establishment of a nation state—and consistently extended thereafter. The United Nations division in 1948 created new ethnic borders in the
Jerusalem area, redefined by large-scale population displacement. The so-called
"reunification" of the city neither revoked this tendency, nor did it lead to the

development of an ethnically integrated urban society. On the contrary: Jewish migration–through the development of exclaves in the annexed eastern part of the city–led to the Zionist development of new territories. Exactly this process reproduces the topographic model of early modern Istanbul. Considering Israel's international political justification as a bulwark of Western civilization, the coincidental consultation of early modern Istanbul as an urban role model is perhaps not so coincidental after all.

1   The following four sections of this essay are based on previously published articles: The sections "The 'Simple Duality' of Old Times," "Discerning Apparent and Real Divisions," and "Ongoing (and Unstated) Material Ruptures in the City" uses citations from the following publication: Orhan Esen, "The Tightrope Walk of the Middle Class in a Fractured Istanbul," in Art, City and Politics in an Expanding World. Writings from the 9th international istanbul biennial (Istanbul: Istanbul Foundation for Culture and Arts, 2005) isbn 975-7363-45-6. The section "The Rise of the Gated Communities after 1980s: Segregation à la Istanbul" uses citations from unpublished parts of the manuscripts for: Orhan Esen, "Learning from Istanbul," in Self Service City: Istanbul, eds. Orhan Esen and Stefan Lanz, metroZones 4, Berlin 2005.

2   In the article entitled "Learning from Istanbul" (2005), the term post-gecekondu is used in order to describe (a) the multistoried building type, which replaces the old conventional gecekondu (literally "built" or "landed" overnight), produced after 1945 to solve the housing problem, i.e., for its use value, and became widespread in the urban periphery. After the 1980s, the multistorey post-gecekondu buildings, produced for their exchange value on the real estate market, replaced these; (b) consequently, the urban environment where these buildings abound–the formerly peripheral gecekondu locations would, after the 1980s, become central areas of the new metropolis; (c) the socioeconomic relations entailed by this kind of urbanization, and eventually, (d) the culture produced within this context.

3   The Mahalle is the smallest urban administrative unit. It often corresponds with the public's perception of a certain area of the city. Generally, it is understood as a traditional, social, and aesthetically intact Turkish borough or neighborhood.

4   The yapsatci is a small construction contractor. The word derives from from yap meaning "do," sat meaning "sales," and ci the suffix for a profession. A yapsatci is therefore a "do-er/salesman." He brings construction services to urban areas where gecekondus, instead of single-family homes, are constructed and renovated through his activities. As compensation he receives a share of the built apartments. Usually he works without capital.

Selected Bibliography

Orhan Esen, "Learning from Istanbul," in Self Service City: Istanbul, eds. Orhan Esen and Stefan Lanz, metroZones Series 4 (Berlin: 2005).

Orhan Esen, "Pot of Babel," in Self Service City Istanbul (Berlin, b books: 2005).

INNOVATION
DESTRUCTION

The intense conflict has produced a city that alters its physical form in an accelerated and panicked-ridden fashion. In Jerusalem, roads, walls, fences, settlements, neighborhoods, or private houses can be constructed or demolished virtually over night. The city's population has almost tripled since 1967, with the Jewish population growing by 135%, and the Palestinian population increasing by 233% during the same period. But growth, modernization, and expansion are inseparable from the struggle for territorial and demographic control between two nations, which each defines Jerusalem as its own legitimate capital and symbolic cultural center. Beyond the political polarization and mutual negation however, a thin and unconscious exchange is underway that is manifest in the everyday. The result is an unintentional urban productivity—a common culture located between the extremes of total rejection, on one hand, and subtle, unconscious hybridity, on the other.

THE THORN AND THE FLOWER

IN THE PRICKLY PEAR CACTI OF ASIM ABU SHAQRA

Zakaria Mohammed

In the struggle over land between the Jewish immigrants and the natives of Palestine, symbols played an important rule. The production and reinterpretation of these symbols has been a crucial battlefield since the rise of the Zionist project in Palestine, and continues as such today. Because the subject of the struggle is the land itself, there has been no way of avoiding both parties' use of the earth's natural elements as ideological symbols.

Here we will make a case study of the prickly pear cactus, exploring how each side developed symbolism around the plant—symbolism heavily invested with specific history and background. We will approach these issues through the works of Asim Abu Shaqra, a painter among the Palestinian Arab minority that was not expelled from its lands during the 1948 creation of Israel. Abu Shaqra was born in the village of Um al-Fahim in 1961, and passed away in 1990. He spent the last two years of his life busy with one main motif: prickly pear cacti potted in vessels.

Cactus, 1988
Asim Abu-Shaqra (oil
on paper, 120 × 80 cm,
collection of the art-
ist's family)

A growing corpus of Israeli-Palestinian interpretative literature has arisen out of Abu Shaqra's potted cactus. The battle over the cactus as a national symbol centers on Abu Shaqra's art. What does his symbol mean? Does it originate from a Palestinian background or a Jewish environment? Is it a Palestinian achievement, or does it belong to Israeli Jewish culture? A heated battle has been pitched over Abu Shaqra and his tiny flowerpots.

The most extreme example of an Israeli perspective on Abu Shaqra's work is represented by the writings of Israeli critic Sarit Shapira, as quoted by Ellin Ginton in her contribution to the exhibition catalog, "Asim Abu Shaqra." The prickly pear cactus is a Jewish symbol,

Cactus, 1988
Asim Abu-Shaqra (oil
on paper, 120 × 80 cm,
collection of the art-
ist's family)

Shapira begins, and Abu Shaqra's journey towards it is a journey to the Other and not the self. Her argument is that the prickly pear cactus symbolizes the Israeli *sabra* (native-born Israeli) and, further, that the *sabra* expresses a concept of "the collective Israeli prototype." As such, Shapira insists on isolating Abu Shaqra from his national milieu and attributing his insights to Jewish Israeli culture. "Abu Shaqra's *sabra* is an identifying mark of Otherness," Shapira explains, "since he, as an Arab, applies it to himself, while originally and in common usage the image refers to the Israeli Jew. "But Shapira does not stop there, writing that Abu Shaqra's choice of the *sabra* "may attest to the lack of personal or collective identifying mark of his own" (Ginton, 1994:88). Thus, by referring to the *sabra*, Abu Shaqra has stripped himself of his own skin and chosen instead to wear that of his rival—nothing more. The cactus, then, is an outsider, and by identifying himself with it, Abu Shaqra is somehow deserting his original identity.

Another Israeli critic, Tali Tamir, does not share Shapira's extreme interpretation. In a gesture of reconciliation, she seeks a way to share the symbol: "Shapira...is mistaken in attributing authorship of the image of the *sabra* to Israeli culture...Examination of its sources in Palestinian culture reveals that there, too, a wealth of concepts exists around this image...[I]t operates as an ironic and critical image of the stolen identity of the Arab who wishes to see himself as the *sabra*, as Shapira shows, while at the same time remaining an internal Palestinian code symbolizing suffering and deeply-rooted tenacity" (Ginton, 1994:88).

According to this analysis, Abu Shaqra shed half of his skin, yet preserved the other half. Tamir acknowledges Palestinian culture and its own separate language and code. But we must note that Tamir agrees with Shapira's central thesis: Abu Shaqra has a deep desire to identify himself with the Other, the *sabra*, by clothing himself in its trappings. As such, Tamir rescinds with one hand what her other hand has offered.

Ellin Ginton offers yet another perspective, based on a comment made by Abu Shaqra himself in an interview with Tali Tamir. "The *sabra* fascinates me," he said, "because its amazing prickly pear cactus enchants me with its shocking ability to flower out of thorny death" (Ginton, 1994:91). Ginton argues that Abu Shaqra's main contribution to this symbolism is his transformation of the cactus plant into a cross. His potted cactus is the crucified Christ. Abu Shaqra, therefore, has enlisted the cactus in his contribution to western art traditions. "Like Jewish and Israeli artists, from Chagall to Tumarkin," writes Ginton, "Abu Shaqra could and did make use of the themes of the sacrifice...as images of personal and national death. His unique quality lay in his ability to present an alternative to the changed symbol of the crucifixion in the form of a cactus" (Ginton, 1994:91). But even here, when Abu Shaqra's reference is the crucifix, he continues to wear the garb of the Other. He is not expressing himself in his own tongue but in a foreign tongue, mainly the language of Israeli and Jewish artists, despite that the crucifixion motif can be found in Arabic literature going back at least one thousand years.

Yet Abu Shaqra was building a new metaphor in direct opposition to the Israeli one, but because this metaphor is so fresh and unprecedented in Palestinian art, it has been misunderstood. Israeli critics are accustomed to seeing Palestinian art as a direct political art; when they are faced with something more subtle and complex, they fail to interpret it properly.

THE PRICKLY *SABRA*

In Israeli culture, the name "*sabra*" was given to the first Israeli generation, the Palestinian-born children of Jewish immigrants. They "toughened up"—or *ikhshowshanou*, in the words of Usama Bin Munqidh, a famous knight and

nephew of Saladin, as he describes in his memoirs the Crusaders who lived for
a long period of time in Palestine and became like the native inhabitants of the
country. The Jewish *sabra* were able to grasp the thorny fruit of the prickly pear
cactus and peel it with their bare hands, just like the Palestinian peasants. At
first this was a literary metaphor, transferred to the plastic arts as an image of a
ripe cactus fruit with thorns pointing outward. The symbol emphasized a duality
between the sweet, soft interior and cruel, thorny exterior.

Equally important, the metaphor of the *sabra* reflected the spirit of the Jewish
ghetto in Europe as much as the reality of Jewish settlement in Palestine. In a
manner of speaking, the cactus fruit has the form of the ghetto, which also maintains a sweet interior (through nationalism, solidarity, mutual support) while
bristling in thorny watchfulness against a hostile exterior. The first Jewish settlements in Palestine were also a type of a ghetto, their thorns pointing outwards,
but all sweetness on the inside.

This aspect is crucial because to ignore the echoes of the ghetto in the
Israeli cactus metaphor is to miss the differences between it and the Palestinian metaphor created by Abu Shaqra. For Abu Shaqra, the Israeli metaphor is an
oppressive one. Its barbs were aimed at him, as an Arab villager. Accordingly,
Abu Shaqra constructed his metaphor in direct opposition. The comment cited
by Ginton suggests another dualism, the flower and the thorn, in the face of the
Israeli dualism, sweetness and barbs. While the Israeli metaphor glorifies the
prickle, Abu Shaqra is most concerned with the blossom. In his eyes, the thorn is
a negative element, not defensive ("the thorny death") and the golden flower of
his cactus is rising against this death. Thus, Abu Shaqra undermines and tries to
overcome the Israeli metaphor. There is no splendid inside and violent outside.
His dualism is that of life in the flower versus death in the thorn.

Because of that emphasis, Abu Shaqra seems concerned in his paintings with
eliminating or transforming the cactus thorns into something softer. Many of the
fruits depicted in his work are void of thorns; if they appear at all, the barbs are
withered, not tense and aggressive. These are gentle thorns that can be taken in
hand with complete ease, or transformed and rendered into something else.

In one of the paintings, the prickly pear appears to lend its thorns as rays of
light to the lamp appearing above it (Asim Abu Shaqra,Tel Aviv Museum of Art catalog,
1994:42). In another work, a sun is setting to the right of the painting, while on
the left the cactus flower receives the last rays of the disappearing light (catalog,
1994:34). Here, too, the rays of the setting sun substitute for thorns.

In another portrait taken from Abu Shaqra's sketchbook (catalog, 1994:73), the
thorns of the cactus pear drop off, transformed into small, beautiful crosses on
a background resembling a blue carpet. In some other paintings, we find transparent thorns, more closely resembling soft, silky threads than barbs of cruelty.
The portrait "Cactus Pear" 1989 featured in the catalog of the Khalil Sakakini
Cultural Center for Abu Shaqra's 1999 Ramallah exhibition, depicts thorns scattered
over the background and merged into the threads of a Persian carpet.

In short, a closer look at Abu Shaqra's prickly pear cacti raises doubts that
the artist wanted us to interpret his paintings in light of the conventional meaning of *sabra* found in Israeli literature, which emphasizes the *sabra* thorns or the

contradiction between interior and exterior. Moreover, on the whole, Abu Shaqra appears to resent prickles. Among the artist's early sketches, we find a drawing of a genie armed with weapons ordering a barefoot man to walk on planks of thorny cactus fruits. In the sketch, the cactus has no flowers. The representation here is obvious: it is an Israeli soldier and a Palestinian man. The soldier, as he appears in this sketch, is precisely the tough Israeli *sabra*. He is rough and cruel, and his prickly pear cactus thorns bristle in others' faces and prick their feet. This sketch is especially important for understanding the origins of Abu Shaqra's metaphor. It provides a reasonable explanation for the "disarming" of Abu Shaqra's cacti barbs.

Cactus, 1988
Asim Abu-Shaqra (oil on paper, 120 × 80 cm, collection Israel Musuem, Jerusalem)

The sketch also might help us in understanding the "thorny death" in Abu Shaqra's famous quote. He is the outsider in the Israeli metaphor, and the thorns of this metaphor are directed at him. As a Palestinian, he and other villagers suffered a great deal from the experience of "sweetness on the inside" and the "thorny, hostile exterior." Sweet democracy was meant solely for the Jewish interior and oppressive military rule was directed at his village. Hence, he seeks to eliminate or to soften the cactus prickles, focusing instead on its flowers in an alternative dualism of interior versus exterior, soft versus cruel, and esoteric versus exoteric.

Soldier and Cactus, by Asim Abu-Shaqra (exhibition catalog Khalil Sakakini, Cultural Center, Ramallah, 1999)

PATIENCE AND STRENGTH REBORN

It is not strange that the Palestinian cactus metaphor was produced by an artist from the Palestinian minority, which remained on the land, and not by an artist from the West Bank or Gaza or the Palestinian diaspora. The cactus' rich metaphor is the legitimate son of the 1948 *Nakba* (Disaster) caused by the establishment of Israel on Palestine's soil. This minority watched as the prickly pear cacti flowered in the 500 emptied Palestinian villages, their golden blossoms like candles set out to light the return of the departed exiles. In every deserted or destroyed Palestinian village, the cacti—once defensive barriers against cattle or intruders—continued to bloom, a reminder of the past. The metaphor was there, lying in wait, to be plucked by an artist. Fortunately, Abu Shaqra was present to paint it for us. He picked the blossom-candle and set it in a flowerpot on the window.

"'Asim potted cacti in a sunless zone, where the major source of light is obscured, as in a partial eclipse," observed Palestinian artist and critic Kamal Boullata (2001:120). This is the light of daybreak and nightfall. In this sunless zone, Abu Shaqra's cactus flowers illuminate the night, at the same time Palestinians in the diaspora were lighting lanterns in their tents. The cactus appears as a lighthouse, or night watchman holding his torch, recalling the kerosene lamp of Gazan painter Ismael Shammout.

But in Abu Shaqra's work, the overt symbol was veiled and fraught with meaning. "Asim Abu Shaqra succeeded in altering the course of Palestinian art and raising it from the status of nostalgic-political art to that of a universal art ciphering political codes in deeper levels," observed Tali Tamir (1994:17,94). This was his main achievement, but it was also the source of his work's critical misinterpretation. It was as if the critics could not accept that a metaphor of such depth could be produced by a Palestinian brush. It was as if the thorn had struck again.

The roots of the connection between the prickly pear cactus (or *sabr* in Arabic) with patience and endurance (also *sabr*, written with the same root) in Abu Shaqra's work lies in allying "verbal heritage with visual language," as Boullata observes (Boullata, 2001). The words are connected in their implied endurance of injury, bitterness, and weariness, accompanied by the hope that circumstances will change. Most probably, the Hebrew word *sabra* derives from the Palestinian word for cactus.

The notion of linking patience and endurance to the genus cacti is a rich concept in classical Arab culture. We recall the saying of the great eighth century Gazan, Imam al-Shafie, which is frequently written in calligraphy and hung in homes:

I will be following, patient, until patience itself is unable to bear my patience / And I'll keep doing that until God allows for my concern / I am patient until patience knows that I am able to stand a thing much bitter than bitter sabr itself.

"*Sabr*" in this verse refers to a bitter aloe with medicinal uses, but its Arabic name has been applied to the cactus family as a whole.

As compared with its meanings in the Palestinian environment in Israel, the cactus metaphor was altered slightly in the West Bank and Gaza. A new generation fighting the Israeli occupation emphasized one element of the metaphor: the ability of the cactus to endure adversity. The silent patience found in the village of Um al-Fahim was transformed into defiant steadfastness (*sumud*) in Nablus and Ramallah. Thus the cactus metaphor adapted to its environment to become a national symbol.

In this light, appropriation of the prickly pear cactus as a solely Jewish symbol stirred bitterness among Palestinian intellectuals. Critic Anton Shammas writes: "And since the Palestinian cactus...has become instead a common nickname for those born in Eretz Yisra'el and raised in it, and nothing more—Someone had to transfer the cactus to the pot. Someone had to shake us and tell us that it's over and done with; that now there is no return, neither to the map nor to the land— just to be placed on the windowsill..." (Shammas, 1998: preface)

One can sense the anger in these words over the theft of a symbol and the forceful transformation of what was once Palestinian property into something obviously foreign. But what Shammas has missed, in my opinion, is that Abu Shaqra did not place the prickly pear cactus on the windowsill as a sign of absence and shelved memory, but as a lantern of hope. Abu Shaqra managed to construct a fresh, rich metaphor in opposition to the Israeli one. On the one hand, he managed to restore the stolen symbol of the *sabr* cactus. On the other hand, he inverted the Israeli meanings of this appropriated symbol. The Jewish cactus metaphor emerged from a foreign European background with its roots in the Warsaw ghetto. Jewish settlements in Palestine were a replica of this ghetto where the toughened *sabras* spread their hostile thorns to the Arab villagers, while turning their sweetness inward to their fellow Jews. Abu Shaqra's disarming of the *sabra's* thorns and "lighting" of its pale blooms is a subtle and even playful act of defiance.

I leave you with the thought that this political struggle over land has managed to transform the Palestinian cactus into an architectural object—a ghetto for Israelis and a lighthouse for Palestinians. Neither is this strange, since the journey traced here between ideology, symbol, and shape is the very path traced by the architectural dimensions of the Israeli-Palestinian conflict. This dimension is manifested in plain view for any visitor to see—between the Palestinian villages and the Israeli settlements overlooking them, and between the Old City of Jerusalem and the settlements that encircle it.

Selected Bibliography

Kamal Boullata, preface to "Asim Abu Shaqra," in *Tel Aviv Museum of Art Catalog* (1994).

Kamal Boullata, "Asim Abu Shaqra: The Artist's Eye and the Cactus Tree," *Journal of Palestine Studies* 30 (4) (2001).

Ellin Ginton, "The Asim Abu Shaqra Passion," in Asim Abu Shaqra, *Tel Aviv Museum of Art Catalog* (1994).

Anton Shammas, "The Impossible Reconciliation between Abu Shaqra's Cactus and Avi's Dogs," *Um al-Fahim Show Catalog* (1998).

Tali Tamir, "The Shadow of Foreignness: On the Paintings of Asim Abu-Shakra?," in Asim Abu Shaqra, *Tel Aviv Museum of Art Catalog* (1994).

PRESENT AND ABSENT

HISTORICAL INVENTION, IDEOLOGY, AND THE POLITICS
OF PLACE IN CONTEMPORARY JERUSALEM

Thomas Abowd

Jerusalem is a place where memory, colonizing power, and historical invention have interacted in myriad ways through successive waves of foreign domination. As the primary site of contest and confrontation between Palestinians and Israelis since 1948, Jerusalem has become an urban center where an intense conflict between competing national imaginations rages. The politics of monuments in Jerusalem is part and parcel of the construction of history and has served a vital role in producing the past in a contested land.

Not only do such sites of national remembrance project a particular notion of what has come before, monuments—like historical archives—are also very much about the future. But what is curious about the Israeli ideological landscape, is not simply that such places have been inscribed on and scattered across an occupied Palestine, but how these places have so often served both as sites of remembrance and, simultaneously, as locales of loss.

In this article I focus on one particular Palestinian home, owned by the Palestinian Baramki family of Jerusalem and BirZeit. I examine how this structure straddles different eras in the city's history and different, deeply politicized spaces. I will also look at how the once-familial space has served multiple functions convenient to Israeli colonial power since its seizure in 1948.

Instances of stolen Palestinian properties transformed into Israeli national sites are not uncommon. Many of these places have, over several decades, been remade and dedicated to the memory of Israeli achievement, sacrifice, or longing. Arab properties—particularly homes—have proven critical in the Zionist "memory mill." As the Israeli state took over thousands of Arab homes throughout Jerusalem in 1948, the city was reconfigured discursively no less than physically. In Jerusalem, as elsewhere, the space of the Arab home has been integral to the vast efforts to both settle and silence Palestine. Over the years therefore, the city has not simply been a contested physical place but also a highly prized idea. As such, it has been brought into being through the discourses that describe it; through an articulation, for instance, of certain narratives of Israeli independence (komimeyot), defense (gonen), and redemption (guela).

These three terms are, incidentally, the names the Israeli state has given to three former Arab neighborhoods in today's West Jerusalem, cleansed of their Palestinian population in 1948. Today, the homes of Palestinian exiles have been filled with Israeli Jewish citizens of the state. Israel, as I will argue, has only been able to "overwrite" the history of Palestinian existence in Jerusalem and change

the meaning of specific locales because it was first able to make the Arab population disappear. Epistemic violence has followed in the wake of the violence of
large-scale displacement.

THE PRODUCTION AND DESTRUCTION OF THE PAST

Palestinian homes have, since 1948, been appropriated and transformed into
Israeli sites of all kinds: kindergartens, centers for psychoanalysis, clubs for new
Jewish arrivals (*olim*) in the country, Holocaust memorials, restaurants, and
even shelters for animals. These transformations have been, in each instance,
a metonym for the larger processes of colonial appropriation in the city. In a few
cases, these houses have served a strict ideological function, underscoring the
productive nature of representational power.

The truth of the past, the "real story," cannot as Trouillot (1995) cogently
asserts, simply be retrieved whole and unsullied as if pulled from history's "file
cabinet." Memory is mediated through a host of present-day issues, political
concerns, and prejudices, and is thus often highly contested and fluid. Epistemological issues and concerns about such sources are indeed real. But history is
also not completely "up for grabs," "undecidable," or simply an effect of dominant
epistemologies. Though the memories of both national communities must be
examined in a critical way, their limitations do not necessarily discount that
which those affected by traumatic events have to say about such experiences.

THE BARAMKI HOUSE

A home owned by the Palestinian Baramki family has served varied functions for
the Israeli state since it was taken from its owners in the spring of 1948. I wish to
examine what its fate (and that of the family who once lived there) might tell us
about the politics of history construction and the way memorials to Israeli military
power involve as much an active forgetting as they entail a steadfast remembering.

The structure was built in 1934 in the neighborhood of Saad Said. During the
first Arab-Israeli War in 1948, this neighborhood and the homes and buildings
that comprised it were split between the Jordanian-held east and Israeli-held
west sides of the city by a "no-man's-land" of barbed wire and fences that
fractured the city for the next 19 years. The Baramkis were one of thousands of
families in Jerusalem who fled familial spaces during the violent spring of 1948
for what they believed were temporary havens.

Andoni Baramki, a young Palestinian architect of renown, designed the home.
Like the many other structures in the Jerusalem area that were also his creation,
this one featured a distinctive, hybrid use of Corinthian columns and Arab-style
arches and verandas. Baramki experimented with the use of red and white
stones, which he often utilized in the same arch or façade, and which would
become one of his architectural trademarks. His work still dots Palestine's landscape of loss, particularly in the former Arab neighborhoods of West Jerusalem,
such as Baqa and the German Colony, which are today populated by Israeli Jews.

The Baramki house, as it happened, came to rest precisely on the edge of the
emerging frontier between the Israeli and Jordanian-ruled segments of the city
during the years the city was physically divided between "east" and "west" (spatial

designations that had never meant anything before the city was partitioned in 1948). This arbitrarily defined boundary, drawn in a perfunctory manner across a formally undivided landscape by Israeli and Jordanian generals, actually ran along the outer edge of this Baramki property.

Mammoth, well-fortified, and strategically positioned, the Baramki's imposing three-story, stone structure was commandeered by the sentinels of the budding Jewish state only weeks after its Arab occupants had fled. In the days after the border was established, the Israeli military transformed the house into an army post. Weapons were placed behind the home's thick limestone walls and aimed across a mixture of mines and barbed wire that separated Israeli forces from those of the Jordanians only meters away. The doors were reinforced and its front entrance sealed. The structure's exquisite arched windows were filled in with concrete and made into turrets so that only a thin aperture, narrow enough to accommodate a gun and the gaze of a marksman, remained. The interior was cleared for the hous-ing of troops. The "state of emergency" along the city's dividing line and the hits absorbed by the home-turned-fortress eventuated in the gradual wearing down of the structure's exterior.

Travelers wait in line to enter Israeli-controlled Jerusalem through Mandelbaum Gate, just next to the Baramki fam-ily home. (Source: G. Baramki)

With very few exceptions, neither Jew nor Arab was permitted to cross over to the other side of the city, an arrangement that held from May 1948 until June 1967. Though the division of Jerusalem prevented Israeli Jews from visiting the Old City and the Wailing Wall, sealing the border also ensured that the Arab homes on Jerusalem's west side (from which tens of thousands of refugees had fled) could not be contested because the families were deemed "absentees" by Israeli law.[1]

In the wake of the flight of the refugees, the Israeli Army reconfigured the Baramki home discursively no less than physically. Emptied of its Arab occupants, the

The run-down splendour of the Baramki home, 1967. (Source: G. Baramki)

home took on new meanings and began to be known by those on the Israeli side of the border as the "Tourjeman Army Post."[2] Its military significance was bound up with the Mandelbaum Gate complex, which existed just north of the property and was the sole crossing point between the east and west sides of the city. However, though tourists, pilgrims, and other foreigners were permitted to cross here, Jerusalem's residents—Palestinians and Israelis—were precluded from entering the other side.

MEMORIES OF WAITING

Exile is a condition shared by many Palestinian Jerusalemites. But there is some-thing fairly distinct about the Baramki case. Unlike nearly all other Palestinian families made exiles and refugees in 1948, the Baramkis had the dubious privilege of being able to see their home on the Israeli-held side of the "no man's land" during the years of the "divided city" (1948-1967). Risking sniper fire, family members would occasionally visit places on the east side's borderlands and peer across the frontier at their lost property.

Much mystery existed among Palestinian exiles concerning Jerusalem's division and their return to their homes. Over the years, questions of *when* they would return gradually became questions of *if*. Would the wall of separation ever be brought down? Would they ever be able to return? The dividing line was something one could see from numerous vantage points and the tens of thousands of Palestinian exiles resident in East Jerusalem regarded it as a continual reminder of their condition of displacement.

JUNE, 1967: MAKING THE LAND "WHOLE"

The years of the "divided city" were to end suddenly and dramatically. During six days in June 1967, Israeli forces conquered Jordanian-held East Jerusalem in lightning fashion. Within a few weeks of taking the east side (and after some internal Israeli debate), the division of concrete and barbed wire which had for 19 years separated the two sides was brought down by the victors. The city, declared Israeli officialdom, had now been "reunified" and "liberated."

Once the streets of East Jerusalem had been quelled and the physical partition was removed, thousands of Arabs and Jews raced across to the other side in curiosity. Thousands of Palestinian refugees who had waited nearly two decades to return made their way back to their former neighborhoods and homes. Hundreds of thousands of Israeli Jews streamed to the Western Wall and the Jewish Quarter of the Old City within the first few days of what Israeli officials referred to as the city's "liberation."

The Israeli conquest of the east side had seemingly opened up possibilities for Palestinian exiles to reclaim properties taken from them in 1948. Many refugees relate that initially there existed a pervasive belief among the displaced that they would finally be able to repossess their homes after 19 years of exile. They had not, after all, repudiated their claims to these properties. United Nations resolutions called for their right to return, and the Palistinian's had kept the keys and deeds from the pre-1948 period that signified ownership. But the reality of reclaiming their property was rather more complex. Palestinian Jerusalemites would, ironically, remain exiles within the newly reconfigured Israeli municipality—refugees within their own city.

The Baramkis, too, crossed over the old frontier with their keys and deeds. They made the short walk through the former no-man's-land they had once peered across. They were, family members relate, forbidden access to their home by military authorities still stationed there. Legal attempts were made to reclaim their property, but the Israeli state refused to hand over the badly-damaged home to the Baramkis, claiming alternately that it was still required for purposes of Israeli "security"; that it was in need of repair and thus a hazard; and finally, that ownership of the property had shifted since the Israeli grid of legality had been imposed on Jerusalem. If Palestinians like the Baramkis stood any chance of retrieving property, the onus was placed on them to prove (to Israeli officials, in Israeli courts) that they were wrongly classified as "absentees."[3]

RE-CONFIGURING JERUSALEM: THE DISCURSIVE CONSTRUCTION OF A REGIME OF POWER

Following the 1967 War, the city's physical dimensions began to undergo significant alterations as well—discursive no less than physical. Only weeks after seizing East Jerusalem, Israeli law was extended to this segment of the city and the occupied populations were subject to a host of new rules and prohibitions. The 60,000 "Arab inhabitants," as Israel referred to them, who came under Israeli rule at the moment of conquest, were transformed almost overnight from citizens of the Jordanian monarchy into "permanent residents" within the enlarged Israeli municipality.

The physical division that had fractured Jerusalem was now gone. But the elimination of that form of forced separation between Arab and Jew gave way to emerging practices of drawing and policing other kinds of frontiers within a physically unified urban space. These acts included extending Israeli segregationist legislation over the whole of the Israeli-ruled city.

In addition to the vast reordering of spaces in Jerusalem, a parallel ideological effort, a policy of knowledge construction, seemed equally at work in the "reunified" urban center. Its raw material was so often not that which was new, but places and sites that existed decades before the Israeli state was established. As the borderlands were swept away and military emplacements were dismantled, one such post was kept intact along the line of the previous divide: the Baramki House, known by then as the "Tourjeman Post."

What precisely such a memorial was meant to convey symbolically for succeeding generations of Israelis—"for posterity"—was not clearly articulated at the time. But it was now certainly evident that two mutually exclusive visions of this structure and its past converged at the same locale, one foregrounded and the other silenced. The Baramki property was no longer seen simply as a home—or even as a home at all. Weathered by war, stripped of elements and traces that would indicate this was once a familial space (including the removal of the family who owned it), the structure's role as a military garrison had begun to assume a "taken for granted" quality. As the son of the home's architect related in the late 1990s: "You know, this question of being defined "absent" or "absentee" by the Israeli Government is unbelievable. Imagine, my father at the time [1967], a 70-year-old person going to the Israelis and telling them "here I am now and I want my property" and them telling him that, no, you are an "absentee." And he said "How am I absent? I am present!" He could not understand how he was absent and present at the same time" (Baramki, 1997)! The Israeli Government never did permit the owner to step foot in his house again, and the elder Baramki died an exile in 1972.

DOMINATION ON DISPLAY: "THE TOURJEMAN POST MUSEUM"

The encounter between the Baramkis and the Israeli state is emblematic of the multiple ways in which Palestinians are simultaneously "present" and "absent" in Jerusalem. The Israeli law defining Palestinian exiles as "absentees" underscores the legal marginality Arabs inhabit in the Jerusalem of Israel's imagination. But this marginality also points to the ways in which certain understandings of the city are remembered and recognized, while others are simply "absented."

Members of the Baramki family were "permitted" to cross the former divide to West Jerusalem in 1967. But they were allowed access to their home only in the early 1980s. The circumstances of their return were as odd as they were painful for the owners. As with hundreds of other Palestinian homes, the Israeli Custodian for Absentee Property had turned the house over to the Israeli government for "public purposes," long before the actual Arab owners were able to return to their property. In the early 1980s, the home underwent another transformation. Without notice, knowledge, or the permission of the owners, the Israeli Municipality stealthily reconstituted the dilapidated, former "Tourjeman Post" into what became known as the "Tourjeman Post *Museum*." This site, the Israelis declared, would now serve as a monument meant to memorialize the "reunification of Jerusalem." The structure's interior and exterior were designed in ways that recall what life was like in the city during the 19 years it was fractured between east and west sides. Museum brochures and the plaque on the front door refer to the structure as "Dedicated to the Theme: Jerusalem—A Divided City Reunited."

The Baramki home presently housing the Israeli "Museum on the Seam" (photo: editorial team, 2003)

The home's crumbling exterior was left in its damaged state—"for posterity"—while a donation from a German family enabled the Israeli municipality to reconfigure the interior. In the literature that the city produces for external consumption, it is never mentioned that the structure was in fact the home of a Palestinian family.

NAMING THE FACT

Guns, mortars, and other weapons used during the 1948 and 1967 wars were exhibited, a sort of display of "purity of arms." These were the weapons, visitors were told, of a reluctant army, one that fought a war against enemies who refused peace and compromise. Remnants of the home's history as military emplacement were plentiful, including the reinforced turrets placed within the former arched windows. But all of these renovations were in a sense two times removed from the original home's interior. Though constructed in the space of a gutted house, the Israeli state officially established this representational site within a former army emplacement. Its appearance reflects and memorializes that past. A transhistorical notion of Jewish identity and entitlement to Jerusalem is deployed powerfully at this locale. The claim to ownership of the city has, by this account, a biblical basis stretching back 3000 years. No other people's notion of connection to Jerusalem, maintain Israeli officials and much of its citizenry, has nearly the same legitimacy.

The museum (transformed again in 2002 into the new "Israeli Museum on the Seam") allows the visitor to use the actual physical structure of this home-turned-outpost-turned-museum to better understand the Israeli narrative of longing and redemption. At the end of the exhibit, all are invited to gaze out from the narrow slits in the filled-in windows of the top floor, apertures that once served as turrets and from which, during the dark days of the divided city, Israeli soldiers peered out bravely at an enemy, apparently as "faceless" today as then.

By reenacting the practice of gazing across a once-divided landscape, visitors are meant to understand the significance of this site for the security of the budding state. Today, however, those who gaze out from behind these former turrets (themselves former windows), see a seamless whole, a unity achieved through Israeli victory. One "sees" just what the beleaguered Israeli nation is said to have once seen, and which it now memorializes. From this vantage point, Israeli collective memory and the myths that inform it ossify into "historical truth."

CONCLUSION

The Baramki House and the museums that have been constructed within its space exist simultaneously. The utilization of the home historically embodies two different but interconnected modes of domination. Serving first as an instrument of military conquest, it policed the borders imposed on the city by the dominant national community. Today, the once-familial space is deployed in the service of epistemic violence, used to produce and police certain ideological and historical boundaries. The monuments to Israeli military victory do more than simply deny the home's familial past. They elaborate a dominant series of myths that "evaporate" the history of the Palestinian people more generally, while providing legitimacy for Israel's occupation of the entirety of the city.

A Palestinian family home of former architectural splendor, designed by a now-deceased master of Palestinian architecture, serves today as a component of a different architecture of knowledge production, a scaffolding of truth-making, a foundation for epistemic violence. It continues to rest on the frontier of competing historical imaginations and memories, anchored in place, but simultanously on the moving edge of Israeli colonial power.

1   The 1949 Rhodes Agreement between Israel and the Arab states called for bringing the wall down. Israel refused to implement this, or to adhere to the UN resolutions calling for the return of Palestinians displaced in 1948.

2   Tourjeman was a Jewish man who lived and owned property in the neighborhood before 1948.

3   Meeting this Israeli standard for ownership was accomplished by Palestinian exiles in only a handful of known cases. To be successful, the Arab owner had to demonstrate sufficiently in Israeli courts that when he or she fled West Jerusalem in 1948, he or she had not gone to a country "at war with Israel." Such read the provisions of Israel's "Absentee Property Law" (originally the "Enemies Property Law"). I came upon only one family, the Daouds, who owned a property in Talbieh, who were able to reclaim it after a several-year battle and after they proved that they had fled in 1948 to El Salvador, not a state "at war" with Israel at the time of her birth.

Selected Bibliography

Gabriel Baramki, interview with the author, July 27, 1997.

Michel-Rolph Trouillot, *Silencing the Past: Power and the Production of History* (Boston. Beacon Press, 1995).

THE ISRAELI "PLACE" IN EAST JERUSALEM

Alona Nitzan-Shiftan

How does new territorial control become inexorable fact?[1] How does such fact, based on confiscated land, turn into "a national home"? How does this "home" embody the Israeli "place" even as Palestinians contest possession of the genius loci? This essay examines the legitimizing professional discourse of the Israeli settler society. It focuses on the architectural practices that empowered the first Israeli-born generation—the generation entrusted with Israelizing Jerusalem after the 1967 War. In its efforts to localize Israeli architecture, this generation faced a double-bind. On the one hand, it criticized the high, developmental modernism that had hitherto shaped the state; on the other, it sought a situated modern architecture inspired by the Palestinian vernacular (and thus belonging to the Arab "other"). This impasse provokes intriguing questions in postcolonial theory about how colonizers appropriate the culture of the colonized in order to define an authentic national culture of their own.

1. David Anatol Brutzkos, Upper Lifta, 1960s reprinted from *Israel Builds* (Israel: Ministry of Housing, 1965)

THE SEARCH FOR PLACE

Architect Moshe Safdie expressed this predicament succinctly when describing the approach to Jerusalem (later, he would play an instrumental role in its Israelization).

"[T]he road ascends to a crest overlooking the western hills of the city. Down the slopes, a deserted Arab village hugs the hill, small and larger cubes made of the stone of the mountain: domes, arches, vaults, the mosque's tower, shaded passages, all in harmony with the landscape and the sun" (1973:216).

Safdie contrasted this idealized picture of a vacant Lifta [Fig. 1] with the achievements of Israel's Ministry of Housing. "At the summit of the hill," he pointed to David Anatol Brutzkus's housing in Upper Lifta (Romema), "is a series of long four-story apartment structures built in the late fifties. They do violence to the mountain. They are foreign, as if imported from some rainy, cool European suburb" [Fig. 2] (1973:216).

What Safdie articulated was a generational refusal to espouse the high modernism of Israel's nation-

2. Lifta (reprinted from David Kroyanker, Jerusalem — Conflicts over the City's Physical and Visual Form (Jerusalem: Zmora-Bitan, 1988))

building years. Although already established by Israel's first architectural history text as a pervasive Israeli architectural tradition (Hashimshoni, 1963:199-229), it fell short of addressing the aspirations of a younger generation whose members sought a "new" tradition authenticated by deeper roots. In order to conceive of an identifiable "Israeli architecture," they turned instead to the tradition of the "place" as found in villages like Lifta, and later in the townscape of the Old City.

Eventually, the search for the Israeli "place" evolving from the late 1950s undergirded the conceptual framework most prevalent in post-1967 Jerusalem. Instead of uniform modernist housing blocks, architects experimented with building clusters, hierarchical circulation, and broken masses. The minister of housing explained the state's building methods in East Jerusalem, prescribing low-rise, stone-clad building. "Also incorporated," he added, "are elements of Oriental building such as arches, domes, etc." These "building types are especially adjusted to the topographic condition and the slopes of the sites" (Haaretz, February 2, 1968), [Fig. 3-4]. The clear reference to the hitherto rejected Palestinian built culture intrigues: how could such built tradition be accepted as a model for the post-1967 architecture of Israeli Jerusalem?

A PROFESSION SEEKING THE ARCHITECTURE OF "THE PLACE"

In the late 1950s, the first Israeli-born generation of architects (the *sabra*) saw in the decade-old Israeli state a homeland fundamentally different from that envisioned by the founders of Labor Zionism. For the 20 years prior, Zionist architects in Mandate Palestine had embraced a modern architecture promising a new beginning—a departure from both bourgeois and "Oriental" life, which they believed had contaminated Jewish life in the Diaspora. *Sabra* architects claimed that the resulting "international architecture" left no room for "culture," which is what makes human beings into a people and society (Karmi, 1998). It may have created proper housing solutions, they posited, but disregarded the Zionist promise of a "national home" [Fig. 5].

3. Ram Karmi, Gilo Housing, cluster 6, 1970s, Axonometric view

4. General view, both courtesy of Ram Karmi

By 1967, this generational group (particularly its leading professional circle)[2] was gaining the professional power required to lead the building of the so-called "united Jerusalem." Their wish to create a sense of belonging between people, community, and place was inspired by similar efforts overseas. In order to find an unmediated form of "the spatial expression of human conduct" architects (such as members of the European Team 10) emphasized vernacular architecture where life, rather than creative professionals, dictated building forms (Bakema, 1968:24). The result was a shift to Man, with structuralist anthropology providing the theoretical

5. *Israel Builds*, 1958, cover image

ground. Modern architecture, they argued, should cease searching for "what is different in our time" and seek instead "what is always essentially the same" (Van Eyck, 1980:276). The prototypical inhabitant of these environments was a generic Man, whose specific history, culture and politics were ignored in favor of universal truths concerning the instincts of human habitation.

In the US, architecture critics such as Bernard Rudofsky drew upon the Bible and Darwin—the mythological and scientific origins of Western culture—to divest the Modern Movement of its scientific command. Rudofsky's Architecture Without Architects emerged as a major sourcebook for architects worldwide. It held vernacular architecture as "nearly immutable, indeed, unimprovable, since it serves its purpose to perfection" (1964: caption for illustration 1). Similarly enthusiastic were Heideggerian phenomenologists who found in vernacular architecture ontological definitions of "place," of being "at home" in the world. The group Atbat-Afrique in Morocco, whose work combined Arab vernacular with modern architecture, wrote in their statement of principle that "[i]t is impossible for each man to construct his house to himself. It is for the architect to make it possible for the man to make his house a home" (1968:74).

This was precisely the type of "social ethics" that brought the architectural thinking of the European Team 10 and the concurrent trend of New Brutalism to bear so effectively on the architectural discourse of sabra architects. New immigrants, the sabra generation posited, could not and should not comply with an imposed modernist immigrants' idea—a utopia built of ordered white boxes. The sabra generation wanted instead to "transform the Diaspora Jew into a man growing out of the land" (Karmi, 1998), a man whose identity develops as a result of his organic ties to territory rather than adherence to foreign ideas. Only architecture "of the place" could identify Israelis with the territory to which they wanted to belong and possess.

Maqom (Hebrew for "place") refers to the encounter between man and the place where he is.[3] The notion of maqom is fundamental to sabra art and architectural discourse because, as Gurevitz and Aran have argued, Israeli Jews had not succeeded in resolving the ambiguities of their place: the tension between the text and the territory. The "Land of Israel," according to this argument, has always been an abstract homeland, an idea, an aspiration the Zionist movement inherited from the Jewish religion. At the same time, it was an actual place, laden with history, authenticity, and sacredness. If the founding generation was devoted to "the idea," the sabra generation embraced the territory itself. The schism between the two persistently disturbed the process of inhabiting the land. Because the idea, according to Gurevitz and Aran, preceded the place, these efforts were conscious, determined, and ideologically charged—fundamentally different from the effortless "nativeness" gained by birthright and direct ancestry (Gurevitz & Aran, 1991).

This "nativeness" was readily found for sabra architects among Palestinians, whose vernacular architecture, inseparable from the place in which it was created, evinced the rootedness they sought. When Yoram Segal published in the inaugural issue of the journal Tvai a cover story on "The Traditional House in the Arab Villages of the Galilee" (1966:19-22), he emphasized this unmediated connectedness. The *fellah's* (farmer or farm laborer's) ties to his house, which was built and maintained with the *fellah's* own hands, entailed "a relationship of belonging, of identification, and of strong emotional attachment" (1966:20) [Fig. 6]. It was precisely this sort of relationship that the *sabra* architects were seeking. In his recent book, Ram Karmi suggested that "emulating the local gave birth to an empathy toward the lifestyle of the Arabs and the Bedouins, and led to a renewed examination of different identity options" (2001:12). Like Arabic words in Hebrew slang, Palestinian attire on Israeli youth, or Arabic cooking in Israeli

cuisine, the evocation of "the Arab village" in Israeli architectural culture was a protest through which sabras aimed to identify them-selves as natives.

In 1965, for example, Ram Karmi explained in reference to his award-winning Brutalist megastructure in Beer Sheva that he intended to *translate* rather than mimic regional values and molds. He claimed to have found in the

6. Yoram Segal, "The Arab Village in the Galilee," reprint-ed from *Tvai* 1, (Spring 1966)

Arab village typologies that accord with the desert—the cohesiveness of the built material; the shaded, airy bazaar; the dissolution of the traditional facade into a volumetric play in which the sun sculpts ever-changing shadows [Fig 7]. But, Karmi emphasized, this typology was not yet part of the Israeli culture, which "we" Israelis were so laboriously trying to define.

THE AMBIVALENCE OF COLONIAL CULTURAL PRODUCTION

Socialist Zionism had emerged in Europe, and its sweeping Judaization of Mandate Palestine intentionally ignored, even destroyed, indig-enous architecture. Additionally, its modus oper-andi was top down, originating with the Zionist pioneers who saw themselves salvagers of a ter-ritorial tabula rasa.

The *sabra* approach, on the other hand, turned to the local vernacular to build from the bottom up. But this approach was no less con-

7. Ram Karmi, "An Arab Vil-lage," reprinted from Karmi, *On the Architecture of Shadows*

fusing. A genuine national architecture required an unmediated expression of place, but the search for authentic expression yielded perplexing results: native architecture was mostly Arab. The Israeli search within the local Palestinian vernacular for an alternative to Zionist modernism was contradictory; at exactly the time when Arab culture was most denigrated by the Israelis, its local con-nectedness was deeply admired. In the wake of this contradiction, notions of colonizer/colonized or Western/Oriental gave way to the ambivalence of colonial subjectivity.

Scholarly analysis of this condition has emerged in critical response to binary oppositions (see, for example, Edward Said's seminal *Orientalism*).[4] It habitually focused on the inability of the colonized to retrieve an "authentic" identity free from colonial subjugation (Ferguson, 1990; Bhabha, 1994). My interest here is a similar yet inverted ambivalence, studied by looking at the dominant professional discourse rather then at the "natives" as the object of ethnography (Clifford & Marcus, 1986; Stocking, 1983). Accordingly, I focus on the colonizer's dependency on the identity of the colonized in its search to define an "authentic" national identity with visceral ties to the place.[5] The Israeli desire to achieve the Arab's native-ness—which was seen as the ultimate expression of locality—sheds new light on a subject seldom frequented by postcolonial scholarship.

The national and professional sentiments of the *sabra*, I argue, underlined the Israeli architectural praxis that shaped the urban landscape of post-1967 Israeli Jerusalem. These sentiments were developed as an internal Israeli debate between post-World War II architectural culture—its modernist crisis echoed in the *sabra* generational revolt against Zionist modernism—and a national identity built on a formative deficiency which provoked a desire for and fantasy about the Arab native's intimate relationship with the place, its landscape, stone and light. After the 1967 War, when the object of this fantasy, the Arab habitat, became tangible, this seemingly internal-professional debate was caught in the urgent unfolding politics of the Israeli-Palestinian conflict.

SEIZING LOCALITY IN JERUSALEM

Immediately after the 1967 War and Israel's resulting seizure of East Jerusalem from Jordan, Israeli planners were suddenly asked to transform the land by constructing "facts on the ground" that fostered the perception of a city unified under Israeli control. But neither Israel's modernist planners nor the politicians who guided them knew how to express this powerful symbolism architecturally.[6] The minister of housing simply advised his planners to give the unified city an "oriental character" (Haaretz, February 2, 1968). The prefabricated concrete arches soon to be superimposed on the completed plans for the first Israeli East Jerusa-lem neighborhood illustrated the confusion.[7] This situation changed dramatically, however, when the younger generation of architects entered the planning scene. During the 1970s, these architects crafted a coherent architectural vision echoing the readily-accessible Palestinian vernacular—a vision which bewildered Elinoar Barzaki, former Jerusalem region head in the Ministry of Housing: "A culture looks for the symbols of its heroic periods and assimilates them in its local archi-tecture, as Italy, for example, relates to the Roman Empire. In Jerusalem, how-ever, the post 1967 architecture of power absorbed the symbols of the conquered rather than those of the conqueror" (Barzaki, 1998).[8]

Barzaki's was a forceful observation. Presumably, the symbols of the conqueror were the ordered cubical housing blocks of pre-1967 West Jerusalem and the modernist institutional buildings that crowned its government precinct. The symbols of the conquered, on the other hand, were found in the Oriental stone architecture of the Old City's picturesque skyline and environment.

But why would architects "Israelize" a contested city using the architectural forms that were identified with another nation? Moreover, once the Palestinian vernacular was espoused, what mechanisms enabled Israelis to separate it from the culture that produced it, in order to reshape it into an Israeli architecture?

Following, I study three strategies for Israelizing the Arab vernacular: to read it as biblical architecture, as an uncontaminated primitive origin of architecture, or simply as typically Mediterranean.

"BIBLICIZING" THE LANDSCAPE

After the 1967 conquest of Jerusalem's Old City, Israeli Jews rejoiced in a metaphorical return home, especially to the Western Wall and the Jewish Quarter as the symbolic centers of the Jewish nation. The consequent heightened focus on the Jewish Quarter's vernacular architecture prompted a national strategy that weakened the authority of Arab architectural forms over Israeli architecture. When Segal wrote on the Arab village in the Galilee in 1966, or when *sabra* architects simultaneously launched a preservationist approach to the reconstruction of Old Jaffa, they expressed admiration for the human values and identity embeddedness of what they saw as generic examples of the region's vernacular architecture. But when architects of this same generation began reconstructing the Jewish Quarter immediately after the 1967 War, this vernacular was no longer generic; it was seen by Israelis as an embodiment of Jewish history. The tangible presence of the Quarter and the Wall substantiated for Israelis their national confidence and anchored their claim over a disputed land. "The Wailing Wall," said architect Karmi, "symbolizes the place in which I feel direct roots to King David. I can greet him shalom" (Cassuto, 1975:95). Archeological research authenticated this biblical connectedness. While architects were seeking locality on the ground, archeologists sought Jewish history underneath its surface. The two were combined in the reconstructed Jewish Quarter, where archeological finds were embedded, as Nadia Abu El-Haj (2001) recently demonstrated, in the physical fabric and spatial experience of the Quarter.

If the architecture of the Quarter testified to the continuity of Jewish habitation from biblical times, the new sense of locale could be applied to the surrounding Palestinian villages, whose architecture was perceived as biblical, and whose inhabitants served as custodians. The central feature of the national landscape scheme was a green belt around the Old City—previously a British colonial dream— which would visually arrest the Old City of Jerusalem. The Arab village of Silwan was included in this park because "its character gives us a good picture of how the landscapes and villages of Biblical times looked" (Dvir, 1969:24). Educational publications by the army[9] compared this village to the archeologically-informed open-air model of Herod's Jerusalem (Zaharoni, 1990). A 1:50 scale monumental reconstruction of the so-called Second Temple Period— a major tourist attraction in and of itself—confirmed the sameness of Silwan and Herod's Jerusalem, again emphasizing the continuity of ancient building traditions [Fig. 8].[10]

8. Prof. Avi-Yona, Model of Jerusalem During the Second Temple, from "Safdie in Jerusalem," RIBA lecture

Safdie immigrated during his youth to Canada, where he became internationally known for his groundbreaking Montreal Habitat (Expo 1967). Endorsed by the Israeli administration upon his return home in December 1967, he designed the (unrealized) prefabricated Jerusalem Habitat [Fig. 9]. Safdie called the site of his project, next to the Arab village Malha, by its Hebrew/biblical name, Manchat. "Here," he stated, "was the prototype, the ancient village, with which any modern development would have to co-exist" (Safdie, 1989:27). Furthering an architecture derived from perceived primary instincts of habitation, Safdie advanced a Darwinian logic that directly evoked acquaintance Bernard Rudofsky's seminal *Architecture Without Architects*.

In Safdie's eyes, villages of 1948 Palestinian refugees, built with "fairly limited resources" and devoid of historical depth, were "awesome environments" (Safdie, 1979). They proved for him that habitation was a product of "the compassionate search for the way people live their private and public life" (Safdie, 1989:29). Safdie explained his incorporation of advanced methods of construction into this "original" vernacular model of habitation as "an expression of life today, but that would be as if it had always been there" (1979:216).[11] By creating a "fugue with two instruments," one vernacular and one technological, Safdie's Jerusalem Habitat could fulfill the Zionist dream of fusing the ancient with the modern (1979:216). In Jerusalem the "origin" was

9. Moshe Safdie, a comparison between an Arab village (Manchat) and Safdie's hometown of Jerusalem . From Moshe Safdie, Jerusalem: The Future of the Past (Boston: Houghton Mifflin Company, 1989), unpaged

biblical, the modern progressive, and the combination of both serving to validate a people's national life from a remote past to an unforeseen future.

MEDITERRANEANISM

Inspiration from indigenous architecture similarly provided rationale for the ordinary housing which defined Jerusalem's post-1967 vernacular. In 1977, Ram Karmi published the essay, "Human Values in Urban Architecture." Essentially a manifesto, the essay prescribed a list of Mediterranean architectural forms as guidelines for future planning. They were intended to help architects to resolve the most pressing question: that of belonging. How could architects establish an architectural language that encouraged personal expression but also defined a vernacular for the national community? Karmi's reference for such active rerooting was the revival of the ancient Hebrew language, which addressed biblical origin, kinship, and blood. Israeli architecture, Karmi contended, should connect those attributes to the land.

In other contexts, scholars have termed the strategy Karmi chose for this task "Mediterraneanism." He invoked the timeless patterns of Mediterranean architecture as guidelines for a hierarchical ordering of the built environment, from the house to the cluster, quarter, square, street, bazaar, and, finally, to the entire system. Then he compiled a manual of Mediterranean "structural elements" comprised of the alphabet of the Hebrew built landscape: the wall, the gate, the balcony and porch, the stairs and threshold, the street and alleyway.

Karmi's shift in focus from the Arab village to Mediterranean architectural precedent was engrained in a larger architectural culture.[12] Politically, the idea of Israeli participation in a larger Mediterranean culture divested Palestinian architecture of its authority over the *genius loci*, because it was subsumed into a larger geocultural realm (Shavit, 1998). This relocation relieved the Israeli architect of the disturbing conflict between admiration of native architecture and disregard for the larger Palestinian culture that produced it. The association with Europe's cradle of civilization was pacifying and flexible, and could accommodate Israel's early modernism.

THE ETHICS OF ISRAELI PLACE-MAKING

When Karmi moved from the private sector to the heart of bureaucracy, he made an ideological claim on behalf of the architectural profession for the right to shape the physical image of the state. He demanded a complete overhaul of national decision-making. Only then, he argued, "...the creation of a "National Home" and of "place" will achieve its legitimacy as an element that represents and reflects, in physical terms, the cultural aspirations of the community and builds the community in its own land, and expresses its physical and spiritual right to, and ownership over, that land" (1977:44).This was a momentous statement. Karmi identified the maqom sought by his *sabra* generation with the national home Zionism promised. *Maqom*, Karmi argued, was a prerequisite for the national home because only an identifiable Israeli place would provide the moral foundation for ownership over the land. Seeking "the physical and spiritual right to...that land" was, for Karmi, at the very heart of Israeli place-making. "Creating a 'place,'" he reminded us, "is a qualitative, symbolic and emotional process," a task that architects—rather than planners or bureaucrats—should undertake. Architecture, as distinguished from "building," "can reflect and represent the cultural aspiration of a community,"—that is, it can create a symbolic place, not only a conglomeration of dwelling units. Making the built landscape into a maqom was a way to nationalize the territory—a way to Israelize Jerusalem.

POSTSCRIPT

The cachet gained by "architecture of the place" established members of the sabra generational group as Israel's architectural elite, a prominence, which remains to this day. In Jerusalem, however, their architectural program met its colonial counterpart. Their effort to crack the Palestinian code for local habitation on unequal political ground diverted the focus of post-World War II architectural culture away from its humanistic path: it deprived other people of the symbolic ownership of their built heritage.

Recently, architectural critics have begun enumerating the political pitfalls of this localist architectural tradition, in an effort to divest it of its leading role in Israeli architectural practice. According to this view "concern with localness after 1967 reflects the release of dark tendencies that are fundamentalist in essence"

(Zandberg, 2000:42). This criticism separates between the social role of this architecture and its aesthetics, and is a strategic move characterizing the production of criticism during the politically charged Palestinian Intifadas. But does this criticism mark the end of "the tradition of the place," of the search for locality? Not necessarily. The "true" locality is now being attributed to Israel's modernism—the "Bauhaus Style" of the 1930s and 1940s, as well as the state's "gray" modernism of the 1950s. Recent exhibitions and monographs clearly indicate that the tradition of the modern, uncontaminated by the regional conflict or the Orient, is taking command. This recovery has a global appeal. One proponent of "gray modernism" explains that, for a younger generation who "knows that the 1950s are now in style" and whose "memory works in megabytes," this tradition offers escape: "plain and simple—they are sick of fabricating 'local' architecture and getting bogged in the provincial swamp." (Zandberg, 2000:43) The global element in this happy reversal prompts the local to redefine a modernist tradition for an Israeliness in crisis.

1   This essay is based on the article "Seizing Locality in Jerusalem," (Nitzan-Shiftan, 2004). It is part of a manuscript in progress tentatively titled: Designing Politics: Architecture and the Making of "United Jerusalem," which is based on my doctoral dissertation at MIT. I would like to thank Mark Jarzombek, Stanford Anderson, Sibel Bozdogan, Uri Ram, Nasser Rabbat, Caroline Elam, and Kevin Chua for their helpful comments and insights. Special thanks go to the architects who guided me through the culture of their generation, particularly to Dan Etan, Ram Karmi, Avraham Vachman, and Yaakov Yaar.

2   The core of a professional architectural circle that was active during the 1960s consisted of Dan Etan, Yizhak Yashar, Ram Karmi, Ora and Ya'akov Ya'ar, Avraham Yaski, and Amnon Alexandroni. Moshe Zarhi and Yaakov Rechter and invited guests frequently participated.

3   This definition has appeared particularly in connection to Dani Karavan's work.

4   In the wake of Said's Orientalism (1978), many studies have demonstrated the Western/Oriental dichotomy in different contexts and locales. For the Israeli context, see Ella Shohat (1989), Gil Eyal (1993), and Yigal Zalmona and Tamar Manor-Fridman (1998). Particularly important in this context is Dan Rabinowitz (1998).

5   For an ethnographic account of this professional generation see Nitzan-Shiftan (2002, 2004).

6   For the architectural debates underlying the Israelization of Jerusalem see Nitzan-Shiftan (2005).

7   The Ministry of Housing was eager to build quickly on land confiscated immediately after the war in order to create a continuous built-up area between north Jerusalem and Mount Scopus. It therefore recruited completed housing plans that Itzhak Perlstein had designed for another site and added to them prefabricated arches in order to provide Eshkol Heights with the appropriate Oriental look.

8   Barzaki studied in Europe during the 1968 events and was recruited by Ram Karmi upon her return to join his team at the Ministry of Housing. Later she became the city engineer of Jerusalem and (at the time of this interview) headed the architectural school at Tel Aviv University.

9   The publication of the Israel Defense Force, Bamahane, preached love of the country. It published stories and detachable photographic centerpieces from "the Land of Israel." These posters became major visual stimuli in the military physical environment; in Israel military service is obligatory for most.

10   The open air model was reconstructed and largely imagined in the absence of accurate archeological data by the archeologist Professor Avi Yona. A recent appraisal in a publication dedicated to "knowing the country" is that by Gavriel Barkai and Eli Shiler (2001).

11   For Safdie's design for the Western Wall Plaza, see Nitzan-Shiftan, (2002), p. 216.

12   Karmi's search for homeness in Mediterranean architecture had roots in his education at the Architectural Association in London during the early 1950s.

Selected Bibliography

Abtat Afrique, "Statement of Principle," in Alison Margaret Smithson and Team 10, Team 10 Primer (Cambridge, MA: MIT Press, 1968).

Nadia Abu El-Haj, Facts on the Ground: Archaeological Practice and Territorial Self-Fashioning in Israeli Society (Chicago: University of Chicago Press, 2001).

Gideon Aran and Zali Gurevitz, "Al HaMaqom (Israeli Anthropology)," Alpayi 4 (1991).

Homi K. Bhabha, *The Location of Culture* (London; New York: Routledge, 1994).

Jacob Bakema, in Alison Margaret Smithson and Team 10, *Team 10 Primer* (Cambridge, MA: MIT Press, 1968).

Reyner Banham, *The New Brutalism: Ethic or Aesthetic* (New York: Reinhold Pub. Corp., 1966).

Gavriel Barkai and Eli Shiler, "A Tour in Second Temple Jerusalem in the Holyland Hotel Model," *A Periodical for the Study of the Land of Israel* (Jerusalem: Ariel, 2001).

Elinoar Barzaki, interview with the author (August 20, 1998).

David Cassuto, *The Western Wall: A Collection of Essays Concerning the Design of the Western Wall Plaza and Its Surrounding* (Jerusalem: The Jerusalem Post Press, 1975).

James Clifford and George E. Marcus, *Writing Culture: The Poetics and Politics of Ethnography* (Berkeley: University of California Press, 1986).

Arieh Dvir, "Overall Plan for the Jerusalem National Park," in *Proceedings of the First Meeting, June 30 - July 4, 1969* (Jerusalem: The Jerusalem Committee, 1969).

Gil Eyal, "On the Arab Village," *Teoria ve Bikoret* 3 (1993).

Russell Ferguson, *Out There: Marginalization and Contemporary Culture, Documentary Sources in Contemporary Art* 4 (New York, N.Y.; Cambridge, Mass: MIT Press, 1990).

Mia Fuller, *Moderns Abroad: Architecture, Cities, and Italian Imperialism* (New York and London: Routledge, forthcoming 2007).

Haaretz, "Planning and Building Methods in East Jerusalem" (February 2, 1968).

Aviah Hashimshoni, "Architecture," in *Art of Israel*, ed. Benjamin Tamuz, (Massada: Israel, 1963). (The English version is "Architecture," in *Art of Israel*, eds. Benjamin Tamuz, Max Wykes-Joyce and Yona Fischer (Philadelphia: Chilton Book Co., 1967)

Ram Karmi, interview with the author, Tel Aviv (July 7, 1998).

Ram Karmi, *Lyric Architecture* (Israel: Ministry of Defense, 2001).

Ram Karmi, "Human Values in Urban Architecture," in *Israel Builds 1977*, eds. Amiram Harlap and Hari Frank (Tel Aviv: Ministry of Housing, 1977).

Alfred Mansfeld and Anna Teut, *Al Mansfeld: An Architect in Israel* (Berlin: Ernst & Sohn, 1999).

Brian McLaren, "Mediterraneita and Modernita: Architecture and Culture during the Period of Italian Colonization of North Africa (Libya), (Ph.D. dissertation, MIT,- 2001).

Alona Nitzan-Shiftan, "Israelizing Jerusalem: The Encounter between Architectural and National Ideologies 1967-1977," (Ph.D. dissertation, MIT, 2002).

Alona Nitzan-Shiftan, "Seizing Locality in Jerusalem," in *The End of Tradition*, ed. N. Al Sayaad, (New York and London: Routledge, 2004).

Alona Nitzan-Shiftan, "Capital City or Spiritual Center? The Politics of Architecture in Post-'67 Jerusalem," *Cities* 22 (3) (2005).

Dan Rabinowitz, *Anthropology and the Palestinians* (Ra'ananah: HaMerkaz LeHeker HaHevrah HaArvit, 1998).

Bernard Rudofsky, *Architecture without Architects: An Introduction to Nonpedigreed Architecture* (New York: Museum of Modern Art, 1964).

Moshe Safdie, *Beyond Habitat* (Montreal: Tundra Books, Collins Publishers, 1973).

Moshe Safdie, *Safdie in Jerusalem*, Slidcas 3 (London: Pidgeon Audio Visual, 1979) (extracted from a talk given to the Royal Institute of Architects)

Moshe Safdie, *Jerusalem: The Future of the Past* (Boston: Houghton Mifflin, 1989).

Edward W. Said, *Orientalism* (New York: Pantheon Books, 1978).

Yoram Segal, "The Traditional House in the Arab Villages in the Galilee," *Tvai* 1 (1966).

Yaakov Shavit, "The Mediterranean World and 'Mediterraneanism': The Origins, Meaning, and Application of a Geo-Cultural Notion in Israel," *Mediterranean Historical Review* 3 (2) (1998).

Ella Shohat, *Israeli Cinema: East/West and the Politics of Representation* (Austin: University of Texas Press, 1989).

George W. Stocking, *Observers Observed: Essays on Ethnographic Fieldwork* (Madison: University of Wisconsin Press, 1983).

Aldo van Eyck quoted in Kenneth Frampton, *Modern Architecture: A Critical History* (London: Thames and Hudson, 1980).

Irit Zaharoni, *Israel, Roots & Routes: A Nation Living in Its Landscape* (Tel Aviv: MOD Publishing House, 1990) (This edition is based on the Hebrew book: Derech Eretz: nofe artzenu.)

Yigal Zalmona and Tamar Manor-Fridman, *Kadima: The East in Israeli Art* (Jerusalem: Israel Museum, 1998).

Esther Zandberg, "The Lost Dignity of the Shutters," *Ha'aretz Weekend Supplement* (October 27, 2000).

THE PLANNING DEADLOCK
HOUSE DEMOLITIONS IN THE PALESTINIAN
NEIGHBORHOODS OF EAST JERUSALEM

Nathan Marom

More than 500 houses were demolished in the Palestinian neighborhoods of East Jerusalem between 1987 and 2004. Every house demolished is also a family left in ruin, a family that has lost not only the roof over its head but most of its savings too, not to mention the place where its memories dwelt or where its future dreams were invested. Over 500 demolished houses means thousands of people, all residents of the city of Jerusalem, who had to pay a high price for the conduct of their city's planning system; a system which they do not understand, and which does not display much understanding of them.

In recent years, there has been a dramatic rise in the number of house demolitions carried out by the Jerusalem Municipality. Throughout the 1990s, the average number of house demolitions was 23 per year. Since 2001, there has been a sharp rise in the figures to 35 houses in 2001, 34 houses in 2002, 51 houses in 2003, and nearly 120 houses demolished in 2004. It is, of course, no coincidence that house demolitions have increased since the Al-Aqsa Intifada erupted in late 2000. The immediate and obvious reason for house demolitions is that the houses were built without permits, as required by Israeli planning laws and procedures, like most formal planning systems in the world. Indeed, many of the Palestinian residents of East Jerusalem build their houses without permits, either after trying to obtain one and failing to, or, for various reasons, without trying at all. This has lead to a phenomenon of building without permits on a massive scale. The Jerusalem Municipality, for its part, justifies house demolitions as its duty to enforce planning laws and procedures, ensure the proper and balanced development of the city, and maintain the rule of law.

Yet, house demolitions and the phenomenon of building without permits on a massive scale, must be examined in a wider context. The Jerusalem Municipality's planning policies since 1967 reveal profound problems and difficulties, both structural and contingent, which make it very difficult (if not altogether impossible) for a Palestinian resident of East Jerusalem to obtain a building permit.

Over the years, the Israeli authorities have adopted a range of planning policies that have constrained the development of Palestinian neighborhoods and led to severe housing shortages. These policies, and the problems they engender, have been addressed elsewhere.[1] My purpose is not to restate the issues, but rather to suggest that at present these policies have reached a deadlock. This planning deadlock is not an end result but a mechanism in itself, which shapes the way the Palestinian neighborhoods of East Jerusalem have developed in recent years through a cycle of "illegal" construction and retributive demolitions. There are three ways in which this planning deadlock manifests itself. The first relates to the inability of the Palestinian residents of East Jerusalem to obtain building permits. Here the deadlock operates as a "catch" in which people must decide whether to build without a permit and risk demolition or not to build at all. The second relates to the Jerusalem Municipality's constraining policies, which have led to a situation wherein most Palestinian construction takes place "outside" the system. Here the deadlock operates as a "failed policy" working against its own makers, since the "necessity" of enforcing the law "necessitates" an impracticable number of house demolitions. The third manifestation of the planning deadlock is a "trap," in which seemingly "professional" planning tools and discourses are used in bad faith in order to promote Israeli political aims at the expense of the Palestinian residents of the city. One could also see the urban policy of Jerusalem as "trapped" by the dictates of a contentious national policy.

THE PLANNING DEADLOCK AS "CATCH"

There is no doubt that planning in East Jerusalem entails extraordinary difficulties due to the unique political and juridical status of the territories that were annexed-by-occupation to the city in 1967. These difficulties have been exacerbated by a combination of planning restrictions, bureaucratic constraints, political biases, and deep socioeconomic gaps and cultural differences. For analytical purposes, these difficulties can be located along a "planning and enforcement sequence": from the preparation of urban plans and their statutory approval, to the procedures by which plans are "translated" into building permits, to the routine inspection of new construction and planning law enforcement, to the demolition of houses in cases of unlawful construction.

While this planning and enforcement sequence is a bureaucratic process that applies to the city as a whole—West and East, Jewish and Palestinian—one must consider how the individual Palestinian resident of the city fares along the way. Unlike in West Jerusalem or in the new Jewish neighborhoods of East Jerusalem, where most of the construction is publicly initiated and managed by contractors on a large scale, in the Palestinian neighborhoods of East Jerusalem most construction is individual, on privately owned lands, and usually small scale.

Thus, a Palestinian resident of East Jerusalem, wishing to build a new house or expand an old one, is likely to encounter difficulties at one or several of the stages along this sequence—beginning with the existence of a detailed plan for the area where he wishes to build, through the zoning scheme of the plan and whether it allows for residential uses, the legal status of the land in the land registry, the existence of sufficient infrastructure in and around the site intended for construction, and, finally, the high administrative fees associated with the process. Any or all of these factors could get in the way of obtaining a building permit, either in advance or retroactively, so as to sanction a building violation after the fact.

For example, a Palestinian landowner may discover that the land he intends to build upon is designated as "open landscape," where no construction is allowed. Thus, he can only build his house elsewhere, where the plan has zoned a residential area. However, because the real estate market in East Jerusalem is limited, and further restricted by traditional patterns of land ownership, the landowner will not likely find land that is both designated for residential use and for sale. And even if he does, he would not be able to buy that parcel with the money he would make selling his parcel, because the construction prohibition on his land makes its value quite low, and the scarcity of land upon which construction is permitted makes the value of the other land quite high. The landowner is left with land he cannot build on, and no compensation. At this point he must choose: forego his wish to build a house for his expanding family, or build without a permit and risk having the house demolished and his life savings squandered.

The planning and enforcement authorities, for their part, ignore these difficulties and place the responsibility and culpability for failing in this process squarely on the shoulders of the Palestinian residents of East Jerusalem. In such circumstances, house demolitions are an extreme form of blaming the system's inadequacies on its victims.

THE PLANNING DEADLOCK AS "FAILED POLICY"

From 1967 to 2001, only 3,100 building permits were issued to the Palestinian residents of East Jerusalem. At the same time, the Palestinian population has tripled, from some 70,000 in 1967 to 215,000 in 2001. It is unlikely that 3,100 building permits were sufficient for meeting the housing needs of nearly 150,000 new residents.

Notwithstanding these 3,100 building permits, an estimated 15,000-20,000 "illegal" housing units were built in Palestinian East Jerusalem in the last 35 years. This gap between what was permitted to be built and what was actually built, between formal and informal construction, makes clear that the permits issued do not meet, indeed are far from meeting, the real housing needs of Palestinian Jerusalemites.

"Illegal" construction on such a massive scale does not indicate contempt for the rule of law, as the Municipality would have it (usually adding that this contempt for Israeli law is encouraged and even promoted by the Palestinian Authority).[2] It indicates, rather, a profound failure on the part of the planning system itself that most of the construction in East Jerusalem takes place outside its procedural bounds. By failing to meet the housing needs of the Palestinian residents of East Jerusalem, or to offer solutions to the objective problems that keep them from obtaining building permits, the formal planning system actually "channels" most construction outside its sphere of control, only to try and combat it through demolitions. Needless to say, the authorities have made no effort to incorporate informal construction into existing plans.

In its effort to justify house demolitions, the Municipality emphasizes the large number of houses built in East Jerusalem without permits, while downplaying the small number of building permits issued over the years. In the decade between 1992 and 2001, the Municipality issued some 1,400 building permits in Palestinian East Jerusalem. In that same decade, it detected some 5,300 building violations[3], took judicial action against some 3,800 such violations, issued 620 demolition orders, and demolished some 240 structures.

The first ratio (1,400 permits—5,300 violations) implies that for every building permit the Municipality issues in East Jerusalem, it detects 3.8 building violations. The second ratio (1,400 permits—3,800 judicial actions) implies that for every building permit the Municipality issues in East Jerusalem, it goes to court 2.7 times against the residents of that part of the city. The third ratio (1,400 permits—620 demolition orders) implies that the Municipality issues a demolition order for every 2.3 building permits it issues. The fourth ratio (1,400 permits—240 demolitions) implies that the Municipality demolishes one house for every 5.8 building permits it issues.

There is yet another aspect to the deadlock with regard to the planning authorities. This is to do with the fact that even with the hundreds of demolition orders it has issued, the Municipality can only demolish a small fraction of "illegal" houses. Of course, the thought of demolishing 15,000-20,000 "illegal" houses (between 45%-60% of all Palestinian housing units in East Jerusalem) is unthinkable, even to the most extreme hardliners in the Municipality, at least one would hope.[4] Moreover, the Municipality carries out only about a third of the demolition orders it issues, and thus fails to "enforce the law," even to its own understanding.[5] The outcome is that, quite often, house demolitions are carried out in a sporadic, even random, manner, functioning mainly as deterrence. Those affected are usually the weakest and most disadvantaged residents, who cannot afford proper legal defense.

Thus, a picture emerges of very limited possibilities for legal construction, compared to a multitude of building violations detected, legal actions taken, and demolition orders issued and implemented. Instead of an efficient, evenhanded planning system we see a draconic, discriminatory enforcement system, where building inspectors, prosecutors, and demolition crews have replaced planners. It is a punitive planning system rather than a facilitating one—a perverted system indeed.

THE PLANNING DEADLOCK AS "TRAP"

The difficulties and failings discussed so far do not occur in a void, but rather within a highly politicized context. Urban policy in Jerusalem since 1967 has not been limited to the orderly development of the city and the well being of its residents. Rather, it has been informed by a national-ideological agenda to ensure Israel's rule over the "unified" city, and to ensure a clear Jewish demographic majority in the face of higher Palestinian birth rates.[6] This is acknowledged quite readily by all involved when it comes to the "grand scheme" of things, but denied quite fiercely when it comes to local plans (such as town building schemes) for the Palestinian neighborhoods of East Jerusalem. Thus, seemingly professional tools, and a seemingly professional discourse are frequently used in a biased and discriminating way.

One can find discrimination in almost every dimension of planning policy and procedures in East Jerusalem: unreasonable delays in the preparation of plans (followed by requirements for yet more detailed plans, without which building permits cannot be issued); distorted zoning schemes which designate large tracts of peripheral urban lands as "open landscape" or "green areas," where construction is not permitted at the expense of potential residential uses; miserly allocation of "building percentages" in plans, which means that houses can only be built sparse and low, so that Palestinian neighborhoods will retain their "rural character"; endless postponement of laying infrastructures and roads, without which orderly construction is impossible; harsh standards for proof of land ownership, as a prerequisite for obtaining building permits (in a society based on traditional forms of ownership, and in a political climate of mistrust and well-founded fears that land will be confiscated by the authorities); and overenforcement of planning laws in Palestinian neighborhoods compared to slack enforcement in Jewish neighborhoods.

Comparisons between specific plans prepared for adjacent Jewish and Palestinian neighborhoods in East Jerusalem reveal considerable differences in nearly every dimension: zoning scheme, building density, public services and public spaces, urban character, etc. By way of generalization, such comparisons demonstrate that the guiding principle in planning Jewish neighborhoods in East Jerusalem is to maximize building capacity while maintaining a high standard of living, whereas in the Palestinian neighborhoods, no such efforts exist. In other words, Jewish neighborhoods are planned to be "publicly dense and privately spacious," whereas Palestinian neighborhoods are planned to be "publicly sparse and privately dense," i.e. "rich" in open areas (where no construction is allowed) and "poor" in built floor space.[7]

Another bias can be found in the enforcement of planning laws, especially house demolitions. Between 1996 and 2001, 82% of building violations were found in the Jewish neighborhoods of Jerusalem, and only 18% in Palestinian neighborhoods. Yet, 80% of the demolition orders were issued against structures in Palestinian neighborhoods, and only 20% in Jewish neighborhoods.

Urban needs have been willingly sacrificed by the planning authorities for political considerations antithetical to any rational and professional planning practice. The demand that Palestinian residents comply with these politicized plans (under the threat of demolition), as if they were apolitical and of benefit to them, is what makes them a "trap."

URBAN POLICY "TRAPPED" BY NATIONAL POLICY

It is the biased and discriminatory use of seemingly professional tools that "traps" Palestinians into the deadlock described. But at the same time, it "traps" the policy itself into untenable political goals, which ultimately lead to its own failings. For many years, national policy has dictated almost every detail of urban planning in Jerusalem. Yet the results are quite dismal, as even those who subscribe to a vision of a "unified" and "demographically balanced" Jerusalem under Israeli rule, would have no choice but to admit.

Thus, while the Palestinian population continues to grow, urban development in East Jerusalem is stymied by the many constraints forced upon it, making the prospects of future development even grimmer. Under the current circumstances, massive "illegal" construction by Palestinians (whether interpreted as "resistance" to Israeli (mis)planning or as a "pressure valve" through which planning constraints come undone) is at once an inevitable result of the planning deadlock and an "excuse" for the system's failures. An air of fear and moral panic surround all urban issues related to East Jerusalem, and it is the city of Jerusalem and its residents—Jewish and Palestinian—who come out the big losers.

The time has come for a paradigmatic change; a change in which equitable and participatory planning will replace the biased and penalizing policy that has trapped itself, and the residents of the city, into a deadlock. If to date Jerusalem's planning policy has been dictated by a unilateral national policy, perhaps the converse is also true: positive changes in Jerusalem's urban policies could open up new possibilities for coexistence between the two national communities that share the city, but also beyond the city, for Palestinians and Jews to live in peace.

1   See, among others, Benvenisti, 1996; B'tselem, 1997; Bollens, 2000; Cheshin et al., 2000; Khamaisi and Nasrallah, 2003. For a flawed analysis sponsored by the Jerusalem Municipality, see Weiner, 2003.

2   For the Municipality's view on this, see Weiner, 2003.

3   Building violations range from an entire house being built without a permit, to adding on to an existing house without a permit.

4   In June 2005, the threat of mass demolitions was hanging in the air when the Jerusalem Municipality announced its intention to demolish 90 homes in the Palestinian neighborhood of Silwan, bordering on the Old City (Rapaport, 2005). Due to public outcry, this threat has been removed, at least temporarily. Yet it does leave the impression that the Municipality is hell-bent on breaking new demolition records.

5   The implementation of house demolitions in East Jerusalem depends on many external factors and is influenced by the general political climate. "Security" considerations also play a part: the availability of police forces to protect the demolition crews is an important factor, since each demolition is not unlike a small military operation.

6   This last aspect of the policy is euphemistically termed "demographic balance" and has informed the underlying logic of almost every plan made for the city, including the new Jerusalem City Plan 2000.

7   For a detailed comparison between adjacent Palestinian and Jewish neighborhoods, see Marom, 2004.

Selected Bibliography

Meron Benvenisti, *City of Stone: The Hidden History of Jerusalem* (Berkley, Los Angeles: University of California Press, 1996).

Btselem, *A Policy of Discrimination: Land Expropriation, Planning and Building in East Jerusalem* (Jerusalem: Btselem, 1997).

Scott Bollens, *On Narrow Ground: Urban Policy and Ethnic Conflict in Jerusalem and Belfast* (New York: State University of New York Press, 2000).

Amir Cheshin, Bill Hutman, and Avi Melamed, *Separate and Unequal: The Inside Story of Israeli Rule in East Jerusalem* (Harvard University Press, 2000).

Rassem Khamaisi and Rami Nasrallah, *The Jerusalem Urban Fabric: Demography, Infrastructure and Institutions* (Jerusalem: International Peace and Cooperation Center, 2003).

Nathan Marom, *The Planning Deadlock: Planning Policies, Land Regularization, Building Permits and House Demolitions in East Jerusalem* (Jerusalem: Bimkom—Planners for Planning Rights and Ir Shalem, 2004, in Hebrew).

Meron Rapaport, "City to Raze Homes of 1,000 Residents in East Jerusalem Neighborhood." *Haaretz*, May 31, 2005.

Justus Reid Weiner, *Illegal Construction in Jerusalem: A Variation on an Alarming Global Phenomenon* (Jerusalem: Jerusalem Center for Public Affairs, 2003).

Growth and Decay

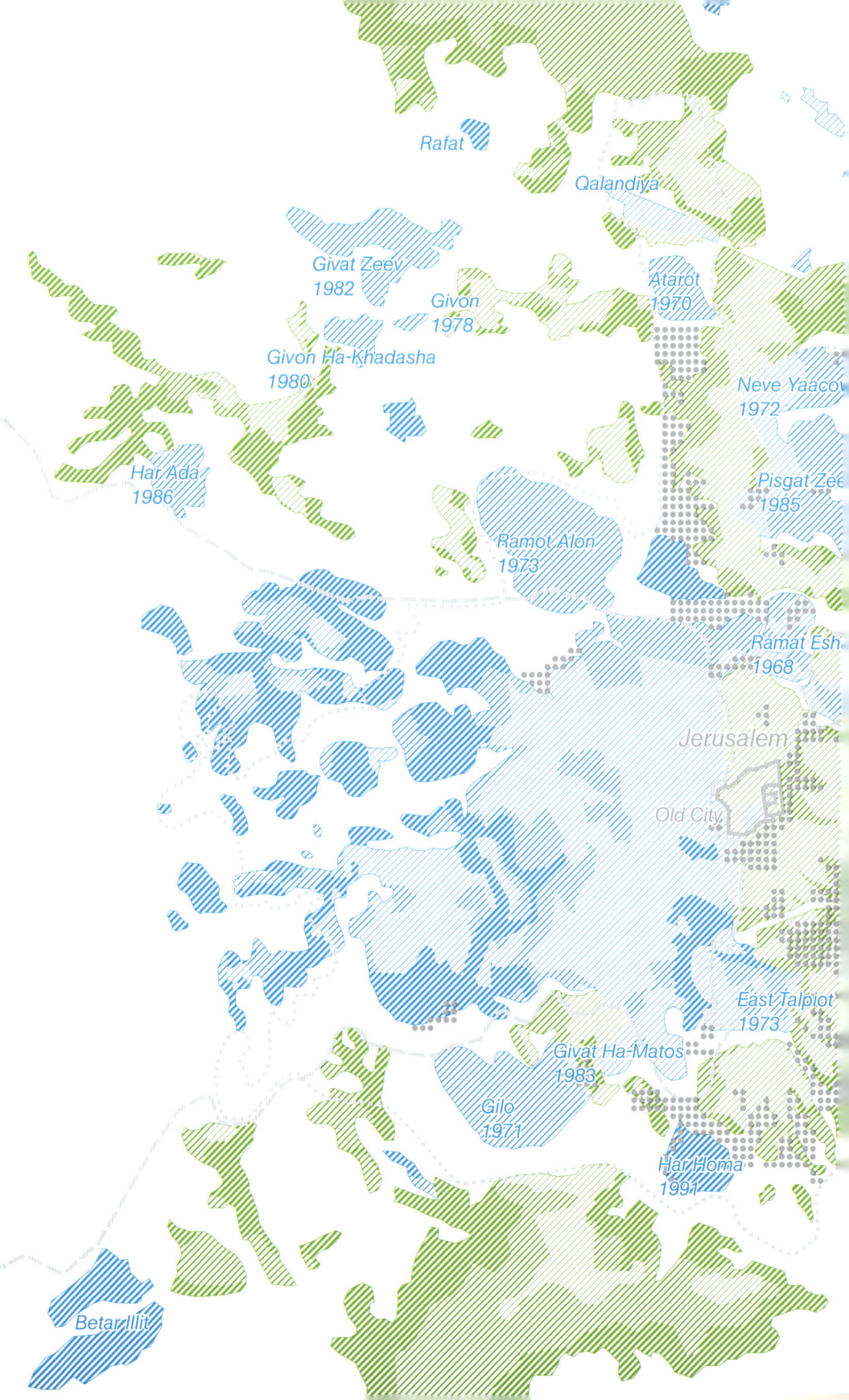

Rafat

Qalandiya

Givat Zeev
1982

Givon
1978

Atarot
1970

Givon Ha-Khadasha
1980

Neve Yaacov
1972

Har Ada
1986

Pisgat Zeev
1985

Ramot Alon
1973

Ramat Esh
1968

Jerusalem

Old City

East Talpiot
1973

Givat Ha-Matos
1983

Gilo
1971

Har Homa
1991

Betar Illit

Urban Transformation
Jerusalem (2005)

Demographic control over Jerusalem has been
one of the most contested issues and a key factor
in the city's rapid growth. A disproportionately
high portion of this growth was in East Jerusalem.
More than 180,000 Jewish Israelis (total Jewish
population: 469,000) were moved into East
Jerusalem into 90,000 new housing units. While
the Jewish population within the municipal
boundaries grew by 135% since 1967, the Palestinian population increased by 233% during
the same period, with 195,000 Palestinians living
in East Jerusalem (total Palestinian population:
237,000). Palestinian growth was mainly fuelled
by a much faster natural growth rate. Large-
scale expropriations for settlement building or
designation of "green areas" prohibited from
development led to extreme density and overcrowding among Palestinians—almost double
the housing density of Jewish Israeli areas.

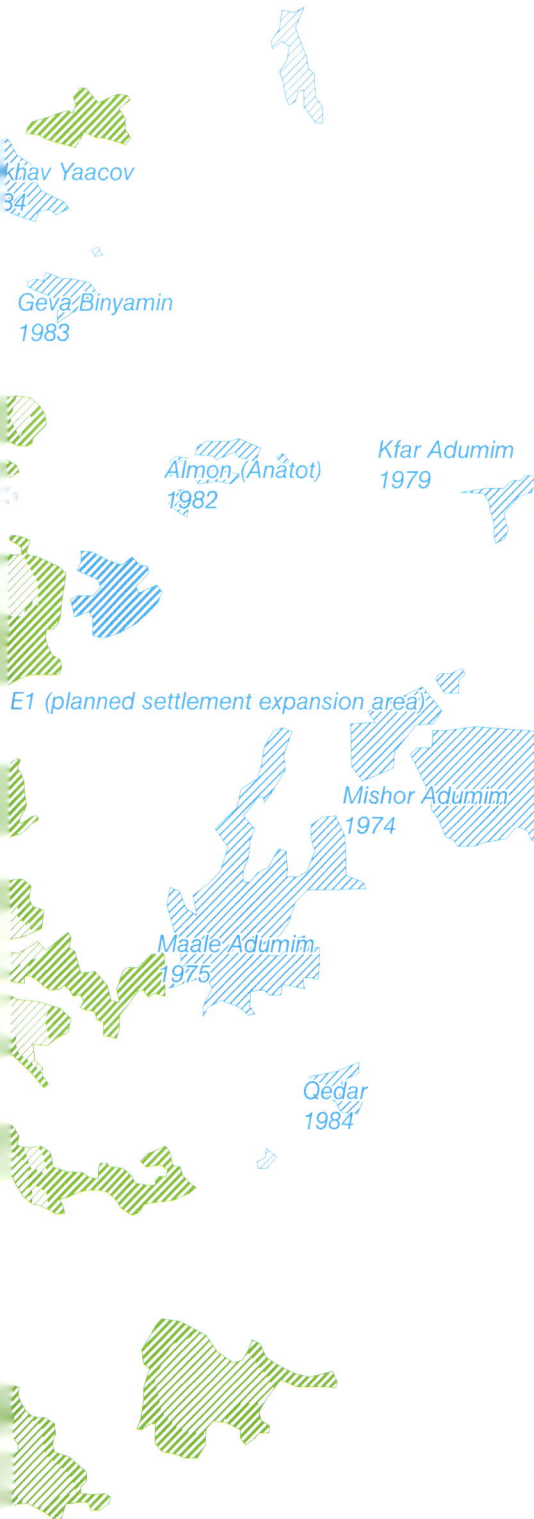

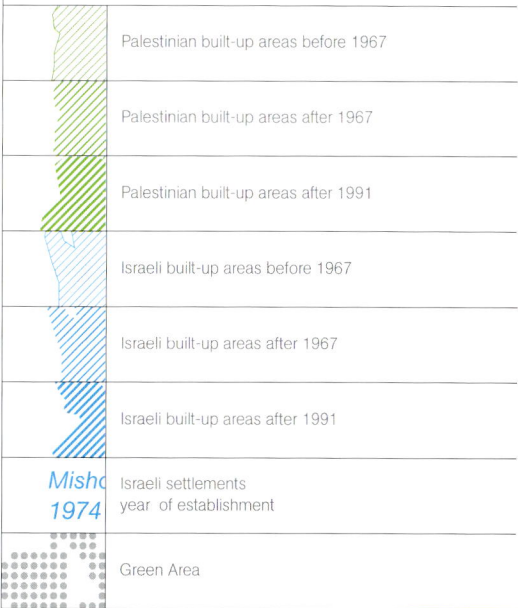

Khav Yaacov
34

Geva Binyamin
1983

Almon (Anatot)
1982

Kfar Adumim
1979

E1 (planned settlement expansion area)

Mishor Adumim
1974

Maale Adumim
1975

Qedar
1984

Palestinian built-up areas before 1967

Palestinian built-up areas after 1967

Palestinian built-up areas after 1991

Israeli built-up areas before 1967

Israeli built-up areas after 1967

Israeli built-up areas after 1991

Misho... Israeli settlements
1974   year of establishment

Green Area

0   1   2   3   4   5 kilometers

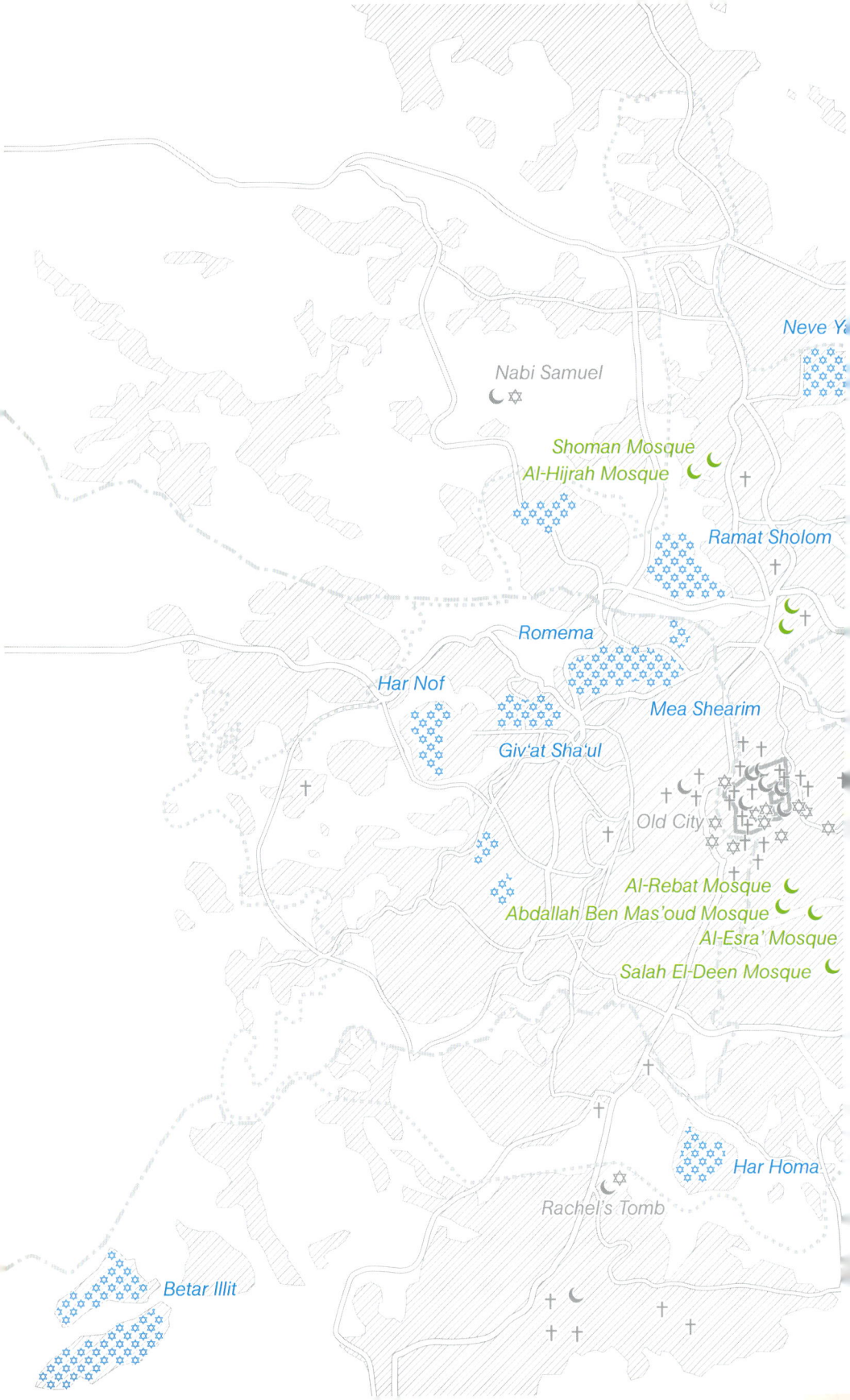

Neve Ya

Nabi Samuel ☪ ✡

Shoman Mosque ☾
Al-Hijrah Mosque ☾ ✝

Ramat Sholom ✝

☾ ✝

Romema

Har Nof

Mea Shearim

Giv'at Sha'ul

✝

Old City ✡

Al-Rebat Mosque ☾
Abdallah Ben Mas'oud Mosque ☾ ☾
Al-Esra' Mosque ☾

Salah El-Deen Mosque ☾

✝

Har Homa

☾ ✡
Rachel's Tomb

✝
Betar Illit

✝ ☾
✝ ✝ ✝

Religion
Jerusalem (2005)

The conflict has profoundly changed the social,
economic and cultural fabric in Israeli and Palestinian areas of Jerusalem, with a particularly
significant impact on secularism and liberalism.
Expanding Jewish religious neighborhoods and
the construction of new mosques or synagogues
are indicative of deep changes in the city itself.
For Palestinians, the closure of Jerusalem has
meant the migration of cultural and political
life to Ramallah. Similarly, thousands of secular
Israelis leave the city annually, mostly for the
Tel Aviv conurbation, and are replaced by the
growing and impoverished ultraorthodox Jewish
community. Jerusalem has become the poorest
of large Israeli cities, dependent on large-scale
governmental subsidies. After several years of
complete stagnation during the al-Aqsa Intifada,
Christian pilgrims begin to flood back to the city,
reving some of the badly hit tourism and hotel
industry in East and West Jerusalem.

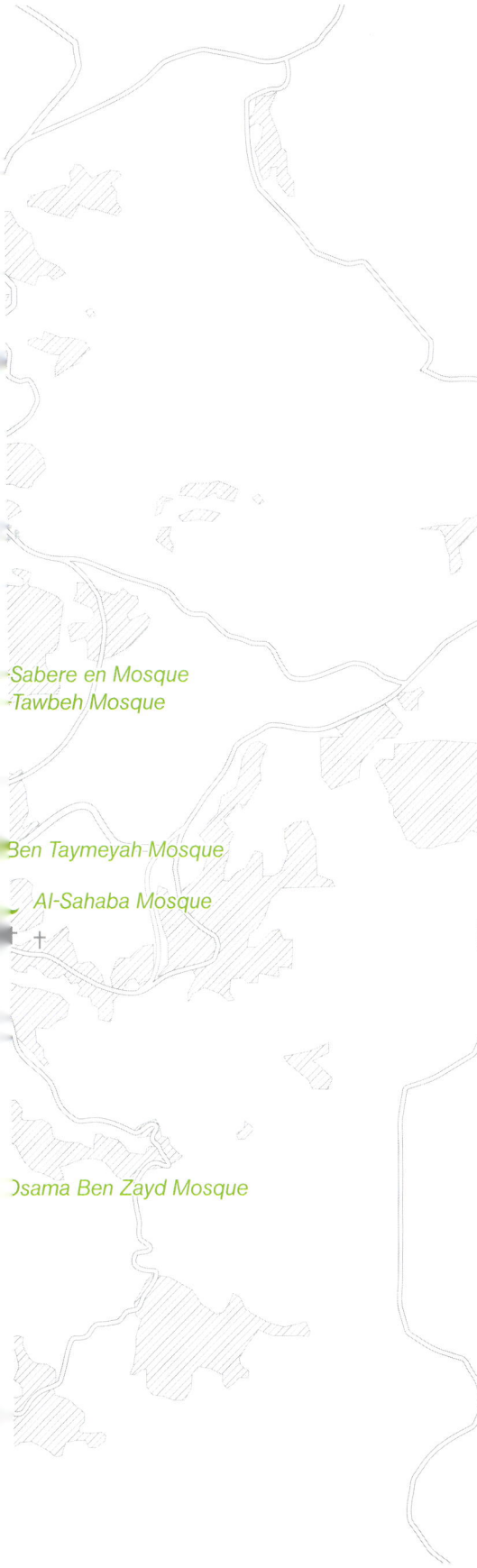

Sabere en Mosque
Tawbeh Mosque

Ben Taymeyah Mosque

Al-Sahaba Mosque

Osama Ben Zayd Mosque

	Important holy sites
chel's Tom	Contested holy sites
	Expansion of Jewish orthodox quarters since 1960
ue ra' Mosqu	New mosques since 2000

0	1	2	3	4	5 kilometers

Sur Bahir
Tsur Bah

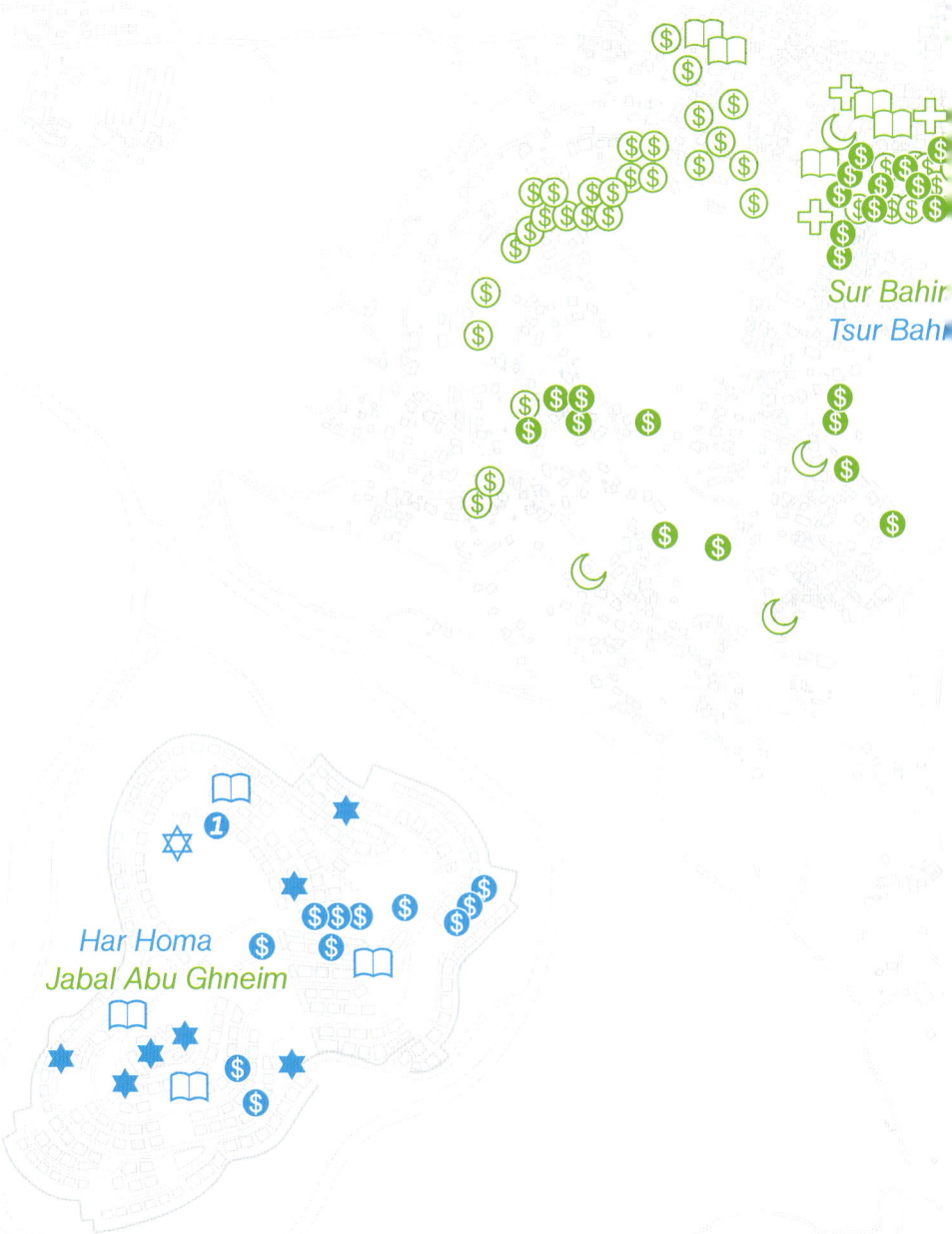

Har Homa
Jabal Abu Ghneim

Forced Urbanization and Religiosity
Sur Bahir / Har Homa (2005)

Conflict in Jerusalem is a catalyst for accelerated urbanism. While struggle over demographic and territorial control has led to the expansive Israeli settlement program, Palestinian building activities inside municipal Jerusalem are limited to existing built-up areas such as Sur Bahir, which gradually acquired urban density. With the al-Aqsa Intifada, the growing difficulty of movement across inner city checkpoints also led to an isolation of Palestinian enclaves and the decentralization of Palestinian commercial activities. While the commercial center of East Jerusalem has declined, commercial growth at the periphery has increased the functional autarky of villages like Sur Bahir. Religiosity has increased not only in the village but also in the settlement. Har Homa's initial market among the secular middle classes failed after 2000, and the settlement is now largely religious. As synagogues were not provided to meet new requirements, informal synagogues have been created in underground car parks or private housing units.

Before second Intifada	After second Intifada	
📖📖	📖	Education
$	$ $	Commerce
✚		Health care
☾		Mosques
✡	★	Synagogues

| 0 | 100 | 200 | 300 | 400 | 500 meters |

Social Structure
Sur Bahir / Har Homa (2005)

The cultural differences between Sur Bahir and Har Homa are clearly expressed in their social structures. Har Homa was planned as a speculative housing project for middle class nuclear families. Beyond shared ethnicity or religious affiliation, there are little or no social connections between apartment residents. Traditional Palestinian villages like Sur Bahir, on the other hand, incorporate social and spatial integration. Four large family clans (*hamulas*) dominate the social composition of the village, each inhabiting a specific part of the village. Land is of vital economic, cultural, and symbolic value. It is rarely sold, and rather shared between the growing extended family. In recent years, this social and spatial order has been challenged by the gradual modernization of village life . In order to maintain Jerusalem residency status, Palestinians poured back into the city, increasing the pressure on the crunched property market. Villagers had to accommodate the new concept of "strangers" (Palestinians without traditional social links to the village) living in their midst.

Distribution of family clans in Sur Bahir

	Abu Tair
	Duwayat, Dabash, Nimer, Hamad
	Al-Fawaqa, Abu Hamed, Atrash
	Bkairat, Jadallah, Ameereh, Abu Kaf, Al-Azaar, Atton, Jber
	New Palestinian immigrants to Sur Bahir
	Distribution of families in Har Homa

| 0 | 100 | 200 | 300 | 400 | 500 meters |

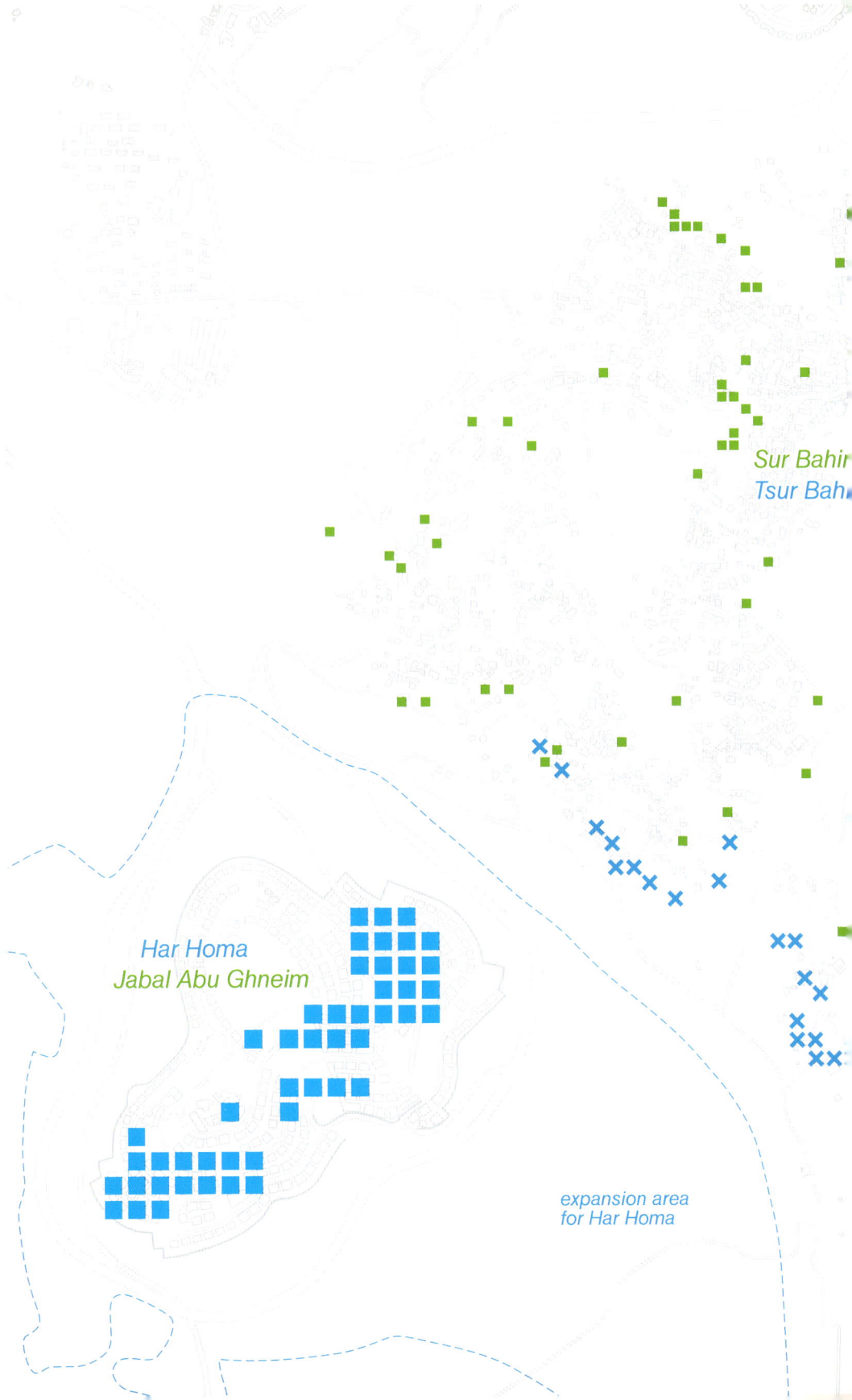

Sur Bahir
Tsur Bah

Har Homa
Jabal Abu Ghneim

expansion area
for Har Homa

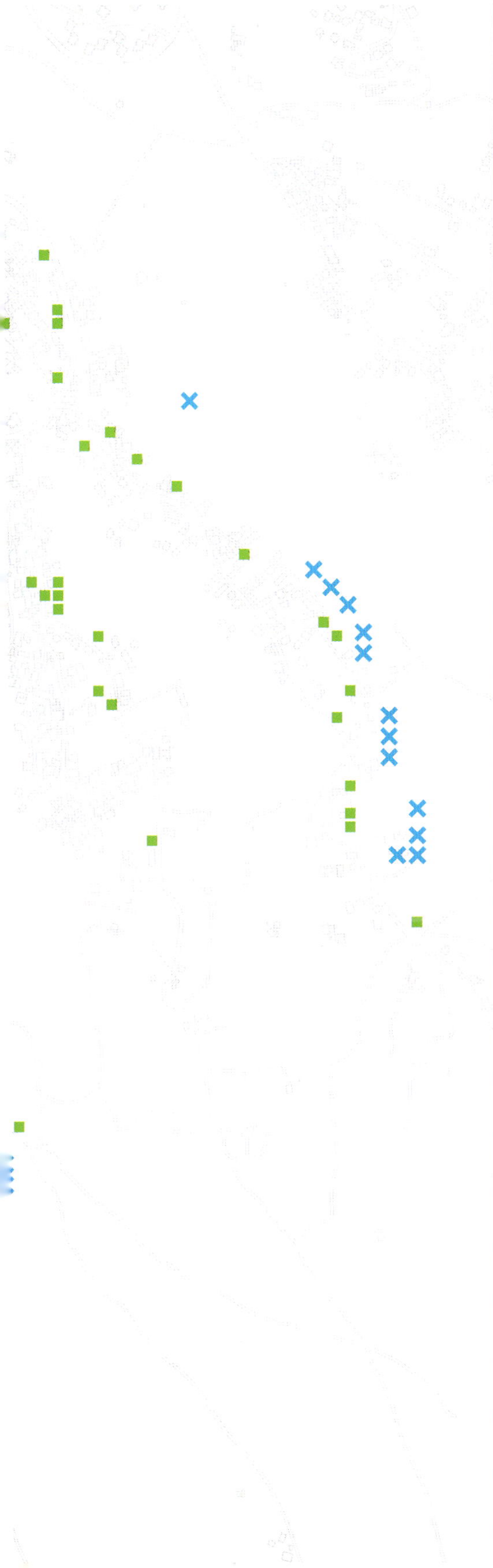

Construction and Demolition
Sur Bahir / Har Homa (2005)

Since 1967, East Jerusalem has been subjected to an accelerated urbanism of growth
and destruction—a permanent state of radical
transformation. Fuelled by the struggle for territorial and demographic control, the eastern
half of the city has experienced unprecedented
construction, paralleled by increasing levels of
destruction and planned demolition. The microcosm of Sur Baher and Har Homa exemplifies
this conflict urbanism. Har Homa already houses
10,000 inhabitants, and expansions are planned
for up to 40,000 people. In contrast, construction for Sur Bahir's growing population is limited
to upgrading and extending existing built-up
areas. While commercial development clings
to Sur Bahir's main roads, private residential
construction is widespread and decentralized,
planned and financed according to the needs
and resources of particular families. Much of
this construction is undertaken without Israeli
building permits, which are expensive and often
impossible to obtain, especially for families with
land holdings outside the imposed building
lines. Illegal structures face punitive demolition
and high fines.

Israeli building sites

Palestinian building sites

Palestinian buildings
demolished by Israeli authorities

0 | 100 | 200 | 300 | 400 | 500 meters

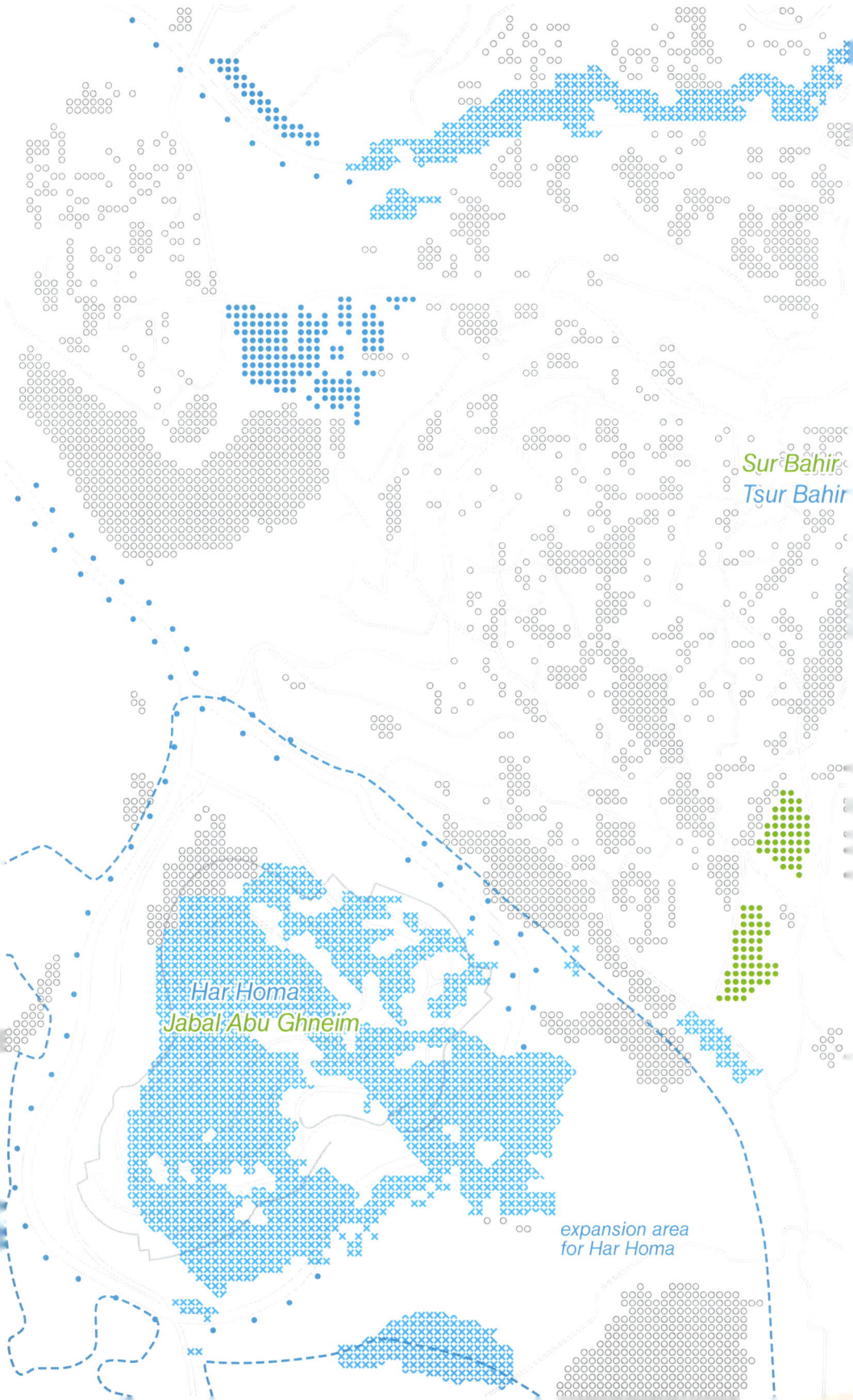

Sur Bahir
Tsur Bahir

Har Homa
Jabal Abu Ghneim

expansion area
for Har Homa

Planting and Uprooting
Sur Bahir / Har Homa (2005)

Recent transformation of the landscape around
Sur Bahir demonstrates the contest over ownership
and cultural identity in Jerusalem. After 1967,
most family land holdings around the village
were expropriated as green areas and land
reserves for future Jewish settlements, destroying
an evolved and carefully nurtured rural landscape of vital economic, cultural and symbolic
value to the villagers. Today, fragmented traces
of this old rural landscape of terraced olive and
citrus groves are juxtaposed with elements of
a newly-imposed Israeli landscape. A highly-
engineered landscape of parks and planted
roadside greenery surrounds Har Homa and
Kibbutz Ramat Rachel. This new landscape
remains decorative: a product of Israeli landscape
planners and artists trying to introduce romantic
landscape features as appropriate backdrops to
European-style suburban living.

Mature trees
(10 to 2000 years)

New Palestinian olive trees
for agricultural use

New Israeli olive trees
for decorative use

Palestinian trees
uprooted by Israeli authorities

0 | 100 | 200 | 300 | 400 | 500 meters

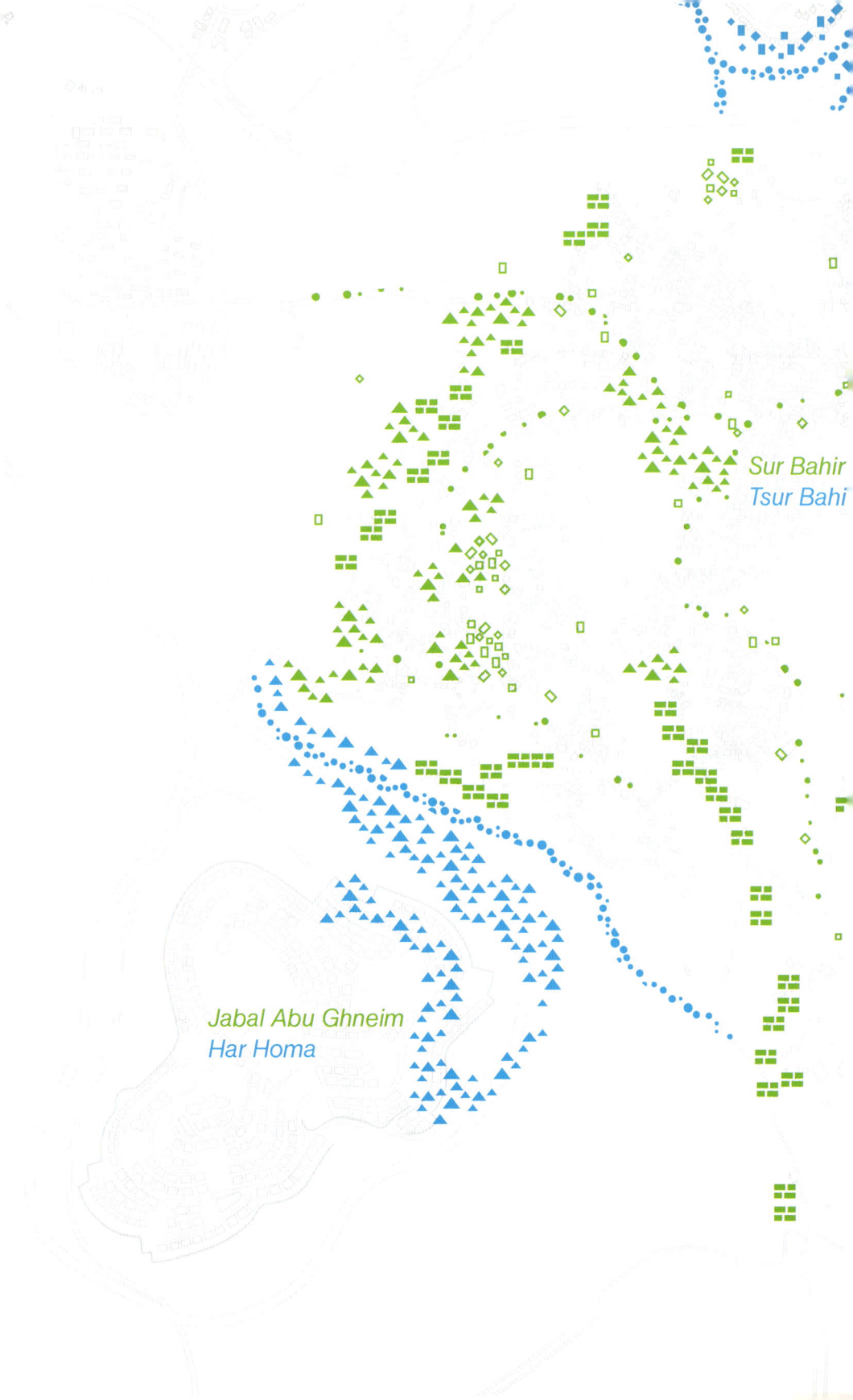

Sur Bahir
Tsur Bahi

Jabal Abu Ghneim
Har Homa

Decay
Sur Bahir / Har Homa (2005)

The decay and neglect of the landscape is indicative of the trauma, fear, and hostility that characterize everyday life at the frontier. The valley between village and settlement has become a no-man's-land filled with building rubble, car tires, domestic waste, etc. from both sides— an emptied, "de-cultivated" territory of fear and uncertainty. Some of this neglect is politically engineered, as Palestinian farmers are prohibited from maintaining their olive groves in the defined security zone around the settlement. But decay is also a symptom of the profound internal cultural and socioeconomic changes underway in villages such as Sur Bahir, which were triggered by the village's annexation into Jerusalem. Employed in the more profitable construction sector, a young generation is become increasingly indifferent to rural family traditions, instead aspiring to a western urban life-style.

Building rubble

Damaged or incomplete roads

Domestic waste

Dilapidated houses

0   100   200   300   400   500 meters

Concept and copyright

Tim Rieniets, Philipp Misselwitz

Sources

International Peace and Cooperation Center IPCC, Nasrallah, Rami, Khamaisi, Rassem, Younan, Michael, *Jerusalem on the Map* (Jerusalem, 2005).

Project Grenzgeografien (International Peace and Cooperation Center IPCC Jerusalem, Bezalel Academy of Art and Design Jerusalem, University of the Arts Berlin, ETH Swiss Federal Institute of Technology Zurich), *Trilateral Student Workshops* (Jerusalem, 2003-2005).

The Applied Research Institute—Jerusalem (ARIJ), *Geopolitical Atlas of Palestine—The West Bank and Gaza* (Jerusalem, 2004)

Shlomo Hasson, *The Struggle for Hegemony in Jerusalem*, The Floersheimer Institute for Policy Studies, (Jerusalem, October 2002).

BETWEEN WAR AND PEACE

CHRONICLE OF A MODERN URBAN CONDITION

Sylvaine Bulle

"BEHIND THE WALLS"

Historical and sociological approaches to understanding Palestinian cities have developed in the shadows of a geopolitical conflict; this conflict has in turn conditioned a specific discursive order. Israeli rule, dictating its own modes of knowledge and power, dominates such analyses through the militarization of space—like the recent construction of the so-called "security fence"—and its effacement of the Palestinian landscape. Analytical understandings of Palestinian cities are thus born into a performing political geography that is blind to the intrinsic characteristics of the land, its temporalities, its social rhythms, and its urban history.

"Reading" a territory in conflict should go beyond political passions or media representations.[1] This process should encompass various points of view, traverse borders, and transform the exterior discourse on objects, forms, or micrological facts. We should assume that military regimes (such as the Israeli occupation of the West Bank and Gaza) cannot occult all the urban and social forms of a territory. There are deep resistances and discrepancies between institutional and political fabrications, and the underlying urban and social rhythms of a place.

Exclusive residence in Al Bireh near Ramallah for PNA leaders and ministers (photo: George Dupin, 2004)

To observe a limited time period in Palestinian society—reconstruction between 1995 and 2000—is to reveal the plurality of Palestinian space. The commonalities are more prominent than the ruptures that lie between Intifada, nation-building, nationalism, and internationalization. Social structures of the ephemeral period of "peace" engendered inequalities no different from those present in less hopeful times. What has changed is that the surge in international stakeholding, and the opening to the world (and by the world) made possible by the "peace" process, considerably altered the urban structure of Palestinian cities. By examining these structural changes, the universal practices of democratization—or put better, forced internationalization—can be unveiled for what they are.

First we find that it is difficult to differentiate between the urban effects of international development and reconstruction efforts (or "pacification"), and the urban effects of domination. But changes in built-up areas are certainly not solely defined by external forces. The Palestinian occupied territories are not only disjointed and isolated by separation barriers, they are also fragmented by other "boundaries," more or less visible, within Palestinian society itself—boundaries that reinforce the social power of one over another. What follows is an attempt to separate these intertwined influences. The "peace" period has been one of internationalization, the introduction of new urban models and globalized life-styles, all of which have influenced ongoing social confrontations beyond (albeit impacted by) the war.

BELONGING TO THE WORLD: FROM SYMBOLIC LIBERATION TO THE "URBANIZATION OF CAPITAL"

In 1993, after the signing of the Oslo Accords between Israel and the Palestine Liberation Organization, the Palestinian occupied territories became the *locus* for the establishment of a provisional state, a "postcolonial" nation in the making. In the newly-autonomous areas, the would-be end of Israeli military rule prompted symbolic liberation. With the promise of independence around the corner, Palestinian elites living in the diaspora converged on the Palestinian dream. It was in the cities, the embodiment of economic hustle and bustle—namely Nablus, Ramallah, Bethlehem, and Gaza—where some 150,000 Palestinian exiles settled, leaving behind homes in Europe, the Gulf, or North America.

The management of local conflicts and civil reconstruction rewards (as mod-eled in international pacification projects in Afghanistan or Lebanon), is based on a "moral universalism,"[2] whose rules are defined by the international com-munity. The "cosmopolitics" that govern reconstruction take three fundamental principles into account: the establishment of economic regulations that will fit an international commercial framework; the free flow of capital and goods; and the democratic election of a new leadership. In the case of the Palestinians, a fourth condition has been added: the normalization or pacification of relations with Israel. The Oslo Accords were written squarely in the context of these universal stakes. They formed a kind of moral contract, an arrangement brokered by the international community and Palestinian shareholders, tying Palestinians to the rest of the world.[3]

These principles were internalized by Palestinian actors. A new class of eco-nomic and political entrepreneur was born in the wake of national reconstruction. This class was tied to an international system, directing the culture of "peace" and its financial benefits. Folded into this system were construction of new infrastructures; urban management; exploitation and ordering of custom taxes, border crossings, and transportation lines; development of communications net-works and licensing; the accumulation of capital; as well as access to symbolic resources. Simultaneously, non-governmental organizations, professional con-sultants, service providers (political experts, lawyers, engineers, etc.) prolifer-ated in the sectors of human rights, education, women's rights, environmental, and health issues.[4] They, too, participated in the management of the city, the construction of a "democratic" and "liberal" space. These actors were crucial in mobilizing the notion of the "public good" in order to develop private enterprises in the name of the public sphere.[5]

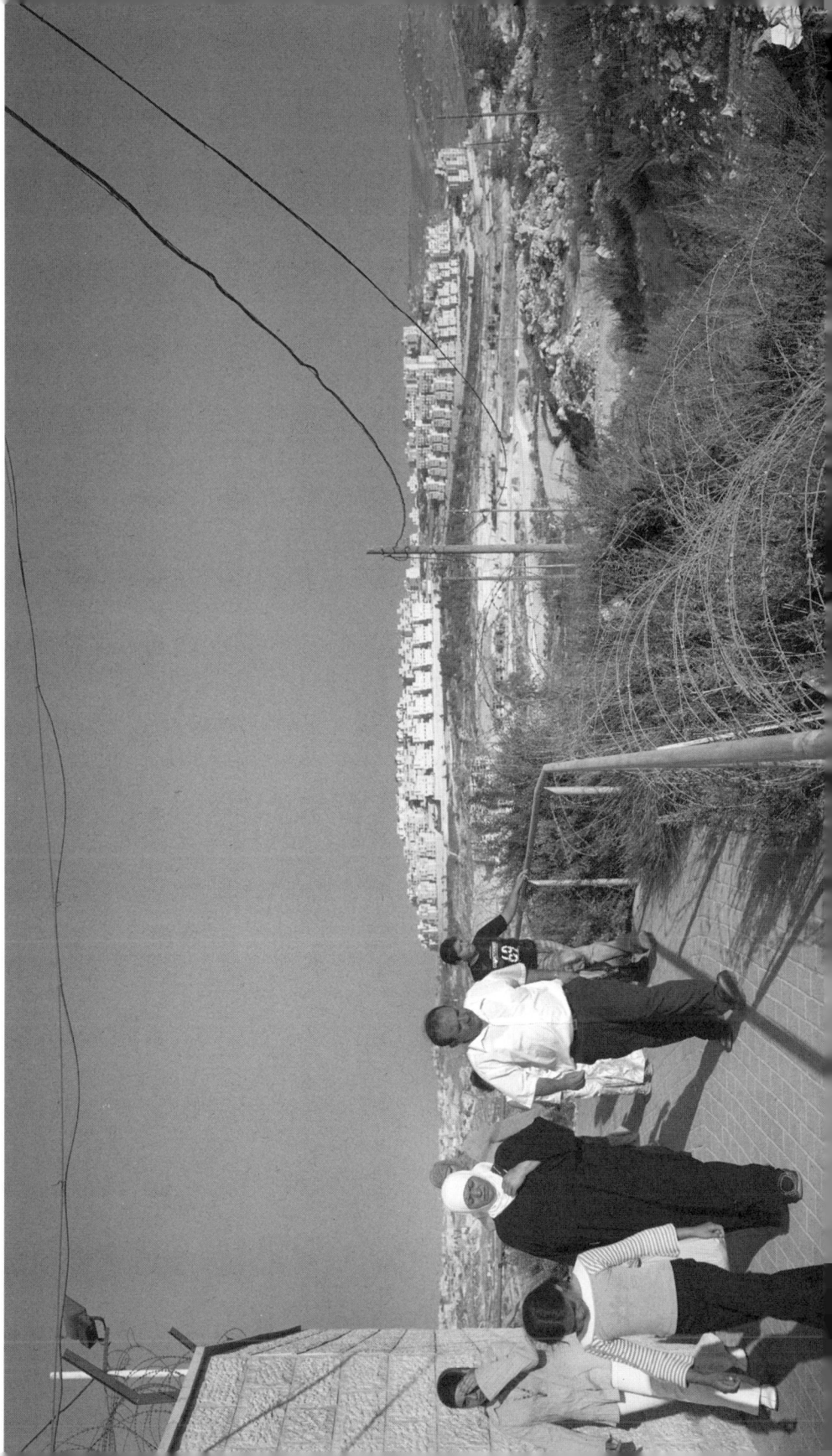

33.9 km: Checkpoint Bethlehem-Jerusalem with Har Homa in the distance

34.0 km: Checkpoint Bethlehem-Jerusalem

The new spirit of the city—a mood between patriotism and capitalism—has been expressed most clearly in the fields of architecture, urban planning, and heritage preservation. As soon as the Oslo Accords were signed, liberalism took precedence over the social concerns prioritized during the first Intifada, and the years of occupation and resistance that preceded it. The national liberation movement was subsumed by a nascent capitalism. The dream of the nation was "realized" through investment, mostly in real estate.[6] The private sector focused on construction, where a global economy directed the development of local commercial and residential areas. Land prices soared. New neighborhoods were built on the periphery of cities and towns without concern for quality, spatial logic, or organic relations to the city.[7]

Luxury condominiums near Ramallah evoking neo-tra-ditional architecture (photo: George Dupin, 2004)

The collision between nationalism and inter-national influences created new social practices, lifestyles, and architectural forms. In this col-lision, universal ideals won out in both private and public spheres.[8] Global culture reinter-preted locally has taken root in open urbanized spaces. Take "downtown" Ramallah for example. The city has been made more accessible than Jerusalem, which was the West Bank's econom-ic, political, and cultural capital until the Oslo years, when most West Bankers were barred from entering the city. In the "transnational" cities of Ramallah and al-Bireh, new urban atti-tudes are legible, where the elite can express their desires and need for public representation. There, they recreate modes of consumption in accordance with their own cultural referents, both regional and international.

Luxury residence in Nablus: The property of a Palestinian entrepreneur overlooking Nablus with stylistic refer-ences to Andrea Palladio's Villa Rotonda (photo: the author, 2004)

The sumptuous residences in the Masioun neighborhood, a bourgeois quarter on the outskirts of Ramallah, have as their proprietors the Palestinian elites of Chicago, Paris, Abu Dhabi, New York, and Frankfurt. The new shopping mall in al-Bireh boasts a series of boutiques and a Western-style supermarket.[9] Politicians and entrepreneurs alike have built monumental properties. One businessman and official's home is a replica of a Palladian villa overlooking the city of Nablus, a site of important Samaritan and Christian interest. The house, built by five European architects, using Italian building materials, means the effective privati-zation of national archaeological treasures and public sites.

A new culture of urban places appeared in answer to international desires, at the same time catering to romantic longings for local architecture, national history, and economic prosperity. Thus, the condominiums of Tel al-Safa near Ramallah evoke a neotraditional architecture aimed at wealthy residents with Western references. The condos, built atop one of the most beautiful hills in the region, the previously-inaccessible site of Gibeon, boasts breathtaking views of Jaffa to the west and the Dead Sea to the east. The promoter, born in Jaffa, is an exiled Palestinian with US citizenship and considerable capital. His building project stems from a nostalgic attempt to revive the image of ancient Jaffa, itself the product of an imaginary world.[10] The luxury residences recreate local vernacular architecture using domes, sandstone, and courtyards. But the complex is built away from the city and its pollutants. It is meant to satisfy its residents' desire for privacy and security.

Similarly, the colossal business complex built near Solomon's Pools between Bethlehem and Hebron is a commercial project that evokes the national imaginary. The pools, which collect water from natural springs, are central to agrarian memory, and a testament to an immemorial presence in Palestine. While the pools are used as picnic grounds for Palestinian families, the mammoth adjacent building managed by PADICO (a Palestinian investment group), with a surface area of 50,000 square meters, was conceived as a closed complex for a primarily foreign clientele. It is a classical example of a "global village," including a hotel, boutiques, business center, amphitheatre, etc. The neotraditional architecture of sandstone and marble is meant to celebrate the

Vacant commercial and tourist complex built in 1998 near the ancestral site of Solomon's Pools, near Bethlehem (photo: George Dupin, 2004)

surrounding landscape, yet threatens that same landscape by the damage caused by construction. The project was halted in 2001 with the outbreak of the second Intifada; its half-built center was subsequently appropriated by Palestinian militants battling the Israeli military stationed in the nearby hills.

"THOSE WHO REMAIN": THE INVISIBLE BORDERS OF PALESTINIAN CITIES

The process of opening Palestinian space to the world was, in the end, yet another form of fragmentation. Luxury buildings and refugee camps of ambiguous status[11] exist side by side. It was thought that the "peace" process would ease housing conditions, making cities more livable, but for the refugees on the urban margins, cramped quarters have deteriorated further. Globalization has not been able to replace citizenship—refugees remain deprived of their civic rights, such as the right to urban planning, in addition to their shelved national rights and claims.

It is clear, then, that this simultaneous process of reconstruction and internationalization is paradoxical. On the one hand, it introduces new modalities of a "universal way of life." On the other hand, it exacerbates the cultural and social disparities between the "indigenous" (i.e. local Palestinians) and the "foreign" (i.e. Palestinians who have returned), the moneyed and/or landholder, and the landless. Globalized transnational forms of reconstruction have in fact accentuated the social and spatial distances that remain between the various social strata.

In wartime, as well as in times of peace, to travel is not a right but a privilege. Permits, projects, tertiary activities remain "practices" reserved for those of a particular status. At the present period, the difficulty of moving from one Palestinian locale to another has exacerbated the differences between the entrepreneurial bourgeoisie and ordinary civilians (the former often possess a foreign passport or some other form of access card, while the latter possess no means of moving past the nearest Israeli checkpoint). Contacts and influence with Israelis are regularly used to attain entry permits or travel documents. In the spatial context of the war of "pacification," the "naked city" (Agamben, 1998) (that of invisible, stateless residents) finds its mirror: *the entre soi*. When the city becomes a battleground, when armed activists fill the densely populated neighborhoods of Nablus, Ramallah, Bethlehem, and Gaza, the local bourgeoisie and returnee elites know how to benefit from their positions: they retire from the urban chaos and take refuge in their new neighborhoods, "among themselves."

One might ask whether the very ideas of cosmopolitism and internationalism are illusory for those excluded from the benefits of "peace." Of course, any politics of reconstruction imposes discrimination, choosing its sites of intervention according to international norms. But in the administration of the "peace" enterprise, the Palestinian actors/operators of reconstruction—Palestinian entrepreneurs and NGOs—have also participated. Most of the time, they have privileged a kind of "urbanization of capital" over social policies, rehabilitated strategic symbol-fetish sites like Jerusalem's Old City, particularly the Dome of the Rock, instead of the "problematic" spaces of the camps.

It is in the refugee camps of Jerusalem where "informal"[12] civilians—those with no civil status other than their United Nations-issued refugee card—exist far from the hybrid global identity.[13] As refugees, they lack resources such as land, and as Jerusalemites (versus Gazans and West Bankers "serviced" by the "peace" process), they do not benefit from housing and employment rehabilitation projects, or other entrepreneurial possibilities.[14] East Jerusalem fits the category of an "informal society," a place where residents are excluded from processes of globalization and internationalization, remaining formal victims of the conflict over sovereignty. The urban euphoria of 1995-2000 has revealed the visible and invisible boundaries that crisscross Palestinian urban areas. The Palestinian city's complex and ambiguous modes of production beg for a reading that is necessarily discursive and exterior.

1   Pierre Bourdieu remarked that ,"[S]ociology is constantly threatened by symbolic commerce of all sorts [...] Prophets of today who mystify knowledge, media and other enterprises of seduction and of the moment [...] have a rare symbolic violence over the social sciences." (Leçon Inaugurale, College de France, April 23, 1982.)

2   See Habermas on international law after World War II and Kantian terms of moral universalism.

3   The limitation of such "Cosmopolitics" is evident from the reinitiation of the Intifada. The failure of the "peace" process should be understood in part as the limits of the idea of universal peace and international law.

4   International aid agencies poured $250 million into more than 1,000 newly created Palestinian NGOs between 1995 and 1998.

5   Habermas' notion of communication at the heart of the production of political functions is useful here. In Palestine, public space does not exist thanks to the actions of the state, but as a product of cultural and economic spheres independent of the (nonexistent) state. This public sphere is associative, civic and transnational.

6   The contribution of Diaspora returnees to real estate investments reached some $170 million in 1996 and 1997.

7   The average price of a 70 square meter apartment in al-Bireh (the Ramallah area) was $900,000 in 2000.

8   In Arjun Appadurai's words: "Where there is consumption, there is pleasure, and where there is pleasure, there is an agency." (Appadurai, 1996:7).

9   Each boutique received a US Aid grant of $15,000 for interior design.

10   "The 19th century on one hand, and the 21st on the other, Tel al-Safa is a neo-village without a mosque or church, but with a tennis court," its developer told me.

11   Today after almost 58 years since their exile, West Bank refugees do not belong to any local jurisdiction but remain dependent on the UN for their urban and social management. They have no civic rights other than those granted to them by host municipalities, when they move into the cities. In Gaza the situation is different, as refugees in both cities and camps have the right to vote in municipal elections and benefit from municipal services.

12   Saskia Sassen in 1998 referred to "informal societies" in urban areas created at the intersection of transnational circuits of globalization (finance, enterprise, etc.).

13   The notion that hybrid culture, i.e. the transnational element that characterizes uprooted populations (such as refugees), induces globalized and flexible practices (Ong, 1999) should be understood as relative; a reasoning similar to that of Appadurai, for whom the imaginary, the displacement of the imaginary community, is a motor for globalization (Appadurai, 1996).

14   Most international donors and agencies active in national reconstruction process do not intervene in refugee camps or Palestinian East Jerusalem because of their provisional status as issues/areas to be negotiated. At the same time, Israel's colonization of those areas is ongoing.

Selected Bibliography

Arjun Appadurai, *Modernity at large: Cultural Dimensions in Globalization*, (Minneapolis: University of Minnesota Press, 1996).

Sylvaine Bulle, "Architectes et Urbanistes Palestiniens. Genèse d'un milieu professionnel (1922-2000)," in *Urbanistes et Architectes de la Méditerranée*, eds. E Verdeil and T. Souami (Paris: Anthropos, 2005).

Jürgen Habermas, *La paix perpétuelle: le bicentenaire d'une idée kantienne*, trans. Rainer Rochlitz (Paris: les Éditions du Cerf, 1996) ["Kants Idee des Ewigen Friedens: Aus dem Historischen Abstand von 200 Jahren," in *Information Philosophie* 5 (December 1995)].

Giorgio Agamben, *Homo Sacer. Sovereign Power and Bare Life* (Standford: Standford University Press, 1998)

Sari Hanafi, "Contribution de la Diaspora Palestiniene a l'Economie des Territoires," in *Les Dossiers du Cedej* (Cairo: CEDEJ, 1997).

David Harvey, *The Urban Experience* (Baltimore: Hopkins University Press, 1989).

David Harvey, *The Urbanization of Capital: Studies in the History and Theory of Capital Urbanization* (Ann Arbour: UMI on Demands, 1994).

Aiwa Ong, *Introduction to Flexible Citizenship: The Cultural Logic of Transnationality* (Duke University Press, 1999).

Saskia Sassen, *Globalization and its Discontents: Selected Essays 1984-1998* (New York: New Press, 1998).

TO THE SUBURBS AND BACK

THE GROWTH AND DECAY OF PALESTINIAN SUBURBS AROUND JERUSALEM

Rami Nasrallah

Since the early days of the Israeli occupation of East Jerusalem, this half of the city has been subjected to various Israeli policies gerrymandering its territorial and demographic constitution—policies which hindered its natural development and functioning. In this essay I will investigate one of the most striking yet unresearched phenomena generated by this process: the development of a Palestinian suburbia and its subsequent decline.

MANUFACTURING A HOUSING SHORTAGE

One of the most important forces triggering the suburbanization of East Jerusalem's hinterlands was Israel's urban planning policy, which utilized (and continues to do so today) planning regulations in order to restrict Palestinian development, thus negatively affecting East Jerusalem residents' quality of life. After the annexation of East Jerusalem and its surrounding villages in 1967, the Jordanian municipal council and planning scheme was annulled. All building activities were henceforth prohibited, and East Jerusalem was never fully integrated into the municipality's broader planning system—its planning was only considered from the perspective of where to build settlements for Jewish immigrants. More recently, Israeli planning authorities have begun to prepare separate planning schemes for Palestinian neighborhoods, knitting them together as if East Jerusalem were an immense puzzle.[1] This practice has further guaranteed the neighborhoods' fragmentation and disintegration.

Between 1982 and 1992, only 270,000 of the five-million-square-meters of built-up Jerusalem were designated for Palestinians.[2] The average number of building permits issued for Palestinians were few; in Beit Hanina's northern section, the number of building permits issued from 1967 to 1999 was a scant 500 (this neighborhood had large areas of land open for development). On average, the Israeli Jerusalem Municipality issues 100 building permits annually to Palestinians, as compared with 1,500 to Jewish Israelis.

Not surprisingly then, in the 1980s a Palestinian housing crisis emerged with particular urgency. As a result of the aforementioned discriminatory government policies, between the years 1985 and 1996, 40 to 60% of Palestinian Jerusalemites were compelled to reside outside of the municipal boundaries. There they found fewer Israeli-determined restrictions on building, greater availability of land, and lower taxation rates and building fees.

FORCED SUBURBANIZATION IN THE JERUSALEM AREA

Thousands of upper and middle class families were forced out of the city's municipal boundaries in search of better housing conditions. In villages such as Ar-Ram, Bir Nabala, and al-Ezariya, land was available for purchase, construction was cheap and—more importantly—Israel had fewer means of restricting development through municipal planning law. Construction could take place quickly and virtually anywhere. New suburbs rapidly sprang up close to the core of these small villages and along main arteries leading to East Jerusalem.

These suburbs developed in two main directions, the first extending between Jerusalem and Ramallah, and located north of and parallel with the municipal boundary. In the early 1980s, this area saw massive construction. The second suburban cluster developed to the east, on the road linking Jerusalem with Jericho and Amman. Here, development began in the late 1980s and expanded rapidly until the second half of the 1990s. The new suburbs began as bedroom communities offering few services, since their new residents continued to

Booming economy at Ar-Ram
(photo: editorial team, 2003)

shop and work inside the Israeli municipal boundaries. These suburbs were developed through the initiative of urban families, accommodating mostly property owners and later attracting young couples through comparatively low rents (prices were less than third of the rent charged in areas within municipal Jerusalem).

Paradoxically, the events of the first Intifada began to change this. While Palestinian commercial strikes restricted Palestinian shops inside Jerusalem (as well as the rest of the West Bank and Gaza Strip) to opening only three hours a day, Ar-Ram's new informal commercial area remained open longer hours. This area eventually became the site of a formal market. Some residential structures along the main road were demolished, and new commercial buildings were constructed. This trend continued and intensified in the early 1990s, only to reach westward, connecting to Bir Nabala.

The suburbs along the Jericho road developed at a comparatively much slower pace. The decisive impetus for these areas' development was the Israeli closure policy imposed in 1993, restricting Palestinian West Bankers from entering the city of Jerusalem—as they were accustomed to doing—in order to work, study, shop, see relatives and friends, receive medical treatment, or pray at the city's holy sites. The fact that this suburban area served as "middle ground" between West Bank towns and the city of Jerusalem contributed to its expansion and development as a major transportation center linking the southern West Bank with the north. Too, the area became a new home for institutions and businesses forced to move out of cordoned Jerusalem in order to continue serving their West Bank clientele or maintain their West Bank employees.

The development of these suburbs accelerated with the establishment of the Palestinian Authority, as many of its ministries and institutions were located in Ar-Ram. Banks and other public and private institutions started to operate from these areas nearby East Jerusalem, encouraged by the Palestinian Authority which saw the space as a springboard to achieve political claims on areas inside the city.

BACK TO THE CITY

In 1996, Israeli authorities unintentionally brought a halt to this suburbanization. That year they retroactively applied a new "center of life" policy stating that Palestinian Jerusalemites must prove by presenting myriad documents that their "center of life" remained within the Israeli municipal boundaries—or risk losing their residency status. Palestinian residents were forced to show that they worked in the city, had paid all their property and municipal taxes, and that their children went to schools in Jerusalem. The move was regarded as a direct attempt to steer the development of suburbanization into a favorable outcome in the ongoing Israeli demographic battle. While previously, Israeli regulations had threatened those living overseas for more than seven years with the loss of Jerusalem residency,[3] the new law considered the growing suburbs foreign territory.

The new regulation caused thousands of Palestinians to panic, pick up their lives, and return to residing inside the municipal boundaries. The East Jerusalem housing shortage was aggravated, prices skyrocketed and overcrowding hit new highs. Many of those returning from the suburbs moved in with their relatives or endured poor housing conditions; some simply maintained two addresses, one of them inside the city. This return flight not only affected residents, but also businesses. Approximately one third of Ar-Ram's businesses and small manufacturing workshops moved from the suburbs to areas within municipal Jerusalem, particularly Beit Hanina and the industrial area of Atarot.

Separation Fence/Wall encircling Ar-Ram (photo: editorial team, 2006)

The recent Israeli construction of the series of walls, fences, barbed wire, patrol roads, and army watchtowers in the Jerusalem area is the logical continuation of the policy of severing East Jerusalem from its West Bank hinterlands, and has thus caused a second wave of panicked flight back to the city. There are now more pragmatic concerns added to the threat of identity card confiscation. The Separation Wall blocks access to the city center through the establishment of permanent checkpoints, which, more often than not, mean long waits and unpredictable travel times.[4] These realities make a daily commute impossible. While maintaining an "alibi" address inside the city boundaries was once a pragmatic solution for some, this is no longer a feasible option.

HYPERCONGESTION

The Shu`fat refugee camp classically demonstrates East Jerusalem residents' initiative in solving their residency problems. In 1999, only 8,000 refugees registered with the United Nations Relief Works Agency lived in the camp, joined by 4,000 nonrefugees that had moved into the camp to maintain their residency rights. Today these numbers have swollen to more than 22,500 camp residents, with a much higher percentage comprised of nonrefugees. Still, this willingness to live in such crowded conditions in order to maintain Jerusalemite status will soon be for naught; the Separation Wall route is expected to place the refugee camp (in addition to the neighborhoods of Dahiyat es-Salaam, and Ras Khamis) on its West Bank side. This will likely start a new wave of movement from the camp to Jerusalem's inner neighborhoods.

By the end of 2003, the average apartment size in the Shufat refugee camp had reached 35 square meters, as compared to 41 square meters in Jerusalem's Old City (excluding the Jewish Quarter). The average number of rooms per house in Palestinian neighborhoods inside the municipal boundaries is 3.2 rooms, as compared to an average of 3.5 rooms per house in the suburbs. Only 10.7% (on average) of houses in Palestinian neighborhoods have five or more rooms. More broadly, the housing density in East Jerusalem is double that in West Jerusalem and Jewish settlements in East Jerusalem.

THE PHENOMENON OF "ILLEGAL" BUILDING

Given these realities, many Palestinian Jerusalemites seek to build, but obtaining the correct building permissions means yet another series of legal hoops to jump through. Faced with complicated bureaucracy, limited available properly planned land, property not yet properly registered, and the high cost of building permits, East Jerusalem residents have instead engaged in widespread unauthorized construction. Prior to 1994, there was almost no unauthorized construction underway. But because some owners of unauthorized homes were allowed by the Israeli municipality to be registered as residents for tax purposes (thus shoring up their residency status inside the municipal borders), others have been encouraged to build quickly and worry about the consequences later.

Between 1996 and 2003, more than 18,000 houses were built without their owners' obtaining permission from the Israeli municipality. Even in the rare cases of permitted building, the permits allow for very low construction density (usually less than 50% building to land ratio), and the owners therefore have built on six to ten times more of the land than allowed. Other structures, particularly those in the northern neighborhoods of Jerusalem (Beit Hanina and Shufat), were built in areas zoned as "open space" green areas. The price of land in these areas ($100,000 per dunam) is one-quarter the price of land in areas zoned for development. Homes here have no public services and are at added risk of demolition (as "illegal" structures[5]), but Palestinians are willing to endure these conditions and the possibility of losing their homes in order to maintain the right to live and work in the city. It is worth mentioning that Israeli municipal building inspectors (aided by the police and the courts) have applied stringent measures to stop the phenomenon of "illegally-built" homes. For example, all vehicles transporting construction materials are required to have a special permit for a specific building site, which is also required to possess a permit. Since early 2004, there has been a major decline in construction without permits as a result of intensified house demolishing and the so-called "enforcement" of building regulations in East Jerusalem.

The most recent rush to move closer to Jerusalem's inner neighborhoods brought on by the construction of the Separation Wall has left entire blocs of housing standing empty in the suburbs, especially in Ezariya and az-Zaim which lie east of the city. Other areas have absorbed new groups of migrant Palestinian workers. West Bankers seeking to take advantage of Ramallah's booming economy are attracted by the comparatively low rents, although most of these properties remain under Jerusalemite ownership. In effect, Ar-Ram has been transformed from a suburb of Jerusalem to a suburb of Ramallah. Before the 1996 "center of life" policy was instituted, more than 60% of the population of these suburbs carried a Jerusalem identity card.[6] If Ar-Ram is our case study, two-thirds of its population of 50,000 to 60,000 were Jerusalemites. But this portion dropped dramatically to under 30% after the partial construction of the Separation Wall in 2003. The decline is expected to continue as Israel completes construction in 2006 and commences operating "border crossing" terminals between Jerusalem and its suburbs.

THE LONG-TERM OUTLOOK FOR EAST JERUSALEM

The momentous changes underway in East Jerusalem and the spatial, demographic, and functional relations between its neighborhoods and suburbs will have a major impact on Jerusalem's geopolitical and functional future. In addition to bringing about the decay of Jerusalem's Palestinian suburbs, the Separation Wall will sever entire neighborhoods that currently fall within the municipal boundaries (home to an estimated 55,000 people prior to the movement underway) from the city center and its services. These changes are so dramatic that their outcomes are difficult to predict. Nevertheless, current trends and expectations help us to understand the possible implications.

First, conditions in the city's urban areas, especially in the inner neighborhoods of East Jerusalem (the Old City, ath-Thuri or Abu Tor, and Silwan) can be expected to deteriorate, creating slum-like conditions. Drug use (already a problem), domestic violence, and crime will likely rise. Fragmentation will reign, characterized by the breakup of East Jerusalem's urban and social fabric, and geographic and functional continuity with its suburbs and the West Bank. Jerusalem will therefore lose its centrality for Palestinians, and its status as their unofficial commercial and political capital.

Second, East Jerusalem's suburbs, which have served as a "bridge" between Jerusalem and the West Bank, will be transformed from areas of strong economic and institutional activity into dead end buffer zones connected to West Bank cities by transportation routes alone, thereby severing their geographic and functional continuity. (Ar-Ram will be an enclave connected to Ramallah by a border terminal at Qalandiya. Bir Nabala will be an enclave with four other small towns, connected to Ramallah by a tunnel running under Road 443. Abu Dis and Ezariya will have one "escape exit," a road running through difficult mountainous topography, linking them to Bethlehem.)

The territorial domination of the Israeli Jewish metropolis will extend over a vast 300 square kilometers, the majority of it located on occupied Palestinian land. The Separation Wall will effectively annex settlement blocs located 25 to 30 kilometers from Jerusalem into Greater Jerusalem. Simultaneously, most Palestinian Jerusalem neighborhoods and suburbs will be excluded from the city, despite their relative nearness (four to eight kilometers from the central Old City). The ongoing settlement process in the city is guaranteed to not only intensify the conflict over Jerusalem, but undermine any remaining prospects for a contiguous and viable Palestinian state.

1   Palestinian neighborhood plans were prepared in different stages; two-thirds of the now-statutory planned area was not planned until the 1990s.

2   After annexation, the Israeli government confiscated more than 30,000 dunams (34% of East Jerusalem's land) (1 dunum = 1000 square meters) of Palestinian land for the building of new Jewish settlements. In addition, large tracts of Palestinian private owned land (7,750 acres = 44%) were designated "green areas" through zoning ordinances; these were later rezoned for the construction of Jewish settlements. As a result, today, Palestinian neighborhoods constitute only 14% of East Jerusalem's area.

3   Revocation of Israeli residency rights means loss of access to the city, and the rescinding of social welfare programs and health insurance. If a Jerusalemite fails to provide documents proving residency in the city, the Israeli interior ministry will declare him or her an illegal resident, deny him or her access to the city and its services, and ask the Palestinian to leave to the Palestinian Authority or Jordan. Since 1967, over 6,500 Palestinians have had their residency rights revoked.

3   Some of the governmental institutions in Ar-Ram moved to Ramallah (under full Palestinian Authority control) for security reasons after the second Intifada broke out in 2001 and as a result of the onerous Qalandiya checkpoint between Ramallah and Ar-Ram. Some important local Christian institutions and schools, and the World Bank and United States Agency for International Development, remain in Ar-Ram's Dahiyat al-Bareed neighborhood. After a court battle, the Israeli Supreme Court decided at the end of November 2005 to include parts of the Dahiyat al-Bareed residential area and these institutions on the Jerusalem side of the Separation Wall, and to erect the concrete structure north of this small part of the suburb.

5   In 2004, more than 150 Palestinian houses were demolished by the Israeli municipality in East Jerusalem after their owners built without permission.

6   According to Israeli statistics, the number of Palestinians carrying Jerusalem identity cards was 181,800 in 1995 and had risen to 237,100 by the end of 2004. This change was solely due to population growth and occurred despite Israeli measures to restrict the number of Jerusalemite Palestinians. As a result, "family reunification" (the granting of residency rights to a spouse or children after marriage to a Jerusalemite) was frozen by Israeli authorities.

This interview with the Palestinian curator Jack Persekian, conducted in person and by email, began as a conversation with Galit Eilat at Anadiel Gallery in the summer of 2005

Eilat: Why do you choose to work in East Jerusalem when it would be possible for you to work in the United States or elsewhere?

Persekian: Jerusalem is my hometown, so it's only natural for me to work here. I started working in the visual arts after working for some time in music. I didn't know at that time where this would take me, and as I pursued it, I was learning, discovering, and charting my career. There are many variables and, of course, uncertainties, but the one thing that provided some consistency was Jerusalem. This might seem a bit nonsensical given Jerusalem's problematic and deteriorating conditions, particularly for Palestinians. Yet my family, my people, and "the comfort of familiarity" are all here. In addition, I think I have made a difference here. I can see the effect of my work on the local art scene, and the impact how my work had on art in Palestine. I have always struggled with whether or not my work would lead me abroad, but seeing its fruition locally and internationally has led me to believe that there is value beyond the personal in what I'm doing here.

Eilat: Could you describe the deterioration of everyday conditions related to your work and life?

Persekian: Where would I start? The deterioration is visible in the ever-tightening closure imposed on Jerusalem and the severance of our life from its natural extensions in the West Bank and Gaza, and the unabashed discrimination of the Israeli authorities (which is deeply scarring my conscience), and everything else in between. My work in Jerusalem cannot reach more than a minute fraction of the Palestinian population, on one hand, and yet there is a huge Israeli audience, which I am not interested in. This is a schizophrenic situation, as I am required to deal with Israelis in most matters related to my life here in Jerusalem—except in my work.

Eilat: How has the second Intifada influenced Palestinian artists' activities?

Persekian: The consequences of the Intifada—from the construction of the Wall [the series of concrete barriers, fences, and military appendages that Israel is constructing around Palestinian population centers in the West Bank], the complete and interminable "closure" imposed on many areas, the deterioration of the economic situation, and accompanying political upheaval—have dug up the terrain. We're still figuring out our way around, negotiating the pitfalls, dirt paths, and swamps. It has, more than ever, fragmented Palestinian society and created pockets of dislocated and disconnected groups, each trying to break out and communicate with the outside world.

Eilat: Do you view the Palestinian art scene as one scene between Gaza, the West Bank, and East Jerusalem? Or has it become a fragmented scene?

Persekian: There is a problem in the question here, because you're falling in to the same trap that the Israelis have set and have maintained for many years: that is, of limiting all issues regarding the Palestinian cause to the people who live in the West Bank and Gaza. It's as if Palestinians living within Israel, scattered in refugee camps in the region and dispersed throughout the Diaspora do not count. Please excuse me for not indulging in these questions that are limited in their perspective.

Eilat: Do you see the Palestinian art scene becoming disconnected from the Israeli art scene? How do you view co-curation or collaboration between Palestinians and Israelis?

Persekian: I am not sure about the formulation of the first part of this question. I don't see a connection between the Palestinian and Israeli art scenes. When the two sides have come together to work on particular projects, it was due to a responsibility (one borne by all good citizens) to voice discontent with and dis-approval of the continuing occupation, violence, and humiliation. My work with the Israeli art historian Gannit Anchori, on the exhibition "Home," was part of a larger project entitled "Sharing Jerusalem—Two Capitals for Two States." A politi-cal concept and proposition was introduced and all of the activities organized were under that umbrella. It was in no way designed to show the sweet face of coexistence, but to gauge public opinion and to raise awareness of the existence of people who are willing to share their city. I am able to see some collaboration, if and when working together can bring about breakthroughs in the political stalemate and alleviation or recognition of suffering and injustice.

Funny enough, in the art and cultural field, that I was responsible for on the Palestinian side for the "Sharing Jerusalem" project, there was a unanimous willingness amongst most of the Palestinian artists and institutions to take part in this initiative, and they did. On the other hand, while individual Israeli artists did participate, no Israeli art or cultural institution in west Jerusalem agreed to participate in or host activities. This leads me to say that yes the Israeli art scene is politically aware but does not necessarily subscribe to my point of view or, for that matter, to yours.

Eilat: Do you think that Israeli recognition of the Palestinian *Nakba* [the 1948 Catastrophe] could start a process of reconciliation? Do you envision resolution through the two-state solution or in one state, where "all inhabitants are equal under the law, the majority rules, and minority rights are protected"?

Persekian: I have always believed that *al-Nakba* should be the first issue addressed and resolved in negotiations between Palestinians and Israelis, with an unequiv-ocal recognition by Israel of its responsibility for the Palestinian Catastrophe. We need, in a just process, to go through divorce, recognize of mistakes made, and then reengage. We need a divorce in the form of a Palestinian state with the green line as its border with Israel. At a later stage, there might be some sort of unification creating one state, where all inhabitants are equal under the law, the majority rules, and the minorities are protected and their interests respected. I don't think this is a utopian vision. Rather, Israel's belief that this land is its property, a country exclusively for the Jews, is utopian. The problem with achiev-

ing a divorce is that the concept of justice cannot be applied to this conflict, as Israel does not recognize any law but its own, or any international resolution.

Eilat: Do you feel "inspired" at all as a curator living in a city of such conflicts and problems? What role does a curator have in this situation?

Persekian: In the early 1990s, I saw the art scene in Palestine as isolated, uninspired, and unchallenged. I decided that I needed to provide a platform, a conduit that allows communication and interaction with the outside world. I also saw that there was a didactic approach to Palestinian representation in the art world, and hence believed that a deconstruction of those models of representation needed to be given opportunity, means, and space. This colossal task represents one of the biggest challenges facing a curator working here, as he or she must embody this conduit between the inside and the outside, becoming a channel for resources and opportunities, and most importantly, a spokesperson on behalf of the art movement.

Eilat: Tell us about the Al-Ma'mal Foundation's collection. Is it a Palestinian art collection? Or an international collection of works produced by the Foundation?

Persekian: Anadiel Gallery (which I established in 1992) began as the first and only independent art gallery in Palestine. Timed with the start of the peace process, Anadiel doubled as both a permanent exhibition space for Palestinian artists and a reference point for all those who wanted to make contact with local artists. But it was actually the renewed interest in the Palestinian people and their affairs brought about by extensive media coverage of the Intifada, which gave the gallery a more important role than just that of selling art and making money. The gallery began with a commercial underpinning, but this idea was soon confronted by the dire economic realities and had to be aborted. Hence, the decision made to maintain the gallery under these conditions was not a simple profit and loss calculation, but included more important considerations, such as the need to provide a venue and an opportunity for local artists to present their work, access to venues, events, and exhibitions abroad through gallery contacts, and prospects of financial assistance (however small) for art projects. It was actually this last consideration that gradually led to the launching of the project of hosting foreign artists in Palestine, initiating exchange programs and residencies abroad, and securing the financial assistance needed to continue the work of the gallery. The gallery started a project of hosting Palestinian artists living in the Diaspora, some of whom had never been to Palestine before. Having secured foreign passports and nationalities, these artists were able to visit as tourists. Mona Hatoum, Nasser Soumi, Samir Srouji, Jumana al-Husseini, and Susan Hijab were among the artists who came, and a very interesting discourse ensued between them and local artists over issues of representation, questions of identity and modernity, and more tangible concerns of articulation, relationship to the land, popular imagery, and national iconography. This gust of change, cutting across all aspects of life, brought about much-needed reflection, revisited dogmas, and spurred a new effort to break down stereotypes and reductive categories, which are so limiting to human thought and expression.

Anadiel gallery was a private initiative, which did not qualify for significant funding from international organizations. Hence a group of artists, architects, and cultural figures came together and established Al-Ma'mal Foundation, primarily to promote, generate, disseminate, and make art in Palestine. Over the past 12 years Anadiel Gallery and Al-Ma'mal Foundation have coproduced and promoted a small, yet important, collection of art works created by local and visiting artists as they engaged with this country, its people, history, and ongoing conflict.

Our plan is to install this collection in the not-yet-established Contemporary Art Museum–Palestine, CAMP (this is a working title), which is conceived as a nomadic, stateless museum awaiting the creation of the Palestinian state. The headquarters for CAMP will be located in host countries for the duration of its nomadic life, until the arrival of Palestinian statehood and a proper venue. The museum will not only give international recognition to the contemporary cultural identity of the Palestinian people, but will preserve and nourish an illimitable discourse and interaction between the disparate experiences of the Palestinian people scattered in various parts of the world and also draws on the experience and interaction of non-Palestinian artists with Palestine, its people and the conflict.

Galit Eilat

"The Israeli art scene relies on the mythical notion of the "West" as its organizing principle, and is shaped as a faithful model of the European art scene. In
this respect, to constitute the Hebrew art scene after a European model is a
quintessential colonialist project, the postulation of the social field as an aesthetic laboratory empty of data and subject to potential utopian applications."
(Chinski: 2002).

Adoption of western practices (the institutional organization of the Israeli art
scene according to a European structure) is supposed to reaffirm the Zionist
project as having moral validity, as a bearer of the Enlightenment torch in the
region, "a western island in an eastern sea" or "the only democracy in the Middle
East." Hence, we have witnessed Israeli art's long rejection of the Arab culture
that lives within and around it, as well as of the culture of Jewish immigrants
from Arab countries, who are perceived as inferior. The representation of the
Arab has undergone numerous metamorphoses, from the pre-1948 image of an
aristocrat tilling his land to the *shahid* (Muslim martyr) of the 2000s.

The 1970s and 1980s are marked in local Israeli chronicles as the birth of an
original, indigenous *sabra* Israeli art, which, in fact, combined *Arte Povera*[1] with
conceptual art. Western art movements made *aliyah* (immigrated) and were
adapted. An important manifestation of this trend was Sara Breitberg's 1986
exhibition, "The Want of Matter: A Quality in Israeli Art," at the Tel Aviv Museum
of Art. This was to have marked a new Israeli narrative which incorporated
concepts and practices from the outside, and finally surpasses the established
Zionist narrative originating in the Diaspora. This new collective narrative continues to dominate the Israeli art field and is the accepted canon of all major
public art and cultural institutions in Israel today.

In this article I would like to highlight another tradition led by individuals
who, for the last three decades, have begun to expand the boundaries of their
work beyond the museum establishment. In this new arena, room exists for
works that cross from art to life, and from the museum and gallery into the
public sphere. This artistic production has been marked by the deconstruction
and rebuilding of conceptual, social, cultural, and political structures. Most con-
spicuous in this trend have been cultural expressions extending from feminist,
ethnic, and Palestinian struggles in Israel. Each group formed an independent
narrative—an intrinsic narrative directed both inwards and outwards—and creat-

ed its own myths and historiography. But this act of construction was motivated by the awareness that the manner in which it had previously been described and interpreted by the canon, by the privileged "Israeli collective," was unsatisfactory and even deceptive. These artists, whether as individuals or part of a group, have worked to generate a unique narrative alongside, or undermining, the central narrative of the artistic establishment (which is, admittedly, the state's official story). The role of the artist today is not to accompany, illustrate, and laud the images of war, but to introduce a critical approach to violence and terror, to oppressive power and the organized state regime, and to repression of the individual's autonomy by the state.

One example of this is the "Jaffa Project—An Autobiography of a City," which was created in response to the October 2000 events in Jaffa when civil unrest broke out in conjunction with the *Intifada* in the occupied territories. Eyal Danon and Sami Buchari[2] initiated a series of video interviews with Palestinian residents of Jaffa who had lived in the city prior to 1948 and the establishment of Israel. These interviews began as an attempt to tell the story of the city, as preserved in the memory of those who were raised there, knew it in its prime, and witnessed its transformation from a Palestinian cultural, commercial, and economic center, to its current state as a squalid neighborhood of Tel Aviv. The desire to create an archive of stories, testimonies, and visual and textual materials based on a variety of sources, stemmed from the recognition that the conditions for future reconciliation and healing required that members of the community be afforded a platform for describing their history, traditions, and version of events in their own words, and from their own point of view.

"Artists Without Walls" is a forum of Palestinian and Israeli artists from various fields who meet in East Jerusalem or Ramallah. Their goal is to protest physical walls and divisions and to foster a dialogue between Palestinian and Israeli societies through artistic means. "April 1st," one event organized by the group, created a virtual window (by means of closed-circuit projectors and cameras) for several hours in the cement wall—which Israel has constructed down the center of the village of Abu Dis—to allow its inhabitants to communicate with one another. Beyond these artistic activities, forum members regard the meetings themselves as important. When 20 or more Israeli artists enter Ramallah (designated Area A under the Oslo accords), both parties put themselves at risk: Israelis violate military law and chance detention by entering the area, and their Palestinian hosts take social and political risks by hosting a large group of Israelis.

The emergence of an alternative voice alone does not however guarantee a change in the existing social order. The existence of an established alternative story, which runs counter to the Zionist version concerning the possession of land does not, in itself, guarantee the undermining or revision of the hegemonic story. The exposure of documents undermining the accepted Israeli version of the 1948 War have failed to bring about a change in the canonical narrative, rather introducing "another way" of reading these historical events.[3] Similarly, the alternative *Mizrahi* (Arab Jewish) voice was absent from public discourse in Israel until the late 1970s. But the presence of this voice in the public sphere and its incorporation within the grand Zionist narrative has not produced a radical change in the narrative itself. The same can be said for the emergence of the feminist debate during the 1980s, which has had no effect on the militaristic character of Israeli society. No matter how these alternative narratives develop, they too are bonded to the larger discourse, each perpetuating the other to some degree.

In the *Over Memory* archive (Maure, 1993:23-8), members of the Sala-Manca group[4] set out to construct an artistic-geographic representation of another memory. The concept of "over memory," coined by Portuguese artist and scholar Joao Delgado, refers to areas in private and collective memory that are perceived as meaningless, but actually fulfill an archival function. *Over Memory* documents aspects ostensibly irrelevant to the construction of history and the memory of place, in an attempt to create a poetics of "over memory" for Jerusalem. The archive contains video, photographic and sound pieces, organized by category, street, description, date and time of documentation.

Yael Bartana's[5] "Trembling Time" (2002) was filmed overlooking a several-lane highway at the sounding of the Memorial Day siren, when Israelis stop to remember those who have died in Israel's wars. Cars slowly come to a halt, their occupants opening the car doors, getting out and standing motionless by their vehicles, then getting back into the cars and driving on. The event is part of a cycle of rituals organized by the state as part of the process of shaping national identity. But while the individual would usually experience these events as part of the collective, Bartana's work and its series of close-ups on the drivers focuses on the individual (Eilat, 2003). It is no accident that protesters against the disengagement plan chose last May to block dozens of roads throughout the country, thus recalling the vision of hundreds of cars stopping simultaneously, a vision linked in the collective consciousness with the Memorial Day siren.

It is amnesia, then, that makes art in the broadest sense possible. Countless improvised and established mechanisms confront amnesia, attempting to present things that are no longer present. These mechanisms isolate what is deemed worthy of reproduction and dissemination, only to perpetuate ideals using the tools of preservation and memory. Since the 1970s, the one-dimensional picture of the past, distributed in Israel in all possible representational arenas, has cracked incrementally. The Lebanon War and the first and second *Intifadas* accelerated the creation of rifts, and these fissures are revealed in cinema, photography, art, literature, and poetry. But these rifts, rather than indicating a transition from the dominant picture to the alternative one, imply that multiple views are concurrently at work, masking and exposing one another.

1   A term coined by Italian artist, Germano Celant, in 1967 to refer to art that was open in terms of material and process.

2   Eyal Danon was born in Ramat Gan in 1972 and lives and works in Tel Aviv. Sami Buchari was born in Jaffa in 1964 and lives and works in Jaffa.

3   "The rules of declassification of various archives enable validation of this historiographic endeavor. In England, the US and Israel these laws enable declassification of documents, usually thirty years after their classification, so that the historical fabric now revealed approximately reaches the year 1962. Thus, since 1978 a researcher of the history of Palestine can cover Mandatory history from beginning to end, using prime British and Israeli archival material. In terms of historical revision one may say that the new harvest has focused on the end of the period, sketching a different picture from the official account of the last Mandate years, and especially of 1948." (Pappe, 1993)

4   Sala-Manca is an independent Jerusalem-based group consisting of two members: Lea Mauas (1974) and Diego Rotman (1972), artists born in Buenos Aires, Argentina. The group engages in various art fields and media. It also publishes a magazine entitled *He'arat Shulayim* on contemporary art and literature. In addition, it curates and produces the *He'ara* events—multidisciplinary events produced independently, without commercial sponsorship or official support.

5   Yael Bartana was born in Kfar Yehezkel, Israel, 1970. She lives and works in Holland and Israel.

Selected Bibliography

Sarah Chinski, "Enaim Atsoumot liRvha: Al Tesmonet haLavqanut haNerkeshet baSedeh haOmanut haIsraeli" ["Eyes Wide Shut: On the Acquired Albino Syndrome on the Israeli Art Scene"], in *Bikoret vTeoria* [*Theory and Criticism*] 20 (Spring 2002).

Salwa Alenat, "biHaim taht haKibush yesh Harbeh Ironia" ["There is a lot of Irony in Life under Occupation"], in *Maarav–An Online Art*, Culture and Media Magazine 1 (2004) www.maarav.org.il.

Ariella Azoulay, "biDeletim Ptuhot: Museunim liHistoria baMerhav haTsiburi haIsraeli" ["With Open Doors: Museums and Historical Narratives in Israel's Public Space"], in *Bikoret vTeoria* [*Theory and Criticism*] 4 (Autumn 1993).

A. Maure, "Paradigma de la memoria y sobrememoria—Bocetos para una arqueologia del olvido," in *Ruptura* 123 (1993).

Galit Eilat, "Mahshavot Al Maqom, Gvarim vTeqnologia" ["Thoughts about Place, Men, and Technology"], in Yael Bartana "Kings of the Hill," exhibition catalog, Herzliya Museum of Art, 2003.

Ilan Pappe, "HaHistoria HaHadasha shel Milhamat 1984" ["The New History of the 1948 War"], in *Bikoret vTeoria* [*Theory and Criticism*] 3 (Winter 1993).

Thomas Abowd (*1967, Ann Arbor, Michigan) received his B.A. and M.A. from the University of Michigan, and his Ph.D. from Columbia University. He is currently assistant professor of cultural anthropology at Wayne State University, Detroit, Michigan. His dissertation is entitled, "Landscapes of Exclusion: The Spatial Construction of Identity and Difference in Contemporary Jerusalem" (2003). He is the author of several works on contemporary Jerusalem, including "Carving Up the Capital: The Politics of Space in Contemporary Jerusalem" in *Middle East Report*, Spring, 2004. His recent work explores racial and class politics in contemporary Detroit.

Sandra Ashhab (*1982, Jerusalem) graduated in 2005 with a bachelor's degree in geology and environmental studies from the Hebrew University, Jerusalem. She joined the Applied Research Institute Jerusalem (ARIJ) in 2005, where she has been working on Palestinian water issues.

Meron Benvenisti (*1934, Jerusalem) was the deputy mayor of Jerusalem from 1971 to 1978, and is currently columnist for the Israeli newspaper daily *Haaretz*. He is author of *Conflicts and Contradictions* (1986), *Intimate Enemies* (1995), *City of Stone* (1996) and *Sacred Landscapes* (2000).

Tamar Berger (*1957, Tel Aviv) lives and works in Tel Aviv. She teaches in the Department of Architecture at the Bezalel Academy of Arts and Design in Jerusalem and has written on issues concerning Israeli urban culture. Her publications include *Dionysus at Dizengof Centre* (1998). She is currently completing her Ph.D. on issue of borders in Israeli society.

Polly Braden (*1974, Perth, Scotland) received her B.A. hons. from East London University and her postgraduate degree from the London College of Printing. She is a photographer and lecturer in photography at the London College of Communication. She has produced several distinguished photo essays and works regularly for national publications (including *ICON*, *The Saturday Telegraph*, and *The Guardian*). She has exhibited widely (including The Institute of Contemporary Arts in London, 2005, and The Museum of Contemporary Photography in Chicago, 2006). Much of her recent work concerns the interface between work, culture, and economics, involving extended projects in China and the Middle East.

Sylvaine Bulle (*1962, Paris) received a doctorate in Sociology and History from the Ecole des Hautes Etudes en Sciences Sociales, Paris and is assistant professor of sociology. She is specialized in urban studies and has initiated and conducted various projects on contemporary urban transformations in the Middle East (Teheran, Cairo, Dubai). She is currently coordinating a program for urban and social sciences about space and citizenship in Palestine, and has recently published the book *Entre monde et patrie: Une socio-histoire du territoire palestinien*, 1920-2002, Centre National de la recherche Scientifique (CNRS) Editions, 2005.

Efrat Cohen-Bar (*1967, Jerusalem) is a graduate of the Department of Architecture at Bezalel Academy of Art and Design and has been practicing as an architect since 1995. In 2000, she became a volunteer for Bimkom – Planners for Planning Rights, and in 2004 has been the coordinator of the Kaminker project for the planning of the Palestinian village of Issawiyah, East Jerusalem. Efrat Cohen-Bar is a member of the forum of Human Rights organizations East Jerusalem.

Zvi Efrat (*1959, Tel Aviv) is an architect and writer. He is a partner at Efrat-Kowalsky Architects, and head of the Architecture Department at Bezalel Academy of Arts and Design. He curated the exhibitions "The Israeli Project" (Tel Aviv Museum, of Art 2000) and "Borderline Disorder" (The Israeli Pavilion at the Venice Biennale, 2002). His most recent publication is *The Israeli Project: Building and Architecture 1948-1973* (Tel Aviv: The Tel Aviv Museum of Art, 2005).

Galit Eilat (*1965, Haifa) is a curator and Founding Director of DAL – The Israeli Center for Digital Art, Israel. She is editor in chief of *Maarav* – an online art and culture magazine, as well as a teacher in the Department of Photography at the Bezalel Academy of Art and Design. She is currently an advisor for the Israel Museum in Jerusalem, as well as member of the artistic board of directors of "Amanut Haaretz," the annual festival for young Israeli art.

Orhan Esen (*1960, Istanbul) studied social and economic history at Bosporus University and history of art and architecture in Vienna. As an activist and researcher, his main interest is Istanbul's rapid urban development and its social, political, and ecological effect. As a freelancer, he collaborates with a wide-range of academic, civic, media, and corporate bodies in research projects, seminars, workshops, and field trips. With "performance without licence" / "ehliyetsiz performans" (2001, Istanbul) he intervened into the political debate on urban mobility. He has recently coedited the book Istanbul: *Self Service City* (2005), dealing with informal aspects of Istanbul's urbanization process.

Michael M.J. Fischer (*1946, Washington, D.C.) teaches anthropology and STS (science, technology and society) at Massachusetts Institute of Technology (MIT). He is the author of two books on ethnography and anthropological theory (*Anthropology as Cultural Critique*, with George Marcus; and *Emergent Forms of Life and the Anthropological Voice*), as well as three books on Iran (*Iran: From Religious Dispute to Revolution; Debating Muslims: Cultural Dialogues in Postmodernity and Tradition; Mute Dreams, Blind Owls*, and *Dispersed Knowledges: Persian Poesis in the Transnational Circuitry*). He is a frequent visitor to Israel and Palestine.

Yaakov Garb (*1960, Johannesburg) is currently a visiting assistant professor at the Watson Institute for International Studies, Brown University, and adjunct professor in the Institute of Urban and Regional Studies at Hebrew University. Drawing on his training in environmental studies and the sociology of science and technology (at Berkeley, MIT, and Harvard), he works on a range of environmental issues, and is currently writing a series of essays on the politics of mobility in Israel and the Palestinian areas.

Stephen Graham (*1965, Newcastle, UK) is a professor of human geography at Durham University, UK. His background lies in urbanism, planning, and the sociology of technology. His research addresses the intersection of urban places, mobility, technology, war, surveillance, and geopolitics. Recent publications include *Telecommunications and the City* (1996), *Splintering Urbanism* (2001) and *Cities, War and Terrorism* (2004).

Derek Gregory (*1951, Beckenham, England) received his M.A. and Ph.D. from Cambridge University, Fellow of the Royal Society of Canada, F.R.S.C., is Professor of Geography and Distinguished University Scholar at the University of British Columbia, Vancouver. He is the author of *The Colonial Present: Afghanistan, Palestine, Iraq* (Blackwell, 2004). His current research centers on the "war on terror" in Afghanistan, Palestine, and Iraq, and on military occupations of Arab cities. He is coeditor of the journal *Society & Space*, and author of *Orientalism Abroad: Cultural Encounter and Political Violence* (forthcoming from Routledge).

Shmuel Groag (*1951, Haifa) is an architect and town planner graduated from the Technion – Israel Institute of Technology in Haifa, specializing in conservation, urban design, and comprehensive urban planning. He taught conservation planning in the Department of Architecture and Art at Tel Aviv University. As a cofounder of Bimkom – Planners for Planning Rights, he continued to explore the link between architecture and politics. His publications include "Planning and Lack of Planning in East Jerusalem and the West Bank as a Political Tool of Spatial Appropriation"(2002) and "Planning Rights in Arab Communities in Israel"(2003). In 2005, he enrolled in an M.Sc. course at the London School of Economics on "Memory and Conservation."

Rema Hammami (*1960, Daharan, Saudi Arabia) is an anthropologist based at the Womens' Studies Institute at Birzeit University in Palestine. She has published numerous articles on gender and Palestinian nationalism, Palestinian civil society, and the politics of Oslo. Her most recent publications include two articles in the forthcoming *The Struggle for Sovereignity: Palestine and Israel 1993-2005*, eds. Joel Beinin and Rebecca Stein (Stanford University Press, 1996). The article in this volume, part of a larger ethnographic project on checkpoints during the second Palestinian uprising, was originally published in extended form in *Middle East Reports* 231 (Summer 2004).

Sari Hanafi (*1962, Damascus) is a sociologist with a Ph.D. from L'École des Hautes Etudes en Sciences Sociales in Paris (1994). He is an associate professor at the American University of Beirut. Until 2005 he was the director of the Palestinian Refugee and Diaspora Center, Shaml, based in Ramallah. He is the author of numerous articles and books on economic sociology, political sociology, and sociology of migration (mainly about the Palestinian refugees). His most recent book (with Linda Taber) is *The Emergence of Palestinian Globalized Elite. Donors, International organizations and Local NGOs* published by the Institute of Palestine Studies, Washington, and Muwatin, 2005.

Jane Hilal (*1975, Beit Sahour, Palestine) graduated with an M.Sc. in environmental management from the Mediterranean Agronomic Institute of Chania (MAICH) Chania, Greece. In 1998 she joined the Applied Research Institute – Jerusalem (ARIJ) where she has been involved in numerous research projects involving land use/land cover analysis, or the analysis of the biological distribution of flora in the West Bank. Currently, she is the director of the Water and Environment Research Unit and has recently copublished the report "Solid Waste Management in Palestine."

Rachel Leah Jones (*1970 in Berkeley, California), M.F.A., is a documentary filmmaker. Her debut film *500 Dunam on the Moon* (2002) tells the story of Ayn Hawd, a Palestinian village captured and depopulated by Israeli forces in the 1948 war that was transformed into a Jewish artists' colony and renamed Ein Hod. Currently, she is working on *Ashkenaz* a documentary about whiteness in Israel and *White City, Black City*, a filmic adaptation of Sharon Rotbard's book of the same name, that undoes the myths of Tel Aviv by telling its untold story: Jaffa.

Rassem Khamaisi (*1958, Kaffer Kanna) received his doctorate in urban geography at the Hebrew University. He works as an urban and regional planner and lecturer at the Department of Geography at Haifa University. He set up the "Strategic Planning and Information Unit" in Um Al Fahem and the "Center for Strategic Planning for Arab Localities in Israel." He heads the Academic Committee at the International Peace and Cooperation Center (IPCC) in Jerusalem, where he has coedited many publications such as *The Jerusalem Urban Fabric* (2003).

Nathan Marom (*1971, Salford, England) lives in Tel Aviv. He received his B.Arch. from the Bezalel Academy of Art and Design and an M.Sc. in urban development planning (University College London) and is currently pursuing a Ph.D. at Tel Aviv University on the topic of urban policy and urban exclusion in globalizing Tel Aviv. He has researched and written *The Planning Deadlock: Planning Policies and House Demolitions in East Jerusalem*, a report published by Bimkom – Planners for Planning Rights (2004).

Naama Meishar (*1963, Israel) earned a Bachelor's degree in landscape architecture from the Technion – Israel Institute of Technology (Haifa) and has been practicing as a landscape architect for a number of years. She is now completing a master's degree in Cultural Studies at the Hebrew University. Meishar has published articles concerning the tensions between development of Arab villages and the natural reservation policy of the State of Israel, the tensions between the Mizrahi and Ashkenazi landscape cultures, as well as art and movies reviews. She is a volunteer activist at the organization "Bimkom – Planners for Planning Rights."

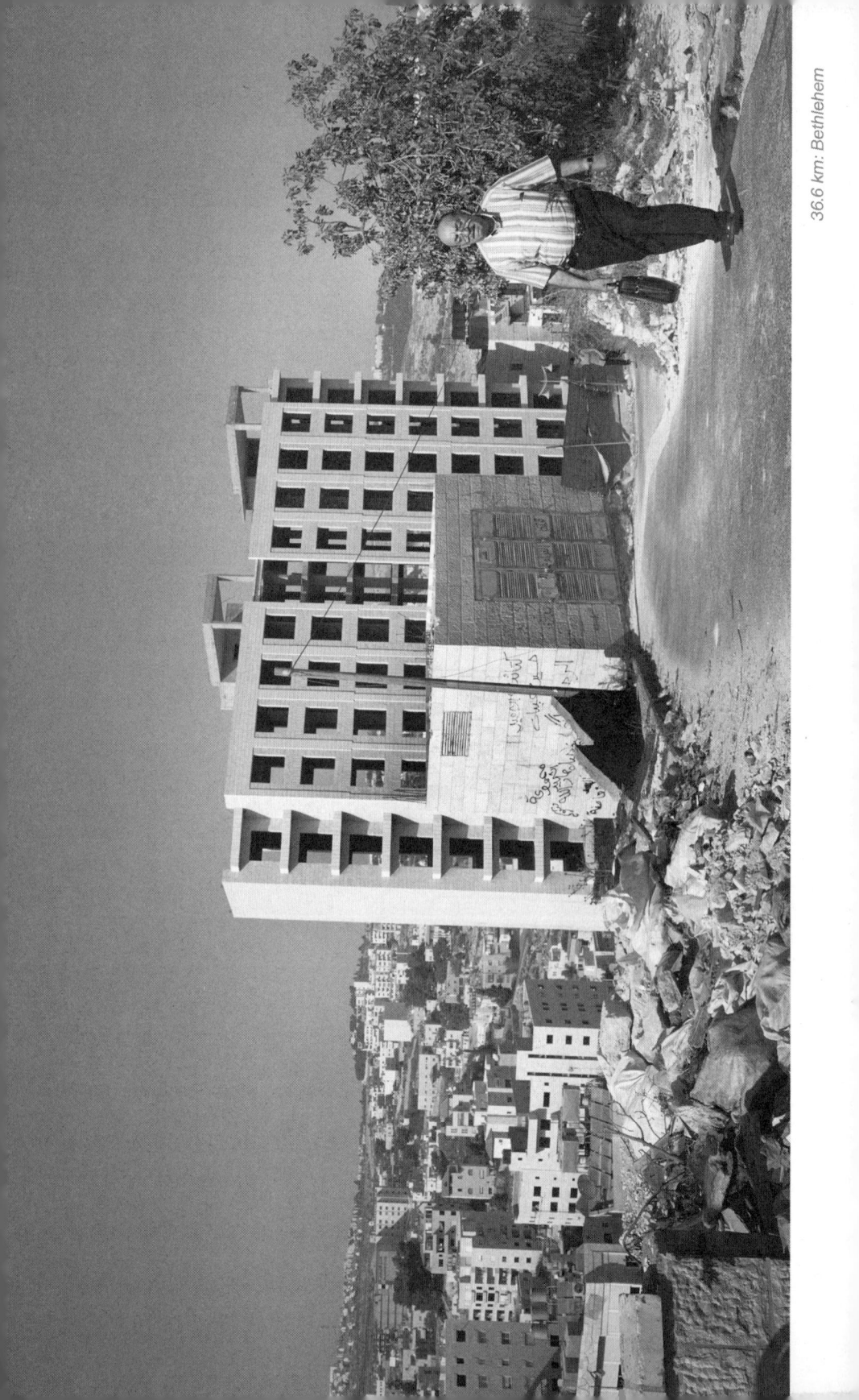

Philipp Misselwitz (*1974, Jena, Germany) trained as an architect at Cambridge University and the Architectural Association. Since 2001, he has taught at the London Metropolitan University, the AA, and the University of the Arts Berlin, and is a founding member of "urban catalyst" – a platform for research activities, exhibitions, publications, and debates including the international conference "Fun Palace Berlin 200X" in October 2004. In 2002, he initiated the European, Israeli, Palestinian cooperation project "Grenzgeografien," and curated the international conference "Cities of Collision" (2004). In 2003-04, he was a member of the Cambridge based research project "Conflict in Cities." His curatorial activities include "Shrinking Cities" (local curator, 2003-04) and "Liminal Spaces" (cocurator, 2006-07). He is currently initiating and coordinating a UN research project investigating development strategies for the informal urbanism of refugee camps.

Zakaria Mohammed (*1950, Nablus) was allowed to return to his country in 1994 after 25 five years in exile. He has published four poetry collections and two books concerning affairs of Palestinian culture: *On the Palestinian Cultural Questions* and *The Rooster at the Manara Square; Critical Reflections on Politics and Culture*. He is interested in the plastic arts, and has written a weekly column on cultural affairs in a daily newspaper. He worked as a senior editor for many cultural magazines in the quarterly *Al-Karmel*.

Rami Nasrallah (*1968, Jerusalem) is head of the International Peace and Cooperation Center (IPCC) in Jerusalem. He studied at Hebrew University (M.A. in Political Science and Middle Eastern Studies). From 1993 to 1996 he was political advisor and Israel Desk Officer at Orient House in Jerusalem, and became director of the Orient House Special Unit (1996–1998). He is a research associate of "Cities in Conflict" based at Cambridge University, and has published and co-edited amongst others *The Jerusalem Urban Fabric* (2003), *Jerusalem on the Map* (2005).

Issam Nassar (*1961, Jerusalem) lives and works in Ramallah and the U.S. where he teaches history at Bradley University, and is currently a visiting professor (2006) at University of California at Berkeley. From 1998 to 2003, he taught at the Center for Area Studies at al-Quds University in Jerusalem, and since 1998 has been Associate Director of the Institute of Jerusalem Studies (Jerusalem/Ramallah). His most recent publications include *Different Snapshots: The History of Local Photography in Palestine, 1850-1948* (Beirut: Kutub, 2005).

David Newman (*1956, London) trained at the University of London, and Durham University, and is now Founding Chair of the Department of Politics and Government at Ben-Gurion University in Israel, where he is professor of political geography. Newman has published widely on territorial dimensions of the Israel-Palestine conflict and the peace process, currently working on the development of modes for Israeli-Palestinian cross-border cooperation (funded by United States Institute of Peace [USIP]), and on alternative peace discourses amongst religious groups in the Middle East (funded by the EU Partnership for Peace project). Since 1999 he has been the editor of *Geopolitics*, a quarterly journal published by Taylor Francis (Routledge).

Alona Nitzan-Shiftan is a senior lecturer at the Faculty of Architecture and Town Planning at the Technion – Israel Institute of Technology, where she heads the history and theory studies program. She holds a Ph.D. and an S.M.Arch.S. from MIT, a B.Arch. *cum laude* from the Technion, and was recently the Mary Davis and the Kress Postdoctoral Fellow at the Center for Advanced Study in the Visual Arts (CASVA) at the National Gallery in Washington. Her publications appeared in *Architectural History, Theory and Criticism, Harvard Design Magazine, Jama'a*, and *Thresholds* as well as in edited volumes such as *The End of Tradition*.

Amir Paz-Fuchs (*1971, Tel-Aviv), received his D.Phil. from Oxford University, and is a lecturer on law at the Ono College of Law, as well being Vice-Chair of Bimkom – Planners for Planning Rights. He has written on conscientious objection and on welfare reform, and his research focuses on the legal and philosophical analysis of human rights.

Jack Persekian (*1962, Jerusalem) is a curator based in East Jerusalem. His curatorial work deals mainly with contemporary Palestinian art. He is the founding director of the Al Mamal Foundation for Contemporary Art, and the Anadiel Gallery, both based in Jerusalem. His international curatorial work includes the conceptualization and the visual arts part of "Disorientation" (2003) for Haus der Kulturen der Welt, Berlin, and the 2005 Sharjah Biennial 7 (United Arab Emirates) where he was chief curator. He is the artistic director of the coming sharjah biennial 8 in 2007.

Bas Princen (*1975, Zeeland, NL) lives and works in Rotterdam as an independent designer/photographer, focusing mainly on the field of the transformations of the urban landscape. His current work includes photographic research on the regions Tirana/Durres (Albania), Beograd (Serbia), Los Angeles and Houston (US). His work has been published in various architectural magazines and has been shown at the Venice Biennale of Architecture (2004), Archilab Orleans (2004), and "Shrinking Cities" Berlin (2004). His recent monograph *Artificial Arcadia* was published by 010 publishers (2004). Bas Princen is represented by van Kranendonk Gallery, The Hague.

Tim Rieniets (*1972, Hilden, Germany) is an architect and urban researcher currently working at the Institute for Urban Design at the Swiss Federal Institute of Technology Zurich (ETH). He has been a lecturer at the Anhalt University of Applied Sciences, Department of Design in Dessau (MAID), and guest lecturer and critic at various academic institutions and conferences. From 2002 to 2004 he was a member of the project team "Shrinking Cities" where he directed a global research study on the phenomenon of urban shrinkage, which has been published and exhibited several times. He is currently working on the *atlas of shrinking cities* coedited with Philipp Oswalt (2006). Since 2003, he has been a coordinator of the project "Grenzgeografien."

Irit Rogoff holds a university chair in visual culture at Goldsmiths College, London University, and is director of an Arts and Humanities Research Board (AHRB) funded international research project "Cross Cultural Contemporary Arts." She writes extensively on conjunctions of critical theory and contemporary arts with particular interest in issues of geography, location, performativity, and cultural difference. Rogoff has written on German Modernism (*The Divided Heritage*, 1992), museums, and the politics of display (*Museum Culture—Histories/Theories/Spectacles*, 1994). She is the author of *Terra Infirma: Geography's Visual Culture* (2001) and is presently working on a study of the participatory entitled *Looking Away—Participating Singularities and Ontological Communities*. She is currently curating "De_Regulation - with the work of Kutlug Ataman" (Antwerp, Herzylia, Berlin, 2006-07) and "Academy—Learning and Teaching" (Hamburg, Eindhoven, Antwerp 2005-06).

Michael Romann (*1935, Jerusalem) studied economics at the Hebrew University (B.A.), and at the London School of Economics L.S.E. (M.A.). He received his doctorate in urban studies at the Sorbonne. He is the coauthor (with Alex Weingrod) of *Living Together Separately—Jews and Arabs in Jerusalem* (Princeton University Press) as well as several articles on various aspects of Jewish-Arab relations. He is currently involved on a research project on the "Geography of Fear."

Sharon Rotbard (*1959, Tel Aviv) is an architect, publisher, and writer practicing in Tel Aviv. He teaches architecture at the Bezalel Academy and is editor of *Architectures*, the architectural and non-fiction series at Babel publishers, Tel Aviv. Rotbard has published numerous articles and essays on architecture and related issues in various international magazines. His most recent book is *White City, Black City* (2005).

Charmaine Seitz (*1974, Nairobi) is an American journalist who has been tracing stories on Jerusalem for over ten years in her work for the *Economist*, *In These Times* and other publications. Currently managing editor for the *Jerusalem Quarterly*, she previously served as administrative director for *bitterlemons publications*, and as managing editor of the *Palestine Report*.

Yehotal Shapira (*1962, Kiryat Tivon, Israel) is a practicing architect, planning projects combining theory and practice, and working on community participation planning projects. He received his M.A. in cultural studies from the Hebrew University. Presently a Ph.D. student at the Technion, he has published essays on architecture and cultural criticism, focusing on spatial and cultural aspects of Israeliness and architecture as well as on Palestinian traditional building heritage, contemporary Palestinian architecture issues, and the cultural spatial aspects of the Israeli-Palestinian conflict. He is currently a board member of Bimkom – Planners for Planning Rights.

Salim Tamari (*1945, Jaffa) is the director of the Institute of Jerusalem Studies and professor of sociology at Birzeit University. He is also a visiting professor at the University of California at Berkeley (2005), and editor of *Hawliyyat al Quds* and the *Jerusalem Quarterly*. His recent publications include *Jerusalem 1948* (2001), Mandate Jerusalem in the *Memoirs of Wasif Jawahariyyeh* (with Issam Nassar, 2005) and *The Mountain Against the Sea* (University of California Press, forthcoming, 2006).

Eyal Weizman (*1970, Haifa) trained as an architect at the Architectural Association, London, and received his Ph.D. from Birkbeck College, University of London. He is a professor of architecture at the Academy of Art in Vienna, and Director of Goldsmiths College Centre for Research and Architecture, London University. He has been working in private practice with Rafi Segal in Tel Aviv, completing among other projects, the rebuilding of the Ashdod Museum of Art. He initiated the exhibition and publication of *A Civilian Occupation*, following research and a mapmaking project for the human rights organization, B'tselem, on violations of human rights by architecture and planning in the West Bank.

Haim Yacobi (*1965, Jerusalem) trained as an architect and urban sociologist in Jerusalem and at the University College London. He received his Ph.D. at the Department of Geography in Ben-Gurion University (Israel) and has been teaching at its Department of Geography and at the Department of Architecture at Bezalel Academy of Art and Design. He has published widely on planning and human rights issues and recently edited the book *Constructing a Sense of Place* (2004). Haim Yacobi is a cofounder of Bimkom – Planners for Planning Rights and is currently a post doctorate at the Center of Middle Eastern Studies at Berkeley University California.

Oren Yiftachel (*1956, Haifa) is a professor of geography and public policy at Ben-Gurion University (Israel). He has previously taught at (amongst others) Curtin University (Australia), Columbia University, University of California at Berkeley, and was a research fellow at Royal Melbourne Institute of Technology (RMIT) in Melbourne, The US Institute of Peace, Washington DC, and the Van Leer Institute, Jerusalem. He is the founding editor of the journal *Hagar/Hajer: International Social Science Review*, and is an editorial board member of *Society and Space* and many other academic journals. He has published widely. His current research focuses on the study of the historical and political development of the land system in Israel-Palestine and the comparison of different ethnocratic regimes and cities, which will contribute to his forthcoming publication *Ethnocracy: Land, Politics and Identities in Israel/Palestine* (2006).

IMPRINT

Editors	Philipp Misselwitz, Tim Rieniets
Editorial team	Zvi Efrat, Rassem Khamaisi, Rami Nasrallah
Language editing	Charmaine Seitz, Rachel Leah Jones
Stylistic editing	Laura Bruce
Design	Tom Unverzagt
Thanks to	Senan Abdelqader, Heide Albertin, Hassan Abu Aslah, Rana Abu Ghazaleh, Peter Bayerer, Kees Christiaanse, Friedrich Dahlhaus, Anselm Franke, Jörg Gläscher, Arthur Goldreich, Nilly Harag, Eva Kästner, Wolfgang Knapp, Kinneret Lahad, Karoline Mueller-Stahl, Ayala Ronel, Georg Schwarz, Salim Tamari, Michael Thoss, Ruth Ur, Eyal Weizman, Michael Younan, Shimshon Zelniker
Partners	Berlin University of the Arts International Peace and Cooperation Center (IPCC) Bezalel Academy of Arts and Design, Jerusalem, Department of Architects ETH Swiss Federal Institute of Technology Zurich, Institute for Urban Design
Made possible by	Robert Bosch Stiftung Allianz Cultural Foundation Berlin University of the Arts ETH Swiss Federal Institute of Technology Zurich, Institute for Urban Design Arthur Goldreich Trust Goethe-Institut Jerusalem

This publication is based on a series of activities that were jointly planned and organised by the main project partners: Berlin University of the Arts, International Peace and Cooperation Center (IPCC), Bezalel Academy of Arts and Design, Jerusalem (Department of Architecture), ETH Swiss Federal Institute of Technology Zurich, Institut for Urban Design (except conference "Cities of Collision").

Atlas

Concept and copyright	Philipp Misselwitz, Tim Rieniets
Design	Tim Rieniets with Annika Seifert, Dominique Meier, Matthaeus Wirth
Texts	Philipp Misselwitz, Tim Rieniets
Local project team	Karen Lee Brachah, Mona Dajani, Yehuda Greenfield-Gilat, Sami Murrah, Michel Salameh, Charmaine Seitz (timeline), Shahd Wa'ary and the student participants of the workshop series "Grenzgeografien – geographies of conflict."

Cities of Collision

The international conference "Cities of Collision" was held in November, 2004 at the Van Leer Jerusalem Institute, Jerusalem

Curator	Philipp Misselwitz
Coordination	Rana Abu Ghazaleh, Kinneret Lahad, Shulamit Laron, Philipp Misselwitz
Curatorial Team	Zvi Efrat, Rana Abu Ghazaleh, Kinneret Lahad, Philipp Misselwitz, Rami Nasrallah, Wendy Pullan (Research Project "Conflict in Cities"), Tim Rieniets, Eyal Weizman and Anselm Franke ("Territories Live") Haim Yacobi, Shimshon Zelniker
Additional partners:	The Van Leer Jerusalem Institute (Host of the conference), Goethe-Institut Jerusalem

Invited participants and contributors to the conference (jointly invited by "Territories Live"):
Fida' Abdel-Latif, Pal Ahluwalia, Amin Amin, Ariella Azoulay, Tamar Berger, Khaldoun Bshara, Sylvaine Bulle, Zvi Efrat, Anselm Franke, Yaakov Garb, Rana Abu Ghazaleh, Stephen Graham, Derek Gregory, Jeff Halper, Sari Hanafi, Jad Ishaq, Jessica Jacobs, Adrianna Kemp, Thomas Keenan, Rassem Khamaisi, Kinneret Lahad, Philipp Misselwitz, Rami Nasrallah, David Newman, Alona Nitzan-Shiftan, Adi Ophir, Bas Princen, Wendy Pullan, Tim Rieniets, Irit Rogoff, Sharon Rotbard, Florian Schneider, Basak Senova, AbdouMaliq Simone, Salim Tamari, Milica Topalovic, Eyal Weizman, Haim Yacobi, Oren Yiftachel, Shimshon Zelniker

Grenzgeografien – geographies of conflict

The trilateral student workshops were conducted between August, 2003 and November, 2005 in Jerusalem and Berlin.

Initial concept and overall project coordination	Philipp Misselwitz
Coordination	Rana Abu Ghazaleh, Philipp Misselwitz, Tim Rieniets
Tutors for workshops	Senan Abdelqader, Amin Amin, Rana Abu Ghazaleh, Riman Barakat, Nilly Harag, Philipp Misselwitz, Tim Rieniets, Ayala Ronel, Zvi Efrat, Michael Younan
Invited speakers	Fida' Abdel-Latif, Amin Amin, Daniel Bauer, Meron Benvenisti, Eldad Brin, Dror Etkes, Rassem Khamaisi, Adriane Littman Cohen, Alona Nitzan-Shiftan, Diego Rotman, Danny Seidman, Shahd Wa'ary

Student participants: Amro Abu Alia, Eyad Abu Soud, Shireen Al-qadi, Barbara Elisabeth Ascher, Ghada Bannoura, Yfaat Baron, Karen Lee Brachah, Daniel Busche, Christina Castellvi, Yonatan Cohen, Markus Deml, Inna Dubinsky, Christoph Dubler, Ronnie Elgavish, Simona Fadida, Iddo Ginat, Sharon Golan, Omer Gorali, Yehuda Greenfield-Gilat, Eyal Gvirsman, Stefanie Hamm, Dan Handel, Kevin Herbst, Peter Herman, Nadera Karkaby, Dan Keynan, Anas Khader, Annegret Kirchner, Ilia Kireev, Gunnar Klack, Ziv Leibu, Tamar Loeb, Ines Lüder, Dominique Meier, Asaf Molcho, Nihal Msallam, Sami Murrah, Johann Reble, Marita Roth, Michel Salameh, Anina Schuster, Annika Seifert, Aya Shapira, Farah Shawar, Sharon Shlossberg, Roi Singer, Philipp Stargala, Anja Traffas, Marta Uriarte, Marek Vogt, Shahd Wa'ary, Claudia Waldvogel, Matthaeus Wirth, Hanna Younan, Heike Zieher, Shlomit Zonenshtein, Ahmad Zubeidat

Additional Support

The Van Leer Jerusalem Institute

Bundeszentrale für politische Bildung BpB

DAAD
supported within the (DAAD) program
"European-Islamic Cultural Dialogue"
with funding from German Foreign Office

Mondriaan Foundation